MAR 1979

D1568995

Also by Edward Rice

The Man in the Sycamore Tree

Mother India's Children

John Frum He Come

Temple of the Phallic King (editor)

The Ganges

Journey to Upolu

Marx, Engels and the Workers of the World

No One Like Margaret

Cities of the Sacred Unicorn

EASTERN DEFINITIONS

EASTERN DEFINITIONS

◂ ▸

A SHORT ENCYCLOPEDIA OF RELIGIONS OF THE ORIENT

A guide to common, ordinary, and rare philosophical, mystical, religious, and psychological terms from Hinduism, Buddhism, Ṣūfism, Islam, Zen, Taoism, the Sikhs, Zoroastrianism, and other major and minor Eastern religions

EDWARD RICE

1978
DOUBLEDAY & COMPANY, INC.
GARDEN CITY, NEW YORK

Library of Congress Cataloging in Publication Data

Main entry under title:
Eastern definitions.

1. Religions—Dictionaries. 2. Asia—Religion—
Dictionaries. I. Rice, Edward E., 1918–
BL31.E24 290′.3

ISBN: 0-385-08563-x
Library of Congress Catalog Card Number 77–19359

Designed by Joseph P. Ascherl

Copyright © 1978 by Edward Rice
All Rights Reserved
Printed in the United States of America
First Edition

Ref.
290.3
E132

CONTENTS

10.00
KANSAS CITY (MO) PUBLIC LIBRARY

FOREWORD

Eastern Definitions deals with the major and minor religions of the "oriental" world, a world that includes the Islamic nations of North Africa and spreads across all of Asia and Southeast Asia. The two major Western religions, Judaism and Christianity, with their sects and schisms, are not touched upon except incidentally.

The terms encountered in this work are in most cases those most likely to be met by the average curious reader of both popular and scholarly works written in or translated into English. There are today many terms, especially from Hinduism and Buddhism—karma, kōan, Ōṃ, yoga, zen, Ṣūfī, etc.—that are virtually commonplace, especially among the younger generations. Yet few people can adequately define them, much less pronounce them. Thus the words and terms defined here are those one might encounter in any work dealing with either the philosophy, religion, history, mysticism, or culture of the lands of Asia in which these faiths are (or have been) an integral part of daily life. However, any such selection also involves a certain amount of personal preference, and to some extent depends on an editor's own background, reading, education, travels, and the influences to which he has been subjected. Whatever, with an eye to future editions, the reader is encouraged to suggest further entries or categories and to question what is here presented.

We have made every effort to explain each term in the light of its own milieu. Many words are untranslatable into ordinary English, yet translated they must be. Terms like dharma or karma, for example, get tossed off in the West as "duty" and "fate," yet they are pregnant with three millennia of subjective and objective implications, which must be reduced to definitions the reader can understand and accept. A concept like "God," which is more or less clear, even self-explanatory, in the Judaeo-Christian West, has no simple definition in Hinduism of whatever period, and in Buddhism does not even exist, for "God" is an idea so elusive and irrelevant that the Buddha refused to discuss it. In Islam, on the other hand, God appears just as the West knows Him, with even more power, omniscience, and majesty, if that is possible. In the Orient, reality, sin, the self, the soul, time, eternity, and so on may or may not resemble Western concepts. In the great faiths of Asia, in fact, one repeatedly comes across quite contradictory and frustrating definitions: Something might be both existent and nonexistent. In approaching these themes the reader cannot give way to his own frustration: He must accept the fact that Eastern concepts work very well for Easterners, and that he must try to set his own mind into neutral and hope to let other cultures, other Ways state their case.

* * *

The problem of transliteration from other alphabets is one that has baffled scholars for centuries, despite heroic attempts to establish common systems. We have attempted to be consistent, a feat equal to maintaining a consistent weather pattern. In some cases the popular English-language conventions are followed. Tongue-twisters like Ṛkveda get the common Rig Veda, and other scholarly interpretations like Kṛṣṇa and Viṣṇu become Krishna and Vishnu, and so on. One surrenders in the face of the odds.

EDWARD RICE

ABBREVIATIONS

Arab.	Arabic
Buddh.	Buddhism
Chin.	Chinese
Chr.	Christian, Christianity
Conf.	Confucian, Confucianism
Hind.	Hindu, Hinduism
Ind.	Indian
Isl.	Islam
Jain.	Jainism
Par.	Parsee, Parseeism
Sans.	Sanskrit
Sikh.	Sikhism
Ṣūfi	Ṣūfism
Tao.	Taoism
Tib.	Tibetan
Zor.	Zoroastrian, Zoroastrianism

NOTE

Hyphenated Arabic (Islamic or Muslim) terms and names that begin with al- (or as-) are listed under the letter that begins the succeeding part of the term or name; e.g., al-Insan is listed under *I*, not *A*.

The Western (Gregorian) calendar is employed for all dates, including Arabic and Islamic. See the entry for calendar for the problem of dates.

The worship of different sects,
which are like so many small streams,
move together to meet God,
who is like the Ocean.

Rajjab

EASTERN DEFINITIONS

A

Ab, Isl. Father. One of the Divine Names (q.v.) of Allāh.

'abada, Isl. Worship, literally "to serve as a slave," meaning in this context not a series of acts but a perpetual state of remembrance and adoration of Allāh.

'abd, Isl. Servant or slave; a term forming a frequent element in Muslim names, e.g., 'Abdallāh, the Servant of God. Man's status as 'abd before God makes Islām, submission, the only possible relationship.

'Abd Allāh, Isl. One of Muḥammad's secondary names, meaning the Slave (or Servant) of God, with the implication that the Prophet (like all other Muslims) must prostrate himself in complete self-effacement before Allāh.

Abraham, in Islam. See Ibrāhīm.

Abū Bakr, Isl. Muḥammad's father-in-law and the first of the khalifs. He was the Prophet's intimate friend and almost the same age, being but two years younger (born c. A.D. 572). Muḥammad later married his daughter 'Ā'ishah during his exile at Medina. The Prophet was conscious of a strong affinity in Abū Bakr to both Ibrāhīm (Abraham) and Isa (Jesus). He said of his Companion, "He is not your superior by reason of much fasting and prayer, but because of something which has been fixed in his heart." After Muḥammad's death in 632, Abū Bakr, elected the first khalif (or successor), pulled the shattered Islamic community together, not, however, as a religious leader but as a secular one. It was he who suggested that the Qur'ān, which up to that time had been memorized by various Companions and disciples, be written down and collated; however, it was not until the reign of 'Uthmān, the third khalif, that the definitive text was agreed upon.

ācāryas, Hind. A group of South Indian (Tamil) theologians who succeeded the Ālvārs, starting about the tenth century A.D. They provided a philosophical basis for the personal theism of the Ālvārs and tried to combine the doctrine of bhakti with those of karma and jñāna. Nāthamuni is known as the first ācārya and as the disciple of Madhura-kavi-ālvār, and is credited with arranging and editing the Ālvār hymns and setting them to music in the Vedic manner for use in temple worship. Tradition states that he entered the image of Vishnu in the temple at Shrīraṅgam and became one with God.

The original ācāryas were Vedic, but the term popularly represents the group of gurus of Tamil-nad in South India, who formed a new class of guru. The success of the movement resulted in a shift of the centers of learning from the altars of the sacrificial grounds of the brahminical teachers to the more democratic places of pilgrimage and bathing, the tīrtha. Unlike Vedic worship, which has little interest in iconolatry and image worship but stresses ritual sacrifice, the movement focused its attention on temples with their special deities. One of the greatest of the ācāryas was Rāmānuja. See also Ālvārs, bhakti, Rāmānuja.

adab, Isl. Pious courtesy, stressed especially among the Ṣūfīs (q.v.).

Adam, Isl. The first of the nabis or prophets in Islam, in a series of twenty-five that includes Jesus (as Isa) and culminates with Muḥammad, who is the strongest and most responsible. In the Qur'ān, Adam is the archetypal man, weak and forgetful rather than rebellious. In XV 29 Allāh vivified Adam with the Divine Spirit: "I breathed into him of My Spirit." By virtue of having created Adam in His Image, in the Spirit of Being, Allāh made him His representative on earth for, as the Muslim divine Jīlī wrote, "Had not his Beauty shone upon Adam's countenance, The Angels never had bowed down prostrate before him." This obeisance is not idolatry to Adam but the adoration of God's indescribable Face. See Allāh.

Ādi-Buddha, the primordial Buddha, the Buddha without beginning, a largely Mahāyānist concept. The Nepalese view the Ādi-Buddha as the first and self-existent protector of the world; he is also found in Java and Tibet, and is especially prominent in tantric Buddhism. The world emanates from the Ādi-Buddha, his meditation creating the five Buddhas of Meditation (Dhyānibuddhas), which in turn each produce the Five Bodhisattvas of the Meditation (Dhyānibodhisattvas), who manifest themselves on earth as the five human Buddhas or manushi-Buddhas. Gautama Śakyamuni is the fourth of these; the fifth will be the Maitreya or Metteyya, the last of the present cycle of evolution. Of the others, the most significant is the Amida Buddha, the central figure of Pure Land Buddhism. See Amida, Namu Amida Butsu, and Pure Land Buddhism.

Ādi-Granth, Sikh. The most sacred of the Sikh scriptures, more commonly known as the Granth Sāheb. Ādi-Granth means Initial (or First) Book; Granth Sāheb, Noble Book. See Granth Sāheb, Sikhs.

advaita (also advaitavāda), Hind. Variously defined as non-dualism, the doctrine that posits the Ultimate Reality as one and undifferentiated; non-dual-absolute. Advaita received its clearest statement in the works of the Vedantin Sankara (c. A.D. 750), and was further elaborated upon (and confused) by disciples and later imitators. As the current interpretation now stands, advaita teaches the following:

1. Brahman alone is real, and the world is false. The world is māyā—i.e., a purely illusory manifestation of Brahman caused by transcendental avidya or ajñāna (or nescience). Therefore, advaita means strictly monism and implies acosmism. Statements such as "Verily, the whole world is Brahman" and "I am Brahman" are to be accepted literally.

2. Brahman is the material cause of the world, is nirguṇa (translated best as "impersonal"), and thus there is no true possibility of establishing interpersonal relationships with Brahman. The jīvatman as experienced in avidya appears to itself as a finite principle of consciousness, activity, and passivity but is really identical with Brahman, the Supreme Atman. See ajñāna, ātman, Brahman, jīvatman, māyā, Śankara.

advaitavāda, Hind. See advaita, above.

āgama, Hind. Originally and strictly a tradition of knowledge or practice handed down from teachers to pupils, beginning with the Vedas and equated with them or said to be the "true" Vedas by certain disciples. Later āgama denoted a school of text and devotional practices, largely Shaivite but including those of other deities, which was outside the scope of Vedic teachings. Shiva, Vishnu, and Devī (or Śakti) were the principal deities involved. All schools of Shaivism, Vishnaivism, and Shaktism drew freely upon the authority of the āgamas to buttress their interpretation of Vedānta according to one's personal deity. The Vaishnavas, Shaivas, and Shaktas all have their sacred āgamas. In general, the āgamas are divided into four aṅgas or limbs—jñāna or knowledge; yoga or concentration—i.e., the esoteric teachings; kriyā or practices connected with the founding of temples and the installation of idols; and caryā or methods of worship of the deity, this limb involving also a man's religious, social, and personal conduct and practices. Much of the originally voluminous āgamas of all schools has been lost over the ages.

Agni, Hind. The Aryan fire god, also worshiped by the Persians until the time of Zoroaster. Agni has three forms: celestial as the sun, atmospheric as lightning, and terrestrial as fire. He is all that burns or devours or digests: sun, heat, stomach, lust, and passion. His three Spheres are Earth, Sky, and Space, the worlds respectively of men, spirits, and deities. He is the priest of the gods and the god of the priests, and serves as liaison between the gods and man. The Vedic fire sacrifice was personified as Agni; the crackling of the fire, with its oblations of ghī (a kind of clarified butter), was considered to be the voice of Agni. He is the most important of the Vedic deities—more hymns celebrate him than any other god—and presides over all the sacraments and all the great events of life, and at the end of a man's life, it is Agni, through the flames of the funeral pyre, who accepts the body as an offering. The counterpart of Agni is Soma, the gentle, devoured substance, who is consumed by the other god. "All this universe, conscious and unconscious, is made of fire [Agni] and offering [Soma]," says the Mahābhārata. See also Soma.

Aḥad, Isl. One, a Name of Allāh expressing Him as essentially One, Single, and unencroachable by the least object.

Aḥadiyya, Isl. The Transcendent Oneness (of Allāh). It is pure non-duality, excluding all concepts such as those of essence and quality, Creator and creation, and so on. The Islamic divine, Jīlī, defines Aḥadiyya as "God was and there was nothing with Him." Aḥadiyya is paired with Waḥidiyya and the Immanent Oneness. In Aḥadiyya even the Divine Qualities are nonexistent. See Allāh.

ahiṁsā, Hind., Jain., and Buddh. Generally, nonviolence (or non-injury), a doctrine that involves many ramifications and has undergone much development and change. Ahiṁsā likely goes back to the cities of the Indus Valley before the Aryan invasions; the transition from the blood sacrifices of Vedic society to ahiṁsā (and vegetarianism and veneration of the cow and other animals) was a very slow process. Ahiṁsā surfaces clearly in the sixth century B.C. in the teachings of the Jains, who show a number of affinities to the Indus culture. Early Buddhism also contained many nonviolent doctrines. Ahiṁsā (from the Sanskrit negative a- and hiṁsā, violence) has both active and passive aspects. Properly speaking, in its most current usage given by Mohandas Gandhi, it means "reverence for life," a characteristic also seen in early Jain and Buddhist teaching. The central Jain text, the *Sūtrakṛtāṅga* (The Book of Sermons), which epitomizes Jain doctrine, says, "If a man kills living things, or slays by the hand of another, or consents to another's slaying, his sin goes on increasing." The Jains' *Sūyagaḍaṅga* states, "In hurting them [other creatures] men hurt themselves, and will be born again among them." Even fires are forbidden, for, "The man who lights a fire kills living things," nor may a man cut or use a plant for pleasure, for he will slay many living things in doing so. Another Jain text, the *Ācārāṅga Sūtra,* says, "All things breathing, all things existing, all things living, all beings whatever, should not be slain or treated with violence, or insulted or tortured or driven away."

The convert to Jainism Kumārapāla (1143–72), according to Jain sources, though something of a tyrant, enforced ahiṁsā so rigorously that he mulcted two merchants of all their wealth for killing fleas and in general enforced ahiṁsā to the point of violence. He is believed to have fasted to death, for the Jains do not believe that self-destruction violates the doctrine of ahimsā. However, it was the far more popular and vigorous Buddhism, not Jainism, that propagated ahiṁsā throughout the Indian world. The Emperor Ashoka (c. B.C. 268–233), a convert to Buddhism, did penance for having waged war after his conversion, and forbade the killing of most animals in his realm, allowing only certain ones to be slaughtered in limited quantities and only for food.

In Hinduism, the development of the doctrine of ahiṁsā came later. Briefly, violence interferes with dharma (roughly, right action). Violence in thought, word, and deed disturbs the proper functioning of the individual and of society and helps to negate dharma. However, from the point of view of the upper castes, there is a practical side to ahiṁsā: The doctrine of nonviolence helps mold the lower castes to the will of the upper, especially the priests'; the lower castes were bound to ahiṁsā, while the higher ones were not. It was in the not-so-recent past a common practice, for example, to stone, abuse, or even torture a lower-caste member who violated caste regulations (such as walking on an upper-caste road or entering a higher-caste temple); in extreme cases, such as a śudra's reciting a verse from the Vedas, the offender's tongue might be cut out. Until the time of Gandhi ahiṁsā remained more or less on this level, with its practice a matter of choice among the powerful and of necessity for the poor; it is still not widely practiced, and had its greatest application during the Indian struggle for independence from Britain.

The most famous practitioner of ahiṁsā has been Mohandas Gandhi, who was born in Gujarāt, the traditional seat of Jainism. Gandhi was influenced by Jain doctrines and found the idea of ahiṁsā both morally and philosophically attractive, and an effective political weapon. Gandhi, reviving not only ahiṁsā but another long-abused practice, that of satya or truth, wrote, "My religion is based on Truth and Non-violence. Truth is my God and Non-violence is the means to reach him." Elsewhere he stated: "Non-resistance is restraint voluntarily undertaken for the good of society. It is therefore, an intensely active, purifying, inward force. . . . It presupposes ability to offer physical resistance." And: "Non-violence is the greatest and most active force in the world. One cannot be passively non-violent. . . . One person who can express ahiṁsā in life exercises a force superior to all the forces of brutality." And: "Non-violence cannot be preached. It has to be practiced." And: "Non-violence is impossible without self-purification." It was a running theme throughout his adult life; The curious reader is referred to his many writings, especially his autobiography, *The Story of My Experiments with the Truth.*

In the practice of yoga, ahiṁsā was known as one of the five restraints. The ancient sage Vyāsa (traditionally the author of the Mahābhārata) stated, "Ahiṁsā means not cause any pain to any creature, by any means or at any time. The restraints [yama] and the disciplines that follow have their roots in ahiṁsā and tend to perfect ahiṁsā." Ahiṁsā is personified in Hinduism as the wife of Dharma (in this case, Righteousness), both being minor incarnations of the god Vishnu. See also Ashoka, Buddhism, Gandhi, Jainism, yoga.

ahl al-Ḥadīth, Isl. A term for the force in Islam that presents itself from time to time as the exponent of "orthodoxy" based on the current interpretation of tradition—i.e., Sunna' (q.v.), as opposed to the more mystical and less legalistic and philosophical groups found in the numerous sects of the Shī'a (q.v.). On the other hand, the followers of ahl al-Ḥadīth also oppose too much emphasis on reason and logic over the weight of tradition. A common though not always accurate term for this orthodoxy is Sunnī, those who follow the sunna'. See Shī'a, Sunnī.

ahl al-Sunna', Isl. Another term for ahl al-Ḥadīth.

Ahmadiyyas, Isl. An Islamic sect of Kashmir, in India, with a strong reverence for a wandering holy man named Yūz Āsaf, who is identified with Jesus Christ. Yūz Āsaf died in Kashmir, according to the Ahmadiyyas, a belief also subscribed to by many of the local Hindus. A mosque, built in the fourteenth century A.D. by Kutb-ud-din upon the remains of a Hindu temple he had destroyed and named after the Syed Ali Hamdani, a Persian credited with converting many Kashmiris to Islam, contains a walking stick said to have been used by Jesus as Yūz Āsaf; it is exhibited to the public upon rare occasions. D. M. Lang of the University of London believes that the story of Yūz Āsaf is "simply based upon an abstract from a familiar Arabic version of the Barlaam and Josaphat romance, and has no connection with the life of Jesus Christ at all." See *Balavariani,* Jesus Christ, Islam.

'ain, Isl. A synthetic Arabic word meaning eye, fountain, self, and origin, and in a synthesis of all, the Divine Essence (of Allāh).

ajapa, Hind. The voiceless utterance of japa, the act of reciting a mantra or prayer. See japa.

Ajita (nicknamed Kesakambali, with the hair blanket), a sixth-century B.C. Indian materialistic philosopher. Ajita taught a thoroughgoing materialism. He denied karma altogether, stating that there was no merit in almsgiving, sacrifice, or offering, no result or fruition of good or evil deeds, that man does not pass from this world to the next, and that there is no afterlife. At death the four elements of man (earth, fire, water, and air) return to their respective origins, while the senses vanish into space. "When the body dies, both fool and wise alike are cut off and perish." See also karma.

ajñāna, Hind. Ignorance of the true nature of the Self or of Reality. Also, unknowing, the perceiver of forms of illusion, derived from māyā, the power-of-illusion. In the Abysmal Immensity, ajñāna is not absence of knowledge but represents a state beyond knowledge, the nature of which is transcendent Being. See also jñāna and māyā.

Akbar (1556–1605), Moghul Emperor of northern India. As a boy in Kabul (Afghanistan), Akbar was exposed to Shī'a teachings and to Ṣūfī mysticism. However, when he began to rule in India, his chief officials were Sunnī. Several of Akbar's wives were Hindus. After an ambitious and successful career as a military leader, statesman, and sponsor of the arts, he suddenly turned to religion. He sought unsuccessfully for a personal vision of the power of God, visiting holy sites and holy men alike. A religious eclectic, he surrounded himself with men interested in other religions, particularly Hinduism, even though his court was Muslim, and eventually built a Hall of Worship at Fatehpur Sikri, near Agra, for religious discussions with Sunnī 'ulamā, Ṣūfī shayks,

Hindu pandits, Parsees, Zoroastrians, Jains, and Jesuit priests from Goa. He made open conciliatory gestures toward his large Hindu population, forbidding the killing of cows, abstained from meat himself on certain days, and celebrated non-Islamic festivals. On one of his periodic visits to the Punjab, while sitting under a fruit tree in meditation, he had a mystical experience, long denied him; he became convinced that he was an instrument of God and no longer needed the usual intermediaries. The arguments in his court between Shī'as and Sunnīs repelled him, and he now proposed a syncretic—monotheistic—system, the Dīn-i-Ilālī, the Divine Faith, which was Ṣūfic in inspiration, with Zoroastrian rituals, but generally vague in conception. Akbar announced, "We ought, therefore, to bring them [all the varied beliefs] into one, but in such a fashion that they should be both 'one' and 'all'; with the great advantage of not losing what is good in any one religion, while gaining whatever better in another. In that way, honor would be rendered to God, peace would be given to the peoples, and security to the empire." For the benefit of the whole empire, "gods, ceremonies, sacrifices, mysteries, rules, solemnities, and whatever was required" would constitute the new, perfect religion. Although Akbar created the first viable pan-Indian state since Ashoka (in the North, however) he was never able to bring Muslims and Hindus together. The Divine Faith had little appeal to the masses, and Muslim-Hindu religious and cultural rivalries remained after his death, being exploited to the fullest by the British during their later rule.

'Ali, Isl. Muḥammad's cousin and later son-in-law. He is traditionally known as the first person to accept the Prophet's call. He is also the Fourth Khalif. 'Ali married Fāṭima, Muḥammad's daughter. At the crisis precipitated by the Prophet's death in A.D. 632, the leadership of the community and the succession went to his closest friend, Abū Bakr (q.v.), to whom he had given the responsibility of directing the Act of Prayer. Abū Bakr was thus the first khalif or successor. The two next khalifs were Omar (named 634, assassinated 644) and 'Uthman, another son-in-law of the Prophet'. When Omar was murdered, 'Ali was elected khalif but was unable to gain recognition and support from rival factions, and thus a split in Islam began that has survived to this day. 'Ali submitted to arbitration, with the Qur'ān as the supreme judge, and was forced to renounce his rights. His supporters, the Shī'a, became one of the two main movements within Islam, the other being the Sunnīs. However, a group with the Shī'a, the Khārijites, who had previously backed him, now turned against his cause and assassinated him in A.D. 661 at Cufa. Henceforth 'Ali was known as one of the great martyrs of Islam.

Alif, Isl. 1. The first letter of the Arabic alphabet. In Ṣūfī mysticism alif is the symbol of Allāh as the One Who Alone is, and of Him Whose Being no being precedeth, or, in other cases, the Divinity in All Its Aspects.

2. A key piece in the subhah, the Muslim rosary. It is the size and shape of a finger, being the hundredth "bead" after ninety-nine smaller ones (ninety-nine being the Names of Allāh). Many subhahs have smaller alifs after the thirty-third and sixty-sixth beads for shorter prayer cycles.

Al-'Alim, Isl. The Omniscient, one of the Divine Names of Allāh.

Allāh, Isl. Allāh is, simply, God. He is identical with the God of Judaism but not with the Trinitarian God of the Christian churches, or at least those that include Jesus and the Holy Spirit equally in the Godhead. God is One. The Qur'ān stresses repeatedly that Allāh can have no plural, and there is no grammatical plural for the word. In Arabic, as the Qur'ān emphasizes, God is, Al-Wāḥid, the One. The Sura of Unity (Qur'ān 112) says directly, "Say: Allāh is One, the Eternal God. He begot none, nor was He begotten. None is equal to Him," a formula that deftly denies the central fact of orthodox Christianity. Tradition says that to confess this particular phrase is to shed one's sins as one might strip a tree of its leaves in autumn. The Oneness of God is the basic theme of Islam and is repeated five times a day in the Shahādah—Lā Ilāha Illā Allāh, There is no god but God.

Prior to the Prophet Muḥammad (c. A.D. 570–632) there was, among the population of the Arabian peninsula (largely pagan, with a small sprinkling of Jews and Christians), knowledge of a supreme deity, known as Allāh, the God. (Muḥammad's father was called 'Abdallāh, the Slave of God.) However, other deities shared the loyalties of the peninsula's polydemonic people, among them Al-'Izzat, goddess of power, Manāt, goddess of fate, and Allāt, goddess of fertility. Also, the ancient shrine of the Ka'ba, which contains the famous Black Stone, later to become the central point of the Muslim on pilgrimage, had been from prehistoric times an object of adoration and worship; it was situated in a temple surrounded by 365 idols. Belief in various supernatural spirits, among them a type known as jinns, some of which could possess a man's soul, was common. This pre-Prophetic age was known as Jāh iliyyah, Time of Ignorance.

Though he encountered much opposition, Muḥammad cut through the superstition and ignorance of the various peoples of Arabia to stress and reaffirm the uniqueness of Allāh. The Prophet preached not the mere fact of His existence, but His sole existence—no god but God. To worship otherwise was sinful, erroneous, and sheer folly. The Qur'ān constantly emphasizes the all-encompassing power, love, and uniqueness of God. He is One Sovereign, Creator, Sustainer, Provider, Lord, ruling and revealing—He Who rules and He Who reveals. He is The Compassionate, The Merciful. The First and the Last—the Outward and the Inward. The Living, the Comprehending, the Self-sufficing, the Abiding, the High, the Mighty, the All-Powerful, the Exalted, the Praiseworthy, the All-compelling, the Guardian, the Victorious, and so on, there being ninety-nine Names of God. Most importantly of all, to stress His love and judgment and his very nearness to man ("He is as close to a man as his jugular vein"), He is Al-Haqq, the Real.

The existence and maintenance of all in the world are attributed to Allāh, on whom all depends. Belief in a partnership of other deities is condemned as shirk, the worst of all sins. Sura 4 contains the warning, "The Messiah, Jesus the son of Mary, was no more than Allāh's apostle and His Word which He cast to Mary; a spirit from Him. . . . Allāh is but one God. Allāh forbid that He should have a son!" The Messiah is but "a servant of Allāh." Allāh created man and all that is in the world for the service of man. Superstitions and magic are also contrary to belief in God and His omnipotence. All of nature exists for the benefit of man and is to be explored and exploited with this in mind.

Although man, first of all, accepts God on faith and without questioning, there are also certain proofs. The existence of everything in heaven and on earth and all the complicated movements and natural processes that take place are evidence for the existence of God.

Allāh is eternal and has no beginning, no end. He is self-subsistent and is One in all aspects. Nothing resembles Him. Everyone and everything depend on Him, but He depends on none and has no need of anything. Allāh is all life: He is seeing, hearing, speaking, omnipotent, and omniscient. Man and the world and the heavens are caused to exist by His benevolent will.

It is through creation that Allāh reveals Himself, but man tends to ignore Allāh through his own weaknesses, and consequently Allāh has to send certain righteous men—the nabis or prophets—to guide His people and to bring them to, or keep them on, the right path. The nabis (there are twenty-five, beginning with Adam and ending with Muḥammad) and include (to give them their Judaeo-Christian names) Abraham, Moses, John the Baptist, and Jesus.

Allāh works with a predetermined plan which takes into consideration the collective benefit of all mankind. This is known as the belief in Qadar, or Divine Will. Muslims have been reticent to speculate upon Qadar, as it is beyond human competence and privilege, believing instead the injunction "Do not cogitate upon God but upon His Creation," and knowing also that earlier communities had perished because they involved themselves in discussions of Qadar. So, man cannot speculate on God's motives—"What He does cannot be questioned." And Allāh says, "Be, and it is." His will is inscrutable. Nothing exists but by His providence. All arises directly from Allāh, there being nothing but Allāh and His creation. Man is His dependent creature. However, man is nevertheless a responsible creature, not a being helplessly at the mercy of a predetermined fate, as the Qur'ān teaches time and time again. It is man's free choice to work out his life and afterlife in the balance of Allāh's omnipotence. It is man's grave responsibility to solve the tension of this great duality.

The dichotomy between God and man cannot be more clearly defined than in Islam. There is no blending of man's soul with God's, no monism, no negation of duality, no absorption into the godhead, as in Hinduism. And where Buddhism avoids the question of a supreme power altogether (despite the myriad gods), Islam clearly defines it. What is stated in the Old and New Testaments concerning the nature of God is hammered home in the Qur'ān. There can be no doubt that Allāh is the Most High, the All-Powerful. "He is God in heaven and God on earth; He is the Wise One, the All-knowing, Blessed be He to whom belongs the kingdom of the heavens and the earth and all that lies between them! He alone has the knowledge of the Hour of Doom. To Him you shall all return," says Sura 43.

Moreover, there is no "intercessor" between man and God, no one to purge man of his sins or to reconcile him with an angry deity. If man sins, he can obtain forgiveness by appealing directly to Allāh and by abandoning his evil ways. And man gains "nearness" to Him by sacrifice, self-denial, and obedience to His commands. See Ibrāhīm, Jesus, Ka'ba, Muḥammad.

Allāhu Akbar, Isl. A brief invocation, God is Most Great, said at the beginning of the five-times-daily prayers; it is also recited four times ("four magnifications") at the funeral service. Allāhu Akbar is known as the takbīr (q.v.).

al-'almal, Isl. Agreed practice, based upon interpretations of the Sunna' (or Trodden Path) from the three sources of the Prophet himself, the living tradition commencing with the earliest generations of Islam, and the deductions from these. The concept of al-'almal is used equivalently with that of ijmā', consensus. See ijmā', Sunna'.

Ālvārs, Hind. A group of Saivite poet-saints who lived in the Tamil country of South India between the fifth (second in some versions) and the ninth centuries A.D. The term Ālvār means one who has a mystic, intuitive knowledge of God and who has submerged himself in contemplation of the Divine. There were twelve major Ālvārs and a number of minor followers. They likely stem back to pre-Vedic times, to the Harappans of the Indus Valley, for they represent a type of low-caste, nonbrahminical spirituality that was originally contrary to orthodox Hinduism but later entered the mainstream, like other elements that survived among the conquered peoples. The first three Ālvārs were all born of flowers in

South Indian tanks, at the ancient shrines of Kāncī, Mahābalipuram, and Madras. Though a prince (the King of Travancore) and a brāhmin are counted among the Ālvārs, most are either śudras or untouchables, and one, a woman, is a foundling. The Ālvārs were a major influence in the bhakti movement. Rāmānuja called their works the "Veda of the Vaishnavas." Ālvār prayers are simple and full of the intense personal devotion of bhaktism. Their poetry embodies the teachings of the Upanishads and are sung to different melodic modes, their recitals being endowed as part of regular temple services. To the Ālvārs, the entire world is conceived as the Body of God, and they offer themselves to Him like a young woman submitting to her lover. The devotee is oblivious of everything except God, his love for Him being beyond space and time. Nammālvār, the most important and the most prolific of the school, sang of God with form and without form.

"He is not a male. He is not a female. He is not a neuter. He is not to be seen, He is, and is not. When He is sought, He will take the form in which He is sought, and again He will not come in such a form. It is difficult to describe the nature of the Lord." Periyālvār (also known as Viṣṇu-citta) could see "this body of mine become the holy shrine of the great Lord, the Cowherd Krishna," and he sang, "This is not the ancient city [of sin]; it has now become the home of the Lord as a protected place." One of the most noted Ālvārs was the low-caste foundling Āṇdāl, who, to the credit of the bhaktis in the caste-ridden, male-dominated society of the time, could by her sanctity alone command a great following. A parallel movement in Tamil-nad were the Neyanars, who were devotees of Śiva. See also Āṇdāl, bhakti, Upanishads.

Ama-terasu-ō-mi-Kami, Shintō. The Sun Goddess (literally, Heavenly Shining-Great-August-Deity). The most important of all the Shintō divinities, Ama-terasu is the daughter of Izanagi and Izanami, the gods of creation, who gave birth to the islands of Japan, as well as to the many divinities. Ama-terasu, so bright and great was her luster, was sent to Heaven to govern; she was later joined by her younger brother Tsuki-Yumi, the Moon God (a minor deity). A second brother, with whom Ama-terasu had some fights, is Susa-no-wo, a deity so cruel and fierce, having caused the deaths of many people and the destruction of the landscape, that he was banished to the Nether Land of Darkness. Ama-terasu is the supreme deity of all the ordinary people and of the royal family. The Emperor is descended from her grandson and is the high priest of her cult. In his attempt to solidify Buddhism in Japan, the Buddhist monk Gyōgi (A.D. 670–749) invoked the aid of the Goddess. After meditating at her shrine at Ise (q.v.), he was able to inform the Emperor that Ama-terasu (speaking in Chinese verse!) had accepted Buddhism as a superior form of Shintō. Shortly after this, the Goddess appeared in all her brilliance in a dream to the Emperor to proclaim that the Sun and Buddha were identical. However, this rapprochement did not survive. In A.D. 780 Ama-terasu put a curse upon her land because a Buddhist temple was to be constructed near the Ise shrine. In 811 she had worship of the Pole Star (a Chinese custom) forbidden. She remained the great protector of Shintō, the people's faith, forbidding Buddhist priests to enter the Ise shrine. In connection with her cult, euphemisms had to be employed for Buddhist concepts: The Buddha himself was "the Child of the Center," the Scriptures were but "colored paper," nuns (whose heads were shaven) were called "long-haired women," and the bonzes were not allowed even to approach the environs of Ise without wearing a wig. See Shintō.

Amida, Buddh. The Buddha of Infinite Light (Sanskrit, Amitābha, Eternal Light), a figure who appeared in various Indian Buddhist texts about the second century A.D. Amida emanates from the meditation of Ādi-Buddha (q.v.), the original Buddha, being one of the five Dhyānibuddas, Buddhas of Meditation. The Gautama Buddha, as a human (manushi) buddha, is on a far lower scale than Amida. Amida as the Buddha of Infinite Light holds a unique place. (The theme of Light shows a Persian—Zoroastrian—influence.) He is characterized by the color red, and by the lotus and the peacock, his identifying attribute and symbols, and reigns over the Western Paradise, Sukhāvati.

His cult was of minor importance in his homeland, but he became popular in Nepal and Tibet as one of many buddhas worshiped by the people, and passed into China as A-mi-t'o-fo, the central figure of the Pure Land sects, and thence into Japan, where his cult became major. The Indian work the *Greater Sukhāvatīvyūha Sūtra* relates the story of the sage Dharmākara who lived in uncounted ages past. He was of such spiritual stature that he could have entered buddhahood but refused, vowing that he would wait until he could achieve such buddhahood as would make him lord of a paradise, to which all who meditated upon him ten times should be admitted. The work was translated into Chinese, along with other works, one of which describes a series of sixteen meditations (dhyāna) upon the Amida Buddha, which lead to entry into Paradise. In the various texts Amida is the personification of infinite mercy, compassion, wisdom, and love, which led to his becoming the focus of worship through the Pure Land sects. By the seventh century A.D. he had come to replace the Gautama Buddha and the Maitreyya Buddha (the Buddha to come) among the popular cults. The repetition of his mantra "Namu Amida Butsu" (I take refuge in the Amida Buddha) even once (though ten times is the usually stated figure) ensures the devotee accession to the Paradise of the Pure Land. Salvation by faith, as in devotion to Amida, is a unique concept in Buddhism and not found elsewhere. See Buddhism.

Amitābha, Buddh. See Amida, above.

Amritsar. The sacred city of the Sikhs, in the Punjab in western India, containing the Golden Temple (Harimandira or Darbār Sāheb). The temple was founded by the fourth Sikh Guru, Rām Dās (1534–81), in the pond of Amritsar in 1579; the pond has since been lined with marble, and the temple stands connected to the shore by a causeway. The dome of the structure and the upper levels are covered with fine filigree and enamelwork in gold. After the building was completed, the Sikhs were on several occasions driven out in the wars with the Muslims. In 1740 the local Mogul commandant had turned the Temple into a dance hall but was assassinated by two Sikhs in disguise. In 1758, a Sikh named Baba Dip Singh, wounded in battle, led an avenging troop through the Temple, where he finally let go of his already severed head "and went to the eternal abode of martyrs." In 1765 the Sikhs reconquered the Punjab and have held the Temple since. In the richly decorated upper hall, Sikh sādhus sit reading the Granth Sāheb in half-hour shifts until it is completed, a process that requires two days and two nights. See Granth Sāheb, Sikhs.

ānanda, Hind, Jain., Buddh., etc. Delight or pure joy, unalloyed with material concepts.

Ānanda, Buddh. The first cousin and favorite disciple of the Buddha, serving as both teaching assistant and personal attendant of the Master. Ānanda agreed to minister to the Buddha on the condition that he receive no personal benefits nor special comforts because of his intimate role. He saved Buddha's life in an assassination attempt. When the Buddha preached, the Master would sketch in the outline and leave Ānanda to develop the theme. Ānanda is credited with preserving by memory and with faultless accuracy four of the five Discourses (Nikāyas) of the Pali canon, the passages being prefaced by the words, "Thus I have heard—." Ānanda is credited with persuading the Buddha to accept women into an order. Although Ānanda was unequaled in learning—he had memorized eighty-two thousand of the Buddha's own dhammas and two thousand of those of his fellow disciples—he was not an arahant (a "worthy one," who is in the highest of four spiritual stages) and was thus excluded from the First Buddhist Council assembled after the Buddha's death. Enemies falsely accused him at the Council of not taking better care of his Master. Ānanda later achieved the state of arahantship; he died in midriver between two rival kingdoms, and his ashes were evenly divided.

Ānandamayee Ma (in English, the Most Blissful Mother), Hind. A Bengali mystic (born Nirmala Sundari Devi), considered by her disciples as an avatāra of Shakti, the manifest energy of the Divine, also as Parabrahmā, the Transcendental Immensity—"Lord Krishna in the personality of Mother," and so on. To the majority of her devotees she is God in the form of the goddess Kālī. She was born in 1896 in what is now Bangla Desh, of a poor brahmin family. At a very early age she behaved like an ecstatic, fell into trances, and showed other signs of mystical behavior. However, her family decided that such tendencies should be discouraged, and at the age of thirteen she was married to Ranani Mohan

Chakravarty, a simple village boy. The marriage was not consummated, the husband (commonly called Bholonath) taking vows of celibacy as a sannyāsī and regarding Nirmala as a guru. Her mystical experiences continued on a more intense level; she went into deeper trances, developing the ability to reach samādhi instantaneously without preparatory meditation. In one such mystical passage, while in the forest, she plunged her arm deep into the earth; warm red water, a sudden "eruption of the sacred," welled up, and on the site Nirmala had an ashram built, this being an "axis mundi." Knowledge of her experiences spread, and pilgrims began to visit her. At the age of twenty-six she entered a stage of structural spiritual discipline (or sādhana) but without a guru, for she was her own guru; eventually she bestowed religious initiation (or dīkṣā) upon herself. Then came three years of complete silence.

Westerners unused to authentic Indian spiritual states might suspect that she is mentally unbalanced, yet close observation of Ānandamayee Ma shows her to be a woman completely in control of her mental and spiritual faculties, without a trace of defect. It is only physically that she has, in a sense, acted oddly, for she does not feed nor dress herself nor even brush her teeth, these and similar activities being done for her by disciples. Though physically dependent and in an infantlike stage, she is still spiritually advanced, even to the skeptic. However, her teachings, often buried in seemingly aimless banter or musings, is orthodox Hinduism: *There is motion in rest and rest in motion. Everything is contained in everything. Whatever a man thinks, feels, or realizes about the Supreme is true from his particular standpoint and has full significance for him. Belief means to believe in one's own Self; disbelief means to mistake the non-Self for one's Self. Melt by devotion the sense of separateness, or burn it by knowledge—then you will come to know your Self.*

Like most Indian mystics past and present, she has no interest in caste or other social problems, stating that all will work out in due time according to God's will. Her disciples have built many ashrams for her thoughout India. The main center is: Shree Shree Anandamayee Sangha, Vārānaśī (Benares). See also avatāra, guru, Kālī, Shakti.

anattā, Buddh. The doctrine that there is no individual permanent soul that migrates after death to another body. Gautama Buddha denied the reality of a self or soul inhabiting the person; instead the individual is viewed as a temporary collection of momentary events, the five khandas or aggregates—form, sensation, perception, volition, and consciousness. These khandas are constantly in flux in their causal relationship to each other. The doctrine of anattā is peculiar to Buddhism.

Āṇḍāl, Hind. A bhakti mystic and saint, one of the most noted of the Ālvārs. She was a low-caste woman, by tradition a foundling adopted by the brahmin Ālvār Viṣṇucitta, but highly respected and honored by her male contemporaries. Originally known as Godā (giver of cows, of light, illuminations, and revelations), she chose virginity over marriage and concentrated her love on Krishna. She composed two sets of hymns. The first, the *Tiruppāvāi,* describes her preparations for gaining Krishna as lover and husband which are an adaptation of the ancient practice of young women going to the river for ritual baths and thence to the temple to pray for a mate. Godā oriented the practice to search for mystic union with God, ending in ultimate liberation (or moksha). In her hymns, union with God is the true aim of the soul, the yearning for infinity, perfection, and unmixed bliss, and freedom from all cycles of birth, disease, and misery. The second group, the *Nācciyār Tirumoli,* describes the mystical marriage with God as Kāmadeva, the Lord of Love; here God hunger replaces sexual hunger. The spiritual marriage of Godā was celebrated by her foster father in the temple at Śrīrangam. It is said that she merged in the image. At this point she was known as Āṇḍāl. See also Ālvārs, bhakti.

animals, as cult objects. In Hinduism, Zoroastrianism, and Buddhism, animals play various roles, some of clearly totemic origins, others in roles stemming from fertility rituals. In Hinduism, which contains much archaic material, animals have an important part, primarily derived from totems. Such would be the bull, cow, monkey, elephant, and snake. As avatārs, the fish, tortoise, and boar are incarnations of Vishu, his first three. In the Rāmāyaṇa (q.v.), the monkeys and bears who are allies of Rāma were undoubtedly tribal indigenes who bore the names of the animals as totems, a practice continued to the present. The elephant-headed Gaṇpaṭi (who has the body of a man) may be traced to a shamanist practice, in which the priest danced in the head and skin of the animal; this custom may explain the representations of the god Shiva (cf. entry under Indus Valley), who is seen on the stamp seals wearing buffalo horns, an iconic form found also in later Indian art. The snake is found throughout Hinduism: the god Vishnu sleeps on a snake, serpent deities abound, and Buddha was protected by the hood of a giant cobra during his period of enlightenment. Sacred cobras are found at many temples, where they are tame enough to take milk from the priests.

Also of interest in Hinduism is the aśvemedha (q.v.), the horse sacrifice. In Zoroastrianism the four-eyed dog (q.v.) plays an important role, and in Shintō, deer (q.v.) are sacred to the Kasuga shrine.

For more specific entries, see also cow, deer, Gaṇpati, Hanumān, horse, tortoise. Also, the entries under numbers, 108, vegetation, sleep, pipal, and tulasī contain information of similar primordial practices and veneration.

Anu-Gītā, Hind. A sequel to the *Bhagavad Gītā* inserted into the Mahābhārata as part of Book XIV to hammer home the lesson of the victory, with Krishna again instructing Arjuna. The *Anu-Gītā* is divided into three parts: instruction given by a siddha to his brahmin, by a brahmin to his wife, and by a guru to his pupil. The work also repeats the general theme of Book XII on the subject of moksha (roughly, liberation). The *Anu-Gītā* praises both brahmins and brahminism and thus is obviously an attempt by the priestly caste to affirm its superiority. The work is usually ignored today, having the reputation of being both dishonest in intent and insipid. See Mahābhārata, *Bhagavad Gītā.*

apsara, Hind. A water nymph or celestial houri (or hetaera) who inhabited water in some form, most often an artificial lotus pond —i.e., a tank or puskara, less often a river. The apsaras were associated with primitive fertility rites, and by Vedic times likely represented a fusion between the women of the early pre-Aryan peoples and the men of the invading Aryans. They were described as irresistibly beautiful creatures who would entice men to intercourse and then destroy them. Verses in the Vedic hymns indicate that after a ritual wedding ceremony and ritual union with an apsara, the male, in some cases, would be sacrificed. Later the apsaras were attached to temples, were skilled in music and dancing, and would be visited by men after they had enjoyed a ritual bath in the temple's puskara. The Great Bath at the Indus city of Mohenjo-daro fits the pattern of the apsara cult. The woman could not marry and settle down, though certain ancient Indian dynasties are said to have descended from the temporary union of an apsara and a prince. See also devadasi.

al-'Arabī Ibn, Islamic poet and mystic. (He has been called "the greatest mystical genius of the Arabs.") He was born in Moorish Spain c. A.D. 1164 and died in Damascus in 1240. His family had Ṣūfic traditions. His father, determined to give his son the best education available (possibly in Iberia more than anywhere else at the time), first sent him as a young boy to school in Lisbon, where he studied Islamic law and theology. Still in his teens, al-'Arabī went to Seville for Qur'ānic studies, and then to Córdoba for jurisprudence under a noted shayk, El-Sharrat. During his school days, al-'Arabī passed his free time among Ṣūfīs, and began to write poetry. He lived in Seville for some thirty years, with law as his profession and mystical poetry as his avocation. His poetry, which took many forms, was Ṣūfic in content and associations. On the surface it spoke in erotic and mundane terms; actually it employed Ṣūfic images and Ṣūfic code terms and phrases. Much of al-'Arabī's poetry can be read as ordinary love poems. In his attempts to reach scholars, for he had become deeply involved in philosophic concepts, he ranged from ancient mythology to Christian themes. As with Ṣūfic writing and thought, there is a primary meaning, taken literally by the uninitiated and the literal, covering unmeasured mystical depths. Some of his work, written in a state of trance, contained meanings that he did not understand until the words could be analyzed later. Reveries and dreams produced other works. "A person must control his thoughts in a dream," he once remarked. "The training of this alertness will produce awareness of the intermediate dimension."

On the surface, though he tried to appear as a conformist in religion, his unusual ideas gained him many enemies among the orthodox, who thought he was a secret heretic. He was denounced as "a deliberate liar and chief among heretics and a hardened Ṣūfī." His theology has been defined as emphatically rejecting "the distinction between essence and existence," affirming that "essences are created at the time of their existence," and attributes "an essence to God, which, as in the case of created beings, is indistinguishable from Divine Existence. Thus, by making existence unique in the case of each being, it eradicates even the slightest tendency to pantheism and develops into a form of existentialism." Al-'Arabī developed the idea of the universe as the macro-anthropos or macro-persona. In relation to this view of the cosmos, man is the micro-anthropos. Thus al-'Arabī reversed the traditional teaching that the Universe is centered on man; instead, man is within the Universe. Criticism of al-'Arabī's doctrines spread from the orthodox to the Ṣūfīs. Al-Sammānī (d. 1336) accused him of "confounding God with the world" by identifying the Divine and the human. Al-'Arabī's thinking about Muḥammad as the Perfect Man had brought this charge. This belief states that the Perfect Man—i.e., the Prophet—is he in whom the Divine Light shines. Muḥammad is the visible aspect of Àllāh. The goal of the mystic is to be united with and in the Perfect Man, who is the personification of all phenomena in the manifestation of the real, and above all, a copy of Allāh, a cosmic power on which the universe depends for its existence. Al-'Arabī saw individual souls as being nothing more than divine emanations. At the moment of mystical union there exists no distinction between the soul and Allāh. It is in the person of man that the image of God becomes conscious of itself.

In his thirty-eighth year al-'Arabī went on pilgrimage to Mecca. News of his extremist teachings had preceded him, and in Egypt he was accused of heresy; an orthodox fanatic tried to assassinate him. In Mecca he joined a community of immigrant Persians, among whom was a beautiful young woman to whom he wrote a series of love poems that scandalized the orthodox. However erotic they may seem on the surface, the poems were but an expression of his mystical search for the divine. In Syria, to counter the attacks of the orthodox, he wrote a work known as the *Interpreter,* in which he adopted orthodox terminology; however, the *Interpreter,* like the love poems, had its own hidden meanings, and it emerges as a manual of inner truths apparent to Ṣūfīs.

arahant, Hind. and Buddh. A variant spelling of arhant (q.v.).

Āranyakas, Hind. Esoteric texts—forest books (from Sanskrit araṇya, forest)—that appeared about B.C. 600. They were composed by forest hermits in a reaction against, or sometimes development of, the ritualism and sacerdotalism of the Brāhmanas. Esoteric in content and concerned with the inmost nature of man, the texts stress the internal and secret meaning of sacrifice, giving ritual a symbolic rather than actual meaning, and ignoring external performances. These mystical interpretations of the Vedas led almost immediately to the Upanishads. See Brāhmanas, Upanishads.

āratī, Hind. A devotional ceremony in Hindu worship, with the waving of lighted candles and incense before the object of devotion. It is most commonly performed at dawn and dusk in Hindu shrines and temples, and at the beginning and end of most religious ceremonies. The second *a* of āratī is not pronounced.

arhant, Hind. and Buddh. (In Pāli Buddhism, arahant.) The word in its Sanskrit form was originally used as a term of respect, being applied to saints such as the Jain Mahāvīra and the Buddha. It now means "a worthy one." It came to have a special meaning in Pāli Buddhism as the last of four stages of spiritual attainment, following sotāpanna (stream enterer), sakadāgāmi (once returner), and anāgāmi (nonreturner). The first three stages may be reached by the layman, but the state of arhant is usually the accomplishment of the monk.

arhat, Jain. A soul who has not quite attained final liberation but who has received illumination, and is above the ordinary human level. Such souls enter mundane life at certain cosmic periods for the good of all mankind, desiring to serve the world and looking upon their fellows with love and kindness.

Arjuna, Hind. The great warrior of the Pāndavas. The conversation with his charioteer, Krishna, concerning Arjuna's moral dilemma in going to war against his relatives, forms the basis of the *Bhagavad Gītā* (q.v. for a fuller discussion).

Artha Śāstra, Ind. *The Science of Material Gain* is a rough translation; the subtitle is *The Conduct of the Ideal King.* The authorship is credited to the late-fourth-century B.C. Magadhan Prime Minister Kauṭilya, also known as Cānakya, who, in laying out the most efficient methods for ruling, carries the doctrine of dharma (q.v.) to its farthest point without cant or ambiguity: it is the dharma of some men to rule, of others to be ruled and exploited, a doctrine found in softer terms in the *Bhagavad Gītā* in Krishna's rambling exhortation to Arjuna. Abstract questions of morality and ethics such as Gautama Buddha and other "reformers" might have raised are never considered.

The *Artha Śāstra* is one of the world's earliest books devoted to the art of ruling. Down to the smallest details, it develops the techniques for gaining and maintaining the governing hand over one's subjects through the establishment of a monolithic, totalitarian state. Spies, secret police, the breaking up of the alliances of one's enemies, litigation, torture, taxation, and the fomenting of quarrels between friends are among the methods in which a prince gains and keeps power. Officials and government servants are to be used and discarded. Tribes and clans must be destroyed, and the ruler must settle his lands with people of the lowest castes, for they are least able to object or revolt; the best villages are those that are "helpless," for they can be best exploited for taxes, labor, grain, and wealth. The pacifistic Emperor Ashoka (q.v.) employed some of the techniques of the *Artha Śāstra* but rejected others. The work was damaged in the copying over the centuries, about a fifth to a quarter being estimated as lost, and finally disappeared, until a copy of the Sanskrit text was found in 1905; study of the work shed much light on ancient Indian statecraft and morality. The Indian social historian D. D. Kosambi (a Buddhist) commented, "Some of the *Arthaśāstra* methods, including strong drink and poison, were used in the U.S.A. against the 'Redskins' for much the same reasons as in ancient Magadha."

Arthava Veda, Hind. The last of the four Vedas (q.v.). It is a collection of charms and magic formulas necessary for the success of daily life.

ārya, Buddh. An individual noted for saintly wisdom and insight, and transcending the state of bhadra (q.v.) in wisdom and strength of character.

Āryans. The second-millennium invaders of northwestern India, whose exploits are commemorated in the Vedas (q.v.). The term ārya means noble or well-born. The Āryans immediately established their domination over the peoples they conquered, the result being the unique social system known as caste. The victims of the marauding Āryans were not, from the evidence now coming from the excavations of the cities of the civilization of the Indus Valley (q.v.), mere primitives but the possessors of a high and complex standard of life. However, since for several millennia the only source of information was the Āryans' own documents, the Vedas, it had been assumed that they were the superior peoples and the originators of what is now called Hinduism. Today it is conceded that the core of Hinduism is probably the religion of the Indus peoples, with a strong infusion of Āryan beliefs. See Hinduism, Indus Valley.

Āryā Samāj, Hind. A reformist, Hindu revivalist movement (the name means Noble Society) founded in 1875 by Swami Dayānanda Saraswatī (1824–83), a Shaivite brahmin from Gujarat. It is based on a return to the Vedas, with a reinterpretation of the sacred texts to correct the misrepresentations that had accumulated over the centuries. Non-Indian ideas are excluded, but the society can claim, for example, that firearms and electricity were described in the Vedas. Attacking the many corruptions encrusting Hinduism, Dayānanda preached that the Vedas were sanātana dharma (eternal law), with all that was necessary for salvation, which he alone could properly interpret. He denounced image worship, caste, child marriage, pilgrimages, and the concept of the avatār, though he insisted upon the doctrines of karma and rebirth, which are post-Vedic. Shortly after Dayānanda's death in 1883, a split between two factions in Āryā Samāj brought the progressives to the fore; they have made a special effort to reach out to fallen-away Hindus and low castes, and are one of the few groups that will accept non-Hindu converts, even Christians, who, however, have no standing in the eyes of the orthodox. The movement has been especially strong in the Panjab and among Panjabis, who suffered much at the hands of the Muslims in the past. Thus the movement is violently anti-Muslim, as well as anti-Christian. However, it looks forward to the establishment of a universal church based on the Vedas, and without distinctions of caste, race, color, or previous religion.

āsana, Hind. 1. Yogic posture or physical pose used in meditation. Āsana is the third of the eight limbs of yoga. There are various kinds of āsanas, some easy, some difficult, the most famous being the padam āsana or lotus position, in which the devotee sits with feet intertwined, back rather rigid, and arms outstretched over the knees, or with his hands together, one atop the other. The eyes are partially (sometimes fully) closed. The classic padam āsana is most difficult to achieve and is beyond the capabilities of the Westerner who comes to yoga late in life; he may find himself forced to wrestle with the demands of the āsana rather than using it as an aid to meditation. Thus many gurus will suggest that one sit in the most comfortable position, with the back straight but not forced. The purpose of the āsana is primarily to provide a calm basis for meditation, not to perform acrobatics. Patañjali (fourth century A.D.) stated, "Proper posture requires that one be seated in a position which is formal but relaxed." A Sāṁkya sutra says, "Any posture which is easy and steady is an āsana; there is no other rule," while Swami Vivekananda advises, "Let the whole weight of the body be supported by the ribs, and then you have an easy, natural posture, with the spine straight." Other āsanas such as the lion and the serpent, common in such disciplines as Hatha Yoga and so on, require training from childhood and are learned under a guru. See Patañjali, yoga.

2. A small carpet or mat used as a seat by a person in meditation.

Ascension of Muḥammad, Isl. In A.D. 620, led by the angel Jibril (Gabriel), Muḥammad made a mystical journey from Mecca to

Jerusalem, riding the steed Burāq. There are several traditions concerning the journey and his Ascension to Heaven. The original source is a verse in the Qur'ān, Sura 17, "Glory be to Him who made His servant go by night from the Sacred Mosque [of Mecca] to the farther Mosque [of Jerusalem] whose surroundings We have blessed that We might show Him some of Our Signs." Some Muslim commentators give a literal interpretation to this passage; others see it as a vision. When the Prophet related the events of his Night Journey and Ascension to his followers, many derided him; the earliest ḥadīth (q.v.) state that the experience was mystical only, the Prophet's body remaining physically in Mecca. However, four centuries later, the *Fiqh Akbar II* (q.v.), an important statement of Islamic creed, says plainly that the Ascension is a fact and who so rejects it is a schismatic.

Several traditions are possibly involved here, the first of the Night Journey (isrā') on Burāq, led by Jibril. Burāq was half donkey, half mule, and was the beast on which several earlier prophets had ridden. At Jerusalem Muḥammad met Ibrāhīm, Musa, and 'Isa (Abraham, Moses, and Jesus), and several other prophetic figures. A second tradition is that of the Ascension to Heaven; it is known as mi'rāj (literally, ladder). A ladder of light brought the Prophet up to a door of Heaven, which was guarded by an angel. Heaven was divided into seven circles: In the first, Muḥammad saw the terrible flames in which sinners were burned; in the second, he met 'Isa and Yahya (John the Baptist); in the third, Jusuf (Joseph); in the fourth, Idris (Ezra); in the fifth, Harun (Aaron); in the sixth, Moses, and in the seventh, Ibrāhīm. It was on the mi'rāj that Muḥammad was instructed to order his followers to pray five times a day.

Such is the core of the belief. Much accretion has piled upon the canonical ḥadīth. In some versions Burāq carried the Prophet from Mecca straight to Heaven; in those in which the Prophet ascends by ladder (which is sometimes literal), Burāq is tied to a stone in the ruins of the Temple.

The Islamic world celebrates the feast of Mi'rāj each year on Rajab 27 (see calendar). There is much mystical literature concerning the event; the Ṣūfīs (q.v.) see in it a mystical ascent of the soul from the mundane world to communion with the Divine. The twentieth-century Spanish Islamicist Abbé Asín Palacios places the sources of Dante Alighieri's *Divine Comedy* in the ḥadīth of the Prophet's Ascension.

Whatever interpretations Muslims put upon the Night Journey and the ascent to Heaven, there are echoes of shamanism (q.v.) in the concept of the mystical voyage and the mystical rising to another world. The steed, the ride, the climbing of a ladder (of light, in this case), and the seven heavens are all elements found in shamanism and may have been carried through Zoroastrianism (q.v.) and Mithraism into the Middle East. See Muḥammad.

Ashoka. See Aśoka.

ashram, Hind. (Sanskrit, āśrama.) 1. An abode or residence, commonly the abode of a saint, sadhu, ascetic, or guru who is usually engaged in some form of religious instruction. Though ashram may mean merely a simple place where the holy man and his students or disciples (chelas or siśyas) meet and reside, the term more commonly denotes the Hindu equivalent of a monastery or hermitage, and may, as in those at holy sites like Hardwar and Rishikesh on the upper Ganges, be highly complex, with schools for religious education, chains of guest houses, medical care, transport across the river, and a host of charitable enterprises. The ashram of whatever size is dependent on voluntary contributions, the dāna, from both individuals and rich business communities. Some ashrams have publishing houses and manufacture ayurvedic (traditional) medicines. Commonly at any ashram it is the guru, with his knowledge, experience, and above all darshan (roughly, spiritual charisma) that is all-important. His mere presence, his recognition of the disciple, his touch and glance are what are sought out, facts that can easily lead the unscrupulous guru or sadhu to take advantage of others. Living in an ashram can be simple and deeply spiritual but, as Richard Lannoy has observed (*The Speaking Tree* [New York, 1971]), "Life in an Indian ashrām is not all sweetness, dreams and garland-giving; on the contrary, it is more like the clamour of a railway station, the lesson of which is that inner concentration can be achieved in the midst of hectic activity by the constant practice of certain techniques [yoga], all of which have a physical basis."

2. The four stages of life (here āśrama is more commonly used) more or less accepted as the usual path for the ordinary man of the three upper castes, the dvijā or twice born; śudras and outcastes are denied the privilege. The first stage is that of brahmacarya, a period of discipline and education in which the boy (women are excluded from the four stages), after attaining the age of reason and receiving the sacred thread of his caste, leaves home to study at the foot (literally) of his guru. It might be remarked in passing that such training is rapidly disappearing in favor of school and university for those lucky enough. In the ashram the boy takes metaphysics and religious instruction, basic yoga, and probably grammar, logic, phonetics, arithmetic, higher mathematics, and literature; Sanskrit will be included, along with the study of ayurvedic medicine and plants and herbs. Such is the ideal, observed less now than in the past.

His training completed, the brahmacaryīn, now in his midteens, returns to his father's house, is married into the proper family, and raises his own family. He is at this period in the second stage, that of the gārhasthya or householder and active worker. Gārhasthya is considered the mainstay of the four āśramas, for it is the basis of the social structure and engages a man's life at his most productive and energetic years. The other āśramas depend on it for sustenance. Ideally, of course, material success is considered ephemeral. The system does not advocate celibacy, for that is outside the āśramas and is a custom reserved for the special few.

After his children are grown and his familial duties completed, the householder is encouraged to begin a period of withdrawal from the world, his wife having been sent to live with one of the sons or with another relative. This is the stage of vānaorasthya or retreat from mundane ties. Finally the man takes up sannyāsa, the life of the hermit, in which he is likely to retire to a secluded place, often in a forest or on a mountainside or riverbank. "He will desire neither death nor life, but will await his appointed time as a servant awaits his wage," say the ancient *Laws of Manu*. "Rejoicing in the things of the soul [atman], caring for nothing, eating no meat, with the soul his one companion, intent on [eternal] happiness, so will he live. . . . By curbing the senses, by destroying affection and hatred, by doing no harm to any living things he will conform himself to deathlessness. . . . Thus by giving up gradually all attachments, liberated from all the pairs of opposites, he will abide in Brahman."

Basically the āśramas concentrate on leading the individual to gain his own salvation: that of other people is not his problem or concern. Women are virtually excluded from the āśramas; their role is to attain salvation by their selfless service and devotion to their husbands and children, after which they may be reborn as a male, to then enjoy the gradual ascent of the āśramas.

Aśoka (or Ashoka). Indian King (ruling B.C. 272/268–233/232), of the Mauryan dynasty, who forged the first universal empire on the peninsula by means of bloody and cruel wars against his neighbors. After a particularly savage war against Kalinga in eastern India, in which 100,000 were killed, several times that wounded, and 150,000 left homeless, he was so horrified at the price of his conquest that he eschewed violence as a policy and adopted Buddhism. He reorganized and reformed the government, ending the *Artha Śāstra* form of rule, encouraged and stimulated art and architecture, laid out new trade routes, built hospitals and schools, and in general following the Buddhist Middle Way, tried to make life better for his subjects—"Whatever exertion I make, I strive only to discharge the debt I owe to all living creatures," he said. Though he accepted all sects without distinction, he actively propagated Buddhism as a peaceful and nonviolent way of life; he discouraged the killing of animals as well as of people. His message of peace and universal love was inscribed in several languages on a series of stone monuments that were placed throughout his empire. He established Buddhist monasteries and centers of learning, sent missionaries to Ceylon, Southeast Asia, possibly to China, and to Greece and other Western nations. Tradition states that he called the Third Buddhist Council (at Pātaliputra, now Patna) to purify the doctrines from heresy. See ahiṁsā, *Artha Śāstra,* Buddhism.

aśrama, Hind. An alternate spelling of ashram, which can be either one of the four stages of life, or a residence for monks. See ashram.

Aśvaghosa, Buddh. A Brāhmin (c. A.D. 100) converted to Buddhism. He resided at Benares and is the author of the *Buddhacarita,* a biography of the Buddha, and of the *Mahāyānaśraddhotpāda Sastra* (The Awakening of Faith). He is called the Twelfth Ancestor, or the Twelfth Patriarch, in the Ch'an line that begins with Gautama Buddha and ends with Bodhidharma (q.v.).

aśvamedha, Hind. The horse sacrifice, a rite performed by the priests on behalf of kings and chieftains during the Vedic period; it was practiced sporadically into the eighteenth century, when the last celebration was held in Rajasthan. The rite is widely mentioned in ancient Vedic literature; the *Taittiriya Saṁhita* (otherwise the *Veda of the Black Yajus School*) is primarily concerned with aśvamedha and its associated practices, including the construction of the proper altar (in the shape of the bird-god Garuḍa) and the soma rite. In Chapter XIV of the Mahābhārata, the rite is performed by Yudhisthira with the aid of Arjuna, under the direction of Krishna.

The custom of sacrificing horses is wasteful and uneconomic, and a burden to any but the greatest or wealthiest social groups. In essence it is a celebration of tribal unity and a demonstration of power—one might say, conspicuous consumption—by the communal owners of livestock, and is intimately connected with a desire for the weal of the tribe, the fertility of crops and cattle, and the superiority of the ruler over his rivals.

THE RITE. A specially bred white stallion was allowed to roam free—casually directed by the warrior princes—for a year, followed by the king's fiercest and most skilled warriors. In the example in the Mahābhārata, which was probably based on a specific incident, or at least the common practice, King Yudisthira is advised to have the sacrifice performed; a horse is sent away, followed by Arjuna, who is to conquer all the kingdoms the horse leads him to. Arjuna returns after a year, with the horse, and the sacrifice is celebrated in the presence of the kings he has subdued. While the horse and the warriors wander about, the king undergoes a self-punitive asceticism and experiences rites of purification. Traditionally the ceremonies are conducted by four brahmins, each priest being from a different brahminical subcaste. The horse is brought to the sacrificial enclosure, a type of maṇḍala (q.v.) drawn in elaborate rites, to be worshiped by the king's four wives, and then killed, either in a blood sacrifice or, more commonly, by smothering. The senior of the queens lies down in symbolic intercourse with the dead horse. Whether this coupling was simulated or an actual entry into the queen's vagina with the dead animal's penis is impossible to say; some texts indicate a literal intercourse, others pantomiming. Considering the literal interpretation of tantric texts at a later date (some of which stem from similar primitive fertility practices) and the importance of the rite to the tribe, an actual penetration is not to be ruled out. A prayer used at the rites may be taken in either sense: "Come, lay thy seed well in the channel of the one who had opened her thighs. O thou, potent of manhood, set in motion the organ that is to women the nourisher of life. It darts into the sheath, their hidden lover, darkly buffeting, back and forth."

The queen has, at least symbolically, if not literally, absorbed into herself the consecrated powers of the male. The priests dismember the carcass, remove and cook the marrow, which is then eaten by the king as the soul stuff or soul force on behalf of his people. At the end of the ceremony, the king's wives are taken to bed, again with appropriate rites, by the four brahmins.

Interpretations of the aśvamedha vary. It is, to begin with, an exhibition of sheer power. Not only were the neighboring rulers overcome, but so were the king's own people terrorized. During the sacrificial processions, the two lower castes, the vaiśyas and the śudras, were placed between the brahmins and the kśatriyas "to make them submissive"—the vaiśya "tributary to another, to be eaten up by another, to be oppressed at will," and the śudra, "the servant of another, to be removed at will, to be slain at will." The rite was indispensable for the aggrandizement of territory and the maintenance of power, for not only were lands added, but other kings were also forced into submission and their people taken for the winner's fields, shops, and factories. Yet the macabre rites of aśvemedha could be sublimated later, as in the *Bṛhad Āraṇayaka Upaniṣad* (Great Forest Text), where they became a metaphysical exercise. Here aśvemedha means meditation, where the entire universe is offered as the horse, and desires are sacrificed and true spiritual autonomy is obtained.

By the time of Gautama Buddha (c. sixth century B.C.), aśvamedha was dying out in the protest against brahminical excesses. After a revival in feudal India, and the last sacrifice, a marble horse was installed in commemoration at Jaipur.

ātman (or ātmā, rare), Hind. The true Self, one's true Self. Self-awareness, Supreme Existence of being that is of the nature of self-awareness and self-delight. Such are the simple definitions, but essentially atman is "undefinable." The *Taittirīya Upaniṣad* (c. B.C. 600) says that ātman is "that from which speech, along with the mind, turns away—not able to comprehend." Still Hindu speculative philosophy has had an age-long preoccupation with definitions of ātman, and continues to speculate. Ātman, more fully, is "that which pervades all; which is the subject and which knows, experiences, and illuminates the subjects; and which remains always the same." Originally the term had been used to indicate even nonintelligent inner cause, such as clay in jars, earth in clay, water in earth, and once meant life breath. Later, briefly, it acquired connotations of feeling, mind, soul, and spirit, but without precision. In many of the Upanishads the meaning of ātman is uncertain, since it may designate either the supreme and transcendent spirit or the finite individual self of man. The *Bṛhadāraṇyaka Upaniṣad* states, "Ātman is not this, not that. It is unseizable, for it cannot be seized; indestructible, for it cannot be destroyed; unattached, for it does not attach itself; it is not bound, does not tremble, is not injured." Often it is coupled with Brahman, for the two are intimately entwined: the same reality is known subjectively as ātman and objectively as Brahman; the pair may be used as synonyms. See Brahman.

Aṭṭār, Farīd ad-Dīn (c. A.D. 1110–1220). A Persian Ṣūfī, the author of *The Parliament* (or *Conference*) *of the Birds* (Mantiq at-Tā'ir) and some 114 other works. Aṭṭār was born, and died, near Nishapur in Persia. The name means chemist (he inherited his father's pharmacy shop), but he also employed the name in a Ṣūfic sense. Impressed by the simplicity of a wandering Ṣūfī who came by his shop, Aṭṭār gave up his profession to withdraw into a hermitage to mull over his place in the world and to study. Later he founded an order of his own. He died at the age of 110, slaughtered in 1220 by the Mongols in their first explosion into the Western world.

The Parliament of the Birds is an allegorical work describing a quest for the Divine, symbolized by the Simurgh, a monstrous, mythical Persian bird, but standing for the Absolute Essence. The work, based upon early Ṣūfic quest themes, is a compendium of mystical experiences, expressed in code terms and phrases, veiled to all but the initiates, and presents the stages in the development of a Ṣūfī. Briefly, the birds, who represent mankind, are called together by the hoopoe—i.e., the Ṣūfī master—who proposes a search for the mysterious king, the simurgh, the bird of Persian myth. (In Persian si-murgh means "thirty birds," but the term is not translatable into colloquial English.) Most of the birds, though pleased with the possibility of having a king, decline the undertaking for various reasons. The hoopoe's answers expose the falsity of each bird's excuse. However, thirty birds do set out on the pilgrimage across seven mystical valleys, each representing a stage in spiritual development. The first four are the Valley of the Quest, the Valley of Love, the Valley of Intuitive Knowledge, and the Valley of Detachment. By the time the birds reach the fifth valley, that of Unification, they see that what has previously appeared to be diverse is actually only one. In the Valley of Astonishment all previous concepts of knowledge are destroyed, to be replaced by the comprehension of love in a new sense. The last valley is that of Death, or more properly, that of Ṣūfic annihilation of fanā —i.e., extinction in God, a common Ṣūfic theme. "Our eyes are blind although the world is lit by a brilliant sun," said Aṭṭār. "If you succeed in glimpsing Him, you lose your wisdom; if you see Him entirely, you lose yourself." He said, "Annihilate yourself, such is perfection. Renounce thyself, that is the measure of thy union with Him, and that is all." And, "He whose heart is lost in the ocean of immensity is lost there forever and will remain there at rest. In this calm sea he will find nothing but fanā. If he is ever permitted to return from his annihilation, he will know the meaning of creation, and the myriad secrets will have been revealed to him." When the perfected soul falls into this ocean, "it will lose its special existence and will participate in the motion of the ocean's waves. In ceasing to exist alone, it will henceforth be beautiful. It exists and does not exist. How that can happen is impossible for the soul to conceive." Such concepts are strongly reminiscent of the Hindu bhakti mystics (q.v.). See Ṣūfism.

AUM, Hind. The chief of all mantras, the universal sound. Glosses on the sound and this spelling are endless—for example, it is said in an Upanishad to contain the eight subtle sound elements. *A* is the first, *U* the second, *M* the third. The nasalization (bindu, q.v.) is the fourth; the sound (nāda), the fifth; the duration (kāla, or time), the sixth; the resonance (kālātīta), the seventh, and its timelessness resonance, the eighth. Some glosses have only the five first components. It is better spelled ŌṂ (q.v.).

Aurobindo Ghose (1872–1950), Hind. A Bengali political extremist who became a noted yogi. Aurobindo Ghose—commonly known as Sri Aurobindo—was the son of an English-educated, Western-oriented Bengali doctor who sent him to Britain at age seven for his education. Aurobindo was isolated from all Indian influences, but after his studies at Cambridge he returned home, now aged twenty, "denationalized," as he put it, and determined to recapture his Indian heritage. He learned Sanskrit and read the Upanishads and the *Bhagavad Gītā*. He entered the civil service in the princely state of Baroda, but as anti-British agitation increased he joined the nationalist movement. Though young Ghose was extremely shy, he tried public speaking against the enemy. A holy man advised him to empty his mind of all thought in order to receive supernatural inspiration, and he often spoke as the spirit moved him, his mind a blank. He viewed nationalism in religious terms: "Nationalism is not a mere political program; Nationalism is a religion which has come from God. . . . Nationalism is immortal; nationalism cannot die; because it is no human thing, it is God who is working in Bengal. God cannot be killed, God cannot be sent to jail." He attacked "the pernicious delusion that a foreign and adverse interest [England] can be trusted to develop us to its own detriment" and preached "self-development and defensive resistance." He saw the struggle for freedom as a great and holy yajña, or ritual sacrifice, in which boycotts, Swadeshi, and education were a part. He preached passive resistance as either the final method of political salvation ("Our attitude is a political Vedantism") or failing that, the final sādhanā or spiritual discipline.

In 1910, his interests having become fully religious, he abandoned Bengal, his wife, and his family, and went to South India to the (then) French colony of Pondichéry, where he spent the rest of his life. He was visited in 1914 by the French mystic Mira Richard, who returned in 1920 and took over Aurobindo's ashram. Mme. Richard, known as the Mother, became an equal partner in his life, and each saw the other as an avatāra, an incarnation of the Divine.

Aurobindo had been experiencing a series of intense spiritual experiences, beginning with "a vast calm which descended upon him when he first stepped on Indian soil after his long absence." (He wrote about himself in the third person.) The experiences intensified, so that by 1910 he was driven to renounce politics in favor of the ashram. By this time he had had "the realization of the silent, spaceless and timeless Brahman gained after a complete and abiding stillness of the whole consciousness and attended at first by an overwhelming feeling and perception of the total unreality of the world." This was followed by a second deep experience, this in the Alipore jail where he had been imprisoned by the British—"that of the cosmic consciousness and of the Divine as all beings and all that is." Meanwhile, two other realizations were developing within him, even while in jail, which were to culminate in what is known among his followers as "the Descent of the Overmind [or Supermind]." He was experiencing continually "the supreme Reality with the static and dynamic Brahman as its two aspects and that of the higher planes of consciousness leading to the Supermind." The Descent of the Overmind occurred on December 24, 1926. Although Aurobindo constantly refused to discuss the subject seriously, and always turned away his disciples' questions, it was apparent that "the Divine (Krishna or the Divine Presence or whatever you like) had come down into the material" —i.e., into his body. Two years later he withdrew from many of his activities, turning the ashram over to the Mother. While Aurobindo saw the Mother as an avatāra (see entry under Mother), she stated without equivocation that he was "the birth of the Eternal upon earth," being "a birth that recurs for ever from age to age upon earth." And "What Sri Aurobindo represents in the world's history is not a teaching, not even a revelation; it is a decisive action direct from the Supreme."

TEACHING. Aurobindo's ideas may be found in two primary forms, that of Integral Yoga, in which, as he said to his disciples, "Knowledge, Bhakti, light of Consciousness, Ananda and love, will and power in works—meditations, adoration, service to the Divine all have their place." He was much influenced by his fellow Bengalis, Rāmakrishna and Vivekānanda (see both), but though he drew upon them for inspiration, he refused to say that his more fully developed system was superior to theirs. The other mode of expression of his thought is in his greatest work, *Life Divine*, a highly complex presentation in which he lays out his thesis of the divine energy at work everywhere, manifesting itself in an ascending order in matter, through various stages of life to consciousness and finally supraconsciousness, which will eventually reveal the identity of the Absolute with the Universe. It is through yoga (i.e., Integral Yoga) that man will transcend his fragmentary knowledge of the universe and his individual consciousness, to bathe in the bliss that pervades all. The laborious evolution from the present low state of humanity to the supramental state will be carried on by a small elite, the seed of a new race. This is the concept that motivated the selection of candidates for the ashram at Pondichéry (now Pondicherry), and the plan for the "planetary city" that the Mother conceived after Aurobindo's death. In the *Life Divine* social and political movements are fruitless, for they ignore the divine energy that rules the cosmic evolution and thus cannot lead man to union with the universal Shakti. Only the spiritual elite can gain man's true destiny.

Avalokiteśvara, Buddh. A major bodhisattva, the close companion of the Amida (or Amitābha) Buddha (q.v.), and a popular figure in Mahāyāna Buddhism. The name, which is Indian, has various meanings: either "the Lord who looks down upon the world with compassion," or "he who is looked to for help." Avalokiteśvara is known for his potent compassion and wisdom and his miraculous powers in aiding mankind in distress. He has a multitude of attributes, including the protection of humanity from natural disasters and the granting of fertility to barren women. As a Buddha form, he is an aspect of the Buddhism of Faith, with a vast attraction for people who seek the key to salvation in devotion rather than in self-reliance and self-development. As the special companion of

Amida, his picture is placed at the bedside of Buddhists on the point of death, because he leads the dead into the Paradise of the Pure Land. The Tibetans believe the Dalai Lama (q.v.) is an incarnation of Avalokiteśvara and connect him with the mantra ŌṂ man-ni pad-me hum (q.v.). In China he is known as Kuan Yin, and in Japan as Kannon, where he plays a central role in both Pure Land and Tendai sects. In Cambodian temple art, princesses, their breasts bare, were sometimes represented as Avalokiteśvara. His cult reached as far as Java (once an Indian colony), where, in Indian fashion, in one temple designed in the shape of a maṇḍala (q.v.), he is shown with eight arms and is accompanied by Tantric figures. In various art forms he may have six or eight arms; texts describe him as having a thousand; he is shown with nine or eleven heads (as well as a single one), and in some Tantric aspects he has a horse's head. See Kannon, Kuan Yin, Pure Land.

avatār (or avatāra), Hind. A manifestation of God on earth, a theophany. The origin of the doctrine is unknown, but an early example has been found in the Zoroastrian Bahrām Yāsht (roughly sixth century B.C.), where the war god Verethraghna, equated with the Vedic Mithra, appears in both human and animal forms (such as a warrior and a raging boar). In the great Hindu epics, the Rāmāyaṇa and the Mahābharata (both developed in the period following B.C. 500), the doctrine is clearly enunciated, especially in the *Bhagavad Gītā,* which states: "When goodness grows weak, when evil increases, I make myself a body. In every age I come back to deliver the holy, to destroy the sin of the sinner, to establish righteousness." The doctrine reached its fullest development during the Purāṇic period (A.D. 300–1200). Maddhva (thirteenth century) taught that the Lord, completely independent and perfect Being and pure consciousness, also possesses a purely spiritual organism or body, which He can manifest as avatār while remaining one and undivided. The belief in many avatārs reconciles the unity of the divine with the multiplicity of local divinities, thus absorbing tribal, community, and racial gods, heroes, kings, leaders, sages, and saints. Of the many avatārs, those of Vishnu, solar and cosmic deity, protector and sustainer of the world, god of the ocean and of the luminous sky, are best known, among them being the gods Rāma, Krishna, and the saint Buddha. Some lists give twenty-four Vishnu avatārs, others but ten, with the last, Kalki, still to come. The belief today that Mohandas Gandhi was an avatār is growing. Other recent avatārs include the nineteenth-century Rāmakrishna and the twentieth-century Ānandamayee Ma, both mystics from Bengal.

The avatārs of the epics are intermediaries between the divine and man. God manifests himself in forms that can be appreciated by even the most unsophisticated. For well over two thousand years Rāma and Krishna have been the beloved and adored manifestations of the Divine, knowable, almost touchable by the ordinary man, no matter how servile his stature. In the *Bhagavad Gītā* it is stated that avatārs such as Krishna have no prārabdha karma (the stored-up karma of past lives that unfolds in the present life) and has never been subject to the law of karma. God is made flesh many times in different ages and in different forms (even other than human), the purpose being to protect and save all of creation through His earthly role. The "body" or shape is not real human nature but is composed of heavenly matter (or viśuddha sattva) and is a temporary manifestation only. The Hindu can accept Christ as an avatār under these circumstances, but according to Christian theologians familiar with the doctrine, Christ, "the Word made flesh," both human and divine, cannot be considered an avatār in Christian teaching.

Avatārs are countless, for besides the popularly known figures any saint or spiritual teacher is an avatār to some degree, being at least in part if not fully an embodiment of the Divine. See Ānandamayee Ma, *Bhagavad Gītā,* bhakti, Krishna, Vishnu.

Avesta, The, Zor. The sacred scripture of the Zoroastrians (q.v.). Of the original work only the fraction used in the liturgy has survived. Zardushti tradition varies about the original, one source stating that an archetypal copy was kept at the royal Persian library at Ishtakhr, the other that there were two, one at Persepolis and the other at Samarkand. Whether one or two, the manuscript was written in gold ink on twelve thousand ox hides and was destroyed by Alexander the Great in B.C. 330. However, a third of the text was retained in the memories of the priests, and this was transcribed again. There is, however, no strong evidence of the actual existence of the primitive written version for at least a century after the age of the Prophet Zoroaster himself (B.C. 626–551), the work presumably being transmitted orally from one generation of priests to another. The language of the Avesta is Zend, an eastern Iranian dialect in which no other works, not even rock inscriptions nor tablets, have been found. Most, but not all, of the Avesta was translated into a later Persian, Pahlavi, about the ninth century A.D. but reflecting theological views of earlier periods; the Pahlavi books contain a number of commentaries, large parts of which show an evident misunderstanding of both the language and the intent of the original Avesta.

The Avesta has always presented a serious problem to scholars, as to the latter Zoroastrians. It and other texts had been known to and studied by the Greeks, and later by the Islamic Arabs, some of whom, such as the Ṣūfī Muslims, were influenced by Zoroastrian doctrines. Zoroastrian studies came alive in 1700 and immediately thereafter when European scholars, fascinated by the survival of the once great faith among the Parsees of Surat in India, began to seek out the original sources of their beliefs. Zoroastrian studies were put on a professional basis by the French linguist and scholar Anquetil-Duperron, who in 1754 (he was then twenty) came upon a facsimile of four leaves from a Parsee manuscript. He became obsessed by the idea of opening up Zoroastrian and Parsee studies to the world. In order to get to India, he enlisted in the French East India Company, fought in the French and English wars raging on the subcontinent at the time, and after three years of service, was able to join the Parsee community in Surat, where he stayed another three years, struggling to obtain from the Parsees both knowledge and manuscripts. His efforts at last successful, he spent another four years in study, then returned to France in 1864 with the whole of the Avesta, along with copies of other works. In 1771 Anquetil-Duperron published the first translation of the Avesta in a European language.

A dispute immediately broke out over the work, for half the scholarly world rejected the authenticity of the Avesta, claiming not only that there was no other text of any kind in Zend, but also that it introduced concepts, gods, laws, and rules, folk tales that were unheard of, even in translation, through Greek and Arab sources but also did grave injustice to the celebrated simplicity, purity, and wisdom of the great sage Zoroaster. However, once the disputes died down and further research was done, the Avesta became a central focus of oriental scholarship, and links were found not only in its primary language, Zend (in both archaic and later forms), to Sanskrit but also in many of its themes and even in the names of gods and spirits to the Hindu Rig Veda. The discovery and translation of ancient Persian rock inscriptions in a tongue akin to Zend, spoken from the mouth of the great Darius (B.C. 522–486) and his successors, which included summary descriptions of the religion of Zoroaster (though he is not mentioned by name), helped confirm the authority of the Zend Avesta. However, no matter how historic the Avesta might be, the problem of linguistics is one that has haunted scholars, and will continue to, for it has been impossible to determine the precise meaning of many words, and even much playing about with comparative philology has failed to solve the tremendous number of blanks in interpretation. The later Zoroastrians, who did not maintain a tradition of Zend studies (as the Hindus did with Sanskrit), only compounded the problem with mistakes in transcription, erroneous commentaries, and a general disregard for the original meaning.

At some point, however, an Avesta canon was drawn up consisting of twenty-one nasks or books, a summary of which exists in the Dēnkart, an encyclopedia designed to salvage what was essential in Zoroastrianism from impending loss; the text of the present Dēnkart dates from the ninth century A.D. The Dēnkart includes a summary of the Avesta extant at the time of its own compilation.

The surviving Avesta is about one tenth the length of the Bible. The oldest portion, written in a somewhat more archaic form of Zend than the remainder of the work, consists of a collection of songs or hymns, the Gāthās. Most scholars agree that the Gāthās are the work of Zoroaster himself. The Gāthās form the core of the Yasna, the primary liturgy. A related, shorter liturgical section is the Visp-rat (or Vispered), which repeats much of the Yasna. The Yasna also contains, inserted between the Gāthās, another early section, the Haptañāiti Gāthā, which is composed in the same old form of Zend but is probably not by Zoroaster, for the theological content differs markedly.

The second most important section, in a later form of Zend, is that known as the Yashts; accompanying the Yashts is the "Little

Avesta," the Khurda Avesta, a collection of hymns addressed to various deities. The final section is the Vidēvdāt (erroneously called the Vendidad), the Law Against the Demons, in a form of Zend written by a much later group of individuals who, from the vast number of mistakes and the awkwardness with which they handled the language, seemed to have little understanding of Zend. The Vidēvdāt is primarily a code of laws and regulations, ceremonial purifications and other rituals, and returns to the kind of polytheism that Zoroaster, in the Gāthās, had rejected in favor of a monotheistic God. See also Parsees, Zoroaster.

avidyā, Hind. Ignorance; individual ignorance. Definitions of avidyā, often given as a synonym for ajñāna, have absorbed Indian philosophers in endless and, one might say, profitless speculation, without much common concurrence. Avidyā, said Saṁkara, is beginningless but can end at any moment when a man attains spiritual illumination. Avidyā causes man to move farther away from the Self and obscure his knowledge of the truth. In the *Bhagavad Gītā* we find that all our sufferings and limitations imposed by our ego come from avidyā; consequently man must seek knowledge, with which hatred, injury, and greed are incompatible. Maṇḍana states that avidyā is called illusion (māyā), also false appearance (mithyābhāsa), because it is neither the characteristic nature of Brahman nor an entity different from Brahman. It is neither real nor absolutely unreal. He states that the locus of avidyā is the individual soul (jīva). Ultimately the jīvas are identical with the Brahman but phenomenally they are diverse, diversity being the product of avidyā. There are two kinds of avidyā; absence of knowledge and positive wrong knowledge. Vāchaspati also says the locus of avidyā is in the soul, but the illusion is psychological, for which each individual is responsible. A dilemma arises: Avidyā resides in the soul, but the soul is the product of avidyā; what Vāchaspati sees is an endless chain of false illusions in which each succeeding illusion is due to its preceding illusion. Sureshvara states that avidyā is beginningless error and is indescribable, as it is neither real nor unreal. It is an inconsistent category, a self-contradictory principle, for if it had been consistent, it would not have been avidyā at all. The many succeeding philosophers are mainly concerned with refuting one another. Vidyāraṇya ends the series with the statement that avidyā is a beginningless power that cannot stand dialectical scrutiny, cannot be described in any way, and is therefore false. When true knowledge dawns, avidyā with all its world products is realized as something that never was, never is, and never will be real.

āyāt, Isl. An Arabic word meaning, literally, miraculous signs, but applied to the verses of the Qur'ān, especially by Ṣūfīs.

ayurveda, Hind. The traditional system of medicine in India, based upon the Vedas (q.v.); the science of longevity was esteemed as the fifth Veda. The knowledge of ayurvedic medicine up to the intermediate stage is still compulsory among certain Vedic brahmins. Treatment is performed with the three basic sources—herbs, roots, or fruits—in combination with mantras or prayers sung or chanted (or sometimes whispered) from the Vedas, especially the Artharva Veda. Some drugs are undoubtedly efficacious, others useless. Ayurvedic medicine is complicated by confusion over which plant may be the one meant in the sacred formula; e.g., the Sanskrit term ananta, for a plant used in the treatment of spasms, may actually mean any of fourteen different plants, from a type of grass to a tree, depending on the area of India in which it is sought. The Buddhist canonical work *Vinaya* describes the education and practice of the physician Jivaka, who was appointed by the Emperor Bimbasāra to attend Gautama Buddha. Jivaka cured the Buddha of constipation by having him inhale the fragrance of a medicated lotus blossom. The work also states that he cured patients of "head disease," fistula (with an ointment), and jaundice, and performed surgical operations on the brain and also on the intestines to free then from entanglement. The Emperor Ashoka (q.v.) sent fully equipped medical missions to the five states of Greece "for relief of suffering of all creatures, man and beast," so his Rock Edicts II and XIII report (c. B.C. 260).

B

Bāb, Isl. and Bahá'í. A term meaning "gateway" employed by the Imāmī Shī'a of Iran to designate a certain kind of spiritual teacher or leader. (The Imāmī Shī'a are so called because they preach the immanence of a hidden Imām, who will appear to complete Muḥammad's mission and save the world.) Extremists among the Imāmī Shī'a took the concept of Bāb, the Gateway of Divine Revelation, to denote a stage of self-propulsion in the manifesting of the Divine Being. A devotee of the cult, 'Alī Muḥammad of Shīrāz (born A.D. 1820 or 1821), made a pilgrimage to the holy cities of Persia and then to Mecca, where his religious enthusiasms were awakened. Upon his return to Shīrāz in 1844 he assumed the title of Bāb and began to preach his own particular Way. His views were eclectic, his doctrines leaning toward a mystic pantheism, with elements of gnosticism (q.v.), and were of a high moral level, being so liberal as to include steps toward the emancipation of women. He soon gained a following among those who felt oppressed by the Shī'a mullahs; bloody conflicts developed, and the Bāb was arrested and taken to Tabriz, where the governor condemned him to be shot. On July 9, 1850, he and a disciple were hoisted on ropes to hang before a wall; a squad of soldiers fired at both people. The disciple died immediately, but the Bāb's ropes were cut by the bullets, and he fell to the ground unhurt. He lacked the wit to proclaim that he had been saved by a miracle and so escape. He was again hoisted to the wall. The soldiers refused to fire at him; a second squad was needed to complete the execution.

The sect descended from his teachings, the Bahá'í World Faith, states that in the persecutions that followed, more than twenty thousand of his disciples were also massacred. Bahá'í doctrine claims that the Bāb "began to teach that God would soon 'make manifest' a World Teacher to unite men and women and usher in an age of peace." Among the Bāb's followers were two half brothers, Ṣubḥ-i Azal and Bahā' Allāh (in Bahá'í spelling, Bahá'u'lláh), who determined to carry on the Bāb's work. The first half brother maintained the doctrines intact, but his sect, the Azalis, are now few in number. However, Bahā' Allāh, drawing upon other sources, proclaimed a new universalist faith, independent of Islam and open to all men of whatever social class. The movement was named Bahá'í after him. See Bahá'í.

Bahá'í. A universalist faith founded in 1863 by the Persian Bahá'u'lláh (the Glory of God), a disciple of the Bāb, a much-persecuted renegade from an apocalyptic sect, the Imāmī Shī'as. Bahá'u'lláh announced to his fellow disciples that he was the chosen "Manifestation of God" for his age and called upon people to unite, claiming that only one common faith and one order could bring an enduring peace to the world. He foresaw that terrible wars would sweep the face of the earth and destroy the institutions and ideas that now keep men from their rightful unity. His teachings, with their emphasis on a just social order, met success among the peasants and impoverished city-dwellers of Persia, and the more orthodox clergy forced him to flee. He went first to Baghdad, then to Constantinople, to Adrianople, and finally to 'Akkā, where he was imprisoned, dying in 1892. However, wherever he went, he made converts. The Prophet's son 'Abdu'l-Bahá took over, was also imprisoned, but upon release in 1908, introduced Bahá'í to Europe and America, enjoying a fine harvest of conversions from people of all faiths and none. 'Abdu'l-Bahá died in 1921, passing on the mantle to his eldest grandson, Shogi Effendi, as first Guardian of the Faith and interpreter of the teachings. The Effendi reorganized the administrative structure of Bahá'í, making it an actual reflection of the Prophet's teachings for a world order.

Bahá'í doctrines are simple and direct, emphasizing social-mindedness rather than theology, mysticism, or ritual. The primary vision is one of God, even though men may call Him by different names, and one world attained through a world religion, i.e., Bahá'í. The world begins with the individual, who must have high moral standards and a new basis of belief. Since there is but one God, all Manifestations of God have each taught the same religious faith, developing and adapting it to meet historical and cultural demands. The unfolding of religion from age to age is called "progressive revelation." Bahá'u'lláh is the Manifestation of God for our time. Mankind is one: people of different races must enjoy equal educational and economic opportunities, equal access to decent living conditions, and must have equal responsibilities. No race or nation is superior to another. There is no priesthood or professional clergy, nor are there any rites or rituals, services being merely readings from the Bahá'í and other world Scriptures. Bahá'u'lláh's own teachings reflect a radiant, universalist optimism: *The earth is but one country; and mankind its citizens. The best beloved of all things in My sight is Justice; turn not away therefrom if thou desirest Me. My love is My stronghold; he that entereth therein is safe and secure. Breathe not the sins of others so long as thou art thyself a sinner. I have made death a messenger of joy to thee; wherefore dost thou grieve. Make mention of Me on My earth that in My heaven I may remember thee. O rich one on earth!—The poor in your midst are My trust; guard ye my trust. All the prophets of God proclaim the same faith. Ye are the fruits of one tree and the leaves of one branch. So powerful is unity's light that it can illumine the whole earth. The light of a good character surpasseth the light of the sun.* See also Bāb.

Balavariani, Chr. An early medieval romance, existing in numerous languages and versions, about the Indian hermit Barlaam and his royal pupil Prince Josaphat, who together were supposed to have converted India to Christianity in some vague past. Their feast days are marked in a few Christian churches with great solemnity, and their relics are known to exist. The ascetic way of life advocated in the *Balavariani* has influenced the Manichaeans, the Byzantine and Georgian Christians, the Muslims, the Cathari, the Albigensians, and recently, Count Leo Tolstoy (see his *Confession*). The earliest texts exist in Syriac, Georgian, and Arabic; other redactions, of various lengths, include Pehlevi, Old Turkish, Greek, and Latin. Scholars are now agreed without exception that the *Balavariani* is but an idealized, freely adapted, edited, and baptized version of certain episodes in the life of the Gautama Buddha, Josaphat equaling Bodhisattva. See Buddha; see also Ahmadiyyas.

baqā', Isl. Literally, "remaining." A Ṣūfic term expressing eternal life in God, or rather, as God. The word signifies pure subsistence beyond all form. It is the spiritual state to which the Ṣūfī aspires. It is preceded by al-fanā (q.v.), or "extinction." Baqā' is analogous to the Hindu state known as mokṣa (q.v.)—i.e., deliverance or release.

barakah, Isl. A blessing (bestowed by a holy person).

bardo, Buddh. A state defined by Tibetan lamas as that intervening between death and rebirth. The *Bardo Thödol* (The Tibetan Book of the Dead) deals with this state and the means for dying in such a manner that one passes through bardo and escapes from the karmic cycle into the final stage of nirvāṇa. *The Tibetan Book of the Dead,* compiled and edited by W. Y. Evans-Wentz, has been published by Oxford and is readily available.

bareshnum (or barashnum) ceremony, Zor. It is correctly known as barashnum nu-shaba (or no-shva), the Ablution of the Nine Nights; among the Zoroastrians of India bareshnum is also translated as "an exalted state of consciousness." It is a period of nine days of rites of purification and retreat, originally found in the Vidēvdāt (q.v.) and to be followed with the utmost scrupulosity. Originally, as in the Avesta (q.v.), the rite seems to have been celebrated only in cases of great defilement, as when a man touched a corpse or a woman gave birth to a dead child, or was practiced to ensure the absolute ceremonial purity of a priest before performing a sacrifice. Later it was open to all adults; the Persian treatise *Sad Dar* (c. ninth century A.D.) states "it is strictly incumbent upon mankind, on man and woman, to perform the barashnum ceremony," this at least once in a lifetime in order to purify the soul for entrance into paradise; otherwise the impurity contracted by life in the womb and nursing at the mother's breast will not be removed (milk was considered blood turned white, and therefore impure, since blood defiles). Today, in Iran, the rite may be contracted to a single day, and is usually confined to the priesthood; in India it is celebrated by priests of the highest rank, the yaosdāthregar (q.v.), either in preparation for the observance of some other important rite or to atone for defilement or for the breach of the priestly rules.

The ceremonies are complicated and elaborate, and may vary depending on locale and country. At the Zoroastrian center of Yazd in Iran the rites are performed at a primitive, circular, mud-walled structure; at Udvada in India, one of the earliest and most important Zoroastrian colonies, the ceremony is held at an elaborate rectangular enclosure. The Iranians place less emphasis on this rite as upon many other Zoroastrian rites, despite the authority of the Avesta. Like many rites, such as the founding of a fire temple or of a Tower of Silence (dakhmah), the first step is the drawing upon the ground of a type of maṇḍala by a priest who, with an assistant, is in a state of purity after a ritual bath, and various prayers. The priest sketches furrows in the ground with two sticks, one with a pointed iron "nail" at the end and the other a large spoon; they are held in the shape of a cross. The small rectangles, each of three furrowed lines, are drawn first. Around these is drawn another rectangle, and around that a larger one, which contains at one end a vacant area where the ceremonies are to be held without disturbing the smaller enclosures. Stones are now set out in a line (in the center in India, along the edge in Iran) in alternating groups of five or three, so that there are ten piles of five and eleven of three. At the far end of the maṇḍala a single large stone is placed; here the priest is to bathe. On the left hand side of the exterior rectangle a special path is marked out for the four-eyed dog (q.v.) that plays such an important role in so many Zoroastrian ceremonies.

The priest to undergo the ceremony now arrives and enters the "charmed" field at the end opposite the large stone. He is stripped of his clothing, takes consecrated bread, and then begins his ritual procession across the field, jumping or hopping from one group of five stones to the next; he may not touch the piles of three. At the first six groups of five he is given nirang (q.v.), consecrated bull's urine, from the spoon at the end of the stick mentioned above (in India he receives only nirang; in Iran he is given a few drops of water as well); the nirang is rubbed on his body, and he drinks some. The spoon is tied to the stick with a cord "nine knots long," so that the other priest need not enter the field.

At the seventh pile of stones the priest rubs sand on his body, and at the next three, water. The four-eyed dog is led along the outside path close enough for the priest to touch; the dog absorbs the negative emanations the priest is discarding in the ritual. At the large stone at the end of the field the priest has a full bath, dresses again, touches the sacred bareshnum rods, and then retires to the temple adjoining the field to pass nine nights in prayer and austerities, which will bring him to the state of bareshnum, or purified consciousness.

INTERPRETATION. This ritual, so obscure even to the ordinary Zoroastrian, and containing elements objectionable, distasteful, or puzzling to the outsider, has a number of symbolic meanings. The Iranians rarely practice it, and the Parsees have not been eager to probe the possible symbolisms, but a few scholars (J. J. Modi, 1937, and Dastur Kurshed S. Dabu, 1959) have offered the following tentative suggestions. The passage across the field represents the progress of the ego from the lowest to the highest state. The eighty-four stones typify the progress of evolution parallel to the Hindu belief in the eighty-four thousand incarnations of a soul before liberation. The ingredients rubbed on the body stand for the handicaps discarded: the urine, animality; the sand, gross matter; water, passions and emotions (which are considered fluid). At the last stage, the priest stands stripped of his lowest nature. The two innermost rectangles represent the influences of nature and of earth, the next the solar system, and the outermost the cosmic or universal field. The priest proceeds from personal elements to the impersonal and finally to the boundless, from the purely selfish personality of man to that wider one of the world, and thence to the vast cosmic sphere. At the end even this is left behind, and man stands on the stone that represents unity, boundless, eternal existence, devoid of individuality and of the person itself. The ego, the "I," disappears as the priest prays "I must become that." The role of the dog is important too, for the animal signifies wisdom (baodangh), the intuitional watchdog accompanying the pilgrim along the path but outside the bounds of involvement. In the end, the bareshnum nu-shaba is a means of gaining divine authority from the Invisible Guardians of the universe. See Zoroastrianism.

bātinī, Isl. A pseudomystic. In Ṣūfic terms, one who takes the inward meaning alone while ignoring the outer aspects. Only by combining both aspects can perfection be attained.

Baul, Ind. The word means "mad" in a nontechnical sense, "afflicted with the wind disease," and is probably derived from the Sanskrit vayu (wind). The Bauls are a mystical folk movement in Bengal, primarily of low-caste or casteless people of both Hindu and Muslim background. Their origins are unknown, nor do they care, for they are unlettered and unfettered, moving, as they say, with the wind. They have no special divisions of society such as caste or class, attend no particular temple or mosque, and in general honor no special deity, though as Bengalis they have a unique attachment for Durgā and Kālī. Their ideal is to be sahaj—i.e., simple and unattached—"for the body is the temple where the spirit lives—" with no Scriptures, for they listen to the message of the heart. "My heart is a lamp, moving in the current,/drifting to some landing place I do not know./Darkness moves before me on the river,/it moves again behind. . . . My Friend is ocean to this river./My Friend is the shore to this shoreless river./The current bends again." They sing constantly as they wander; the most common instruments are a small sitarlike instrument made of a gourd, and drums. They have no place of pilgrimage, for "At every step is my Mecca and my Kāśī; sacred is every moment." They were probably influenced by the bhakti movement, though similar cults can be traced as far back as the Arthava Veda. Tradition and learning are passed on from generation to generation by gurus, who are not teachers in the formal Hindu sense but men learned in holiness gained by wandering and suffering. Until the beginning of this century the Bauls were made fun of by upper-class Bengalis, but Rabindranath Tagore was deeply impressed by and influenced by their uncluttered vision and spontaneity, and now they are much admired.

Benares. One of the most sacred of Indian cities, located in Bihar on the northern bank of the Ganges. Benares is the British spelling; the Indian Government today prefers Vārāṇāsī, and it was known earlier as Kāśī, named after the sacred kāśā grass (*saccharum spontaneum*). It was probably founded about the eighth century B.C., although Indian tradition claims it is the oldest city in the world. Today it is a major pilgrim center, Hindus from all over India coming there not only to bathe in the Ganges along its shores and to pray in its numerous temples, but also to die;

those who can afford it live in ashrams; the poor sleep in certain streets and usually die quickly, since death is welcomed. The fame and sanctity of the city have come since the twelfth century, for up to then it was overshadowed by the renown of many others. Silks, cottons, and other products, including an orange-brown dye, kāshāya, which gave the color for the first Buddhist robes, once made the city a leading industrial center and inland port. Kāśī is Siva's city, the god's most sacred temples being located there, including a shapeless mound, Kedāra-nātha (also identified as a liṅga, a sign). Symbolically the inner Kāśī is the point where the three subtle arteries of the body join: The earthly Kāśī unites the earthly Ganges, the subterranean or underworld Ganges, and the celestial Ganges or Milky Way. Mystically Kāśī represents the city of knowledge—i.e., the head. The Buddha preached his first sermon near the city, in the Deer Park at Sarnath. See Buddha, Gaṇgā, Shiva.

bhadra, Buddh. One who is noted for such qualities as goodness but is not at the stage of ārya (q.v.).

Bhagavad Gītā, Hind. "The Lord's Song," or "The Song of the Lord." It is the most popular and sacred book for Hindus, and is the Indian work most widely known and read by the outside world. Although it is an interpolation into the Mahābhārata (q.v.), it stands as an independent work consisting of a dialogue between Krishna, the eighth avatāra of Vishnu, and the noble warrior Arjuna, who is about to enter into battle against his cousins, an act he considers reprehensible and immoral. Arjuna raises the question of human actions: How can he kill his blood relatives (teachers, fathers and sons, grandsons; grandfathers, wives' brothers, mothers' brothers, and fathers of wives), his own kinsmen, in the terrible act of war? He seeks an answer of Krishna, saying, "Neither the kingdom of the earth, nor the kingdom of the gods in heaven could give me peace from the fire of sorrow with which this burns my life." The entire social structure—from the family to caste—will be destroyed, and he concludes by saying, "I will not fight, Krishna." Such is the underlying theme, that of a man's duty (here as a warrior) and the sorrow he sees ensuing in fulfilling it. It is a theme, this moral struggle, that has engrossed the Indian mind and soul for two millennia, and some of the non-Indian world as well.

The *Gītā,* as it is popularly called, is composed of eighteen chapters, composed independently of the Mahābhārata and inserted into it as Chapters 25–42 of Book VI. The date of its composition is unclear and not likely to be placed accurately. Scholars, working from the same text (that used by the eighth century A.D. commentator Śamkara—no earlier version is known), have drawn contradictory conclusions. Juan Mascaró (the Penguin translation, 1962) states, "As there are no references to Buddhism in the *Gītā* and there are a few archaic words and expressions, some of the greatest scholars have considered it pre-Buddhist, i.e., about B.C. 500. The Sanskrit of the *Bhagavad Gītā* is, on the whole, simple and clear, like the oldest parts of the Mahābhārata. This could be added as an argument for an early date." On the other hand, the Indian critical historian D. D. Kosambi, in his commentary (Bombay, 1962), dates the work "as somewhere between 150–350 A.D., nearer the later than the earlier date. . . . The language is high classical Sanskrit such as could not have been written before the Guptas [fourth and fifth centuries A.D.]," and adds that Chapter II, 55–72, recited daily as prayers at Mahatma Gandhi's ashram, is Buddhist and that "the theory of perfection through a large succession of rebirths [that is, karma] is characteristically Buddhist." The noted philosopher S. Radhakrishnan states, "From its archaic constructions and internal references, we may infer that it is definitely a work of the pre-Christian era. Its date may be assigned to the fifth century B.C., though the text may have received alterations in subsequent times."

However, even this point is open to controversy. The Indian philosopher Dr. Chandradhar Sharma has stated, "Dr. Belvelkar has tried to show that there are no interpolations in the *Gita*. We are also tempted to agree with Dr. Belvelkar." The German scholar R. Otto (London, 1939) believes that there was an "Ur-Gītā" consisting primarily of Chapters I–II, 38; X, 1–8; XIII, 1–51; and XVIII, 58–73. This basic core narrates Arjuna's doubt whether or not to fight and so become guilty of the ruin of his family and of law and order, with Krishna's reply that he should carry out his duty because all human beings are but instruments in the fulfillment of God's eternal designs, a point he makes by revealing himself as the Supreme in all his glory and power and as the original abode and absorbing abyss of created beings; as the mortal Krishna again, he delivers a philosophical summary concerning pure and impure knowledge, pure and impure wisdom, and emphasizes the nature of karma, saying that it is Arjuna's nature and duty to fight. Otto sees eight major additions, representing eight different schools of philosophy, plus some glosses. These revisions, of whatever school and at whatever date, have enabled the individual and society at large to draw the conclusions and support most wanted from the *Gītā*. While Otto and others have approached the text critically, trying to identify the various sources and interpolations, Kosambi puts the matter into another, ethical and moral context, believing that it is a late brahmin forgery and that "This divine but rather scrambled message with its command of expository Sanskrit is characteristically Indian in attempting to reconcile the irreconcilable, in its power of gulping down sharp contradictions painlessly." Sharma disposes of this and other criticisms, whether textual or ethical, thus: "The root-fallacy lies in believing that theism and pantheism, that qualified monism and unqualified monism are opposed to each other. At least they are not so in Indian Philosophy. . . . Similarity merges in transcendental unity and all qualifications merge in the Absolute."

Whatever the date of composition and of additions and revisions, the *Gītā* belongs to a long age of changing sociological conditions, from that of the priestly, Vedic world, centered around the sacrificial fire, in which the perfect observance of ritual was essential to salvation, to that of the world of kings, courts, warriors, princes, armies and battles, and forest sages and teachers. It is also the first great exposition of the doctrine of bhakti—i.e., of devotion to God. Rather than salvation gained by fees paid to the priests, salvation came by attention to duty and the recognition of past acts upon which the present and future are to be based. Still, this is a highly dependent and structured society, essentially feudal in its loyaties and obligations. The caste system its frequently emphasized, with each man's role in it and his need to fulfill his caste duties properly. At the same time, however, the individual's attitudes toward God are given a new direction: in place of knowledge (as exemplified by the scholars as the way), the individual may reach and become merged in God through his loving devotion, or bhakti, a way that was to develop into a widespread movement encompassing people on all levels and eschewing caste roles. The *Gītā* offered Krishna as God, but others were to find God through their devotion to Shiva or to Shakti or her various forms.

The scene for the working out of the *Gītā* is a battlefield near what is now New Delhi, which in turn is founded upon a series of ancient cities (even today a field is celebrated as the site of the actual war, though its authenticity is beyond proof). The war, traditionally ascribed to the twelfth century B.C., but again not provable, would, as described in the Mahābhārata, have involved an army of nearly five million men (and an equal number of camp followers) in an eighteen-day battle, a doubtful possibility considering the small population of ancient India. Most scholars agree that there was a battle of some sort, but Gandhi and others have dismissed a literal war by stating that the battle was nothing but an allegory, in which the battlefield is the soul and Arjuna is man's highest impulses struggling against evil.

What the central theme might be, despite the authority with which one scholar or another might state it, is still a question. "To put it bluntly," says Kosambi, "the utility of the *Gītā* derives from its peculiar fundamental defect, namely dexterity in seeming to reconcile the irreconcilable." The Panjabi poet P. Lal, in the Introduction to his translation (Calcutta, 1965) states, "The *Gītā* has only one purpose: to get Arjuna to fight. It is fitted neatly into the grand design of dharma-kshetra Kurukshetra"—i.e., the struggle between the field of righteousness on one side and the field of the Kurus (Arjuna's family) on the other, righteousness vs. practicality, two incompatibles warring each against the other. Christopher Isherwood, commenting on his translation with Swami Prahbhavananda (1944), sees the work as one of nonattachment, "Which will lead us to true wisdom . . . the ultimate Reality. . . . The law of Karma will cease to operate. We shall realize our true nature, which is God." He dismisses the many injunctions to observe the laws of caste and the command to go to war as Arjuna's duty as a warrior. "The *Gītā* neither sanctions war nor condemns it. Regarding no action of absolute value, either for good or for evil, it cannot possibly do either." Mascaró states, "The essence of the *Bhagavad Gītā* is the vision of God in all things and of all things in God." Sharma's view is this: "The fundamental metaphysical teaching of the *Gītā* is that 'of the unreal there is no being and of the real there is no non-being,' *BG* II, 16. . . . The ideal of the *Gītā* is not negativism, asceticism, or escapism. It is not negation of actions, but performance of actions in a detached spirit." What it comes down to is that the *Gītā* is an extremely personal work, to be approached in a personal manner.

Translations are not wholly satisfactory, and discrepancies make some passages seem like selections from unrelated works. Worth reading, however, are those by S. Radhakrishnan (which has a better and more profound commentary than most), P. Lal, Juan Mascaró, and the collaboration by Swami Prabhavananda and Christopher Isherwood. Most commentaries seem forced, and bear an air of unreality (cf. those by Isherwood, Aldous Huxley, and Mascaró); however, the chapters on the *Gītā* by Richard Lannoy (*The Speaking Tree,* 1971) and D. D. Kosambi (*Myth and Reality,* 1962) are superior.

Bhagavan, Hind. God, contemplated and invoked as the supreme object of man's worship and devotion. Bhagavan is one of the most generally employed terms for the Lord as the Blessed One, the Adorable One; also, the All-Powerful. The term, derived from Sanskrit bhaga (share), originally may have meant the one who is entitled to a full right in tribal property; in post-Vedic times there was an official known as the bhāga-dugha, the King's apportioner, whose job it was to share out the gifts brought by the tribal chiefs at the time of the horse sacrifice. Bhāga came to mean a term of respect for a dignitary, a ruler, and then a god, and is now used as a form of address for a holy man. In the bhakti cults Rāma and Krishna are often addressed as Bhagavan by their devotees, though Bhagavan is not synonymous with any one name or any one avatāra or other manifestation of the divine. It clearly designates the one personal supreme deity, the Parama Puruṣa or Parama Ātman, also as Īśvawara. Bhagavan is also Brahman, the supreme and eternal ground of all reality, absolute, transcendent, unconceivable, unmanifest, unique. As Paramatman, Bhagavan is the Self abiding in the heart of every being, and as Īśvawara, the supreme Ruler and Controller of nature and of the universe. The work that best expresses the concept of Bhagavan is the *Bhagavad Gītā,* where he is the good and gracious Lord, He whom many virtually touch, friend and divine lover, savior and refuge, charming, compassionate, and beautiful to behold. See *Bhagavad Gītā,* Brahman.

Bhāgavata, Hind. The leading Purāṇa, composed in South India in the ninth or tenth century A.D. It is written in a lofty and difficult form of Sanskrit, in twelve sections (skandhas) divided into 320 chapters comprising 18,000 slokas or verses. The tenth skandha, of ninety chapters, tells the story of the Lord Krishna, and is one of the most popular of all Hindu works, ranking next to the *Bhagavad Gītā* (q.v.). Though composition of the work is accredited to the legendary Maharshi Veda Vyāsa, author of the Mahābhārata, the two works are centuries apart, and the *Bhāgavata* is a complex synthesis of many streams of Hindu thought, and many literary forms, from the purest bhakti hymns to numerous stories, retellings of ancient myths, with much emotion, some eroticism, and a good mixture of anthromorphism. As a Vaishnavaite work, it sees the world as a manifestation of Vishnu, with emphasis on Krishna as the most perfect avatāra (q.v.). The doctrine of līlā, divine sportive play, explains the creation. One of the ideas expressed in the *Bhāgavata,* unusual for its time, is that people have a right to demand as much of the basic necessities of life as they need; the accumulation of wealth is theft and should be punished.

The view of Krishna here is radically different from that of the *Bhagavad Gītā.* In the *Bhāgavata* we see him in a more human and in a semidivine aspect (instead of fully divine), where he partakes of ordinary life, with special emphasis on his childhood and his youth, where he is the handsome and somewhat lecherous cowboy who can make love to the 16,108 gopis. See Krishna, Vishnu.

bhajan, Hind. A religious hymn chanted in honor of a deity, either local or universal (Kālī, Durgā, Rāma, and Krishna would be among the most popular), carried to the pitch of emotion which, if not entering into an actual state of ecstasy, at least borders upon it. Bhajans are sung in the local dialect or language and are expressions of various bhakti cults. The Rajput Queen Mira Bai (q.v.) was a famous composer of bhajans. Today they may be heard at almost any temple as part of normal worship; LP records of the foremost bhajan singer, the South Indian M. S. Subbulakshmi, are available in the United States and other Western countries. See bhakti.

bhakti, Hind. Devotion to and love for God. The path of devotion as opposed to the path of knowledge (jñāna). Bhakti is an expression of love and adoration centered upon the Supreme Person rather than on the Supreme Abstraction. It is a popular—folk—movement, traceable to the post-Vedic period, though it probably originated earlier among the pre-Vedic, pre-Aryan peoples of the Indus and elsewhere, and reaching a peak of expression in the Middle Ages. Bhakti is manifested in worship and adoration of various deities, the most popular being Vishnu, Shiva, and Shakti, all originally nonbrahminical. Shiva and Shakti are definitely non-Vedic in origin, and there are but few hymns to Vishnu in the Vedas. The bhakti movement was long opposed by the brahmins, for it disregarded traditional Vedic rituals, often ignored caste differences (many of the bhakti saints and leaders were of the lowest castes), and stressed devotion over knowledge. Calm speculation about the all-pervading Brahman was eschewed in favor of mystical exuberance. However, when the movement first began to gain popularity, it attracted brahmins in number. The *Bhagavad Gītā* is the first major expression of bhakti, with its concentration on the adoration of Vishnu, who appears in the work in the person of Krishna. Over the centuries the movement grew to great power in South India among the Ālvārs (q.v.) and thence throughout the country, developing not only Vaishnavite but also Shaivite and Shakti forms. The movement was carried by wandering holy men through the means of songs and music and the recitation of the great texts. Bhakti is essentially the religion of the great masses of India, for it enables the individual to approach the Divine directly and to become a part of his warm all-encompassing love. Tiru-Mular, a Shaivite mystic of the Middle Ages, sang: "The ignorant say that Love and God are different;/None know that Love and God are the same./When they know that Love and God are the same,/They rest in God's Love." More formal but obscure bhakti texts can state: "The nature of bhakti is absolute love for Him," and "Bhakti is supreme attachment for the Lord." The bhakti poet Nammālvār sang, "My Lord, though endless pains afflict me,/I will not cease to look for thy mercy." One of the underlying themes of bhakti is that of avatār, God manifesting himself upon the earth in some form (even animal as well as human) in order to aid mankind in a time of troubles; Krishna is the supreme example of avatār, but avatārs are endless and beyond count. Besides the *Bhagavad Gītā* as the major bhakti text, the *Bhagavata Purāṇa* is given equal importance. Tradition assigns its authorship to the same Marharshi Veda Vyāsa who is credited with the *Gītā,* but internal and external evidence show that the Purāṇa can be dated at about the ninth or tenth century A.D. In sum, it is a grand synthesis of the many themes and schools of bhakti, and contains not only bhakti laid out in its fullest, but also many legends, folk stories, discourses, theological and philosophical asides, and scraps of unconscious anthropology and sociology, centered around hundreds of avatārs, saints, heroes, gods, and holy people. Today it is a fertile source of stories for Indian films. Hundreds of other bhakti works have been composed, plus the many thousands of truly moving poems and songs by the bhakti poets and musicians. Special reference might be made to the Ālvārs, Kabīr, and Mira Bai.

Besides its challenge to the brahminical institutions, bhakti has also presented a conflict with basic Hindu beliefs, especially that of karma (roughly, the working out of one's destiny in the light of past deeds). According to karma one is fated to undergo the suffering consequent to one's past lives, for whatever good or evil one may have done. But in bhakti, karma is set aside, for the devotee expects that the Lord will return Love for love and to alter or ignore the predestined course of karma: Will the Lord abide by the ironclad law of karma, or will He bestow his grace upon the bhakta? The question has fallen into the hands of the priestly castes, without resolution. Bhakti, like other aspects of Hindu religion and life, has been categorized ad infinitum, in numerous categories that seem to multiply, being divided into ninefold divisions, which in turn have been divided into nine times nine, and so on. However, this scholasticism is generally ignored by the masses.

bhikku, Buddh. Roughly, a Buddhist monk. The word is Pāli, from the Sanskrit bhiksu, a beggar. A bhikku is a lay follower of Gautama Buddha; he follows a special way of training, practices, and meditation. The bhikku passes through two stages, the first as a novice, when he is received into a Buddhist brotherhood, joining most orders no earlier than sixteen, though some may take children as young as five; the members of the lower order are usually called sāmanera (cognate with a Sanskrit word to wander). The young monk dresses in simple robes and accepts the precepts of the community. In some of the Theravāda Buddhist lands of Southeast Asia it was the custom for virtually all young men to become sāmameras for a short period, from three months to three years, and then to return to the duties of married life.

At about the age of twenty, if the young monk wants to continue in the monastic life, he petitions his brotherhood for full admission. He must be seconded by his spiritual master and another monk. He must be free of obligations (no serfs, debtors, soldiers, etc.) and free from contagious diseases and bodily infirmities, and must have the permission of his parents. Though both the new bhikku and the community assume that his ordination is to be permanent, he still may leave voluntarily later, or even be expelled for some grave offense. But from now on, so long as he remains attached to a brotherhood, he will follow its discipline. Practices differ in each country, but in general the life of the bhikku follows that of Buddha and his first followers (parenthetically, Buddha broke through the barriers of Hindu religious life, which confined it to the upper castes, by allowing anyone to join a brotherhood; among the first members were not only several kings, but also low-castes or outcastes, among them a robber, a scavenger, a dog eater, a fisherman, a cowherd, and a barber). Though Buddha advised a middle—normal—way for all, bhikkus are celibates. The bhikku attempts to eliminate all hindrances to perfection, since he has acquired his present body through his own cravings (thus leading to rebirth) and will eternally pass through the cycle; he strives to purify himself of all earthly attachments in his monastic life. He wears simple clothing, yellow or saffron robes (being limited to three, one outer, two under); he may even dress in cast-off clothing or remnants of shrouds. His food comes only from house-to-house begging; he must go to all houses on his path rather than to the most opulent, and take whatever food is offered him. He will live and sleep anywhere without discrimination, as the brotherhood dictates. In general, bhikkus reside either in a vihāra (literally, abode) with other bhikkus, or in a secluded place such as a forest, cave, or even at a charnel or cremation ground. For most, life on the road is the standard, each bhikkhu wandering for some eight or nine months until the monsoon season, when he returns to the vihāra.

The bhikku must have (and is restricted to) Eight Essentials as possessions: his three robes; a begging bowl (usually of thin iron or tin with a brass cover); a cloth belt; a needle and thread; a straight-edged razor; and a water strainer, this to rescue insects that might have fallen into his drinking and cooking water. All of these items are required and must be replaced immediately if lost. He is likely to have a few other objects: a water flask or small kettle, an umbrella (sometimes called the crot), a sitting cloth, a washrag, a candle lamp, some medicines, toothbrushes, and even a small clock and a penknife. Two or three books will finish the list of possessions: The most common is the *Patimokka,* a manual of discipline listing two hundred offenses, the breaking of any of which he will have to confess to his community; the *Patimokka* will be in Pāli, and the bhikku will have another copy in his own language. He will also carry another book of the Buddha's teachings, the *Dhammapada* being one of the most popular.

The monk's day begins well before dawn, perhaps as early as two or three A.M., when he starts prayer and meditation, the first act being prostration to the Tri-Ratna (the Three Jewels, or Gems); the brief chant is sometimes called the Three Refuges—"I go to the Buddha for refuge, I go to the Dhamma [Teaching] for refuge, I go to the Sangha [Brotherhood] for refuge." He may also check himself against the Five Hindrances (sometimes the Five Precepts)—"Take no life; take not what is not yours; do not act basely in sexual matters; do not lie; do not drink spirits." If he feels drowsy at his early rising, he is likely to walk back and forth while praying, a practice traced to the Buddha. At dawn the bhikku lights incense, offers a candle, and prostrates himself in honor of the Buddha, the Dhamma, and the Sangha. More prayers follow, and eventually, before the sun has risen too far, he sets out to beg food, a task that has to be completed before noon, and then he returns to his abode, either his isolated hut or cave or the vihāra. He is enjoined to but one meal a day, and a simple one at that. In the afternoon he may engage in simple jobs, but not manual labor, repairing his robes or making small religious or secular objects (such as statues of Buddha, lamp stands, or candle holders). Normally he sits on the ground while working (and praying), but if he is tired from the day's efforts or about to suffer the common contemplative's problem of "experiencing too much of the monkey mind," he will lie down "mindfully" in the position of the Lord Buddha. He will lie on his right side, with a supporting roll of robes (or a pillow) under the upper half of his body, his head supported in the palm of his right hand and his elbow on the ground. "This," the bhikku will explain, "was the lying posture recommended by Lord Buddha and thus balanced it is not possible for one to go to sleep but mindfulness will be maintained."

More meditation follows—it seems to be a truism that the body is "lightened" by it—the monk sitting on a mat on the ground. Then he sweeps out his cell or hut, being careful not to harm any insect or other creature. He next bathes and washes his clothes; he may take some fresh fruit juice fortified by honey. The bhikku's day is climaxed by meditation by the light of a candle and the chanting of Buddhist suttas in Pāli, if he knows the language, otherwise in his own tongue.

bhikṣuṇī, Buddh. A Buddhist nun, who follows approximately the same rules and regulations as the bhikku, or bhikṣu, above.

bhūmi, Buddh. From the Sanskrit. A Mahāyānist term used in a special sense as "stage" in the upward spiritual progress of a bodhisattva; usually there are ten such stages to transcend.

Bilāl, Isl. An ex-slave whom the Prophet Muḥammad saved from a beating, traditionally the first black convert to Islam. Bilāl, an Ethiopian, is also the first known muezzin, the leader who calls the faithful to the five-times-daily prayers. See Islam.

Bilalians. The self-styled name of the Black Muslims, after Bilāl (q.v.). See Black Muslims.

bindi (also tilak), Hind. The red "spot" that Hindu women wear on their foreheads. It is nothing other than a form of the bindu of esoteric origin (see below), of tantra and other mystical disciplines carried over into daily life. The bindi (made of a powder or, today, lipstick or even a bit of plastic in a bindi kit) does not necessarily signify that the woman is married or of a certain caste (though in most areas the unmarried or the widowed do not wear it) but is an affirmation that she is Shakti, the feminine power. The bindi is also the Third Eye, or the Sun or the Moon; as Third Eye it was worn by Gautama Buddha and is usually seen on the images of saints; the male version is often of ochre sandalwood. Among Gujaratis the new husband and wife place bindis (here called tilak) on each other's foreheads during the marriage ceremony. In some areas the bindi is worn from the age of twelve as a symbol of śanti (or peace); it symbolizes blood, to show that "this blood" (of such and such a clan) is passed from mother to child. In Mahārashtra, the bindi is said to be connected with the heart and the vital organs. In the same state and in parts of the North, lower-caste women wear a green bindi tattooed on their foreheads (and green tattooing on their wrists). See Shakti, Third Eye.

bindu, Hind. The esoteric term point, and related to bindi, above. Literally, bindu means a drop or a point. The point—bindu—is a standard religious symbol throughout the world, as in Hinduism, where it is set in the center of a yantra or a mandala as a cosmic axis. The bindu is the all-pervading spatial concept. It is the limit of manifestation: When something exists yet does not exist, it is represented by the bindu. When the Extended Universe collapses in the Great Dissolution (Mahāprajaya), it culminates, so to speak, into the point, bindu, ultimately, to re-form from it. Bindu is also an aspect of Shakti, or Consciousness; in some texts Shakti is called bindu. Bindu is also the creative single seed, the sperm, that is released—or in tantra, retained—during the sexual act. Tantric yantras show the bindu as the center point within the series of triangles denoting the yoni. In meditation the mind is focused on the point or dot—bindu—as the realization of cosmic energy.

Bismi'Llāh, Isl. A popular Muslim salutation, "In the name of God." (Also transliterated as Basmalah or Bismillah.) Next to the Shahādah (q.v.) it is the most common expression among Muslims and is articulated to recognize Allāh's aid in all the varied aspects of man's life on earth. It is the first part of the formula or phrase that begins the Qur'ān (q.v.), "Bismi 'Llāhi 'r-Raḥmānī 'r-Raḥīm" (literally, "In the Name of Allah the All-merciful, the Merciful" [sometimes translated as ". . . the Compassionate, the Merciful"].

Black Muslims. An indigenous movement of American blacks who, under the leadership of the man who called himself Elijah Muhammad, adopted Islam as their religion. Virtually all Black Muslims were originally Christian; they usually took Arabic names, and considered Elijah as the messenger of Allāh. The movement was immediately popular because of its apocalyptic nature, appealing to those suffering from the abysmal social conditions under which many blacks labored; many conversions were made in prisons. Early doctrines stressed the black nature of the movement and were antiwhite. When Elijah Muhammad died in 1975, the movement, under the leadership of his son, Herbert D. Muhammad, took the name Nation of Islam and opened its membership to all races. It also abandoned the violence that had marked its earlier days, and it relinquished many of the businesses it had developed as a means of aiding its members. In 1977, under a new leader, Wallace D. Muhammad, the Muslims took the name World Community of Islam in the West. Many orthodox Muslims have rejected the Black Muslims, and a schism within its own ranks resulted in 1967 when Hamaas Abdul Khaalis, an American black who had been a Roman Catholic before his conversion to the Muslims, charged that the movement was not in fact Muslim and did not follow Islamic practices except superficially. Khaalis, who had been studying under a Pakistani Muslim of the Hanafī rite of the Sunnīs (q.v.), established an American branch of the Hanafīs (q.v.).

blama, Tib. The orthographic version of the term lāma (q.v.).

Blavatsky, Madame Helena Petrovna (1831–91). Russian-born occultist and spiritualist, the moving force behind the Theosophical Society (q.v.). Madame Blavatsky—commonly known among her disciples as H.P.B.—founded the Society in 1875 with the aid of a group of sixteen other people interested in spreading knowledge of the occult. H.P.B. stated that she had been selected by a Buddha incarnation, Tsong-kha-pa, to work under the direction of two Adepts in the Himālayas (known in Theosophical writings as Mahatma M. and Mahatma K.H.) to help save the world. When the Society moved its headquarters to India, H.P.B. attracted the interest of journalist A. P. Sinnett, then in Banaras, by performing various siddhis (q.v.), such as producing a cup and saucer to match a crockery set at a picnic when an unexpected guest arrived. Sinnett noted that occult temple bells would ring anywhere H.P.B. wanted to produce such sounds, without any sign of actual bells. H.P.B. was reluctant to perform such phenomena, as the Mahatmas discouraged them. Siddhis were permitted only when there was a reason, not merely to entertain the curious. The Society, they emphasized, was not a hall of magic but a nucleus of the Universal Brotherhood of Humanity, formed to encourage the study of comparative religion, philosophy, and science and to investigate unexplained laws of nature and the powers latent in man.

One of H.P.B.'s most puzzling siddhis was her correspondence, by "spiritual means," with her two masters. She passed on letters from Sinnett and others to both Mahatmas by "thought transference" and received answers in colloquial English ("bye the bye" is a typical example) impressed *in* the grain of rice paper. (The originals, along with the cup and saucer and other mementos, are now in the British Museum.) According to Theosophical doctrine, Madame Blavatsky appeared during a cycle of spiritual barrenness in the world to sow the seeds of spirituality. Through her spiritual development in former lives she had acquired the occult power known in Tibet as tulku (q.v.), through which she could temporarily but deliberately and self-consciously remove her own egoic consciousness and permit the influence of the Buddha Tsong-kha-pa to act through her. Her disciples see her in three aspects: in her own humanity; as a channel for the ideas of her Masters; and in her own divine, spiritual, Monadic Self.

Among her works are: *The Secret Doctrine, Isis Unveiled,* and *Talks on the Path of Occultism.*

Bodh-Gāya (or Buddha-Gāya). The sacred site in eastern India in today's state of Bihar, where Gautama Buddha received enlightenment. Bodh-Gāya is now a collection of temples and monasteries surrounded by a few shops and the houses of farmers; the larger town of Gāya, a prominent Hindu center of pilgrimage (and the nearest railway stop), is some eight miles away. The central feature of Bodh-Gāya is the sacred asvatta (or pipal) tree under which Buddha sat in meditation during the time when he attained Supreme Enlightenment. Next to the tree is the Mahā-Bodhi Temple, original date of construction unknown, but possibly founded by the third-century B.C. Emperor Ashoka (q.v.).

Numerous rebuildings have effaced the primitive structure. The temple, not a stūpa (q.v.) but a tower of the Hindu type, with Buddhist additions, is 48 feet square and rises 170 feet, with the top stories composed of a slender cone. Adjoining the temple are other sites connected with the Buddha's Awakening, among them the Vajrāsana or Diamond Throne, a stone block five by eight by three feet in height, on which the Buddha sat, other trees under which he meditated, and Mucalinda Lake, on whose shores he spent much time in contemplation. Bodh-Gāya was ravaged by the Muslims in the early thirteenth century and remained virtually abandoned. In 1590 a Hindu monk claimed possession of the temple, and his descendants held it until 1885, when the orientalist Sir Edwin Arnold visited the site and began an earnest appeal for its restoration. The Hindus were ousted with much difficulty. Most of the Buddhist nations contributed to the cause of rebuilding and restoration of Bodh-Gāya.

Contemporary structures include Tibetan, Chinese, Thai, and other monasteries, and rest houses and a museum. Though Buddhist pilgrims come to Bodh-Gāya from all over the Orient, Westerners will find the site difficult to reach but well worth the trip.

bodhi, Hind. and Buddh. The word is derived from budh, to awake, become conscious. In Hinduism it is reality as pure spirit. The term is more commonly employed in Buddhism, where it signifies enlightenment, illumination, or awakening. There are three kinds of bodhi: that of the disciple or hearer of the Buddha; that of the Pacceka Buddha, an enlightenment gained in isolation and independently; and that of samma-sam-buddha, the universal Buddha, which is independently gained but proclaimed also to others. See Buddha.

Bodhidharma (c. A.D. 470–543), Buddh. An Indian Buddhist monk, the third son of a South Indian king. Bodhidharma founded the meditative school known in China as Ch'an (Japanese Zen), after the Sanskrit dhyāna (q.v.). Bodhidharma arrived in China at Canton about 520; initially frustrated in dealing with a local king, who did not understand his blunt, often enigmatic explanations, he withdrew into a cave, where he spent nine years; tradition says he stared at the wall during this period; hence he is known as the "Wall-gazing Brahmin." Biographical accounts, the first of which appeared about a century after his death, include much legendary material. All in all, he appears as a crusty, no-nonsense exponent of Buddhism in its meditative form. Contemporary scholars are divided about his very existence, some saying he is a complete fabrication; others, among them Hu Shih and T'ang Yung-t'ing, believed he actually lived in China from 420 to 479. Such controversy seems pointless: There was much traffic between India and China at the time, both over land and by sea, and the names of other Indian travelers are known; also the techniques of Ch'an have an indisputedly Indian origin.

In any event, Bodhidharma gave Chinese Buddhism, which had become routine and stagnant, a much-needed rejuvenation, though it was his disciples who had the greater effect. Bodhidharma's teachings were based on the *Lankāvatāra Sūtra,* a somewhat fanciful and unsystematic Indian work, which, however, is one of the nine principal texts of Mahāyāna Buddhism; it takes the form of a dialog between Buddha and the King of Lankā (Ceylon). Bodhidharma's methods were simple, being based on concentration in sitting—this was before the development of kōans, mondos, shouts, blows, and other means of awakening the monk into enlightenment. His school of teaching was known initially as the Lankā sect; a text, the *Leng-chia-tzu chi,* found in the Tun-huang caves, details its history and mentions not only Bodhidharma but also the Fifth Patriarch and some of his disciples, including Hui-nêng (q.v.), the sixth. Bodhidharma, carried in the genealogies as the twenty-fourth in apostolic succession after Guatama Buddha, is known as the First Patriarch of Ch'an. (His feast day is celebrated by Zen Buddhists on October 5th annually.) His teachings are summarized in his most famous verses:

Outwardly, all activities cease;
Inwardly, the mind stops its panting.
When one's mind has become a wall,
Then he may enter into the Tao.

A special transmission outside the Scriptures,
No dependence upon words or letters,
Direct pointing at the soul of man,
Seeing into one's own nature for attainment of Buddhahood.

bodhimaṇḍala, Buddh. The site where the Lord Buddha attained Enlightenment, but the term is also applicable to a "truth plot" or any other place of sanctity or enlightenment. See maṇḍala.

bodhisatta, Buddh. See bodhisattva.

bodhisattva, Buddh. (also Pali, bodhisatta.) A buddha to be, or one who is an aspiring buddha. The term was originally used to describe Gautama Śakyamuni's state before he received final enlightenment. It later came to denote anyone who had passed the stage of arahantship, or perfect being. The first-century A.D. Indian sage Nāgārjuna defined bodhisattva as follows: "The change from an ordinary being to a bodhisattva takes place when his mind has reached the stage when it can no longer turn back on enlightenment. Also, he has by then gained five advantages: He is no more reborn in the States of Woe, but always among gods and men; he is never again born in poor or in low-class families; he is always a male and never a woman; he is always well-built, and free from physical defects; he can remember past lives and no more forgets them again." The concept of bodhisattva is primarily Mahāyānist; all good Buddhists are potentially bodhisattvas. A bodhisattva's main characteristic is his intense love and compassion for the mortal world, which he sees as "victims going to slaughter." The bodhisattva wants to "become the savior of all beings and set them free from their sufferings." See Buddha, Buddhism.

bodhi tree. The tree, under which Gautama Śakyamuni sat in meditation and received enlightenment, by which he became the Buddha. The site is at Gāya, Bihar, near the banks of the Neranjara

River. The tree is a pipal or *ficus religiosa* and related to the common fig. Originally it probably had been a simple cult site; after the Enlightenment it became a center of pilgrimage. The Emperor Ashoka sent a cutting with his mission to Ceylon. The original tree was destroyed, along with temples and images, in the anti-Buddhist campaign of the seventh-century reformer King, Narendragupta-Sasanka of Bengal. A few years later cuttings were brought back from Ceylon and planted at the original site (now Bodh-Gāya) by Purnavarman of Magadha, the "last descendant of Ashoka," along with some at other Buddhist foundations. Other versions of the replanting say that the cutting was taken from Gāya during the reign of Devanampiya Tissa and from it other seedlings were raised in Ceylon. These are all legends and not to be relied upon. See also Ashoka, Buddha.

Bön. The indigenous, pre-Buddhist religion of Tibet. Its members are known as Bön-po (less common, Bön-poba). Etymologically the origin of the term is unknown, though European scholars believed it is derived from the shamanistic murmuring of magic formulas. Bön changed markedly with the introduction of Buddhism into Tibet early in the seventh century A.D., and much of what is assumed about its original practices and beliefs is a backward projection of later ideas, thus resulting in some confusion. The Bön-po believe in a celestial deity, a heavenly king or overlord, who stands above but does not interfere in the affairs of the world; he resides in Pagö-pünsum, an eighteen-thousand-foot mountain peak in northeastern Tibet, surrounded by his ministers who live in lesser peaks. Two tutelary spirits live among men, communication with them being achieved by shamans in an ecstatic state. In the pre-Buddhist period, sacrifices, both animal and human, were made to appease various minor gods and spirits and a cult of warrior gods with armies of fighting attendants. The king was conceived of as a divine being, descended from heaven but still linked to it by a silver cord. Eventually, as Bön entered more advanced stages, the cord had to be cut, and from then on, kings were entombed in great burial mounds along with their faithful retainers and various possessions. This stage of Bön was also marked by blood sacrifices, which have been described by Chinese observers. A great sacrifice was held every three years, in which donkeys and human beings were offered to the gods of the three regions, Heaven, Earth, and the Underworld. Sheep, dogs, and monkeys were sacrificed in lesser and more frequent rites. The offerings involved disemboweling of the victim and the scattering of his or its blood into the air. Tibetan Buddhists have reported that such practices still survive, though on a limited scale. The juniper tree contains certain spirits, and the berries, wood, trunk, and branches are offered in sacrifices, the berries also being used as a narcotic to induce trance. Spirits also inhabit rocks, water, other vegetation, and mountains, and guard mountain passes, the various worlds, and the family hearth. The god of the hearth, Thab Lha, has to be appeased with daily sacrifices of butter (the Tibetan tsampa).

After the arrival of the early Buddhists, the priests, Bön (or invokers) and the gShen (sacrificers), gradually abandoned many of the more extreme practices and adapted various Buddhist customs, rituals, and ideas. Meanwhile Buddhism, propagated by missionaries from Nepal and China, borrowed many Bön gods and concepts, though the two sects remained independent of each other and largely hostile. The influence of Buddhism gradually brought the Bön-po to a reorganization of their religion: Temples and later monasteries along the Buddhist style were constructed, and the art of writing, introduced by Buddhist missionaries, resulted in an independent Bön literature of great prolixity and complexity, much of it akin to Buddhism with Bön terminology. Bön forms of yoga and tantra were also developed. By the fourteenth century, Bön had become for all purposes a form of Buddhism, heretical and independent by Buddhist standards: Much of what now passes for Bön has Buddhist derivations, and much of Tibetan Buddhism is actually Bön.

Bön is marked by a lack of historical time. The founder of Bön, Mi-bo gShen-rab, who goes back to prehistory, bears a strong resemblance to the Gautama Buddha; the Bön-po say that Mi-bo gShen-rab came from a far western land called sTag-gzigs, which is vaguely identified with pre-Muslim Persia.

bosatsu, Buddh. The Japanese term for bodhisattva, buddhas devoted to the salvation of mankind. Particularly popular are Jizō and Kannon. See bodhisattva.

Brahmā, Hind. The Creator in the Trimūrti, the largely artificial trinity in which the two other partners are Vishnu, the Preserver, and Shiva, the Destroyer. The worship of Brahmā is the oldest of the Trimūrti; he appears in the Vedas as Prajāpati, Pitāmaha, and Hiraṇya-garbha; he appears in the Brāhmanas, but after that his importance wanes before the emergence of the non-Āryan Shiva and Vishnu. Now he is rarely honored. However, Brahmā has a well-defined role in Hindu cosmology. The world creates and dissolves itself in a long process, called the days and nights of Brahmā. Each day and each night lasts one thousand years of the gods, and each year of the gods corresponds to twelve thousand years of men. Every day of Brahmā, which sees the emanation of the universe from the divine substance and its dissolution again, lasts twelve million years. During the night of Brahmā, all remains are absorbed in the one Brahman (note difference), waiting for its re-creation. Each year of the gods is in turn divided into four yugas. In the night of Brahmā, God remains in dreamless sleep, inactive, all being fathomless rest and boundless peace. During this night, Vishnu lies unconscious on the Cosmic Serpent Shesha. At the coming of dawn a lotus blooms from Vishnu's navel, out of which springs Brahmā the Creator, while Shiva, agent of reabsorption (saṁhāra), springs from his head, to send the universe through the four yugas. The Buddha (in *Dīgha Nikāya*) denied and denigrated the doctrine of Brahmā as Creator. Brahmā's cult is today infrequently observed among Hindus. See also Brahman, Shiva, Vishnu, yuga.

brahmachārī, brahmachārin, Hind. Originally the term signified a student of the Vedas, one who went to Brahman, the holy word; later it came to mean one who is engaged in brahmacharya (q.v.), and most recently, in Mohandas Gandhi's cosmogony, a celibate —either complete, or if married, restrained. The brahmachārī practices a rigorous life at the literal foot of his guru, either at his teacher's own house or at an ashram; the brahmachārī treats his guru as a father and as a god, in absolute obedience and practicing complete chastity. In the primitive periods the brahmachārī was himself considered sacred. The Artharva Veda says that not only does he "sustain earth and heaven," but also "The fathers, the god-folk, and all the gods together follow the brahmachārī." Of interest is the passage that states that his teacher, after accepting him, "treats him like an embryo in his own body" and "carries him for three nights in his belly." The brahmachārī begets Brahman, the waters, and the world, and becomes the god Indra and shatters the demons; "born of the brahmachārī are plants, past and future, trees, the year and its seasons, animals of the earth and those of the heavens, wild and domestic, wingless and winged." The same Veda also states that the brahmachārī's fervor clothes him "in heat" i.e., he was nude; however, when he returned to the world outside, consecrated by the sacred fire, he was bearded and wore antelope skins. Nevertheless, the brahmachārī's celibacy could be set aside, and he engaged in intercourse, either ritually or literally, with a prostitute (the puṃścali) in a ceremony that contained a number of elements of archaic fertility magic.

brahmacharya, Hind. (1) The first of the four stages of aśrāma, meaning an active period of education and discipline. (2) Sexual abstinence. Brahmacharya, explained Mohandas Gandhi, means "control in thought, word, and action of all the sense at all times and in all places," the purpose of such control being the search of Brahman. "Brahman pervades every being and can therefore be searched for by diving into and realizing the inner self. This realization is impossible without complete control of the senses."

Brahman, Hind. The Supreme Reality conceived of as one and undifferentiated, static and dynamic, yet above all definitions; the ultimate principle underlying the world, ultimate reality: "Without cause and without effect, without anything inside or outside," according to the sage Yājñavalkya. "Brahman is he whom speech cannot express, and from whom the mind, unable to reach him, comes away baffled," states the *Taittirīya Upaniśad*. The concept of Brahman is difficult, perhaps impossible to define, and has changed over the aeons; Brahman is now of interest more as a philosophic concept of past ages than as an active principle—to be meditated upon, but not adored or worshiped.

Philological aspects are important. The root of the word is bṛh (to make, to form, to grow). The term brahman meant at first prayer, hymn, magic formula, sacred knowledge (and still means sacred word in some contexts), then the power in them, and finally the Supreme Power. As brāhman the term means sacred utterance, while brahmān means one imbued with the power of sacred speech or of the sacred word. Brahman came to denote both the creator or Absolute, divine substance and a man, the latter being the brahman (more correctly, brāhman, commonly spelled brahmin in English to lessen the confusion), who is of the priestly caste. The concepts are confusing and depend on almost unnoticeable shifts in stress and pronunciation; at the same time they meld into each other, for each is intimately part of the other and yet separate.

It must be emphasized that Brahman is not god, is not Pure Spirit. All words used in connection with Brahman are neuter—It, not He. However, Brahman is not a thing or an object. Brahman is inexhaustible plenitude, the measureless reservoir, both emptiness and fullness. Though Brahman can be inadequately described as primeval Matter and Spirit alike, both external principles, there is no absolute distinction between the two. To call Brahman "the Ground of All Being," as Western vedantists do, is to belittle the immensity of Brahman. Briefly, Western terms, which aim at precision, definition, order, logic, purity, and clarity, fail before the immensity of Brahman, for Brahman, according to Śaṃkara (c. A.D. 788–820), is silence, Nāda Brahman. "'Sir,' said a pupil to his master, 'teach me the nature of Brahman.' The master did not reply. When he was asked a second and a third time, he replied: 'I teach you, but you do not listen. His name is silence.'"

Ultimately Brahman is summed up in the famous phrase neti neti (not this not that). Commenting upon the phrase, the *Chandogya Upaniṣad* states: "It is incomprehensible, for it cannot be comprehended; undecaying, for it never decays; unattached, for it never attaches itself; unbound, for it is never bound. By whom, O my beloved, shall the Knower be known?"

In the Vedas the mythical image of Brahman as sound or word is the skambha, the cosmic pillar that supports the world; skambha is also the cosmic axis and the ontological foundation. Brahman is expressed also by the sacred monosyllable ŌṂ, pregnant with the meaning of eternal worlds, within which all other sounds are contained. Visually Brahman is signified by yantra, the graphic equivalent of the symbols of creation. In the overlapping triangles that form the center of a yantra, symbolizing the union of male and female, the central point (or bindu) signifies the undifferentiated

Brahman. In certain aspects of tantra, the coupling (or samhita) of man and woman expresses union with the gods and with Brahman. See ātman, brāhmin.

brāhman, Hind. See brāhmin.

Brāhmaṇas, Hind. A collection of elaborate prose treatises concerned with the arts and sciences of sacrifice (yajña). They are part of Vedic literature and are among the works known as śruti (revealed). The Brāhmaṇas, eight in number and dating before B.C. 600, exalt the priest above the gods, for the brāhmin alone possesses the secret lore of the sacrifice that is able to bend even the will of the gods. Even the rising of the sun depends on the priestly fire sacrifice—yajña—properly performed. Yajña is central, and all. Sin consists chiefly in mistakes in ritual; immoral acts are sinful only if they affect ritual purity. The god Brahmā, one of the Trimūrti that includes Shiva and Vishnu, is pre-eminent, appearing in the Brāhmaṇas in the forms of Prajāpati, Pitāmaha, and Hiraṇya-garbha; the god later declined in importance and today is rarely worshiped. A running theme is the working out of the cause of the universe and of creation, for which various hypotheses are offered: a primeval artificer, a primitive couple, a "golden germ," a cosmic egg, an organizer of chaos into cosmos, a perfect "One" procreating through desire and asceticism (kāma and tapas), a mind manifesting itself in definable forms, an ascetic whose perspirations and breath materialize as world, a cosmic Person whose sacrificial dismemberment results in the diverse elements of the universe, a unique godhead expressing itself through transcendental power, a Lord of Life producing through the power of the Word. See Brahmā, Vedas, yajña.

brāhmin (or brahmin), Hind. The first or priestly caste; "brāhman" is the correct spelling, but brāhmin is more often employed to avoid confusion with Brahman (q.v.). For a full definition of brāhmin, see caste.

Brāhmo Samāj, Hind. The Society of Brahmā (or the Society of God). A Bengali movement founded in 1829 by Raja Ram Mohan Roy (1772–1833), a Bengali brahmin; based upon a unitarian approach to God. Roy, who was raised in Patna, then a center of Muslim learning, came under the influence of Islamic teachings against images (though he tolerated images for people who needed them); later, in Calcutta, he was exposed to Christianity. Without wanting to abandon his own Hinduism, he sought a purified way free of superstition and idolatry, and drawing upon some aspects of the Gospels. A remarkable scholar, he not only knew Bengali, Sanskrit, and other Indian tongues, but also Arabic, Persian, Hebrew, Greek, and Latin, and he read many of the world's scriptures in the original tongues in his search for unifying doctrines. However, what he was looking for he found in his own background, the eighth-century B.C. Upanishads, which contained the unitarian teachings he had sought. But he did not rely completely upon the past; he advocated that Indians learn Western sciences, such as mathematics, natural philosophy, chemistry, and anatomy. A few years after his death his work was taken over by the young Devandranath Tagore (1817–1905), a saintly man who reorganized the now dispirited Samāj. Tagore did not accept the Vedas, the Upanishads, and other texts as infallible, and he rejected Christian doctrines as compromising the transcendence of God. The Hindu books were guides, the primary authorities being reason and conscience. A crisis came to the Samāj in 1865 when a younger member, Keshab Chandra Sen (1838–84), objecting to certain conservative practices of Tagore's, led a schism of the majority of the members and founded the Brāhmo-Samāj of India. The original group now called itself the Ādi Samāj, or Original Society, and became increasingly conservative. Keshab introduced not only readings from other religions but also certain Hindu folk practices, such as devotional singing and dancing. He also campaigned for the education of women and for their emancipation, and against child marriages and for intercaste marriages. However, to the dismay of his followers, he married his daughter, then thirteen, to the prince of Cooch Behar in an orthodox rite. This led to still another schism, the founding of the Sādhāraṇ (Universal) Brāhmo Samāj, while Keshab's group was renamed the Church of the New Dispensation, the two previous being the Old Testament and the New. The latest schismatic group was run not by a single figure but by an elected group of one hundred members, who chose their own directors. Since then the entire movement has declined considerably in influence, with more schisms and some offshoots in various parts of India. It has almost always been confined to the upper castes and classes of Bengalis and rarely included the people. But its legacy has been a large number of well-educated, intelligent, progressive Bengalis who are open to new ideas, generally eschew the barriers of caste and national group, often marry outside their community, and are active in their country.

Bhrigu, Hind. A legendary sage, born ten thousand (or more) years ago. He is also a minor deity and one of the sages of the Mahābhārata. Bhrigu had a vision of the life of everyone ever to be born, and he wrote it all down. Collections of his visions, the *Bhrigu Saṁhitā* (the Bhrigu Collection), are still extant, some of them running to two hundred volumes; others are in manuscript form; the language is usually Sanskrit but may be a vernacular. With the knowledge of one's horoscope, for Bhrigu is based on astrology, a skilled reader can forecast a client's entire life. Unfortunately the art is dying out, and qualified interpreters of the sage are now scarce; few disciples are eager to assume the burden of the tremendous training necessary to read Bhrigu.

Buddha. (1) The term means the Enlightened or the Awakened. There are many buddhas, running from the Ādi-Buddha (the Original Buddha) to several small groups of five (the Buddhas of the Meditation, the Human Buddhas, etc.) to large numbers of interest solely to certain sects and subsects of Buddhism, primarily of the Mahāyāna schools. (Even the Trappist monk Thomas Merton is said to be accepted by certain Tibetans as a buddha.) The Hīnayāna (Theravada) Buddhists recognize only Siddārtha Gautama of the Śākya tribe of eastern India (on the Nepalese border) as the Buddha; he is the individual generally known as the Buddha, or Buddha, to Westerners. See also Ādi-Buddha, Amida, Buddha, Buddhism, Pure Land Buddhism.

(2) Buddha (or the Buddha). The originator of the Way—the Middle Way—of Indian thought based on transcending the sufferings of ordinary life by ending the cycle of birth and rebirth by attaining a state of spiritual perfection called nirvāṇa (or nibbana). Though there is little doubt of the historicity of the Buddha, the dates of his life span are not definite; the best that can be

said is that he lived eighty years. Indian scholars set his dates at B.C. 560–480. The major, Hīnayāna (Theravada) school of Ceylon and Burma puts the chronology at B.C. 623–543. Other Hīnayānists say 624–544. The Mahāyānists schools of China and Japan and elsewhere prefer 566–486, or even a year later, for birth and death. The Chinese, and some others, celebrate the Buddha's birth on April 8, but May 8 is more common.

Doubts as to the existence of a historical "Buddha" should not be considered seriously, though a brief mention of the problems that intrigue—or plague—Western scholars is in order, for many of them have been puzzled by the success of a school, a Way, a world soul-force of inestimable strength that defies much Western tradition. The problem first arose in the nineteenth century when oriental scholarship broke upon the European horizon. H. H. Wilson in 1856 suggested that the traditional accounts of the Buddha's life were but allegories of Hindu sāṃkhya, a pre-Buddhist philosophical system attributed to the sage Kapila (q.v.), which taught the complete independence and freedom of the human mind and its full confidence in its own powers, life's goal being to put an end to the three kinds of suffering (the pain caused by diseases of the body, mental disturbances and unrest; the pain caused extraneously by men or beasts; and the pain caused by supernatural agencies, the planets and the elements). The events of the Buddha's life can be matched against sāṃkhya in some detail, but Kapila's teachings do not explain away the existence of the human figure of Siddārtha Gautama, the Buddha. The French and Dutch scholars Senart and Kern put the Buddha's life into the terms of a solar myth symbolic of the cakravartin (q.v.), the universal monarch, summarized in the Buddhist phrase "the turning of the Wheel of the Law." The traditional stories of the Buddha, argued Senart, are but mythological descriptions derived from a body of sun legends. In this century the leading European Buddhist Edward Conze, while not denying Buddha's historicity, says that his actual existence is of no importance, for the Buddha is "a kind of archetype which manifests itself in the world at different periods, in different personalities, whose individual particularities are of no account whatever." Though many successive layers of legends have accreted upon the original truth, many other diverse traditions combine to emphasize the fact of a historical individual who was at the center of a system of thought that grew to be unusual, complex, and highly sophisticated. Even the traditions of the many other buddhas may have probable historical foundation. Of the two major Buddhist traditions, the earlier, the Hīnayāna, focuses on a single Buddha, while the Mahāyānist, split into numerous schools, accept the Gautama Buddha as but one (though a major one) of many, without particular emphasis on any special buddha.

BIOGRAPHY. The individual generally called the Buddha was born (whatever the precise date) into the family of a minor Hindu prince of the warrior caste (kśatryia) in the foothills of the Himālayas, on the Nepalese-Indian border, some one hundred miles north of the holy city of Kāśī (now Benares or Vārāṇāsī). Later legend made the father a great king; actually he was but heir to a small kingdom, that of the Śákyas; he was of the Gautama clan, and his given name was Suddhodana. His wife, the mother of the future Buddha, was Mahā Māya. The Buddha is also known as Siddārtha Gautama (the former being his given name), and later as Śākyamuni, the Sage of the Śákyas. The agreed-upon version of the events leading to his birth is that he was the final incarnation of a Hindu sage, Sumedha, who in ages long past had decided in some future birth to become a buddha, an enlightened one, in order to aid suffering mankind. Before the day came for this last incarnation, Sumedha experienced various stages of enlightenment, the details of which need not detain us (the curious reader is referred to Sir Edwin Arnold's *Light of Asia*). This long passage of spiritual development has played an important part in Buddhist doctrines. The birth of the Buddha himself puts us in a definite historical age, though the events surrounding it are, again (at least to the Westerner), fanciful.

Mahā Māya was impregnated in a manner surrounded by miraculous features (the entire sequence of events of the Buddha's conception, birth, and early life was attended by numerous celestial figures, gods, the deities of the ten thousand world systems, minor spirits, spiritual powers, and so on). Mahā Māya did not have sexual relations with her husband, but during a deep sleep, she dreamed that she was lifted from her couch, transported to the Anotta Lake in the Himālayas, and put down to rest on a heavenly couch within a golden mansion on Silver Hill. The bodhisattva, or Buddha to be (that is, the brahmin sage Sumedhra), in the form of a white elephant bearing a white lotus in his trunk, approached from the north, seemed to touch the queen on the right side, and then entered her womb. (In a more prosaic phrase, one might state that the Lord Buddha impregnated himself upon his mother.) Upon awakening, Mahā Māya had lost all desire for intercourse with her husband. These details, a puzzle to the Westerner who queries anything of the miraculous in any religion but his own, are of importance to the Buddhist.

Mahā Māya related the dream to Suddhodana, who told it to the eight household priests. Seven said that the queen had conceived a male child who would become a chakravartin, the universal monarch; one priest, however, foresaw that if the child entered the religious life he would become a buddha in order to remove the veils of ignorance and sin from the world.

The child was born; on the fifth day after his birth, following Hindu custom, he was given a name, Siddārtha. The priests again repeated their prophecies. Immediately afterward tragedy struck the young family: Two days later, Mahā Māya died; her sister Gautami, also a wife of the prince, took over as the baby's foster mother. Young Siddārtha was raised as a warrior prince, taught not only wrestling, archery, and other martial skills, but also writing and arithmetic and the "sixty-four arts and sciences." At sixteen he was married to his cousin Yasodharā. However, as a bodhisattva, the buddha to be, Siddārtha was always conscious of his future state. It was after his marriage that he had the experience of the Four Signs, the four encounters of life-as-it-is, which laid bare the hollowness of his sheltered existence as a prince and turned his mind to the fulfillment of his mission. Despite his father's attempts to prevent Siddārtha from seeing misery and illness, the young prince, on different outings, encountered an aged man, a man ill with fever, and a corpse. These face-to-face meetings with age, illness, and death brought him to the resolution to "seek a way of deliverance." Siddārtha's final encounter was with a bhikku (q.v.), a wandering mendicant who was serene, dignified, and self-possessed, and carrying a beggar's bowl. Such a way, the young man said, "makes me eager for the same course of life." To become a religious "shall be my refuge and the refuge of others and shall yield the fruit of immortality."

Thus came the great Renunciation, when Siddārtha, now fully a bodhisattva, gave up his family, palaces, future kingdom, and accompanied only by an attendant, rode out of the palace. All of these events are described in great detail in the various Buddhist works, which also surround them with vast numbers of attendant gods and heavenly spirits raining down flowers. But the Bodhisattva was not to escape easily without challenge. In one of the great moments in the Buddha's biography, he is tempted by Mara the Fiend, who offers him the four continents and untold wealth. This barrier passed, the Bodhisattva begins his search for the Way, experiencing a path in which he tries the severe austerities of the Hindu holy man, retreat into the forest, and wandering as a beggar. His companions are five wandering holy men. Siddārtha undergoes six years of the most severe austerities, prayer, and penances but is still unable to attain liberation, and his companions desert him.

Awakening finally comes, however, during a period of retreat in the forest under a great tree near Gayā (in what is today the state of Bihar); now Siddārtha is the Buddha in the fullest sense of the term. The trials the Bodhisattva experienced are described at great length in the documents—more temptations by Mara, assaults by demons, attacks by hostile forces under the guise of storms, showers of rocks and fires, and other tests that enhance but do not explain the legends. The new Buddha is to spend forty-nine days in peaceful meditation in the area. He has the message of salvation now, but how is he to convey it, and to whom? And most important of all, just what is the message?

The Buddha set out to find his former companions of the forest, the Five Wanderers. He found them in the Deer Park at Kāśī. They greeted him as "Brother," but he corrected them by saying that he was not "Brother," but "a Buddha of clear vision even as those who went before." The message, which he gave seated before his friends, is an important one in Buddhism. It is known as the First Sermon, otherwise called Setting in Motion the Wheel of the Law (also, Foundation of the Kingdom of Righteousness). It contains the essence of Buddhism. Briefly, the Buddha made the following points:

He warned against two extremes—habitual devotion to the passions, the pleasures of sensual things, a low and pagan way of seeking satisfaction on the one hand, and on the other, habitual devotion to self-mortification, which is painful, ignoble, and unprofitable. "There is a Middle Path . . . a path which opens the eyes and bestows understanding, which leads to peace, to insight, to the higher wisdom, to nirvāṇa." This is the Āriyan Eightfold Path, i.e., "Right Views, Right Aspirations, Right Speech, Right Conduct, Right Mode of Livelihood, Right Effort, Right Mindfulness, and Right Rapture." Needless to say, the Five Wanderers were converted to his mode of thinking and became buddhas. Other sermons, crucial to Buddhist doctrine, immediately followed, one against three yogic fire worshipers (who were converted), another called the Discourse on Fire, and so on. Legendary accretions persist, but so far as historical authenticity of the Buddha is concerned, we are on firmer ground. Disciples began to flock around him in large numbers—a dozen here, twenty thousand there. The followers were soon organized into formal groups, the Sangha or Brotherhood. Wealthy patrons built monasteries and foundations for the Sangha, though in general the monks followed the traditional life of the Hindu holy man. It is doubtful, at that time, that anyone, either the Buddha or his disciples, thought of the movement as anything but another version of traditional Hinduism, stating doctrines as they saw fit, and wandering about from place to place during the dry seasons and returning to a fixed abode in the monsoons. There were many similar movements, even in the same area, such as the Jains (q.v.), who lived in an identical manner (though some of the doctrines were radically different).

Among the Sangha disputes began to arise over discipline and teaching. Should women, for example, be given an equal role or not? They were not, in fact, though some women did play important roles in early Buddhism. In matters of doctrine there had to be a continued effort to keep the Middle Way free of the superstitions of the neighboring Hindus and Jains. A group of newly ordained bhikkus forced a temporary schism by demanding a stricter rule. Near the end of the Buddha's life virtually his entire clan, the Śākyas, was annihilated in a war. At the age of eighty the Buddha predicted his own approaching death, saying to his monks, "All component things must grow old. Work out your salvation with diligence." He went on preaching to the end, but after eating a meal of sweet rice and cake and pork (the latter is a doubtful item—it may have been truffles) he became ill, recovered slightly, and set out toward the next village accompanied by his favorite disciple, Ānanda. The Buddha took ill again, lay down under a tree on the banks of a stream, and shortly afterward died. The death scene is a favorite in Buddhist writings, for it is described in detail, and in art, replete with symbolism; miracles of nature and the heavens surround the dying Buddha, disciples and villagers crowd around, he gives his last discourse again, repeating it slightly differently: "Decay is inherent in all component things! Work out your salvation with diligence." He then went into the Rapture that led to nirvāṇa, the cycle of birth and rebirth having ended. The body was cremated, the ashes being divided into eight portions and given to eight tribal chiefs, each of whom had some special claim to the remains. Tumuli were erected over them, the burial mounds that were to develop in Buddhism into the elaborate buildings of Southeast Asia, Indonesia, China, the Himālayas, and Japan known variously as stūpas or pagodas.

(3) The Buddha in Hinduism. Indian—Hindu—views of Gautama Buddha are mixed and often confused and contradictory. For many Hindus, he is one of the greatest Indians ever to have lived. Buddhism, which is not well known in India today, is accepted as one of many forms of an all-encompassing tolerant Hinduism. A popular view is that the Buddha did not intend to found a new religion but merely sought a reformed, reasonable Middle Path in Hinduism between extremes of pleasure and pain, luxury and austerity, and other problems of human life. The fact stressed by Buddhists, that the Buddha did not mention God, is taken by Hindus to show that he was a Hindu and took God for granted, the obvious not needing elucidation. Many Hindu temples include an image of the Buddha along with those of various deities and saints, and pilgrimages to Bodh Gāya (q.v.) and other Buddhist shrines in India are common among Hindus. Such are some of the noncritical views among a large number of devout Hindus. However, others, especially those with speculative or occultist minds, see the Buddha on vastly different levels.

Though the Gautama Buddha is the ninth incarnation of Vishnu (q.v.) and the first avatār of the fourth or present age, the Kali Yuga or Age of Strife, not all Hindus accept the Buddha avatār as the Gautama Buddha; some of the Purāṇas see the Buddha avatār as one sent to the world in order to mislead men of low birth by opposing the teachings of the brāhmins. The Buddha avatār is the embodiment of illusion and delusion; by preaching a moral Way dependent on one's own efforts—incorrect and unacceptable in Vedic brahminism—he attacked Vedic ritual and the very foundations of a hierarchical society so dependent on rites correctly celebrated by the priests. Thus the Buddha avatār has pushed the world on its path of ruin and destruction in the Kālī Yuga.

On a philosophical basis, orthodox Hindus criticize Buddhism (so far as they understand it in its Indian environment) as eliminating the Absolute as the First Cause of the cosmic series and leaving out the hypothesis of self-alienation. The Buddhists, say such orthodox Hindus, erroneously regard karma as a moral necessity working itself out independently of providence or personal will. Hindus see the Buddhists sharing the Vedāntist view of nirvāṇa as unconditioned, but in distinguishing nirvāṇa from man's conditioned, existence, they err in holding the latter as phenomenal, momentary, and relative.

In popular occultist belief, the Lord Buddha is viewed as the first flower of the tree of humanity. In the process of evolution from the mineral through the plant and animal to the human, there were always two souls predominant. In one, Love was primary; in the other, Wisdom. "In the occult hierarchy," states the noted Hindu academician Ramanuja Srinivasan (b. 1887 in Tiruchirapalli, Madras), summarizing traditional beliefs, "a selection had to be made to fill the post of the Buddha who was in charge of the religious instruction of the world, an office till then held by Kashyapa, a Great One from Venus." Traditionally, Kashyapa (Kaśyapa), the god Vision, is the universal progenitor of men, gods, and demons, all born of his thirteen wives, the women being the daughters of Dakṣa, or Ritual-Skill. Among Buddhists, however, Kashyapa is the first disciple. "The candidate chosen was He known to us as Gautama Siddhartha, One in whom the Wisdom-Love was personified. As Bodhisatwa, he took the vow before Kashyapa to work his way up and to equip himself for the great office of the Buddha. He came to the world several times: as Vyasa in India, as Hermes in Egypt, as Zarathusthra in Persia and Orpheus in Greece." This linking of several saints and holy men as one, or aspects of the One, is found in a number of religions. Vyāsa is a cosmic entity born again and again to arrange and promulgate traditional knowledge—i.e., the Vedas; he is also the arranger of the eighteen Purāṇas and the compiler of the Mahābhārata. Hermes Trismegetus is prophetical leader (possibly mythical) of Hellenic Egypt, and Zarathusthra or Zoroaster, the great Iranian prophet of the sixth century B.C., roughly a contemporary of Gautama Buddha's. Orpheus lived at about the same period; he was a seer who introduced the worship of Apollo and taught reincarnation. Such occultist beliefs had a powerful effect on the synthetic religion of Theosophy (q.v.), which predicates its beliefs upon the Buddha incarnated as a fourteenth-century Tibetan lama, Tsong-Kha-pa.

Buddha, days of celebration. There are three major festivals in the Buddhist calendar: the Buddha's birthday, May 8; the day of his Enlightenment, December 8; and the day of his death, February 15.

Buddha-Gāya. See Bodh-Gāya.

Buddha-kāya, Buddh. The doctrine of the Three Bodies, or Tri-kāya, of Buddha. In this teaching the Buddha exists as Dharma-kāya, the Truth-Body or Self-Being Body; the Sambhoga-kāya, or Bliss-Body, the celestial manifestation of the Buddha-Nature as perceived by celestial beings; and the Nirmāna-kāya, the Assumed-Body, which exists because the Dharma-kāya is too exalted a body for ordinary mortals to come into any conscious contact with. Hence the Nirmāna-kāya is the historical manifestation of Buddha as man, in the person of the Gautama Buddha.

Buddha, relics. Unlike Hinduism, which rarely engages in the veneration of the physical remains of the dead, Buddhism enshrined portions of the body of the Lord Gautama Buddha. His ashes were collected and placed in eight stūpas (q.v.), originally burial mounds for royalty or the great, but which quickly grew to have a primarily Buddhist significance. Four of the Buddha's teeth also survived cremation. One of them was taken by the god Indra, a Hindu deity absorbed into the Buddhist pantheon; a second tooth is preserved in a crystal stūpa in the great palace of the Nāgas, a type of non-Āryan serpent deity, at the bottom of the ocean, and the other two remained among mankind. The third was enshrined in the Temple of the Holy Tooth in Kandy, Sri Lanka. The fourth, after a long series of dramatic events that brought it from Udyāna now in northern Pakistan) to China's Ching-shan Mountain (near Nanking), then to She-shan Mountain in the same area, and later to a monastery near Changan, now rests in a pagoda in the hills west of Peking. The Tooth disappeared from sight, and was forgotten for some 830 years, when it was discovered in 1900 in the bombardment of Peking during the Boxer Rebellion. In clearing up the wreckage of the pagoda, which had been destroyed by the foreign armies, the monks came across a reliquary inscribed in Sanskrit describing its contents and its history; inside was the Holy Tooth.

The history of the Tooth in Kandy is better known. It is enshrined in a garbha, or womb, about 2⅗ inches in diameter. It was stolen by the Portuguese in 1560; the archbishop of Goa (the city was then the leading Portuguese entrepôt of the East), had it crushed to a powder and thrown into the sea. The Buddhists of Sri Lanka (formerly Ceylon) affirm that this was not the Buddha's actual tooth but a substitute. They still honor the Holy Tooth today. The Chinese Tooth has been brought on pilgrimage to Sri Lanka; both teeth bear strong resemblance to each other.

Rangoon possesses a hair of Buddha given to Te Pau, a disciple, who is the legendary founder of the city. The Hair was placed in the highest part of the Swe Dahon pagoda. Buddha's own alms bowl is found variously in Sri Lanka, Kandahar, Persia, and China. A finger bone of the Lord Buddha was brought to China in A.D. 819 by the Emperor Hsien-tsung, against the objections of Taoists and Confucians, who thought it should be destroyed as an example of barbarian superstition. See Buddha.

Buddhism. The Way, not quite a religion in the Western sense, taught by Siddārtha Gautama of the Śākya clan, otherwise commonly called Buddha or the Buddha. The followers of the Buddhist Way are likely to refer to it as Saddharma (roughly, the True Law); members of the southern schools (Hīnayāna or Theravāda) using the Pāli term, Buddhism Dhamma (That Which

Upholds). The essentials of Buddhism were laid out by Gautama Buddha himself in his first group of sermons before his initial followers. What he taught is as follows:

The first sermon, called either Setting in Motion the Wheel of the Law or the Foundation of the Kingdom of Righteousness, begins with a broad statement about two extremes that ought to be avoided. The first is habitual devotion to the passions, the pleasures of sensual things and a low, ignoble, and uprofitable way of seeking satisfaction; the other extreme is habitual devotion to self-mortification, which is painful, ignoble, and also unprofitable (the Buddha is here denouncing a common Hindu practice). The Buddha advocates a Middle Path he himself has discovered, which opens the eyes and bestows understanding, leading to peace, insight, to the higher wisdom, and above all, to nirvāṇa. He calls this the Āriyan Eightfold Path (Āriyan means Noble), which is to say, Right Views, Right Aspirations, Right Speech, Right Conduct, Right Mode of Livelihood, Right Effort, Right Mindfulness, and Right Rapture.

Suffering is a central fact of living. The Noble Truth of suffering is that birth is attended with pain, decay is painful, disease is painful, death is painful. Union with the unpleasant is painful; painful is separation from the pleasant; any unsatisfied craving is also painful. In brief, the five Aggregates of Attachment are painful.

The Noble Truth of the origin of suffering is the thirst to gratify the senses or the craving for material gains. This craving leads from rebirth to rebirth.

The Noble Truth for the annihilation of suffering is to give up, to get rid of, to be emanicipated from the craving thirst that causes so much woe.

The only Path that leads to the passing away of the pain of existence is the Noble Eightfold Path.

Buddhism has no place for the supernatural, and this was a question that the Buddha tackled immediately for the benefit of his disciples. In his sermon On the Nonexistence of the Soul he outlined the problem of consciousness as he saw it. To begin with, the body cannot be the eternal soul, for the body dies. Neither do sensation, perception, the predispositions, and consciousness together constitute the eternal soul, for all these attributes are transitory. And what is transitory is evil. And what is transitory and evil and liable to change cannot be called an "eternal soul." The true disciple will conceive a disgust for the body and for sensation, predispositions, and consciousness, and thus divested of desire will be freed, will be aware that he is freed, will know that becoming or rebirth is exhausting, that he has lived the pure life, and now the cycle of birth and rebirth—of being mortal—is ended.

How one attains nirvāṇa is something that has been worked out differently in the various schools of Buddhism. Some teach a simple but rigorous following of the Way; others enlightenment through regular and constant meditation (the various Ch'an and Zen methods are examples), or through an instantaneous awakening as the result of solving an apparently insoluble mental or verbal problem, the kōan. Buddhism's stressing of pain and sorrow has brought it the often-repeated charge of pessimism and of creating passivity in its followers. However, the Buddha himself, after pointing out the essential truth that for virtually all of mankind suffering is the all-too-common fate, also emphasized that the followers of the Dhamma must still try to follow the Way with zest, or piti, and be cheerful and open, and must also aid others. In place of rationalizing suffering as a test of God or the gods, Buddhism takes it for granted in the world but seeks to eradicate it. Suffering will exist so long as there is craving, both of which are paired and can only be annihilated by following the Eightfold Path.

The Dhamma may be called the law of cause and effect, both of which embrace the entire corpus of the Buddha's teachings. And whether the Buddhas—the Gautama or others—arise or not, the Four Noble Truths exist. The Buddhas can only reveal these Truths, which lay hidden in the abyss of time, and show the Way to salvation. And at the bottom, only the individual can attain his own salvation; the Buddhas can merely teach that there is a Way. It is the individual's responsibility to follow it—"Abide with oneself as an island, with oneself as a Refuge. Abide with the Damma as a Refuge. Seek no external refuge." In other words, look within, for the Lord Buddha, buddhahood, is inside you.

HISTORY. When the Gautama Buddha died (c. B.C. 480), he left behind a well-organized band of followers, the monks or bhikkus (literally, beggars) assembled into a Brotherhood, the Sangha, who were committed to a regulated life of meditation, prayer, supporting themselves by alms, and usually based up on a center, the vihāra, from which they would set off on long periods of wandering except during the rainy season. The bhikkus were typical of Indian holy men but followed the Middle Way preached by the Gautama Buddha, without the customary austerities and other penances, eschewing the extremes of life styles, such as nudity, of some Hindu sects. For about two centuries the Sangha was but one of many similar groups on the subcontinent. However, there was considerable development of doctrine over this period. A canon of sacred texts, later called the *Tripiṭaka* (q.v.), was assembled, based upon the Buddha's words, which had been memorized by his chief disciple, Ānanada, and transmitted orally. A great Council was held shortly after the Buddha's death, and a second one a century later, where a dispute over the correctness of doctrine divided the disciples into two rival sects, whose rivalry hardened as time went by and the monks' own concepts of Buddhism began to develop into different channels. The Theravādas, the Elders, claimed that they maintained the Buddha's own tradition with exactness; they are part of what came to be called the Hīnayānists, or the Lesser Vehicle, while their opponents became the Mahāyānists, or Greater Vehicle. Each major school has numerous subsects, divided not only by differing interpretations of the Buddha's Dhamma, but also by accretions of local customs, rites, folkways, and earlier religions, for much of what had been a pristine Buddhism is now hopelessly entangled with the gods of many forms of animism, of primordial religions such as Tibetan Bön, Tao, Shintōism, and so on.

Buddhism may have remained nothing more than another Indian sect on its way to a full shattering of itself, in an age of many rivals, when in the third century B.C. the Emperor Ashoka (q.v.), distraught over the carnage in his latest war, rejected violence as a means of ruling and turned to Buddhism. Ashoka's lands contained the major Buddhist centers, and principles of the sect, with its Middle Way, its eschewing of violence, and its positive emphasis on the self-sufficient individual, were a major attraction. Buddhism seemed to point to a peaceable kingdom. Under Ashoka's patronage, Buddhism suddenly became a world power. The Emperor called a third Council to settle doctrinal disputes and to try to establish some kind of orthodoxy; he also sent Buddhist missionaries to most of the known world, from Southeast Asia and Ceylon on one side to the Middle East and possibly Greece on the other. He embarked upon a major building program on behalf of Buddhism, founding monasteries, schools, hospitals, and other institutions, and enlarging the highway system to facilitate both trade and ordinary travel. Indian Buddhism survived in strength for another thousand years and then began to decline under the pressure of a Hindu revival, especially the bhakti movements among the peasants; the coming of Islam also affected Buddhism. Meanwhile, being solidly established abroad, Buddhism was to grow with even greater vigor on other soils, in a prolixity of philosophies, forms of mysticism, creative arts, literature, and doctrinal schools, some of great purity, others heavily burdened with folklore, superstition, and magic. Refinements and changes of direction continue to take place within Buddhism. In this century Buddhist councils have met to examine the problems facing Saddharma in a technological, nuclear world. Today much of Asia, from the offshore islands such as Sri Lanka, Indonesia, Japan, the mainland including Korea and even China, the Himālayan nations such as Sikkim, Tibet, Bhutan, and Nepal, and Southeast Asia are either partly or completely Buddhist. It might be added that Buddhism is not a quantitative Way; attempts to count the number of Buddhists in, say, China, Vietnam, or Japan run into frustrating difficulties, for in the first two an individual might be also a Taoist and a Confucian as well as a Buddhist, and in the latter, also a Shintōist. And though China may, on the record, be a completely secular nation, the Buddhist Way, inextricably entwined with Taoism and Confucianism, is still a powerful subsurface force. See also Buddha, Ch'an, Hīnayāna, Mahāyāna, Tripiṭaka, Zen.

Bullah Shah (A.D. 1680–1752). Noted Punjabi Ṣūfī, born near Lahore, into a respectable family said to be descended from the Prophet. His father was a pīr, or religious teacher, and a member of a dervish order. Bullah spent his early days engaged in both Ṣūfī and Hindu practices, often in a graveyard, without finding a spiritual path. After hearing a voice saying, "Seek my lover and you shall meet me there," he set off a pilgrim. He finally found his future guru (the Hindu word is used), Shah Inayat, planting onions. Inayat agreed to take on Bullah as a disciple, but the young man soon made such great spiritual progress that he boasted of it openly, and Inayat expelled him from the zāwiyah; Bullah was eventually restored to favor, saying he was not Bullah but Bhullah (literally, the erring one). Bullah's songs, known as kafis, became popular throughout the Muslim areas of western India, especially Sind and the Punjab, and are still sung among certain coteries of Ṣūfīs. See Ṣūfī.

Burmese position, Buddh. A method of sitting in tsen ch'an or zazen meditation. Unlike the interlocking of legs in the lotus position (q.v.) the legs are not crossed, but the knees are bent to the sides, with one foot in front of the other.

butsuden, Buddh. The hall in Japanese Buddhism that enshrines the image of either a Buddha or a bodhisattva.

◂C▸

cakra (also chakra), Hind. (1) Literally wheel, but symbolically the universal law and its reflection in the moral law of man; the universal power and the focus of spiritual power in human consciousness; the universal sun and the inner light of illumination. Gandhi designed the flag of the Congress Party (it later became the Indian flag) with a cakra—in this case, a spinning wheel—as the central symbol.

(2) In a mystical sense in tantric yoga a center of the body. There are six major cakras—namely, the mūlādhāra, svādhiṣṭhāna, maṇi-pūra, anāhata, viśuddha, and ājñā—which run in a line from the area between the penis and the anus (the mūlādhāra) to the ājñā, which is situated between the eyes and is sometimes called the Third Eye. Above these cakras is still another mystical center, at the top of the skull, the sahasrāra-padma, which is sometimes counted as a seventh cakra.

Each cakra contains a lotus, the petals of which represent different mystical and religious qualities, and are the seats of various deities. The goddess Devī (or Kuṇḍalinī, the Serpent Power) is coiled around the mūlādhāra and when properly awakened in tantrism, ascends in force to the sahasrāra-padma. The cakras are mystical, not literal, and cannot be identified with any organ. There are other cakras of lesser importance, not counted among those listed above. Buddhist tantrics employ only four.

cakravartin, Hind. The universal Emperor. Literally, abiding in the wheel (cakra), often rendered as wheel king or wheel turner, a concept brought to its height by the Mauryan Emperor Ashoka in the third century B.C., who revived the theme as the ruler of the Dharma in his own person. The cakravartin was a form of avatār, especially those of Vishnu (particularly Rāma and Krishna) and resembling the Mahāyānist Buddhas, born at auspicious ages to proclaim the universal empire and its place within the cosmos. The concept survived until late medieval times, when the Rajput kings, who were descended from both sun and moon, claimed the right of cakravartin. The concept was not confined to Hindus alone: Buddhists believed that in a previous incarnation the Buddha was the cakravartin par excellence, the cosmocrat.

calendar, in oriental faiths. The precise determination of certain dates for religious celebrations is of vital importance. Calendars in oriental sects and faiths are based either on a cosmic body (the sun or the moon, which may be divine objects as well and even the source of mankind) or on a date associated with a key figure in the sect's history. Among major calendars of interest are the following:

HINDU. Virtually all Hindus accept a cosmic calendar far beyond the scope of the human mind, the great cycle or kalpa of 420,000 years, which is divided into yugas. Mankind is now in the Kali yuga, which began at approximately B.C. 3,000. At the other end of the scale, the yugas constitute a mahāyuga of 4,329,000 years; a thousand of these make up a kalpa. Kalpas alternate in dissolution and creation.

However, more specific and practical calendars are also in use. The Vikrama calendar began in B.C. 57, the Śaka calendar in A.D.

78, and the Bengali calendar in A.D. 554–55. Since many events, such as horoscopes, marriages, the dedication of temples, palaces, homes, and even office buildings depend on the calendar, the astrologers employ various solar or lunar reckonings according to their region and even caste. The solar months are defined in terms of the zodiac, which closely resembles the Western, since both apparently stem from that devised in Mesopotamia about five thousand years ago. The lunar calendars must be adjusted with an intercalary month every third year or so in order to keep the celebration of feasts at approximately the same period annually. The lunar month is divided into two sections: the bright half, when the moon waxes; and the dark half, when it wanes. Usually it is the new moon that marks the end of the lunar month. Most feasts are calculated by the lunar rather than the solar month.

BUDDHIST. The calendar followed in China, Japan, and some other Buddhist lands is duodecimal, being based on a series or cyles that originated in Babylonia sometime between B.C. 480 and 250. The date of B.C. 480 coincides with the year in which Gautama Buddha died. The years of the Buddhist calendar are named for various animals over a twelve-year period and are repeated after the end of each cycle. According to tradition, when Gautama Buddha was dying, a number of animals followed the people to his death cot. The rat, by popular belief a crafty creature, rode on the back of the ox and jumped in front of it at the last minute to become the first animal. After the ox came the tiger, rabbit, dragon, snake, horse, sheep, monkey, rooster, dog, and wild boar. Each year is believed to have the characteristics of its animal, as do people born in that year—e.g., the Year of the Tiger is tumultuous, the Year of the Rabbit affable, though people born in that year may be gossips and be easily led astray. The "Year of the Donkey" means never. The cycle commences again in this century with the Year of the Rat in 1983 and 1995.

ISLAMIC. The Muslim calendar is based on the year of the flight —hijra—of the Prophet Muḥammad from Mecca to Medina in A.D. 622, which most accounts agree happened on September 20. However, the Muslim calendar dates not from the hijra but from the beginning of the Arab year in which it took place—i.e., from July 16, 622. The Muslim year is lunar, with thirteen months, thus making conversion into Western terms difficult. The Islamic calendar is often called Anno Hegirae, or A.H. A simple but not quite precise formula is to equate A.D. 1300 with A.H. 700 and to allow 100 lunar years for every 97 Gregorian (or solar) years.

Of interest as a reaction to the Muslim calendar, which was in use in Persia at the time, the prophet known as the Bāb (q.v.) devised a new calendar that is in theory followed by his disciples, the Bahá'í. He dispensed with the lunar month and based his calendar on the solar year, but in an odd manner. The Bāb's year consists of nineteen months of nineteen days for a total of 361 days, with the addition of certain intercalary days (four in ordinary, five in leap years) between the eighteenth and nineteenth months. The Bahá'í era commences with the year of the Bāb's declaration of Prophethood, which was A.H. 1260 (A.D. 1844), the day being May 23. The New Year is celebrated on the spring solstice, March 21.

Cao Dai. A syncretist religion of Southeast Asia. Cao Dai means High Place, or Reigning God. The complete name of the sect is Dai Dao Tam Pho Do, signifying "the Third Pardon of God," the central tenet of the faith. Cao Dai originated in 1919 with Ngo-van-Chieu, an Annamese official in the government of French Indo-China. Ngo-van-Chieu was in the habit of holding spiritualist sessions with the aid of young women mediums. At one session the spirit of Cao Dai appeared. A divine voice ordered Ngo-van-Chieu to proclaim a new doctrine to the Indo-Chinese. In Saigon, on Christmas Eve 1925, Ngo-van-Thieu had a second vision in the presence of a number of minor government officials; among the group was a notorious businessman, Le-van-Trung, an opium addict and lecher, who was on the brink of financial ruin because of dishonest business practices. Le-van-Trung was so affected by Ngo's vision that he changed his mode of life and became a member of the cult. The founder soon retired, leaving his disciple to take over. Le-van-Trung put the movement on a solid basis, building a cathedral and chapels and forming an ecclesiastical structure patterned after Roman Catholicism (which had been long established in the area), with a pontiff (himself), cardinals, bishops, priests, seminarians, minor dignitaries, and missionaries. Women were allowed to hold any post except that of Supreme

Pontiff, Le-van-Trung "disincarnated himself" in 1934, and his successor was named by a council of Cao Dai leaders.

Cao Dai developed into a vital force in Indo-Chinese life, its three hundred thousand members before World War II, increasing to some two million at the time of the Vietnam War. In essence, it has become the peninsula's national church. Cao Dai played an important part in resisting the French colonial rule, then the Japanese (after initially welcoming them), and to some extent, the Americans. In the late 1930s the French exiled a number of Cao Dai leaders, among them Prince Cuaom De, who went to Japan; the prewar Grand Master Tac and his closest associates were deported to Madagascar. There are strong elements of millennianism in Cao Dai: a movement called Tien Thien saw Prince Cuang De as a messiah and demanded his return from Japan. At about the same time, the White Hat movement welcomed Japanese intervention and formed a Cao Dai army, which was instrumental in forcing the French withdrawal from Indo-China. Cao Dai leaders attempted to mediate between the postwar Viet-minh and the Viet-nam forces, seeking a moderate middle ground. The cult which has stressed social services, the abolition of colonialism, and an end to the fetters of traditional culture, has helped transform Indo-China from a feudal society into a contemporary state. However, at the present, the various People's governments of the peninsula show little favor to the Cao Dai, and Cao Dai's present strength and effectiveness are unknown.

THE CULT. The sumbol of the Cao Dai is the Eye of God, surrounded by rays symbolic of the omniscience and universality of the Almighty looking over the world. Doctrine is drawn from five major sources: the animism and spiritualism of the people (both indigenous practices of long standing), Taoism, Confucianism, Buddhism, and Catholicism. God has already remitted the sins of mankind through Moses and Jesus in the West, and through Lao-tse and Buddha Śākyamuni in the East. These are incarnations of God as man, but now, in the Cao Dai, God remains as Pure Spirit, the others being the Five Branches of the Great Path leading to Perfection. God as Spirit—also known as the Third Pardon—is the form in which He appeared to Ngo-van-Chieu and Le-van-Trung. God's message is universal, being one of "love, life, and truth" as found in all religions, which are now to be united in Cao

Dai. In the Cao Dai cathedral in Saigon, images of Confucius, Lao-Tse, Jesus, Buddha, Joan of Arc, and Victor Hugo (included because he is known to have been a spiritualist) appear along with numerous representations of the Divine Eye.

Central authority is held in the members of the Cun Trug Dai, which is headed by the Supreme Pontiff, the Giao Tong. However, after the death of Le-van-Trung, the Giao Tong is not a living person but the spirit of the ancient Vietnamese poet-sage Ly-thai-Bach, who was represented on earth by Le-van-Trung.

Prayer four times a day is enjoined upon members. There are also numerous feast days. Mediums play a central role, their messages being received before a basket containing an inkwell and pen; their transmissions are written down immediately on paper.

caste, Hind. The hierarchical system by which Hindu society is divided into four sections and one outside the system. The word caste is derived from the Portuguese casta, from the Latin castus (pure). The word is loosely employed: The common Indian terms are varna (color) for the four major divisions, and jāti for the many subdivisions. The concept of caste is mentioned in the tenth and last book of the Rig Veda, the first known Hindu scripture, and is developed throughout in later works, becoming more and more stratified. The Rig Veda society is described as a giant body: The brāhmins (priests) are the head, the kśatriyas (warriors) the arms, the vaiśyas (businessmen, traders, small landholders, farmers, etc.), the body, and the śudras, the manual laborers, virtually serfs, the lowest. The three higher castes are twice-born (dvijā, q.v.). The śudras are denied this privilege and must await birth into a higher varna. The sage Brighu (q.v.), in explaining the nature of castes (actually varna) in the Mahābhārata, says: "Brahmins are fair, kshatriyas are reddish, vaishyas are yellowish, and the shudras are black." Below these four are what are known as untouchables, whom the strictly orthodox do not consider to be Hindus at all, even though they may worship the same gods. Usually, untouchables have their own temples, section of a village, and paths, and work at the most despicable of all jobs, such as handling human waste, carrion, dead animals, and so on.

BACKGROUND. The origin of caste is obscure. Some experts believe that it existed even before the arrival of the Āryans, who are in most opinions responsible for the institution of caste. Certainly, the Āryans, as white-skinned people, quickly established, or accepted rules for a division of society with the darker people, the various indigenes, at the bottom. However, there was always ample opportunity for certain members of the indigenous people, especially the kings, tribal chiefs, priests, and shamans, to cross over into the Āryan world and to be accepted as brāhmins and kśatriyas by undergoing ceremonies of rebirth such as that of the Golden Womb (q.v.).

Caste is still the most distinctive feature of Hindu life and religious and social structure. In general members of different castes will not intermarry nor take meals with each other. Lower castes may not touch higher members. Any step outside the accepted channels is considered polluting. In spite of legal acts to the contrary, caste is still dominant and has managed to withstand the changes of history. It has permeated such casteless religions in India as Christianity and Islam, and even Sikhism (q.v.), which was founded upon a stated abrogation of caste. Castes usually follow traditional occupations (priest, farmer, potter, metalsmith, sweeper, trader, toymaker, barber, and so on). New castes can come into being, such as those, e.g., of auto drivers. The plight of the untouchables, who still face severe restrictions and discrimination, brought a special effort by Mohandas Gandhi to aid them. Grandhi called them harijans, children of God, but the onus still exists.

ORIGINS. Rather than seeing the explanation of caste in the efforts of a handful of Āryan nomads to dominate a large, restless, and unwilling population by the imposition of varna and jāti, which could be enforced only with difficulty, the reason may be found in the primitive social structure itself. Caste was and still is most rigid in the predominantly non-Āryan societies, in Bengal, Mahārāshtra, and above all in South India. Though the Āryans eventually immigrated to these areas, carrying the concept of priest and warrior, caste is strongest in the lower levels of the population, where caste taboos are highly effective. The origin can be found in the totemic system of the aboriginal tribes, in which totemist exogamy and tribal endogamy are paramount, this keeping groups separate within the system. The South Indian Tamil term for caste is not "color" but kulam (family), indicative of the true nature of caste or jāti. Even among the brāhmins totemic tribal and not Āryan origins can be seen. The seven sages credited as the founders of the seven gotras of the brāhmins (no two lists agree on the same seven) are invariably totemic. Achela was born of an elephant, Kesha Pingala of an owl, Agastya of the agasti flower, Kausika from kuśā grass, and Kapila from a monkey. The term gotra means a cowpen and is the primitive name for an endogamous clan unit.

Totem implies a taboo against eating certain foods by a group. These foods are said to be infused with a soul force of divine powers and must be treated with sacramental care. Thus one cannot allow taboo foods to be taken by strangers, a proscription that eventually includes all foods; neither can one eat food cooked by others outside one's own group. Again, marriage within the gotra is permissible, but not marriage outside.

Totemic gods still survive in profusion in Hinduism, especially among the lower jātis. Ganesha (or Ganpaṭi), the elephant-headed god; Hanumān, the monkey god; and the sacredness of cobras, bulls, and monkeys in general are such manifestations.

caste, Zor. Like the Hindus, the Zoroastrians possess four castes, but actual observance has long passed into abeyance, only the priests being distinguished from the laity, whose three castes have now blended into one. The Zoroastrian castes, which in fact antedated the time of the Prophet (c. sixth-century B.C.), were athravan (priest), ratheshtar (warrior), vastryosh (farmer and peasant), and hutoksh (artisan). The castes were not hereditary, as among the Hindus, and the son of a man of one caste could join another. See Zoroastrians.

caste, Hindu. A member of the three higher or twice-born castes in Hinduism, namely brāhmin (priest), kśatriya (warrior), and vaiśya (service and trade). The fourth caste Hindu. See caste, above.

cetiya, Ind. An earthen mound or tumulus venerated as a cult object or as the tomb of royalty or of a saint. This is the type of structure that developed into the stūpa in India. The term survives in the Siamese name for stūpa, chedi (or phra chedi, venerable stūpa).

Ch'an, Buddh. Ch'an is a condensation of the original Ch'an-Na the Chinese attempt to pronounce the Sanskrit dhyāna, or meditation. Ch'an, one of the major forms of Mahāyāna Buddhism, became Zen (q.v.) in Japan. Its difference from other forms of Mahāyāna lies not in its unique teachings but in the unconventional style and the unusual forms of expression it employs in leading the adept to enlightenment. Ch'an, like its Chinese predecessor Tao (q.v.) and its offspring Zen, defies rational explanation, being, in one definition, something "round and rolling, slippery and slick." Ch'an master Huai Jang stated, "Anything I say will miss the point." What Ch'an and Zen try to teach is a Truth ungraspable, indefinable in nature except by the devotee's own awakening, at which point he has undergone an experience impossible to communicate. Ch'an aims at eliminating the duality of subjective and objective to attain an immediate awareness of Reality. The only Reality is the Buddha-mind, which cannot be apprehended by philosophy, ritual, or even meditation.

The origins of Ch'an in China are obscure. Tradition says it was brought to the country by the Indian monk Bodhidharma (A.D. 470–543), who introduced traditional Indian forms of meditation. However, since the introduction of Buddhism into China in the first and second centuries from India and Tibet, some forms of meditation were probably practiced, especially among the higher levels of sages and holy men; for the Taoists there were many immediate resemblances between Tao and the Dharma of Buddha. Documentation is scarce for the period following Bodhidharma, but Ch'an remained more Indian than Chinese, in form and practice, until the time of the Sixth Patriarch, Hui-Nêng (Eno to the Japanese). Hui-Nêng (A.D. 638–713) gave a radical new "Chinese" twist to Ch'an. His major contribution was that Reality could be obtained suddenly rather than gradually (as Indian Buddhists taught), in an immediate awareness of the inner reality of things. He did not deride conceptual knowledge as such, but the clinging to it. He denigrated both the use of texts and authority, with the single purpose of seeing into one's own nature to reach Ultimate Truth or First Principle—i.e., to become Buddha. He emphasized that the method of teaching had to be through a master, by means, as he himself said, of "a separate transmission outside the scriptures," with no dependence on words or phrases. Teaching was transmitted from mind to mind, "Pointing directly at the Mind in every one of us, and seeing into one's Nature, whereby one attains Buddhahood."

By tradition this wordless teaching originated directly with the Gautama Buddha. When the Buddha was questioned about the nature of Ultimate Reality, "Not a word came out of his mouth." He pointed instead to a bouquet of flowers. "Nobody understood the meaning of this except the old venerable Mahākāśyapa [one of his closest companions], who quietly smiled at the master," Buddha's reply was, "I have the most precious treasure, spiritual and transcendental, which at this moment I hand over to you, O venerable Mahākāśyapa." This treasure was the form of Dharma other than the two main bodies, Hīnayāna and Mahāyāna.

The technique known in Japanese as kōan (Chinese kung-an), in which the disciple is presented with an insoluble problem, question, or situation, was developed to bring instant enlightenment. Some of the most famous kōans originate with Hui-Nêng himself —e.g., "What is your original face before you were born?" (The answer—or *an* answer—is deceptively simple, for it means nothing out of context. "Not thinking of good, not thinking of evil, right at this very moment, that is your original face.") Some traditional kōans have as many as two hundred replies, which may, or may not, satisfy the master. Sometimes a gesture, or no gesture, is an answer.

After the death of the Sixth Patriarch, Ch'an spread rapidly, breaking up into two major schools, the Northern, which emphasized gradually awakening, and the Southern, which taught instantaneous enlightenment. The Southern, claiming Hui-Nêng as its patriarch, attacked the slower methods of the Northern. In the succeeding centuries a variety of sects developed, the so-called Five Schools and the Seven Houses, but by the eleventh century, the subsects had been reabsorbed into the major groups, the Northern known as Ts'ao-tung, and the Southern, Lin-chi. Japanese students studying in China attended both schools during this period and returned home with the doctrines of each. Ts'ao-tung became Sōtō in Japan, and Lin-chi, Rinzai. See Buddhism, Sixth Patriarch, Zen.

chedi, Buddh. The Thai term for stūpa (q.v.).

chela, Hind. A pupil of a guru (q.v.)

Chenrezig (or Chenräzi). Buddh. (spelled in Tibetan, Spyan-ras-gzigs) The national tutelary deity of Tibet. He is the four-armed herdsman, the Lord of Mercy, the Tibetan version of the bodhisattva Avalokiteśvara, the Gracious Compassionate One of India. In Tibet Chenrezig experienced further reincarnations, the most famous of which is the Dalai Lāma (q.v.), the highest spiritual and political leader of the nation. Chenrezig is also incarnated in the famous Tibetan mantra ŌṂ man-ni pad-me hum (q.v.) The repetition of the mantra in both the human world and on the plane of bardo (q.v.), Tibetans have stated will bring an end to the cycle of birth and rebirth, with subsequent entry into nirvāṇa (q.v.). Chenrezig is often depicted with eleven heads and a thousand arms, with an eye in the palm of the hand; they represent him as the Lord of Mercy as ever ready to discover distress and to aid the troubled. See Avalokiteśvara.

Chih yueh lu, Buddh. A collection of Ch'an texts compiled in A.D. 1602. The full title is *Shui Yueh Chai Chih Yueh Lu* (Finger Pointing at the Moon).

Chishtīya, Isl. A Ṣūfī brotherhood founded by Mu'īn al-Dīn Chishtī (d. A.D. 1236). He was named after the village of Chisht in Khorosan, where he was born; he died in Ajmeer, India. Music was central to the order's worship: To produce an ecstatic state, members would sing in honor of Allāh and the Prophet, while the rest of the company would watch with respect until the devotee completed his experience. Members of the order would wander from village to village across northern India, playing flutes and drums to attract people; then they would deliver homilies in the form of stories and legends with Ṣūfic connotations. The Spanish folk figure, the chistu, and the medieval court jester are believed derived from the Chishtīya. The brotherhood was the largest on the Indian subcontinent and included many saints and other luminaries. Because of their confusing of ecstatic experiences with the emotional arousals induced by music, the order went into an eclipse, to be revived in the early nineteenth century. The tombs of its saints are still honored by both Muslims and Hindus; and the founder's tomb in Ajmeer is a noted center of popular devotions; to fulfill a vow the Mughal Emperor Akbar (q.v.) made a pilgrimage to it on foot from Delhi. See Ṣūfīs.

chörten, Tib. A form of the stūpa (q.v.). In Tibet chörtens are constructed over the remains of the dead, or over sacred relics. Chörtens may run in height from a few feet to several stories; they are constructed on a square base, atop which is a high, pointed cone.

Christ, Chr. See Jesus.

Chuang Tzu (also Chuang Chou). A Chinese philosopher c. fourth century B.C., noted as ranking next to Lao Tzu as a Taoist thinker (readings of Chuang Tzu as a Confucianist are erroneous). Ssema Ch'ien's history, the *Shih Chi* (completed c. B.C. 90), noted that his study was all-embracing, but in essentials he went back to the teaching of his predecessor, Lao Tzu. Therefore, Chuang Tzu's writing (over one hundred thousand characters) was, for the larger part, symbolic. He composed "A Fisherman," "Robber Chih" and "Safebreaking" to criticize the followers of Confucius and elucidate, the concepts of Lao Tzu. Such works of his as *Hsu Wü-kuei* and *Keng-sung Ch'u* are purely imaginative and have no basis in fact. He was, however, a skilled writer and skilled in the use of giving new meanings to ordinary phrases. He attacked specific matters and practices advocated by the Confucianists and Mohists [the followers of the utilitarian Mo Tzu, who taught "love without discrimination" as "the will of heaven"], and even the serious students of his day could not extricate themselves from the toils of his argumentation, for his language, in its vastness and freedom of concept, fitted very well his own ideas. He rejected service with kings, dukes, and other officials, no matter how much he was offered, noting that such service resembled being prepared as a sacrificial ox. "Go away immediately!" he said. "Don't dirty me! I prefer to enjoy myself wallowing in the mud rather than be bridled by some ruler. Never in my life will I engage in government service. I will enjoy myself right where I am."

The compilation of his works that have survived bear his name, being called the *Chuang Tzu,* which, briefly, explores "the realm of Nothing Whatever" in territories of the mind where "now and long ago are one." The text itself is often fragmentary or corrupt and thus sometimes unintelligible. Chuang Tzu's own writings have been identified in the earlier chapters, the remainder of the work being of the following two or three centuries. In actuality it does not profess to be by Chuang Tzu but is centered around him, and contains a number of anecdotes, stories, parables, and short poems, which also mention Lao Tzu, Confucius, and other sages, presenting various points of view that are not resolved but that leave open to the reader to decide for himself the relative merits of each position. Thus the book's own point of view is that of impartiality, all being equally valid or invalid. Unlike Lao Tzu's *Tao Te Ching* (late sixth century B.C.). the *Chuang Tzu* discusses the problem of the control of the mind, positing, or at least trying to identify, a force that rules the body just as the eluctable Tao rules the universe. See Confucius, Lao Tzu, Tao.

cit (also chit), Hind. Consciousness, the supreme unconditional consciousness, the Being that is regarded as the real Self, or the soul, different from the rationalizing mind and realized by the superconsciousness or transcendental state. The uncolored light of Pure Consciousness that lies beyond all phenomena. Cit, as pure unconditional consciousness, cannot be the property of the mind, for it is the mind's apparent consciousness.

Cloth-bag Monk, Buddh. A ninth-century wandering Ch'an adept, who was believed to be an incarnation of Maitreya (q.v.), the Buddha of the future. The monk carried his possessions in a bag of cloth; hence his name.

color, as religious and cultural symbol. Colors can possess deep significance, transcending purely decorative values. Among the Chinese, red symbolizes good luck. For Hindus it is the color most often associated with women, who wear a red sari at marriage, and are cremated in a red cloth. Women wear a red bindi (q.v.) on their forehead; the nuptial state is indicated by a red streak (or powder or even lipstick) on the part of their hair. In these instances red represents blood. Red powder, again a blood substitute, is thrown on statues, aniconic stones, phallic symbols, thresholds, etc.

In Hinduism men wear a white garment at marriage, and are likely, at least among the strictly orthodox, to wear white throughout life. Among Parsees white is the color of purity and is generally worn by men and women alike, except for those very Westernized or Hinduized individuals, the men wearing Western garments of various colors and patterns, the women wearing colored saris. White signifies mourning for Hindu women, who will wear a white sari, the period of time depending on caste, area, and linguistic group. In China also, and some other Asian lands, white is again the color of mourning. In Japan white symbolizes death; a bride wears white to signify that she is dead to her family and belongs to the husband alone. Confucius insisted that when fasting clothes be of white linen, scrupulously clean. Among Tibetan Buddhists, monks who are adept in tumo (q.v.), the skill of the inner heat that enables them to exist with only a cotton shirt in the worst of winter weather, wear white as a mark of their accomplishment.

Green is associated in the popular mind with Islam, particularly in India, where it is known as the "Muslim" color; Hindus have been known to refuse to work in Western offices painted green by foreigners ignorant of local customs.

Black is worn by many Islamic women, apparently under the distant influence of Mediterranean Christians, who clothed women in black for centuries. Among Hindus black connotes bad luck and is worn only in defiance of custom. See animals, Name, numbers, 108, sleep, and vegetation for parallel religious and cultural symbols and practices.

Companions (of the Prophet), Isl. The intimate friends of Muḥammad—they are also known as The Seven Great Ones—whom he saw on a personal basis and to whom he gave his Revelations as they appeared. They are the reciters of the Qur'ān, and the ultimate source, next to the Prophet, for the validity of hadīth (q.v.) in the chain of attestation. The senior Companion was Abū Bakr (q.v.), who, after Muḥammad's death, was elected to be kalifah or successor, the choice being made even before the Prophet's body was interred. One of the Companions was Salman-i Pars, said to be a Zoroastrian (q.v.) who left the faith of Ahura Mazdā, tried Christianity, and then joined Muḥammad; it was his influence that prevented the Islamic armies from annihilating the Zoroastrians in Persia.

Confucianism. The philosophical and ethical system based on the teachings of the Chinese sage Confucius (B.C. 551–479). The Chinese term for the system or school is Ju, the word originally meaning a scholar or intellectual during the Confucian period; the term has connotations of "weakling." (The ju's function at court was to direct or assist the performance of the various ceremonies and rites, both secular and religious.) Essentially Confucianism (or Ju) contains much other matter than that propounded by the Sage and has developed extensively from his kernel of teachings. Confucianism is not a religion in the Hindu-Buddhist or Judaeo-Christian-Islamic sense but is both a philosophy pure and simple and an ethical code directed to right living, with emphasis on a rational, tightly structured hierarchical society of unparalleled probity, with due allowance for the vagaries of human nature ("Maids and servants are hardest to keep in your house. If you are friendly with them, they lose their deference; if you are reserved with them, they resent it.") At the top of this structure is the ruler as Son of Heaven, from whom all descends in order. But the ruler should be both paternal and benevolent, governing like a great patriarch.

Confucianism, which had no priesthood and very little mysticism, was not concerned with a future perfection, either of a Heaven or of absorption in the Divine, or any kind of afterlife; there is no "God" or gods, though there are countless deities. Instead it looked back with nostalgia to a lost golden age, to the time of the two perfect kings, Yao and Shun (c. B.C. 2300, but probably legendary); Confucius extended this age to the founding of the Chou dynasty (c. B.C. 1100). The Sage's own writings contain the wisdom of this period. "I have transmitted what was taught me without making up anything of my own," he stated, a position that his mystical contemporary, the Taoist Lao Tzu, dismissed with scorn. But the six works generally accredited to him contain matter that satisfied his own beliefs, being a collection of ethical sayings and prescriptions, rules for ceremonies, songs, historical data (of the barest sort), all of which are enlivened by a great touch of understanding for human frailties and potentialities. His works contain his soaring conception of simple virtues: faithfulness to oneself and to others (chung), altruism (shu), human-heartedness (jen), righteousness (yi), propriety (li), wisdom (chih), sincerity (hsin), qualities that the Sage himself tried to exemplify. This insistence on moral and ethical cultivation was for Confucius a way of life, of truth, which he called tao. This tao is not the Tao of the Taoists, but a moral law applicable to man based on the correctness of human relationships, a law serving mankind just as a natural law served Heaven. And this law was one of a middle way (later to be called the Doctrine of the Mean), which was easily evident in the sayings attributed to Confucius:

> The nobler man first practices what he preaches and afterward preaches what he practices.
>
> A man without virtue cannot long abide in adversity, nor can he long abide in happiness.
>
> Is not he a true philosopher who, though he be unrecognized of men, bears no resentment?
>
> I will not grieve that men do not know me; I will grieve that I do not know men.
>
> To go too far is as bad as to fall short.

After the death of Confucius, his disciples carried on his teaching; by tradition there were eight divisions of the K'ung school, which carried his ideas across China and especially into the courts, where many of the scholars took up posts in the various governments. A number of the men in the following generations, including his grandson Tzŭ-ssŭ, whose major work was the book called *The Doctrine of the Mean* (Chung-yung), were noted as important scholars in the Ju tradition. *The Doctrine of the Mean* is composed largely of sayings by Confucius, with numerous explanatory passages. The theme of the book is a search for harmony, for equilibrium as the supreme foundation of the great universe. "Once equilibrium and harmony are achieved, Heaven and Earth maintain their proper positions, and the myriad things are nourished." Man must be involved in "a thorough study of what is good, inquiring extensively about it, cogitating over it carefully,

A Tibetan lama sits in meditation. He uses the rosary as an aid in gaining depth to his meditation, but eventually he passes the stage where externals are eliminated, all being concentrated within the mind itself. Finally, with the mind controlled, past, present, and future, all external thoughts are also eliminated, and the mind concentrates on mind itself.

The site at Sarnath, near Benares, where Buddha preached his first sermon, was venerated by the building of a stūpa and a great monastic complex. As the result of the persecutions of Buddhists by both Hindus and Muslims, the monastery was abandoned after the eleventh century A.D. It is now being excavated and restored.

Statues of Lord Buddha take different forms according to the lesson intended. We see him in meditation in this figure from an Indian stūpa, seated in the classical lotus position, his legs entwined and his hands holding a small casque as sign of the person who donated the statue (left). The Teaching Buddha, his hands outstretched, is seen in this Chinese figure (right).

Buddha showing the Lotus of the True Way in the palm of his right hand is a common depiction; the statue is Indian, found at Bodh Gaya.

Although the Buddhist Way normally avoids extremes, such as fasting, penances, and mortification of the flesh, some Buddhists, especially the Tibetans, practice difficult means of expressing their belief. Certain monks and pilgrims, like this man, will raise and prostrate themselves by the hour in atonement for their sins.

The prayer wheel is a common ritual object in Buddhist worship. The wheel contains a mantra or prayer written on a slip of paper and is spun rapidly, each turn sending the prayer heavenward faster than the individual could say it himself.

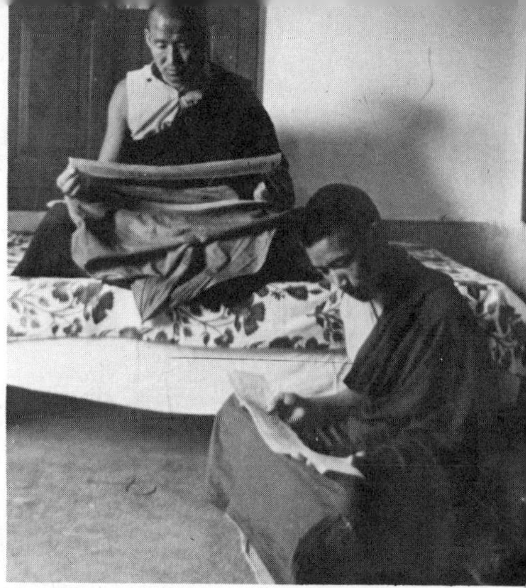

A spiritual master—called a guru in many oriental faiths — instructs a novice. Much teaching is done on an individual basis. These men are Buddhists, but the methods are virtually the same for Hindus, Jains, and other Eastern disciplines, which, in person-to-person encounters, pass on inner doctrines from master (guru) to the pupil (chela or siśya).

Begging bowls are neatly stacked outside a Buddhist monastery in Thailand. Each day, except in the rainy season, the bhikku begs his daily food, a practice more common in the Theravada forms of Buddhism in South Asia than among the Mayahayan sects.

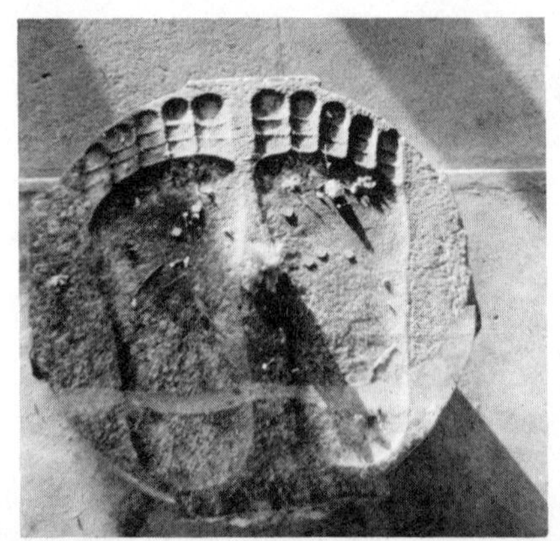

Buddha's footprints are found embedded in stone outside the Buddhist complex at Bodh Gaya, India, where he found enlightenment. The prints are about fifty per cent larger than those of a man of average height.

The Lord Buddha received enlightenment while sitting under a bodhi tree at Bodh Gaya. A branch of the original tree was sent to Ceylon (Sri Lanka) in the third century B.C., and the current tree at Bodh Gaya is believed to have come from a cutting of the Singalese tree, the original having been destroyed by the Muslims in their wars in India.

Cha-no-yu, the tea ceremony, is a by-product of Zen discipline, like the Nō play and the haiku poem. The spirit of cha-no-yu is the cleansing of the six senses from contamination. When the sense organs are purified, the mind itself is free of defilements. Thus cha-no-yu is a spiritual discipline. Tea was brought to Japan from China in the eleventh century A.D. by Japanese Zen masters as a means of keeping monks awake during spiritual exercises and for medicinal purposes. Today, cha-no-yu is practiced by the laity for social reasons.

In many Buddhist lands, especially those that follow the Theravadin forms of the Way, young men are expected to spend from three months to three years as monks, a custom that is dying out under the pressures of the modern world. These are novices at a monastery in Bangkok.

Throughout the Buddhist world, pilgrims and the wealthy have donated small models of stūpas to temples and monasteries to signify their devotion. The rows of figures of the Lord Buddha in meditation ring such a miniature stūpa at Bodh Gaya, India.

making it clear through contrast, and earnestly putting it into practice."

Next to the Master himself, the most illustrious sage of the school was the fourth-century B.C. scholar Mencius (Meng K'o). His major contribution was the statement of the Fourfold Rule of Conduct (also called Four Limbs of a Man), which codified ideas earlier stressed by Confucius. Mencius stated the Limbs succinctly as follows:

> We may say that no man is devoid of a feeling of compassions, nor of a feeling of shame, nor of a feeling of consideration for others, nor of a feeling of plain right and wrong. The feeling of compassion is the origin of human-heartedness [jên]; the feeling of shame is the origin of righteousness [i]; the feeling of consideration for others is the origin of good manners [li]; the feeling of right and wrong is the origin of wisdom [chih]. The presence of these four elements in man is as natural to him as the possession of his four limbs. Having these four elements within him, the man who says he is powerless to act as he should is doing a grave injury to himself. . . . Let a man but know how to expand and develop these four elements existing in the soul and his progress becomes as irresistible as a newly kindled fire or a spring that has just burst from the ground. If they can be fully developed, these virtues are strong enough to safeguard all within the Four Seas; if allowed to remain undeveloped, they will not suffice for the service due one's parents.

Mencius taught the innate goodness of human nature, but the vicissitudes of life and man's own destructive efforts deprave it. The problem is to save the original goodness before it is completely lost. Thus his emphasis on the Four Limbs as the exemplification of Confucian tao.

However, a century later, Hsün Ch'ing believed that the nature of man was basically evil and that whatever goodness man acquired came not from Heaven, as his predecessors taught, but only from training, or in the modern term, conditioning. The social organization, culture, and laws, along with man's intelligence, would overcome his acquisitiveness and sensual nature. Hsün

Ch'ing became an open agnostic, for Heaven was no more than a law of nature, the unalterable workings of a force that the sage could not seek to know. The phenomena of nature were not to be considered as omens for good or bad. "The falling of stars and the groaning of trees are but natural disturbances caused by the modification of Heaven and Earth, the mutation of the yin and yang. These are uncommon events. We may marvel at them, but we should not fear them. When ominous signs come from man himself, then we should be really afraid." Man alone is responsible for his misfortunes, for "If the right way of life is cultivated then Heaven cannot send misfortune; flood and drought cannot cause famine; extreme cold cannot cause suffering; supernatural powers cannot cause calamity."

By this time, an age when a Hundred Schools (of philosophy) were flourishing, Confucianism lost much of its strength, being heavily affected by Taoism and Buddhism. In the sixth century A.D. a revival occurred, but by this time the three major sects were deeply entwined. In the succeeding centuries Confucian scholars went back to many of the early sources, especially Mencius and Tzŭ-ssŭ's *Doctrine of the Mean*. By the twelfth century the sages had re-established Confucianism (now neo-Confucianism) well enough for it to be adopted by the state as its formal cult. It survived in power until the overthrow of the monarchy in 1912. Attempts at about this time to found a Confucian Church patterned after the Christian Churches failed, and today the Sage's teachings are, at least for the moment, thrown into the dustbin of history. See Confucius, Doctrine of the Mean, Mencius, Tao, Taoism.

Confucius (B.C. 551–479). The most famous of the ancient Chinese sages. Confucius is a latinization of K'ung-fu-tzu, his Chinese title, which means Master K'ung. His proper name was K'ung Ch'iu, K'ung being his family name, and Ch'iu meaning Hill, because at birth he had a bulge on his skull; his cognomen has become a sacred word and is rarely mentioned, at least by the Chinese.

Confucius was born of a line of dispossessed aristocrats; his father was a minor military official who died a few years after his son's birth. The child was brought up by his mother, an unusually strong person, who indoctrinated him into respect for the court and for the power of the past. One of his biographers, Sse-ma Ch'ien (first century B.C.), reports that "Confucius was always wont to set up sacrificial vessels in his childish play, and to imitate ceremonial gestures." There is some confusion in Sse-ma about the exact date when Confucius joined government service, but Confucius did so with honor. "Confucius was poor and of low estate and when he grew older he served as petty official of the family Chi, and while he was in office his accounts and the measures were always correct. Thereupon he was made Chief Shepherd; then the beasts grew in numbers and multiplied," says Sse-ma, interjecting the odd information that "Confucius was nine feet six inches tall. All the people called him a giant and marveled at him." The Sage served under a wide variety of rulers, sometimes with success, sometimes falling into disfavor because of court intrigues. One of the standard complaints against him was his insistence on the proper performance of ceremonies at court and the observing of the rules of decorum. Meanwhile, Confucius had engaged himself in a study of music, and his wide knowledge on many subjects began to attract disciples. During the perilous age in which he lived, times of social unrest, wars, and rebellions, when "from the highest dignitaries down, everyone was grasping of power and all had deserted from the true way," he decided the wisest course was to go into retirement. So he "arranged the odes, the records, the rites and music. His pupils grew ever greater in number, while from all sides, from far distant regions, disciples flocked to him." Over the years he is said to have instructed some three thousand pupils on a personal basis, in four subjects: Literature, Conduct, Conscientiousness, and Loyalty. He was free from four things: he had "no foregone conclusions, no arbitrary predetermination, no obstinacy and no egoism. He rarely spoke of fortune, of fate, of "perfect virtue." Also, "He gave no help to him who was not zealous. If he presented one corner of a subject as an example, and the pupil could not transfer what he had learned to the other corners, Confucius did not repeat."

The Sage eventually returned to the government, but his reputation for honesty and probity, and his beneficial effects upon others brought the constant suspicion that he was only seeking his own aggrandizement. As he turned sixty and entered old age, he realized that his time was running short, and he began to assemble the wisdom he considered reflected his own beliefs, editing and anthologizing a number of ancient texts, regulations, ceremonies, songs, and other material. His works are six in number, of varying quality. They are:

The Book of History, sometimes the *Book of Records* (in Chinese, Shang Shu or Shu Ching). Though there is some doubt of the authenticity of the work, since all the ancient manuscripts were burned in the third century B.C. and the text reconstructed from oral tradition, it is still a significant remnant, for it deals with the regulations of wise rulers and the meditations of faithful ministers, along with some hints of a primitive astronomic religion ruled by a priest-king.

The Book of Odes (Shih Ching), a collection of 305 songs (some of them only titles) selected from some 3,000, but without music. This is one of the best-preserved of all the ancient texts. The songs run from folk pieces to ceremonial and religious works.

Record of Rites (Li Chi). A fragmented collection of rituals and songs for court, based on earlier texts, with much post-Confucian material but still in the tradition of the Sage.

The Book of Changes (I Ching, q.v.). A well-preserved and important text from pre-Confucian sources with many later additions. Scholars are divided about the Sage's role in the work. However, parts of it may stem from oral discourses he gave to pupils. Later Confucians applied themselves with fervor to a study of the *I Ching,* and today it can be safely said to have passed the Hindu *Bhagavad Gītā* as the oriental work most popular in the West.

Spring and Autumn Annals (Ch'un Ch'iu). A bare-bones account of events in the state of Lu, the Sage's native land, running from listings of such occurrences as plagues of grasshoppers to famine to the murder of princes. However, by the method of his presentation, whether he mentions the death of a prince as a murder, and by whom, and gives him a title or not, Confucius makes subtle judgments. "The style is historical," he said of the work, "but I have taken the liberty of determining the sense myself."

The final Confucian work is one that was actually written by his pupils. This is the famous *Analects* (Lun-yü), a collection of the Master's sayings originally assembled by his immediate disciples and added to and edited by later generations. The basic theme is one of humanitarianism, a love for the world commencing with the natural feelings of affection within the family and spreading to all mankind. This humanitarianism is expressed publicly in forms and ceremonials reflecting the inner attitude. A harmonious public life is but the outward expression of a harmonious interior life. The supreme example has to be set by the prince. "If the ruler himself is upright, all will go well, even though he does not give orders. But if he himself is not upright, even though he gives orders, they will not be obeyed." When he was asked, "Is there any single saying that one can act upon all day and every day?" Confucius replied: "Perhaps the saying about consideration: 'Never do to others what you would not like them to do to you,'" a remark he made elsewhere in a more positive manner.

Whatever the books taught, it was a practical kind of life for all mankind. Confucius made sense. Yet one important group, the early Taoists, saw Confucius as an object of derision. The famous meeting between Confucius and the Taoist Lao Tzu, though probably apocryphal (but a standard fixture in the accounts of both Sages), illustrates the basic conflict. The versions vary, depending on whether the source is Confucian or Taoist, yet even the Confucian accounts hardly make him seem a man of great sophistication or depth of wisdom or understanding.

Basically the story goes that Confucius, having heard of Lao Tzu, who is now in retirement, goes to see him for advice. Confucius has brought along copies of his own works, which he unrolls and starts to expound. Lao Tzu snaps, "This is going to take too long. Tell me the gist of the matter." "The gist of the matter," says Confucius, "is goodness and duty." Confucius expounds a few sentences, and Lao Tzu crisply cuts him off and says what any mystic might say, to look within, to learn "the Inward Path." And "soon you will reach a goal where you will no longer need to go around laboriously advertising goodness and duty, like the town crier with his drum seeking for news of a lost child." He adds: "No, sir! What you are doing is to disjoint men's natures!"

Somehow Confucius doesn't get the message. He tells Lao Tzu about the six books he has edited, but though he has visited "seventy-two rulers expounding the Way," no one was willing to listen. "It is a lucky thing that you did not meet with a prince anxious to reform the world," says Lao Tzu. "All your lectures are concerned with things that are no better than footprints in the dust. Footprints are made by shoes, but they are far from being shoes."

By the first century B.C. the purity of teaching of both Masters had declined, and both doctrines began to merge, taking on also a popular accretion of magic and superstition. However, the Confucian legend developed over the centuries, with various additions that turned him into a pedantic authoritarian instead of the likable and wise schoolmaster he actually was. As early as B.C. 174 sacrifices were offered to Confucius as a divine power, and he was continually raised higher and higher, becoming, in the amalgam with Taoism, one of the Eight Immortals. Before the empire ended in 1912 he was found in equal place with the deities of heaven and earth. The historian Arnold Toynbee stated that even "under a veneer of Communism, Confucianism [is] still decisively moulding the lives of the Chinese people," who amount "to something between a fifth and a quarter of the whole living generation of Mankind." The Chinese-American scholar Liu Wu-chi conjectures that important elements in Ju (Confucianism) will be incorporated into the Marxian philosophy of the new Chinese Government, that "Despite the difference in their socio-economic background and the incompatibility of their basic tenets, the teachings of K'ung [Confucius] and Marx are similar in their common concern for the practical, material aspects of life, in the monolithic structure of the two systems, and in the political role played by their partisans."

Cosmic Egg, Hind. The universe, both literally and symbolically. In some Indian epics a Cosmic (or World) Egg is the source of the universe. Other texts (summarized by the sage Vyāsa in his commentary on Patanjali's *Yoga-Sūtra,* q.v.) state that the cosmos is enclosed in a World Egg, which includes at its center Rose-Apple Land (Jambudvīpa, q.v., or India), which in turn is encompassed by a sea of salt double its size, the sea being fringed with "marvelous hills" and "the Seven Seas with their waters of sugar-cane juice, of spirits, of butter, of curds, of cream, of milk, and of treacle." The entire configuration "stretches out in the midmost part of the Egg. And the Egg itself is a minute fragment of the primary cause, like a firefly in the sky." In tantra (q.v.) the liberated soul is likened to the Cosmic Egg, his body being the yolk and his sanctity enclosing him visibly like the white. See linga.

cow, in Hinduism. The cow, as the world knows, is sacred to the Hindu, a fact that puzzles the foreigner viewing the numerous bony animals wandering the streets of Indian towns and cities, nuzzling at vegetable and fruit stands in the bazaars and obstructing traffic. The sacredness of the cow is a central and crucial element in Hindu belief today, though it is of comparatively recent origin. Vedic society, which enjoyed blood sacrifices, included cows among the victims, along with humans and horses (see puruṣamedha and aśvamedha). However, for the Vedic Āryans, who had depended on herds of cattle during their long treks into the subcontinent, the cow retained a quasidivine significance. The changes that led to full veneration were partly social, partly religious.

During the primitive Āryan period, cattle could be taken by the kings or the priests without payment for the celebration of yajña, the brahminical ritual of sacrifice. This practice, which was always resented by the people of the lower castes, brought outspoken condemnation by the sixth century B.C. The Jain, Buddhist, and Vaishnavite movements (the latter expressed in the figure of the cowherd god Krishna, q.v.), all sects that had a great appeal to the middle and lower castes, many of whom were becoming affluent in the settled conditions of the age, helped consolidate the increasing taboos against the sacrifice of cattle and the eating of their flesh. The Buddha is quoted in the ancient and canonical *Sutta-nipāta* as saying, "Cattle are our friends, just like parents and other relatives, for cultivation depends on them. They give food, strength, freshness of complexion and happiness. Knowing this, brahmins of old did not kill cattle." The last is a most dubious statement, for in the Hindu *Satapatha Brāhmana,* a pre-Buddhist work, the brahmin priest Yājñavalkya says in answer to a ritual question why the flesh of the cow and the cart-ox should not be eaten, "That very well may be, but as long as it puts flesh on my body I will continue to eat it."

However, the very powerful Jain doctrine of ahiṁsā (q.v.),

which eschewed violence against living creatures, the nonviolent tenets of the Emperor Ashoka (q.v.)—all helped to aid the movement toward veneration of the cow. Mahatma Gandhi (q.v.), who was born in a heavily Jain area of western India, put the situation into a modern focus with his many statements about the cow, insisting that cow protection is "the central fact of Hinduism." For Gandhi, the cow symbolizes the entire subhuman world, and her protection becomes an expression of the "brotherhood between man and beasts, indeed of man's identity with all that lives." Homage paid to the cow was also the "worship of innocence," the "protection of the weak and helpless," and "one of the most wonderful phenomena of human evolution." In today's India there are several organizations devoted to cow protection. The cow has become a political issue as well as a religious symbol, standing as a focal point of the struggle of many of the ordinary people against the modernizing—and "atheistic"—tendencies of the educated classes. and as the rallying cry against the large meat-eating Muslim minority. On a practical basis, the Indian cow is too often but a scavenger, and at best bred for her milk. Consumption of her flesh, as urged by foreigners, is sometimes practiced by low-caste and out-caste peoples, the eaters of carrion. In general, in India, grain that in other countries would be fed on a broad scale to cattle to fatten them is better consumed directly by a largely vegetarian people.

◂D▸

dāgaba, Buddh. A reliquary mound similar to the stupa, but the two are not interchangeable, as the stupa may not always contain relics. The word dāgaba is derived from dhātu (see) and gharba (womb); thus the shrine is the repository of the sacred within the universal vulva. The derivation of the term pagoda (q.v.) as a Portuguese mispronunciation of dāgaba is a supposition only. See stūpa.

dākinī, Hind. A female divinity, usually a type of earth mother.

dakmah, Zor. The Zoroastrian (and Parsee) Tower of Silence (q.v.) for the disposal of the dead. See also Zoroastrianism.

Dalai Lāma, Buddh. The leading lāma (or high "monk") of Tibet, the incarnation of the Tibetan deity Chenrezig (q.v.). The Tibetans usually refer to the Lāma as Gyalwa Rinpoche. Chenrezig as Dalai Lāma (the term means approximately Monk of the Ocean of Wisdom) is now in his fourteenth tulku or incarnation, in a line that began in 1575, the first Lāma being an avatār of a yogin belonging to a group known as the Eighty-four Great Magicians. When each Dalai Lāma dies, his soul passes into the body of a child, who is sought out with much care and with many tests by specially trained lāmas, who examine a large number of likely candidates all over Tibet. The current Dalai Lāma, His Holiness Tenzin Gyatsho, was installed in 1940; he was found on the Chinese-Tibetan border after the regent of the Grand Lamasery in Lhasa had had a vision of the village where the child had been born. He was forced to flee his country in 1959 after a Tibetan uprising against the Chinese, who had occupied the land in 1950. He is now in exile in India. In Tibet the Dalai Lāma had traditionally been the supreme religious and secular power (the Tashi Lāma, q.v., was second to him); today the Dalai Lāma has lost much of his influence, and the younger Tibetans no longer look up to him as the tulku of Chenrezig and the leader of his people.

darshan (Sanskrit, darśana), Hind. Literally, sight or vision. One speaks of having darshan of a saint, sage, or a deity, and so on, which means being in his or her presence and receiving a blessing by the mere fact. It is of crucial importance to the disciples in an ashram that the guru, in darshan, *look* directly at the siśyā, for his glance, no matter how impersonal and disinterested correctly forms an important psychic and spiritual link to the master, and through him, to the Absolute. See guru.

Daruma, Buddh. The Japanese name for the Indian Buddhist Bodhidharma, who introduced meditative techniques into China. See Bodhidharma.

darwaish, Ṣūfī. See dervish.

David-Neel, Alexandra (1869–1969), Buddh. A convert to the Tibetan form of Buddhism, Mme. David-Neel spent some thirty years in Asia after completing studies in Sanskrit at the Sorbonne and in Belgium. As a child she was extremely precocious, interested in oriental and occult subjects. She wanted "to go beyond the garden gate in search of the Unknown." One of her many trips took her from India to China across vast mountain passes and plateaus no European had seen previously. She went to Tibet to do research in the various forms Buddhism assumed in becoming lamaism—i.e., in borrowing doctrinal and ritualistic elements from Bön (q.v.), tantrism (q.v.), shamanism (q.v.), and other Altaic and northern religions that had infiltrated Tibet in unknown ways. Her visit, which included trips to Lhasa and Shigatse, normally barred to foreigners, and interviews with both the Dalai and Tashi Lāmas, grew to an extended stay of fourteen years, two of them in a cave on the Tibetan side of the Himalayas, where she lived as a hermit. As a professed Buddhist, she enjoyed many of the psychic experiences—siddhis (q.v.)—she described in her writings, though she usually spoke of them in third-person terms. What she wrote of lāmas and other holy men and saints and their occult powers she practiced herself, according to close friends, having undergone similar training and possessing many of the same supernormal powers. In one instance, after months of practice, she was able to create the form of a monk, which followed her about and was seen by others. She lost control of it, whereupon the monk grew hostile; it was only after six months of difficult psychic concentration that Mme. David-Neel was able to dissipate it. Mme. David-Neel spoke all the dialects of Tibetan. Among her seventeen books (translated into many languages), the three most famous (available in English) are: *My Journey to Lhasa, Initiation and Initiates in Tibet,* and *Magic and Mystery in Tibet* (also known as *With Mystics and Magicians in Tibet*). The latter is probably her most famous work. Her frequent traveling companion, a young Tibetan monk named Yongden, she adopted as her son. Mme. David-Neel spent her last years at her own lamasery, Samten Dzong, at Digne in France's Maritime Alps, where she died at the age of one hundred.

deer, in Shintō. At the Kasuga shrine near Nara, deer are considered the dwelling place of certain deities, four in number. In Kasuga art, the deer may embody the deity, or the deity may ride upon the animal. In the case of the warrior-god Takemiskazuchi no Mikoto, the deer represents the god himself. This belief, which resembles others in Shintō (e.g., the animism of trees, rocks, and water), is very archaic and antedates the introduction of Buddhism into Japan. See Shintō.

Dēnkart (also *Dinkard*). A detailed summary in Pahlavi, an Iranian border language containing many Semitic words, of the contents of each of the twenty-one volumes of the Avesta, the central Zoroastrian scripture, which has been virtually lost, only the equivalent of three volumes surviving to the present. The Dēnkart in its present form, though it is obviously based upon earlier redactions, dates from the ninth century A.D. See Avesta.

dervish (also darwaish), Ṣūfī. A member of a Ṣūfī brotherhood, especially the Mawlawīyas (or Mevlevis) of Turkey and Afghanistan, who practice a form of "whirling" or spinning dance as an aid to mystical transport. The dance of the "Whirling Dervishes" is known as sema. It was developed by the thirteenth-century Persian mystic Jaīāl al-Din Rūmī, then living in the holy town of Konya in Turkey, where he was a teacher. While passing a gold beater's shop, Rūmī heard the apprentices hammering out the sheets of gold to a special rhythm that seemed inspired. The strokes came to him as the endlessly repeated sound "Allāh." Rūmī immediately began to whirl in the street in ecstasy, the beginning of the dance of the dervishes. He developed the practice for his students.

How one goes about sema is known only to the Ṣūfī initiate (though one can study "Sūfī" dancing in America, say, at the local adult educational extension program). But, said Rūmī, "Sema is a secret. The Prophet Muḥammad said, 'I have time with God and during that time neither angel nor prophet can intrude.' Sema is to attain that place where even an angel cannot go."

After Rūmī's death in 1273, sema was held on Thursday nights at the tekke or prayer hall adjacent to the tomb where his body lay. There were five tekkes in all in Turkey where sema was practiced, until the Ataturk government, in its modernizing campaign, banned it in 1925. After that the dervishes continued to dance in private homes until some of the restrictions were lifted in the 1950s. Since then, the Mawlawīyas have been allowed to dance openly at Konya, where they have become tourist attractions; they even have given performances abroad.

Similar forms of dancing and whirling are practiced in other Islamic areas, especially parts of Africa. The term dervish may often have a perjorative connotation, being applied by non-Muslims to Muslim holy men of apparent unpredictable disposition. In the past dervishes dancing in the heights of mystical ecstasy have been shot by apprehensive colonial administrators. See Rūmī, Ṣūfī.

deva, Hind. A god. In Hinduism the devas are lesser deities and are to be distinguished from God, the supreme uncreated being. The devas, while supernatural, embodied beings who live in the heavens, higher on the scale of evolution than man, are still subject to the round of birth and rebirth. The devas are often involved in a struggle with the asuras (as in the Rig Veda and the Rāmayāna), the devas being the shining ones and the asuras, the titans and the dark ones. The Jains share this doctrine with the Hindus. The term deva is cognate with the Latin root div- (divine); however, among the Iranians, the word came to mean demon.

devadasi, Hind. A temple "prostitute," though that word lacks the full significance of the role played by the devadasi. The term means "slave woman of the god." Devadasi, or a similar occupation, have been found in ancient Sumeria and Egypt. In India, for a long time, devadasis played an important part in daily life, being the only women with an education; they carried on such professions as dance and music (both sacred) and were, in a sense, the repositories of culture, along with certain holy men. Unfortunately they were also forced to serve as prostitutes. Older texts lead one to believe that such women entered the temple willingly, or were members of a caste that supplied devadasis, or were donated by respectable parents at an early age for the glory of the family. All may have been true in the past, but today the devadasi is usually nothing but a temple prostitute, often forced into service by criminal methods. The devadasi is "married" to the temple god—Māruti, the bachelor god (a form of Hanumān, q.v.), is a favorite—in nuptial rites that in many areas (such as Mahārāshtra) are held on the full moon of the night called Randav Punaw in the Hindu month of Mārgashirsh (roughly, December). Hundreds of girls and young women may go through the ceremony together, though the custom of devadasi is officially prohibited today. Recent investigations have shown that the women are either sold by their parents or kidnaped by pimps for the temples. About 70 per cent are untouchables, the remainder of higher castes. Several hundred thousand are now believed to be in temple service. Once the women have been taken in as devadasis, they have no chance of any other form of life, having lost their virginity, being rejected as possible wives for the laity, and unable to return to their families. Devadasi service may take several forms. The woman, if she is of a higher caste, may be used by the priest who ostensibly represents the deity, or he may prostitute her to pilgrims. Recently a few devadaṣis have tried to bring their plight to the attention of the public, but if they leave the temples, they are then homeless, are denied jobs or the chance of marriage, and usually must beg for food and shelter, or even continue as street prostitutes. See also apsara, Garuḍa, Hinduism.

Devī, Hind. The World Mother, or the Great Goddess, the Shining One, etc., who is manifested under other names, such as Durgā, Kālī, etc. All of these figures were probably derived from pre-Āryan cults and may now be regarded as forms and variations of Shakti, the female principle.

dhākir, Isl. A "practitioner of remembrance"—i.e., one who can recite the Qur'ān from memory.

dhamma (Sanskrit, dharma; dhamma is the Pāli spelling), Buddh. Dhamma takes different connotations among Buddhists, especially the southern school, from the dharma of Hinduism. Dhamma is the Way, and is used by Theravādin Buddhists as their term for Buddhism. Gautama Buddha spoke of "my Dhamma," meaning Teaching, but the term is not easily translatable into Western languages ignorant of the vast connotations it commands. Pure living, pure thinking, the gaining of supreme wisdom, deliverance from evil; also, ultimate constituent, causal antecedent, what is phenomenal, are but a few of its meanings. It may also denote law, righteousness, morality, and the human condition. Early Buddhism drew upon surrounding Hindu tradition to employ the term in a more traditional usage: "Dharma is the King of Kings," as the Upanishads taught—i.e., the absolute infallible righteousness of which our earthly justice is but a shadow. While the Hindus concentrated on the other-worldly aspects of dharma, to the Buddhists the term came to have primarily ethical significance. It is not only the driving principle of the universe, but it must be as well the motivating force of the individual. The redemption of suffering humanity is the realization—or actualization—of dhamma. See Buddhism.

Dhammapada, The, Buddh. An important, self-contained book of the *Tripiṭaka* (q.v.) containing an anthology of essential teachings of the Gautama Buddha, with narrative passages. The Pāli version, the most widely known, has 423 verses divided into twenty-six chapters. There are Tibetan and Chinese versions also, slightly different. The verses probably date from the earliest times—i.e., from the period of the First Buddhist Council (B.C. 477), which set most of the Canon. Though *The Dhammapada* may not contain the actual words of the Buddha, it does embody the spirit of his teachings as recalled by the first generation of disciples, being a simple but profound statement of the Four Noble Truths and the Eightfold Path. The wide popularity of *The Dhammapada* places it on the same height for Buddhists as the *Bhagavad Gītā* for Hindus. *The Dhammapada,* which is easily memorized, is the one book most likely to be carried about by wandering monks, especially among the Theravādins. See Buddhism.

dharma, Hind. Social and moral order, law, duty, right, virtue, merit. No one English word can summarize dharma, for it is a concept pregnant with aeons of meaning to the Hindu (as to the Buddhist and Jain). The Sanskrit root from which the term is derived is dhṛ in the sense of bearing, upholding, supporting, that which forms a foundation. Its classical interpretation is righteousness or good ethical practices according to the prescriptions passed down from one generation to the next by means of the virtuous. In this general sense, dharma designates the traditional established order, which includes all duties—individual, social, and religious. Dharma is threatened and endangered by three great moral pitfalls: lust, covetousness, and anger (kama, lobha, and krodha).

Besides the general prescriptions contained in dharma, every man has his own (self) dharma (svadharma), which is determined by his place in the social structure—i.e., his caste. The correct working out of one's own dharma above all other obligations is one of the primary themes of the *Bhagavad Gītā*. The word dharma, now commonly (and not very correctly) used by Westerners in the sense of duty, is mispronounced: Both *a*'s should be short, with an "uh" sound.

The Buddhist interpretation of dharma is slightly different. See dhamma. See also *Bhagavad Gītā*.

dharma age, Buddh. A monastic term for the number of years since a monk or nun was ordained into a Buddhist order or sect. The count is done by the summers passed under discipline.

dhauq, Arab. Literally, taste, but in a Ṣūfic sense a "vertical" consciousness, an extra dimension (of depth or height) one can gain from a mystical rather than a literal or pietistic interpretation of the Qur'ān, ḥadīth (Traditions), and the Holy Names of God.

dhauti, Hind. The yogic exercise of internal cleansing of the body. A thread may be inserted in the nose and pulled through, or a tape swallowed and pulled out again.

dhikr, Isl. Remembrance, recitation; "remembrance of God"—dhikr Allāh—which the Qur'ān insists upon without respite. Among the Ṣūfīs there are many varied techniques of dhikr, which are meant to lead eventually to ecstatic release. The recitation of the Holy Name of Allāh, of His Holy Names, or of verses from the Qur'ān or from ḥadīth (Tradition), or rhythmic chants, music, and dancing (for which the "whirling dervishes," or darvishes, are noted) are some. Another technique is concentration upon a visualization of the written name of Allāh (in Arabic); in the interior vision the characters are enlarged until they fill the horizon. Eventually, after various progressive stages, they disappear, and the disciple is submerged in the World of the Absolute and is strengthened by Its Pure Light. Dancing, swaying, chanting, and such rhythmic exercises are only bridges toward the Grace of Divine Unity, and an aid to concentration. See Sūfīs.

dhyāna, Hind. Meditation in the strict sense, being the seventh of the Eightfold Path of raja yoga outlined by Patañjali (second century B.C.). One stage presupposes the other; dhyāna is crucial because it leads into the rarely achieved samādhi, and thus extraordinary emphasis is placed upon it. Patañjali (in *Yoga-Sutra* II, 2) states: "Dhyāna is an unbroken flow of thought toward the object of concentration"—i.e., it is prolonged concentration, or the undisturbed flow of thought around the object of meditation without a break. Dhyāna has become jhana in Indian Buddhism, Ch'an in China, and Zen in Japan (all of which see).

dīkṣā (also diksha), Hind. Spiritual initiation of a novice by a master, the guru. The student may be called either a siśya (disciple) or a chela (pupil). Dīkṣā is effected through the grace of the guru, who represents the Divine. This implies a twofold function on the part of the guru: The first, or negative, is the removal of the dark forces of obscuration that have kept the ātmā (q.v.) of the siśyā in bondage; this is known as pasa ksaya, and is analogous to the disciple's self-purification. The second, positive, is the establishment of a direct connection with the Sitatma yojana or Supreme Reality. Dīkṣā depends on the intermediary of the guru; however, the Bengali saint Anandamayee Ma (q.v.) underwent the complete ceremony of dīkṣā herself, playing the role of guru and giving herself a mantra.

The ceremony takes various forms, depending on the guru and the milieu. Most simply, it consists of the guru saying a few prayers over the siśyā, perhaps touching his own forehead on the site of the Third Eye (q.v.) and bestowing the mantra, the central act of any form of the rite. Other acts may include the laying on of hands on the initiate's head or shoulders and the chanting of various hymns. In any case, the culmination comes with the giving of the mantra, which is whispered into the siśyā's ear; the mantra is his alone, and he must never reveal it to another person, for its repetition in prayer is the basis of his spiritual life.

Dīkṣā may also occur during instruction, or even by the mere glance of the guru, an act that can free a man of the knots that constitute his ego. Since a guru can confer only as much power and enlightenment as he himself has attained, a guru who bestows dīkṣā too early in his own spiritual career limits his disciple. "It is obvious that he can pass on only as much wealth as he himself possesses." The disciple must wait on the path as long as the guru does not himself advance. However, in the case of disciples possessing greater inner capacities than the guru and with inner dispositions of high quality gained in previous birth, he can surpass the guru; here the initiate needs only the amount of power conferred by his dīkṣā to give him the final boost that will carry him to his goal.

At the time of the initiation the guru must first establish the life of the Supreme Guru in his disciple's body. In tantric yoga the siśyā goes through a more elaborate rite than other disciples experience. On the day before dīkṣā he withdraws to a quiet place; he must sit on a mat of kusa grass and must fast and practice sexual abstinence. The guru gives him a "sleep mantra" (supamantra), which he is to repeat in japa (q.v.), and he ties his crown lock in a knot. The disciple repeats the mantra three times, prostrates himself at the foot of the guru, and then retires to rest. The next day the full rite of dīkṣā is performed, and, as the tantric texts state, the mantra that will accompany the initiate for the remainder of his life is bestowed, "As one lamp is lit at the flame of another, so the divine Shakti [q.v.] consisting of mantra, is communicated from the guru's body to that of the siśyā." Without dīkṣā, japa of the mantra, pūjā (worship) and other ritual acts are believed useless. Certain mantras are forbidden to low castes, such as śudras, and women. However, dīkṣā initiated by a woman (in tantric rites) is efficacious and that by a mother "eightfold so."

Tantric dīkṣā is highly complicated, involving eight stages; on the attainment of the last, the siśyā is fully realized. After an ordinary dīkṣā, the tantric enters a further series, on eight planes, called aghidrka abhiseka, to become, in the final phase, a sādhaka—i.e., one who enters sādhana or preparation for self-realization. In this final stage the sādhaka performs his own funeral rites (śrāddha), and makes oblation (purnahuti) with his sacred brāhminical thread and crown lock. The relationship between guru and siśyā now ends, and the initiate ascends by himself until he realizes the great saying "So'am" (I am He). At this stage, which tantra calls jivan-mukta (liberated while still living), he is known as paramahamsa, the Great Swan, meaning one who is engaged in a mystical way.

In the post-Vedic period, dīkṣā took a different form and had a different intent. The precise origins of the ceremony, and the reasons therefor, are unknown. Most likely, since it is not mentioned in the Vedas but in the later *Aitareya Brāhmaṇa,* it apparently refers to the initiation of non-Āryans—i.e., the indigenous, "Harappan" priests and kings, who by definition would be of low caste or outcaste. Here the re-enactment of the birth process is performed in a ceremony that helps shed some light on the phrase "dvijā" (twice born). The initiate is first sprinkled with water by the brahmins, for he is about to revert to the primal stage—"Him whom they consecrate the priests make into an embryo again." The initiate is led into a consecrated hut, is bathed, his nails are cut, and his head is shaved and anointed. Now "they conduct him to his womb"—he is dressed in a clean cotton garment, over which is placed the skin of a black antelope. "The placenta is above the caul," says the verse connected with the rite. The initiate closes his hand in imitation of an embryo. "Closing its hands, the embryo lies within; with closed hands the child is born." The newly born is brought to a bath, where the skin and the garment are removed. The text is explicit: "The bath signifies his conception, the hut is the womb, the garment the amnion, the skin of the black antelope the chorion." From that point on, the initiate's status is changed: He must have no contact with men of impure caste, nor with women; he avoids answering questions, he must not be touched. Being a god, he takes only milk, a sacred food. One might add that milk is also the food he would have received as an infant. See guru, Hinduism.

dīn, Isl. The practice of religion; sometimes, religion itself. Dīn includes the Five Pillars—confession, prayer, almsgiving, fasting, and pilgrimage. The obligations implicit in dīn bind man to God, Allāh. Dīn is invariably paired with īmām (q.v.), faith.

Dinkard, Zor. A variant spelling of Denkart (q.v.).

disposal of the dead. It is a normal practice to bury, cremate, or otherwise dispose of the corpse on the day of death in virtually every culture but American, except for those strata of the royalty, nobility, or upper classes where the dead may be embalmed or preserved with spices and herbs and kept for long periods; the extended exposure to mourners of the bodies of the minor rājas of Bali is an example.

Primitive disposal consisted of placing the dead in an isolated area where animals and birds might devour the body, especially in lands where the ground was too stony or hard for burial. This was and still is the custom in Tibet among the Bön and Buddhists. The Zoroastrians (see below) have a highly refined form of this custom. For the curious, three methods—cremation, burial, and exposure—will be considered as examples.

HINDU. Among orthodox Hindus, especially those of the higher castes, there are many variations of the following customs, depending on area and social stratum. A person close to death is carried to the banks of a river, the Ganges if possible. Some may be brought to Benares, where certain streets are set aside for the dying. Many sacred sites contain shelters, either crude structures or more elaborate buildings, to house the dying. The ideal locale is always a river. A work called the *Gaṇgā Bākyabali* states, "He who thinks upon Gaṇgā, though he be eight hundred miles distant from the river at the time, is delivered from all sin, and is entitled to heaven." The *Kurma Purāṇa,* in a phrase echoed by other Purānas, claims, "Those who consciously die on the banks of the Ganges shall be absorbed into the essence of Brahmā; while those who die there unconsciously shall go to the heaven of Brahmā."

The dying man (even if at home) should be laid upon a bed of kusa grass (*poa cynosuroides*), the head sprinkled with water from the Ganges and smeared with river clay; flowers and leaves of the basil plant are also scattered about the head. A sālagrāma (q.v.), a sacred shell, is placed nearby. Verses from the Vedas are chanted. Upon death the corpse is washed, perfumed, wrapped in cloth (white for men, red for women, these being the colors of their marriage clothing), and carried to the cremation site, often on a simple charpoy (a type of cot). The cremation site is normally on the banks of a river, otherwise in a forest. The nearest male relative, a son in the case of a man, lights the logs of the funeral pyre with a wand bearing a flame from the deceased's home. The lighting of the pyre is an important act, for whoever performs the rite is usually considered the legal heir. The stomach (called the "navel") often may not burn; it is placed in a river separately from the ashes. In some cases the ashes and scraps of bones are taken to an epecially sacred site, such as Rishikesh near the headwaters of the Ganges, to be immersed. Various Vedic verses are chanted at the cremation; the following is typical: "All that is low must finally perish; all that is elevated must ultimately fall; all compounded bodies must end in dissolution; and life be concluded with death." In the days following cremation various commemorative ceremonies are performed, especially that of śrāddha (q.v.).

Cremation is now the standard method in India, but in the primitive period both exposure to wild animals and burial were common. At the time of the Gautama Buddha (sixth century B.C.) corpse enclosures were still in use, these being places where bodies were placed to be eaten by animals and birds; they were a common site of meditation for holy men. The Buddha himself was cremated according to Hindu rites; possession of his ashes was disputed by his various disciples.

MUSLIM. The Shahādah (q.v.) is recited in the ear of the dying person; the prayer is supposed to be the last words the individual hears on earth. Upon death the body is immediately washed and is wrapped in a piece of unsewn clean cotton and is brought in procession to the cemetery; a shallow grave is dug and the body laid in the trench on its right side, the head pointing toward Mecca. The grave is covered with stones to prevent animals from digging up the corpse. The Prayer for the Dead is recited. Tombs are enjoined, but in many areas, especially in North Africa and among the Ṣūfīs (q.v.), shrines are not uncommon.

ZOROASTRIAN. The disposal of the dead among this ancient religion is of unusual interest and importance, for it expresses very archaic customs as practiced by a highly sophisticated and modern people. Funeral rites among the two branches of the Zoroastrians —the Fārsīs of Iran and the Parsees of India—are virtually identical, being based on the Avesta (q.v.), with minor points of difference due to local custom or the correction of past errors.

When a person seems on the point of death, a priest (usually a mobed, one of ordinary rank) is called in; he recites a prayer on behalf of the dying person in repentance of past sins and pours a few drops of nirang (q.v.), consecrated bull's urine, on the lips of the individual. As soon as death occurs, the mobed goes to the fire temple (q.v.) to perform the ceremony (ravān barsm in Iran, srōsh-drūn in India) for the repose of the soul of the deceased. From the moment of death on, the corpse must not be touched except by those who are traditionally given the task. The body is first cleansed by a corpse washer (murdah-shūr) or clean washer (pakshur), aided by an assistant, both being of the same sex as the deceased. The two washers are tied together by a kustī (q.v.) thread, for one person may never be alone with a body. The washing is done with a woolen glove, and the liquid is not water but gomez, beef urine, dipped by a long-handled spoon from a brass bowl. The body is now dressed in a worn but clean white garment. The kustī is tied around the body.

The ceremony of sag-dīd (q.v.), glance of a dog, is now performed for the first time, as prescribed in the Avesta. In Iran an ordinary street-dog is used for the purpose; in India a dog may be kept by a priest, but not one of any special breed. Morsels of bread are strewn around the corpse, or, according to the older usage, laid on the bosom for the dog to eat. Usually the body is placed in a receiving vault for a short period, but normally the rites must be completed within twenty-four hours, and the procession (pādāsh) to the Tower of Silence begins as soon as feasible. The vault ordinarily has three compartments—one for men, one for women, and one for the corpse; the Avesta enjoins three vaults for each village, a practice not always observed at present.

The body is carried to the dakmah, or Tower of Silence, on an iron stretcher (gāhan). The mourners always follow in pairs, with a kustī held between them; if there is an odd number, then there is a line of three, again with kustīs. The men who bear the body may take turns; they, too, are linked with kustīs. A single man may not carry a corpse, even a small one, for this is forbidden in the Avesta. At the dakmah, there is a final viewing of the body by relatives and friends, with many prayers led by the priests; then the body, after a final sag-dīd, is taken within the Tower by special men, nasā-sālārs (chiefs of the dead), who are well advanced in years and of high moral character. Holding a kustī again, they recite a final prayer, the Shrosh Baj, and then, still praying, one of them takes an iron key, and beginning at the left ear of the deceased, draws three furrows in a circle around the body. The corpse is now brought into the center of the Tower, laid down with its head to the south, and stripped. The corpse carriers withdraw, leaving the body to the vultures. The vultures are said to strip the corpse of flesh in about twenty minutes.

When the bones finally crumble and turn to dust, they are placed in a special niche in the Tower, where the rain finally washes them away. At this point they are not considered corrupting or defiling of the earth.

Zoroastrians, especially the Parsees, are quite sensitive to criticism by outsiders of what others consider to be a primitive, even disgusting method of disposing of the dead. Some of their own observations may be of interest. They consider it an act of charity in disposing of a "useless physical vestiture," the decaying flesh, by presenting it as food to other creatures. This is the speediest method of disposal, it is economical, and it shows the equality of all, rich and poor, the great and the lowly, in receiving the same treatment. It is hygienic, since the corpse has little contact with the environment, there is no odor of burning flesh (as with the Hindus), no contamination of the earth or of water systems (as in Muslim and Christian burials), and it is safe because of the sterilizing effect of the sun's rays.

In the event that a Zoroastrian dies away from a dakmah and cannot be exposed to the vultures, the body is carried to some remote place in the hills or mountains and covered with a slab, but not interred. See Tower of Silence, Zoroastrianism.

djinn, Isl. See jinn.

Doctrine of the Mean (Chinese title, *Chung-yung*), Conf. The work is commonly attributed to Tzŭ-ssŭ (or Tse Ssu), a grandson of the sage Confucius (c. fifth century B.C.). The central section is undoubtedly by Tzŭ-ssŭ, but the beginning and end, which show a non-Confucian mysticism, seem to have been written by a third-century B.C. disciple of Mencius (q.v.). The basic theme of the work is this (presumably a direct quotation from the Master himself):

"To have no emotions of pleasure and anger, sorrow and joy, surging up is to be described as being in a state of harmony. This state of equilibrium is the supreme foundation of the great universe, and this state of harmony, its universal path. Once equilibrium and harmony are achieved, Heaven and Earth maintain their proper positions, and the myriad things are nourished." Apparently unsure of his own ideas, Tzŭ-ssŭ relied heavily upon quotations from his grandfather; however, he eventually forged his own philosophy, "the way of the princely man," which is "widely apparent and yet hidden. [His] ultimate reaches may be examined only in the light of Heaven and Earth." It is only this exceptional individual, who may be a prince or a commoner, "who can make the warp and woof of the great fabric of society, who can establish the great foundation of the world, and who can understand the transforming and nurturing processes of Heaven and Earth. . . . His human-heartedness, how pervading! His depth, how unfathomable! His heavenliness, how overwhelming! Who is there who can comprehend this unless he possesses superior intelligence and sagely wisdom, unless he reach out to the spiritual power of Heaven?" See Confucius, Confucianism.

Dōgen (A.D. 1200–53), Buddh. Founder of the Sōtō sect of Zen Buddhism, he is the leading figure in Zen and is venerated by Japanese Buddhists as a bodhisattva, a buddha-becoming. Dōgen was born into a noble family, his father being descended from an emperor and his mother from a prime minister. Dōgen was orphaned at the age of seven and was ordained a Buddhist monk six years later. He showed such promise that the court regents wanted to adopt him and groom him for the post of prime minister. However, he preferred to remain a monk, though he was frustrated by the life the Buddhists led in Japan. "It is taught that we are all born Buddhas," he complained, "but I have been unable to find among the inmates of Mount Hiei [a leading monastic center] a single person who looks like a Buddha." Dōgen, now twenty-three, went to see the great Eisai (q.v.), who had introduced Ch'an (or Zen) doctrines into Japan. Eisai advised Dōgen to go to China to study. Here again Dōgen was frustrated, for the various Chinese monasteries he visited were rife with worldliness.

But he encountered Ch'an meditation, the techniques of which he brought back as Sōtō Zen (from the Chinese Ts'ao-tung) to Japan in 1227. Dōgen eschewed the extremism practiced by many of the Ch'an monks, who rejected scripture. Dōgen saw equal value in the two basic schools of meditation in zazan (q.v.) and sudden enlightenment through the kōan (q.v.), but he warned, "Stay on top of the Lotus [i.e., the writings]; don't let it get on top of you." Dōgen put aside much of Mahāyāna Buddhism in its Chinese form and returned to original sources, especially as taught by the Theravāda school; he found in the Buddha's posture of sitting the key to enlightenment through meditation, and he came to see less value in the techniques of sudden enlightenment through the verbal byplay of the kōan, which was the method of Eisai's Rinzai school.

Unlike the Rinzai monks, Dōgen believed in the efficacy of the written words if they did not dominate (cf. the Lotus, above). Devoting most of his life to writing, with a remarkable literary output, he produced one of the basic Zen works, the massive *Shōbōgenzō* (Treasury of the Eye of the True Doctrine), which covered all facets of Buddhism, from disciplinary practices to deep insights into the nature of Buddhahood and nirvāṇa, final enlightenment. See Buddhism. Sōtō.

dog, four-eyed, Zor. The four-eyed dog plays an important part in Zoroastrian ritual, and has done so since the earliest days. In the scriptures a dog is the constant companion of man and is his guardian. A dog is counted next in holiness to man and has virtually the same rights and privileges as a man. The Vidēvdāt (q.v.) mentions the ceremonial use of dogs in several passages, particularly in his role as a purifying agent. The Vidēvdāt speaks of the necessity to send a dog through an area or road contaminated by the reposal or passage of a body, either a man's or a dog's; the dog causes latent impurities in the region to fly "away to the regions of the North, in the shape of a fly, with knees and tail sticking out, droning without end." Until the area is purified by the presence of the dog, it may not be occupied by "flocks and herds, by men and women, by the fire of Ahura Mazdā [the Supreme God], by the consecrated bundles of baresma [sacred twigs] and by the faithful." The dog ranks in importance with a man in being a vehicle of such power that his carcass can contaminate. Neither women nor the bodies of other creatures bear the same dreadful curse.

The animal of the Vidēvdāt is "a yellow dog with four eyes, or a white dog with yellow ears." Today the standard creature is the four-eyed dog, though a Parsee priest, Dastur Khurshed S. Dabu, has stated, "We now employ any dog available." The four eyes are simply the two natural eyes and two markings, either above or below them. The emphasis on the white dog with yellow ears has disappeared from Zoroastrian ritual. The dog is of no particular breed. Four-eyed or not, in India, where the majority of Zoroastrians now live, he is nothing more than a docile pariah dog (pie dog) of the type commonly found in any Asian city or village street. "You'd throw a stone at him before you took him home," a Parsee woman remarked to the editor in discussing the four-eyed dog. The animal is kept indifferently by a priest, or by the priest's wife. Yet he is in frequent demand for two important services, which could not be properly observed without his presence. These are at the rite of bareshnum and at the disposal of the dead (see both entries).

From the most primitive and archaic times dogs have played a role in religious rites and rituals, but none to the extent of that among the Zoroastrians. In some cultures the dog is friendly, in others a ferocious guardian of a sacred enclosure. A dog accompanies the gurus of the Aghorīs, a Shaivite sect; a dog is also a faithful companion of the Roman Catholic St. Rocco. Often the dog is connected with funery rites and myths, and in passages to the underworld, whether benign or fearful; in this sense dogs are often attendants of Siberian shamans (q.v.). Attempts to connect the Zoroastrian four-eyed dog to other religions have been fruitless, except for obvious parallels to Hinduism. The four-eyed dog cannot be equated to the fifty-headed (or three-headed) Cerberus of the Greeks, nor to his brother, the two-headed hound Orthrus, who lay with his own mother and begot on her the Sphinx. The dog-headed Egyptian god Anubis, who accompanied souls to the underworld, is as close as one can come to affinities with the Zoroastrian animal. Those ancient Hindus who believed that the soul went to the god Yama, the King of the Dead, feared their way would be blocked by two ferocious four-eyed dogs with wide nostrils.

At this date Zoroastrian priests differ over the interpretation of the dog's role, and the matter is rarely broached by Western scholars, who are more often concerned with texts and not practice. In the past a "gifted" dog was used, but now such dogs are hard to come by. A common belief is that the dog is clairvoyant under the circumstances in which he enters the ceremonies—i.e., he possesses the Third Eye, and when he is a part of the funery rites he can tell whether or not the deceased is truly dead or if the body is merely under suspended animation. A scriptural reason for the role of the dog is that his sight—called sag-dīd—is capable of preventing the "magnetic" defilement of the dead from spreading to the living; the dog absorbs the evil aura that emanates from the corpse. Psychically the animal breaks up the evil forces that surround the body, for when death occurs, the forces of evil can predominate. Other interpretations state that there is what is called in English a "magic circle" that surrounds the corpse so that the disintegration of both the physical and that astral bodies should not harm the living. When the corpse is removed from this insulated invisible field, the dog is brought forth to cut and absorb the electromagnetic residue that remains. On a more ethereal level, the four-eyed dog is a symbol of the human conscience; before the body is consumed by the vultures in the Tower of Silence, the conscience looks back upon the life that is becoming extinct. See bareshnum, Tower of Silence, Zoroastrianism.

Dravidian. A catch-all term applied to both races and languages; today the term refers to the people of South India. The Dravidians are known to have occupied India before the arrival of the Āryans (q.v.) about B.C. 1500. The major cities of the Indus Valley (q.v.), Harappā and Mohenjo-daro, are believed, more by instinct than by actual proof, to have been Dravidian cities; the Āryans either killed or drove the peoples of this vast civilization into the jungles, their survivors forming the bulk of the population of South India; pockets of Dravidian languages remain in the North, especially Brahui. Classical Sanskrit, the priestly tongue, contains much Dravidian; even the great Āryan scriptures and epics show strong Dravidian influence in the form of non-Āryan myths, legends, concepts, and divinities, especially the now-popular gods Shiva, Krishna, Vishnu, and the various Earth Mother figures, such as Shakti, Durgā, Kālī, Pārvatī, etc. Dravidian forms of worship and ritual, especially that of pūjā, which consists of prayer, offerings of fruit, food, flowers, the burning of incense, and individual types of devotion, have by and large replaced many of the more formal Āryan rites, which are highly structured and are centered on sacred fires, and in the past, on sacrifices of animals and humans. See Hinduism.

Durgā, Hind. One of the major goddesses who are but forms of Devī or Shakti, the female principle. Durgā is one of many ancient matriarchal figures brought into the mainstream as the consort of a god, in this case Shiva, and is sometimes known as Pārvatī in her role as wife. Durgā plays a primary part in tantrism and was probably an aboriginal divinity of vegetation and agriculture; in some areas she is still worshiped in the roots of a tree; in others, in the branches. Pigs, goats, and fowl may be sacrificed to her. Her visual aspect is frightening: She is black, her face is terrifying, she wears several wreaths of skulls around her neck, her hair hangs loose, and she is smiling; a serpent serves as a sacred thread; she wears a girdle of dead hands; two infant corpses serve as earrings. She often stands on the whitened body of Shiva, who cannot function without her power. Except for minor details she closely resembles Kālī, with whom she may be equated. In the past, especially in Assam, human sacrifices were dedicated to her until the British ended the practice in 1832. In a ceremony still celebrated in Bengal the people daub themselves with mud and cover themselves with leaves and flowers. Erotic practices are common at such festivals. During the feast of Durgā Pūjā in eastern India clay images of her with sweet and benevolent features (copied after the ideal of the movie actress) are made by various communities, which vie for the best-made and best-dressed figure. The goddess descends to earth to reside in the figure, which is honored for three days, the festival ending with the decapitation of goats and buffalos in her temples, after which the figures are lowered into the river (usually the Ganges or a tributary) and the goddess leaves the statue as it disintegrates.

dvijā (or dvi-jā), Hind. The twice born, a Hindu who goes through a formal initiation into his caste, thus being born a second time. Only members of the three higher castes—brāhmin (priests), kśatrīyas (warriors), and vaiśya (service)—can be dvijā. The lowest caste—the śūdras (servile)—and the untouchables are denied the privilege of dvijā and must await a rebirth into a higher caste at some future date. See brahmin, caste, caste Hindu, and harijan.

◂E▸

Eight Consciousnesses, Buddh. The eight different functional aspects possessed by each sentient being. They parallel the eight stages in yoga (q.v.). The Eight Consciousnesses are: The Consciousnesses of the Eye, the Ear, the Nose, the Tongue, and the Body, this group of five being considered a unit. The sixth is Consciousness of Discrimination; the seventh, the Consciousness of Constant Thought (or Ego), and the eighth, Store Consciousness (Sanskrit, Ālaya-Vijñāna), the basic consciousness or persisting element, which is subject to repeated births and deaths.

Eightfold Path (also Noble Eightfold Path; in Sanskrit, Ārya Aṭṭanga Mārga; in Pāli, Attangika Magga), Buddh. A central tenet of Gautama Buddha's First Sermon, in which he presented the Four Great Truths (q.v.) and the Noble Eightfold Path to his handful of disciples. The following of the Path, he said, will lead to nirvāṇa (Pāli, nibbana, q.v.). The eight points are the following:

Right Understanding, Right Thoughts, Right Speech, Right Actions, Right Livelihood, Right Effort, Right Mindfulness, and Right Concentration. The Path is a systematic exposition of a Way that will direct the smallest glimmering of understanding toward the Supreme Awakening. Of the eight factors in the Path, the first two are grouped under the heading of Wisdom, the next three under Morality, and the last three under Concentration, the very last of which produces ecstatic concentration. This systemization corresponds very roughly to the primitive stages in the development of classical yoga (q.v.), which was to be finally formulated more than half a millennium later. The Eightfold Path, Gautama Buddha said in his sermon, "leads to the stopping of sorrow." See Buddha, Buddhism.

Eisai (A.D. 1141–1215). Japanese Buddhist priest and monk who is generally credited with the introduction of both Zen and tea into his own country from China. On the mainland, Eisai discovered that the only type of Buddhism with any vitality was Ch'an (q.v.), to be nipponized as Zen. Eisai attempted to introduce Zen in its Rinzai form (Lin-chi in China) to the Buddhist monasteries on Mount Hiei near Kyotō but was rebuffed by the traditionalists; he then moved to the new seat of government, Kamakura, where the samurai, the warriors, were among the first to adopt Zen meditative techniques, finding them an aid to military discipline. Eisai's alliance with the warlords did much to propagate Zen throughout Japan. He thought tea "the most wonderful medicine for nourishing one's health," adding, "it is the secret of long life," and "In the great country of China they drink tea, as a result of which there is no heart trouble and people live long lives . . . to build up the heart the drinking of tea is the finest method." However, the famed tea ceremony, which was to become a cult, was introduced by another, Dai-ō, half a century later, and given its final form as a ritual in Zen monasteries by Jō-ō and Rokyu in the sixteenth century. Eisai wrote a number of important works, among them *Kōzen gokoku ron* (Propagation of Zen for the Protection of the Country) and *Kissa yōjō-ki* (Drink Tea to Nourish Life). See Zen.

Ek Oankar, Sikh. The Supreme Being, and the most sacred name in the Sikh Creed. Both the sound and the calligraphy of the word bear profound meanings. Ek Oankar is written in the Gurumukhi alphabet with the numeral 1 followed by the nasalized vowel for O, surmounted by an arc. Ek in many of the Indian languages stands for one, while Oankar is a form of the sacred Sanskritic Ōṃ (q.v.). The Granth Sāheb (q.v.), the Sikh scripture, contains both forms, Ōṃ and Oankar, the latter being preferred. The unity and indivisibility of God are emphasized, with the addition of the numeral 1, and thus formulated the term signifies "the One Indivisible Being." Ek Oankar is placed at the top of the Granth and at the head of all sacred Sikh writings. It is inscribed thus to invoke Divine Blessing and is solemnly pronounced by all who accept Sikhism at the time of their initiation. See Sikhism.

Evans-Wentz, W. Y. (1880–1957). An American anthropologist who attended Oxford as a post-graduate student of the religious experiences of mankind, Evans-Wentz began his field work with the study of the peasants of the (then) remote Celtic areas of the British Islands—Ireland, Scotland, the Isle of Man, Wales, and Cornwall—and Brittany, wandering about on foot in search of authentic fairy-seers. Under a secularized layer of Christianity, he discovered a substratum of medieval paganism. His first work, *The Fairy-Faith in Celtic Countries,* was published in 1911. After that, Evans-Wentz became a kind of gypsy scholar, ranging as far as the Near East. In 1917, supported by the recommendation of an old friend and fellow student, T. E. Lawrence, he journeyed to India, where he found the opportunity to investigate the most intense forms of mysticism. The next year he crossed the glaciers of the Himālayas from Kashmir to the cave of Amar-Nath, with its huge ice-liṅga of the god Shiva (q.v.). He then took up residence as a sādhu near the sacred city of Hardwar on the upper Ganges, where he received yogic training. This was followed by three years as a chela of the Lāma Kazi Dawa-Samdup in Sikkim, until the Lāma's death in 1922. Evans-Wentz remained in the Orient some fifteen years. Many of the occult experiences and powers he mentions in the third person he himself experienced (c.f. Madame Alexandra David-Neel). The Lāma and his chela edited the famous Bardol Thödol, or *Tibetan Book of the Dead,* and also *Tibetan Yoga and Secret Doctrines.* Among Evans-Wentz's other works are the *Tibetan Book of the Great Liberation* and *Tibet's Great Yogī Milarepa.* Evans-Wentz passed his last years at San Jose, California, at a small ashram he had founded.

F

fanā', Isl. Extinction or passing away, a Ṣūfic term for expressing absorption in God. The concept became prominent in the third Islamic century and has held a central place since then. In some forms of Ṣūfism the disciple, on his way to fanā', passes through three stages (often expressed in terms of the three sections of the Islamic rosary): The first asks forgiveness of God and seeks purification; the second, in which the disciple calls for blessings upon the Prophet Muḥammad, lets himself be absorbed into the Prophet in anticipation of the Infinite; and finally, even the Prophet no longer exists, and everything, including the "I am," is extinguished in the Divine Oneness. The twentieth-century Algerian mystic al'-Alawī defines fanā' thus:

"The Prophet said: 'Die before ye die,' and this is the real death, for the other death is but a change of abode. The true meaning of death in the doctrine of the Sūfīs is the extinction of the slave—i.e., his utter effacement and annihilation [fanā']."

The medieval mystic al-Ghazālī (q.v.) defines it in different and simpler terms: "When the worshiper no longer thinks of his worship or himself but is altogether absorbed in Him whom he worships, that state is called fanā'." In fanā' "a man has so passed away from himself that he feels nothing of his bodily members, nor of what is passing without, nor of what passes within his own mind." See Ṣūfīs.

faqīr, Isl. A member of a Sūfic order. The Arabic word means poor. The plural is fuqarā (and the English is fakir). The faqīr is not a mere passive member of his order; his entire life is devoted to a search for spiritual illumination, at first under the guidance of a master, and then, often, entirely on his own. The would-be faqīr enters the order through an initiatory rite (sometimes as simple as a clasping of hands all around) and takes an oath of allegiance to his shaykh. A frequent practice is the spiritual retreat under the guidance of the master; this may take place in an isolated cell, hut, or cave, or the open wilderness; the practice of retreat is known as khalwah. In his isolation, the faqīr fasts and prays, repeating ceaselessly the Shahādah, the Sacred Invocation, and the Divine Name. Khalwah can mean the turning point, or the break, in a man's life between his previously secular career and the opening of his soul to illumination. The trained faqīr enters in hāl, a term with a wide meaning, extending from a state of spiritual concentration to one of enlightenment. Besides meditation and prayer, such techniques as music and dancing are used by some communities of fuqarā to help induce spiritual states. The faqīr lives in simplicity, even poverty, and normally carries on a trade or does manual labor, and is married. Visions are not uncommon in the advanced faqīr. See khalwah, shaykh, Ṣūfī, Sūfism.

Farid, Baba (c. A.D. 1200–80). North Indian Ṣūfī. After passing twelve years living in a niche inside a well without finding the enlightenment he sought, he began to wander about the countryside near Lahore (now in the Pakistani Punjab). He experienced hunger, thirst, and homelessness, and practiced sacrifices, fasts, penances, and vigils, and repeated the Divine Names, before he met a guru who would take him as a disciple. Many of his songs were immensely popular with the ordinary people and are still sung today. A number of them are among the wide variety of Muslim and Hindu devotional poetry included in the Sikhs' sacred scripture, the Granth Sāheb (q.v.). Farid's songs lean to melancholy and thoughts of death. Of a noted courtesan of Lahore, he sang, "The eyes that were so delicate they could not bear the weight of collyrium/today the skull that bore them has been turned into a nesting place for the eggs of the birds." He wrote: "The day a man is born the date of his death is inscribed in his forehead; these words cannot be effaced: marriage with the God of Death must come on the appointed day; entreaties are of no avail. The path by which the soul must pass is thinner than the thickness of a hair." In the mainstream of Indian Ṣūfism, he sang, "Within my body dwells my Beloved," whose grace is mysteriously bestowed, for "Some do not get it even after performing great austerities and night-long vigils, while it is forced on those who lie asleep." See Ṣūfī.

fatwā, Isl. An authoritative legal opinion issued by the 'Ulamā', the body of orthodox Islamic scholars.

fiqh, Isl. Understanding; the process or activity of understanding and deduction. The term was originally general in concept; gradually it came to be restricted to religious thought—belief, practice, dogma, and Islamic jurisprudence. Eventually it grew to denote almost solely the discipline of the Law, closely identified with 'ilm (q.v), or knowledge, and is encompassed in the concept of the sharī'a (roughly, the Sacred Law). See 'ilm, sharī'a.

Fiqh Akbar, Isl. A collection of dogmatic and theological questions attributed to Abu Hanifa (second Islamic century), the founder of the very influential Hanafī school of Islamic law.

Fiqh Akbar II, Isl. An important statement of the Islamic creed, assembled in twenty-nine articles, based upon the teachings of al-Ashari, the leading figure in the formative period of Islamic theology. The work, compiled about A.D. 1000, includes the following points: Allāh is absolute in His decrees of good and evil; He has existed from eternity, and does not resemble His creatures in any respect (i.e., man is not in His image). The Qur'ān is His speech revealed to the Prophet Muḥammad; He speaks without instruments and letters; His speech is increate, though that of the early prophets and others whom He quotes in the Qur'ān is create. Allāh does not force man to believe or not to believe; what man does is of his own volition, for good or evil. God will punish or not as He wishes, but the Prophet may intercede. The faithful will see God in Paradise with their own eyes. Of the Prophet Muḥammad, he, like other prophets, is free from sins of all types—e.g., lack of belief, mistakes, and sordid acts—but may stumble and err. However (despite what certain verses of the Qur'ān say), he never worshiped idols; he never sinned in any manner. His Ascension (q.v.) is a fact, and whoever rejects it is a schismatic. Numerous other credal matters are included in the *Fiqh Akbar,* but these are a few of the major beliefs, which are accepted by a majority of the

Sunnīs but not entirely by the Shī'as, who view the Prophet in a different light, and have developed many eschatological and mystical beliefs not entertained by the larger group. See Shī'a, Sunnī.

fire, Zor. Among the Zoroastrians, fire plays a central role in worship. Fire is personified and referred to as "the son of Ahura Mazdā," a concept found in various Zoroastrian scriptures. Fire is the representative of God, not only His most important creation, but also His physical manifestation. The sun as a form of fire is "the most beautiful body of God." Fire is bright, always points upward, is always pure. The fire in the royal chapel of the Persian emperors was looked upon as the smiter of the enemy; later it became the angel of victory. Fire does not tolerate any rival artificial light in its presence. After the Zoroastrians migrated to India (c. seventh century A.D.), they symbolized the sacred throne of the Iranian shah, lost to the Muslims, by fire, calling it Iranshah, a practice still observed. See fire temple below; also see Zoroastrianism.

fire temple, Zor. Fire temples are the common center of worship among the Zoroastrians in Iran and the Parsees of India; those in the former country are simple structures so as not to irritate the Muslim majority; In India, fire temples may be magnificent buildings; many are influenced by nineteenth-century English colonial architecture. The Parsees do not allow any but members of their own faith to enter the building; the Iranians are much more tolerant. The temple normally consists of an inner sanctuary, plus meeting rooms, hallways, and various chambers. In the more important temples only priests may enter the fire sanctuary itself. The fire is not allowed to die out, and must be fed with "well-dried and well-examined wood," as the Avesta enjoins. It is attended by priests, who may maintain a continual celebration of hymns; each celebrant wears over his mouth the paitidāna, a small white veil prescribed by the Avesta to be worn over the lips when before the sacred flame in order to prevent the breath and spittle from contaminating it.

There are three grades of temples, more precisely defined in India than in Iran:

1. Atāsh Bahrām: fire dedicated to the angel of Victory. This is

the fire of the royal chapel of the Iranian King, where he kept his sword and scepter; no other light but fire is allowed. Atāsh Bahrām is the most important and complex, as the rites for dedication require a year to perform and involve seventeen different types of fire, including those from sources the Zoroastrians consider defiling, such as the cremation ground; also fire from lightning that has ignited wood in a forest and fire from places where a furnace or oven is used, such as a smith's or a baker's. Each of these fires goes through a purificatory rite. On the final day of dedication the various fires are collected at the temple and in an inner sanctum, where only the priests may enter; the embers are placed under a wooden throne of sandalwood beams and logs. Worshipers remain outside the sanctuary but place contributions of fragrant woods on the threshold. The priests, after washing the lower part of the throne, circumambulate it nine times, chanting a litany; a bell is tolled to expel evil thoughts, words, and deeds. The throne has become a type of maṇḍala.

At the end of the ceremony ashes are given to the faithful, who place a pinch on their foreheads. The ashes symbolize the return of the body to its ultimate dust—equality in that rich and poor alike undergo the same death; ashes are also a sign of loyalty to the throne, it being an oriental custom to take the dust from the ruler's feet and apply it to one's head. Lastly, the ashes are the manifold return of a gift, the sandalwood coming back as such. A most important aspect of the ash is that of magnetic emanation; when applied to the vital centers (or plexuses) the ash stimulates the inner life and purifies one's aura. Finally, the ash is a symbol of the link between the faithful and the Invisible Presence.

There are eight first-grade fire temples in India: four in Bombay, two in the old Parsee colony at Surat, and one each at Udvara and Navsari. These temples may have smaller temples attached.

2. Adaran: fire from only four sources, the four "castes." These temples are smaller than the above but similar in intent. No laymen may enter the inner sanctuary.

3. Dād-gāh or Dar-i-Meher, the court of Mithra, the angel of Justice: This is the type of temple for ordinary worship. Consecration is simple, and even the lay Zoroastrian may enter the sanctuary; however, nonbelievers are excluded from every part of the temple. The consecration of priests, marriages, and other cere-

monies are conducted at the Dād-gāh. One of the important rites is that of yasna, the sacred offering. See fire, Zoroastrianism.

Five K's, Sikh. The five signs whereby a Sikh symbolizes his adherence to his faith. They are: uncut hair and beard (keś), a comb in the hair (kaṅgh), a steel bangle on the right wrist (karā), short underdrawers (kacch), and sword (kirpān). See Sikhs, Sikhism.

Five Stupid Vices (Sanskrit, Pañca Kleśa), Buddh. They are: desire, anger or resentment, stupidity or foolishness, arrogance, and doubt.

Five Violations, Buddh. They are: parricide, matricide, murder of a spiritual worthy (arahant), causing disharmony in the monastic community, and striking a Buddha in such a manner that he bleeds. In Pure Land Buddhism (q.v.) any of the Five Violations keeps an individual from enjoying the celestial paradise.

fo, Buddh. A Chinese term for Buddha, which may mean Gautama Buddha, or one of the other Buddhas, such as Amitābha or Maitreya, etc. In actuality, any Buddhist on the threshold of nirvāṇa (q.v.) may be a fo; the term is sometimes applied to a saintly or even royal individual.

food, as daily sacred substance. Especially in the meditative religions, food takes on a cosmic and spiritual significance, being equated with breath and the life forces. In the Upanishads of ancient India the term anna means everything that is eaten, digested, and transformed on the fundamental basis of mutations, not only soul stuff but food. Diet has an intimate connection with the mind in Hinduism, as it does in its related religions, Jainism and Buddhism. Mind is formed of the subtlest portion of food. According to tradition, "Food, when consumed, becomes threefold: the gross particles become waste matter, the middling ones flesh, and the fine ones the mind. When milk is churned, its fine particles which rise upward become butter [a most valued food]. Thus, when food is consumed, the fine particles which rise upward form the mind. Hence verily the mind is food." Also: "By the purity of food one becomes refined in his inner nature; by the purification of his inner nature he verily gets memory of the Self; and by attainment of the memory of the Self all ties and attachments are severed."

The yogis classify diet in three forms: sattvic, rajasic, and tamasic. Milk, barley, wheat, cereals, butter, honey, cheese, tomatoes, dates, fruit, and nuts are sattvic, making the mind pure and calm. Fish, eggs, meat, salt, and sauces are rajasic and excite passion. Beef, wine, garlic, onions, and tobacco are tamasic, filling the mind with anger, darkness, and inertia. In the *Bhagavad Gītā* (q.v.), the Lord Krishna says to Arjuna, "The food which is dear to each is threefold. Hear the distinction of these. The foods which increase vitality, energy, joy, vigor and health, and which are delicious, bland, substantial and agreeable are dear to the pure. The passionate desire foods which are bitter, sour, saline, excessively hot, pungent, dry and burning, and which produce pain, grief and disease. The foods which are stale, tasteless, putrid and rotten, leavings and impure are dear to the tamasic." This admonition, parenthetically, is undoubtedly a brahminical gloss intended to help keep the lower castes in a state of lassitude.

Most yogis advocate four meals a day, during daylight hours, four hours apart. The following menu is typical and standard. Breakfast may be composed of milk, some form of a whole wheat preparation (such as a gruel or bread), honey, and dried or fresh fruit. The second meal or lunch consists of a vegetable soup, a preparation from grains, fresh green vegetables and roots, salads, fresh yogurt, or buttermilk. The afternoon meal would be made of fruit juices, nuts, and grain in some form; this is only a light refreshment. The dinner, which should be taken at least an hour before retiring, should consist of dairy products, a preparation from grain, green vegetables, and fruit. No tea or coffee, alcohol, drugs, or tobacco should ever be taken, a rule that applies also in Jainism and Buddhism. Most yogis prohibit both fasting and overeating as harmful. Moderation is the guide. A general rule is to prepare only two thirds to three quarters of what the empty stomach thinks it wants.

The Jains are much stricter than the Hindus in their diet, since the Jains consider every animate and nonanimate object to contain a soul. Some try to live only on foods that have died "naturally," such as wheat or rice, which cannot be consumed in a living form but must be dried and hence "lifeless." The ordinary Jain diet consists basically of one-sensed life—nuts, fruits, vegetables, milk, and clarified butter (ghī). Fish, meat, fowl, eggs, honey, spirits, and many root vegetables are eschewed. Garlic, onions, spices, and vegetables that might resemble a human or animal form are also forbidden.

Among Buddhists there is a wide variety of practices, with most Buddhists being vegetarians. There has been a controversy over flesh meats: The Lord Buddha died (of diarrhea) after eating, in some texts, a meal that included pork; in others, truffles (which are rooted out by pigs). Some Buddhists have concluded that if the Lord Buddha ate flesh, so may his disciples; others say that since he died as a result of taking forbidden food, a Buddhist should not do so. However, fish, chicken, and eggs have often been a staple in Buddhist lands, with the exception of flesh meat. In Japan, which is both Shintō and Buddhist, beef was not eaten until the time of the first American consul, Townsend Harris, who had a cow slaughtered (c. 1855) for his dinner; he was oblivious of the trauma he caused, but some seventy-five years later the Japanese erected a memorial for the poor beast.

In the Zen Buddhist hall, wine, meat, garlic, onions, scallions, and horseradish may not be taken. A popular text among Buddhists, the *Vimalakirti Sūtra,* sums up the widespread sentiment in the Orient about food and the cosmos: "When one is identified with the food one eats, one is identified with the whole universe; when we are one with the whole universe, we are one with the food we eat." In this sense, if the universe is the Lord Buddha, the food, too, is the Lord Buddha, for, according to the *Lankāvatāra Sūtra,* a favorite of the Sixth Patriarch, Hui Nêng (q.v.), "Both concept and reality are equal as they are in the eye of the Buddhas, there being no difference between them whatever."

For related and parallel mystical concepts outside liturgical practices, see animals, numbers, and sleep.

Four Holy Truths, Buddh. See Four Noble Truths.

Four Infinite Minds, Buddh. They are also known as the Four Immeasurables, or the Four Universals. They are: kindness, pity, joy, and indifference.

Four Noble Truths (or Four Holy Truths), Buddh. As the result of his enlightenment under the bodhi tree, Gautama Buddha realized that there were four Truths existing in the universe. They are: Suffering, Craving, Nirvāṇa, and the Middle Way. In detail they are described by the Buddha as follows (as recorded by his disciples):

1. The Noble Truth of Suffering: Birth is suffering, old age is suffering, disease is suffering, death is suffering, to be united with the unpleasant is suffering, to be separated from the pleasant is suffering, not to receive what one craves is suffering; in brief, the five Aggregates of Attachment are suffering.

2. The Noble Truth of the Cause of Suffering: It is the craving that leads from rebirth to rebirth accompanied by lust of passion, which delights now here, now there; it is the craving for sensual pleasures, for existence, and for annihilation.

3. The Noble Truth of the Annihilation of Suffering (that is, nirvāṇa): It is the remainderless, total annihilation of this very craving the forsaking of it, the breaking loose, fleeing, deliverance from it.

4. The Noble Truth of the Path leading to the Annihilation of Suffering: It is the Noble Eightfold Path, which consists of Right Understanding, Right Thoughts, Right Speech, Right Action, Right Livelihood, Right Endeavor, Right Mindfulness, and Right Concentration.

The first three Noble Truths represent the philosophy of Buddhism, the fourth the ethics of Buddhism based upon that philosophy. Whether the various Buddhas exist or not, the four Truths nevertheless exist in the cosmos. The Buddhas only reveal these Truths, which lay hidden in the dark abysses of time. The Four Truths are dependent on the body itself. The Buddha stated: "In this very six-foot-long body, along with perceptions and thoughts, I proclaim the world, the origin of the world, the end of the world, and the path leading to the end of the world." See Buddha, Eightfold Path.

fuqahā, Isl. A Muslim canonist, invariably conservative in opinion.

fuqarā, Isl. The plural form of faqīr (q.v.).

◂G▸

Gandhi, Mohandas Karamchand (A.D. 1869–1948). The unifying power in twentieth-century Indian nationalism, which he accomplished with a shrewd use for political purposes of Hindu doctrines (ahiṁsā [q.v.] and self-discipline), at the same time, for a few brief decades at least, infusing India with a revived sense of its past greatness and its potentialities. He was born in Gujarat, a stronghold of Jainism (q.v.). His family were banyias, or merchant caste, and fervent Vaisnavites; his father and other close relatives had served as prime ministers to several princely states. Gandhi married at thirteen, his bride being a young girl named Kasturbai, a member of his own caste. His father died one night while Gandhi was making love to his bride, a traumatic experience that he spoke about throughout his life. At eighteen he left Kasturbai and his infant son to go to London to study law, though crossing the "Black Water" earned excommunication from his caste. In England he not only encountered Christianity in more enlightened forms, but was also introduced to English Theosophists (q.v.), who gave him Sir Edwin Arnold's translation of the *Bhagavad Gītā,* a work that was to influence his life. He made English friends, dressed like an Englishman, but despite temptations, remained a vegetarian and a celibate. At twenty-one he returned home. Two years later, unsuccessful as a lawyer in India, he went to South Africa to help a Gujarāti Muslim in a court case. Almost immediately upon landing he encountered his first experience with racial prejudice: He was ejected from a first-class train compartment as a coolie, and spent the night shivering on a cold, windswept railway station. It was an awakening, after his pleasant experiences with whites in London. He then decided to remain in South Africa to help the Indian community.

Though the Indians were subject to numerous racial, economic, and social barriers, they were, because of circumstances, free from the restrictions of caste and custom as in India. Meanwhile, Gandhi moved closer to what was to be called satyāgraha (q.v.), soul force or truth force. Despite the urging of some white Christian friends who hoped he would convert, and though he studied the New Testament and was especially impressed by the Sermon on the Mount, Gandhi became more and more of a Hindu. The Russian anarchist Piotr Kropotkin and especially John Ruskin, whose writings convinced him of the need to simplify his life, were among the seminal influences at this period. It was above all the New Testament and Ruskin that brought him further into the *Bhagavad Gītā* and the conviction that the ideal life was one of selfless service to one's fellow men. He founded an ashram near Durban, simplified his diet, gave up European clothing, and with Kasturbai's permission, took a vow of lifelong celibacy. Meanwhile he began to work out the actions for which he coined the term satyāgraha. He decided that the best method of righting wrongs was to protest nonviolently and to suffer lovingly rather than to submit to injustice. Over and over again, he and his followers, first in Africa and then in British-ruled India, allowed themselves to be jailed rather than obey laws they considered restrictive and anti-Indian. During one of his terms in prison he read Henry Thoreau's essay "Civil Disobedience," which helped reinforce his views that an honest man is duty-bound to resist or even violate unjust laws.

After twenty years in Africa, Gandhi returned to India, where he immediately became involved in the Indian freedom movement. He sided with indigo workers and millhands successfully. His leadership politicized the Congress movement from a group of westernized lawyers and intellectuals hoping for better jobs into a national revolutionary program. Thirty years of nonviolent activity eventually brought about the peaceful transfer of government from Great Britain to the Indians themselves. However, the Muslims refused to live in a communal state with Hindus, and demanded partition. Muslim-Hindu riots swept the subcontinent, and the Congress Party agreed to partition. In 1947 India was divided into a secular (but primarily Hindu) state and a Muslim state, Pakistan, which again was formed of two sections, one in East Bengal, the other in the Sind and Panjab. On January 30, 1948, a right-wing Hindu, enraged by Gandhi's attempts to bring Muslims together with Hindus, shot him dead.

GANDHI'S TENETS. Unlike many of the Congress leaders, especially Nehru, who pushed for an industrialization of India along Western lines, Gandhi stressed a return to the best of the ancient way of life. He wanted a large cottage industry, which would give the peasants (the bulk of India's people) their own control over their livelihood. He reaffirmed traditional Indian customs, such as caste, but worked for the elimination of untouchability, which, he said, "poisons Hinduism as a drop of arsenic poisons milk." He called cow protection "the central fact of Hinduism," since the cow symbolizes the entire subhuman world. One of his most important doctrines was that of ahiṁsā, or nonviolence, which he stated was not negative "but a positive state of love, of doing good even to the evildoer." In his teaching of satyāgraha, he said the major means were nonco-operation, civil disobedience, and fasting, which is the ultimate weapon and not to be lightly used.

Whatever Gandhi taught, he closely identified it with the Divine. "By ourselves we are insignificant worms," he wrote in an essay on the mantra Rāmanāma. "We become great when we reflect His greatness. Men make a fetish of their physical being while neglecting the immortal spirit. Anyone who bears Him in his or her heart has accession of a marvellous force or energy as objective in its results as, say electricity, but much subtler. . . . What an amount of labour and patience have been lavished by men to acquire the nonexistent philosopher's stone. Surely God's name is of infinitely richer value and always existent."

This insistence on the nearness of the Divine and man's absorption in it has led a number of Hindus, especially among the ordinary people who still remember him, to consider Gandhi as a twentieth-century avatār of Vishnu, an unusual concept, for most avatārs today are believed to be forms of Kālī. See ahiṁsā, avatār, caste, cow.

Ganeśa (Ganesh), Hind. The elephant-headed god. See Gaṇpati.

Gaṇgā (anglicized as Ganges), Hind. The most sacred of all India's rivers. The Gaṇgā begins in a cave in the Tibetan side of the Himālayas, dropping from heaven upon the god Shiva's matted hair; the river flows through the mountains in a torrential rush toward the great North Indian plain that ends in the delta on the

Bay of Bengal. From cave to sea is a drop of some three miles. The mountainous flow of the river attracts only the bravest and hardiest of pilgrims; most will begin their tour of the Gaṇgā at Rishikesh (the Place of the Rishis) above the foothills of the Himālayan mountains; the neighboring town of Hardwar (Place of Hari—i.e., Vishnu), fifteen miles downstream, is also one of the stops for pilgrims. Devotees bathe in the ice-cold waters throughout the year. Periodic melas or religious festivals are held at both sites; on the plain at Allahabad, at the junction of the Gaṇgā and the Yamunā (or Jumna), is another popular place of pilgrimage; here, every twelve years, is held the kumb mela, where as many as a million pilgrims (or two million?—no one can actually tell) may meet to pray. Farther across the plain is the holiest city of all, Banaras (q.v.), the greatest of all sacred cities. In Bengal the Gaṇgā meets the Brahmaputra, which has come from the eastern Himālayas, splits into a hundred mouths, and flows into the ocean. Her names change, her sacredness remains. On the branch of the Gaṇgā, the Hooghly, that flows through Calcutta, is the Kalighat; the Bengalis claim that this is the most sacred of all the river's most sacred banks. The Hooghly passes an island near the sea, Sagar, where every January an especially sacred festival, the Gaṇgā Sagar, is celebrated and where pilgrims can wash away their sins in the holy waters. A most revered object at Sagar is the block of stone, daubed in red powder, that is the image of the sage Kapila, whose powers have been justly celebrated in burning away sin and sinners; Kapila is considered an incarnation of Vishnu.

Despite the many festivals, the favored manner of worshiping at the Gaṇgā (as other holy rivers) is to walk up one bank and down the other. Hindus try to die on her banks and be cremated along her shores. Anyone whose ashes are placed in the river will go straight to heaven.

Tantra (q.v.) has made much of the Gaṇgā. In tantra the Gaṇgā is one of the three nādīs or mystical rivers of the human body. She is the Iḍā, the Yamunā the Piṅgalā, and the Sarasvatī the Suṣumnā; they meet at the mūlādhāra, the lowest of the cakras or mystical centers. The Gaṇgā is also the semen flowing from Shiva's liṅga (this sacred seed is stored in the moon). At Kāśi (the ancient name for Banaras; its etymology is the summit of the head) the three forms of the river unite: the celestial Gaṇgā (or

Milky Way), the earthly Gaṇgā, and the Underworld Gaṇgā (Pātāla Gaṇgā). See Benares, Shiva, Vishnu.

Ganges, Hind. The anglicized spelling of Gaṇgā, above.

Gaṇpati. A minor Hindu deity (sometimes also found in Buddhism). He is the son of the goddess Pārvatī (a form of Durgā) and later of the Lord Shiva. Gaṇpati is a jolly, pot-bellied creature, half man, half elephant, is a Lord of the People and a King of the Animals, being considered by forest tribes as the owner of the jungle and its creatures. He is often found at the entrances of villages, his image being smeared with red pigment, red lead in oil, or a cheap scarlet coloring matter—all substitutes for blood, a remnant of primitive sacrifices retained in the worship of such deities. Devotion to the Lord Elephant is ancient. At Poona, in the Kasba, the city's oldest temple, the Gaṇpati figures are nothing more than roughly carved boulders. The Lord Elephant is one of two animal deities so honored, the other being the monkey god Hanumān, the companion of Rāma. Gaṇpati's feast, under various names, is celebrated in late summer. It was originally a harvest festival in thanks for early crops and a propitiation for later ones to come. At high noon an image of the god is placed in a platform in a house. It is surrounded with lamps and mirrors, decorated with red-dyed rice, and offered rice puddings (of which Gaṇpati is said to be very fond). Artisans present their tools to him, and schoolchildren offer their books. In the evening a service of lights (āratī) is performed along with the singing of hymns. A few days later the image is immersed in a river to dissolve. Various interpretations of the cult have been adduced, one being that Gaṇpati (like other animals) is an ancient totem, another that he is descended from shamanism among the tribal peoples; in this connection is the legend of Shiva's horrendous dance in a flayed skin of an elephant. Gaṇpati is also known as Panpati, Gajendra, and Ganeśa (or Ganesh).

gaomaēz, Zor. See gōmēz.

Garuḍa, Hind. The divine bird (half man) upon whom Vishnu rides, sometimes in company with his consort Lakshmi (q.v.); normally they sit in the lotus position of meditation, rarely astride. A certain bird, popularly called a kite but classified as the Malabar eagle, is held to be the same creature as Garuḍa, and sight of him at specific times is a good omen. Garuḍa means "Wings of Speech." An ancient sky deity, possibly of totemic origin, he is known as Garutman in the Vedas. Esoterically he is the Word incarnate (or the Word made bird), being the hermetic utterances of the Vedas —occult sounds that can transport man from one world to another with the speed of light and the power of lightning. Garuḍa is the vāhan, or vehicle, of Vishnu; if the god himself is not atop the bird, his riders may be Vishnu's avatārs, Rāma and Krishna. Garuḍa is the personification of the Sky, the ethereal vehicle of Vishnu as the Sun. The Vedic fire altars constructed for the yajña ritual were built in the shape of Garuḍa, the divine bird lying flat on the ground with outstretched wings, his head pointing east toward the awakening sun. In the past, the temple women consecrated to Vishnu were tattooed upon their breasts with an image of Garuḍa; they were known as garuḍa-basavis (wives of Garuḍa). At night pious brahmins, as they lie down to sleep, offer a short prayer for Garuḍa's protection against snakes. A late development, after A.D. 1600, the result of Ṣūfī influence in India, brought a revival of Garuḍa, who took on some attributes of Simurgh, the mystical bird of ancient Persia symbolic of the Absolute Essence; the quest for the Simurgh was the theme of the Ṣūfī mystic Aṭṭār's *The Parliament of the Birds,* a work well known in the Muslim areas of the subcontinent. See Aṭṭār, Vishnu, yajña.

gāthā, Buddh. A poem or a chant; the term also applies to one of the twelve divisions of the Mahāyāna Buddhist canon.

Gāthā, Zor. A song or hymn in the Avesta (q.v.), most likely the work of the Prophet Zoroaster himself. The Gāthās form the heart of the Zoroastrian liturgy and are the most archaic portion of the Avesta. The Zoroastrian Gāthā has no connection with the Buddhist gāthā, above. See Zoroaster.

Gautama Buddha. The individual generally known as the Buddha (q.v.).

Gāyatri mantra, Hind. The most important of Vedic mantras (it is found in the Rig Veda, 3.62.10); it is the core utterance in the prayers said three times daily by Hindus of the higher castes (low castes and women may not say it). Hindus forced to shorten the complicated daily rituals will still recite the Gāyatri mantra, especially in the morning at sunrise. The prayer invokes the sun god Savitṛ, which is the sound from which the sun was created; Savitṛ is the name given the sun when it is not visible at night and during both eclipses of the sun and moon (when the mantra is also said). The prayer reads: *ŌṂ. O terrestrial sphere! O sphere of space! O celestial sphere! Let us contemplate the splendor of the solar spirit, the Divine Creator. May he guide our minds. ŌṂ.* This mantra is repeated 108 times on a rosary in the morning facing east by the orthodox brāhmin.

geh, Zor./Par. The obligatory prayers, said five times a day, starting with sunrise. The word geh means "watch." The first geh, which is the "time for extracting hoama" (q.v.), runs until noon; from noon until three P.M. is the "period of heat"; thence until sunset, the "period of turning out"; sunset to midnight is the time for the recital of epics and hymns; last, the hours until sunrise are known as "drawing near to dawn." A bell is rung in the fire temples (q.v.) at the beginning of each geh, and every Zoroastrian who has been formally received into the community in the navzote ceremony (q.v.) is obligated to pray. The prayers, which are said facing the sun, change slightly during the day and according to the season.

Each geh has its own protector archangel. In its esoteric significance the geh is the symbol of the spiritual evolution of the soul in its ascent to liberation, light, and wisdom, commencing with dawn. See Zoroastrianism.

Ge-lugs-pa, Tib. See Yellow Hat.

al-Ghazālī (A.D. 1059–1111) (Literally, "The Spinner") ('Abu Ḥamid Muhammad al-Ghazālī), Isl. Islami theologian and mystic, born at Tus in Khurāsān. Beginning at twenty and continuing into his late thirties, he experienced a series of intense spiritual crises, during which he came to doubt the foundations of all knowledge. He was appointed to the chair of professor at Baghdad, where in a reaction to the popular Aristotelian (or neo-Platonic) philosophers he wrote the *Tahāfut al-Falāsifah.* However, he was not interested in attempting a new philosophical system but in correcting what was erroneous in others and in saving what was useful. He came to believe that no metaphysic, purely and rationally constructed, would satisfy man's need of certainty. But the spiritual crisis he was experiencing soon overwhelmed him and he left the university to become a pilgrim and a wanderer among the Ṣūfīs (q.v.), spending twelve years, the traditional period for such training, as a faqīr (q.v.). In his search for inner experience he found a different quality of certainty among the mystics from what he had known within scholastic theology. He made God more personal. As the result of his experience, finding the orthodox formula inadequate and distant, the famous Creed, "There is no god but God" [God=Allāh] became "There is no god but Thou." Al-Ghazālī returns again and again in his works (of which there are many) to the thought of Allāh as Light and Beauty. "The beauty of His works prove that He Himself is Perfect Beauty," said al-Ghazālī, and the contemplation of this Beauty fills men's hearts with love, so that they long to look upon the All-Beautiful. All other lights are but "partial rays of reflections of His Light." Allāh is immeasurably transcendent yet infinitely near. "When My servant calls to Me, I answer him, and to him who seeks forgiveness I will not grudge it, for I am at hand, ready to listen to his request." He drew the wrath of orthodox theologians on one hand (and of contemporary Ṣūfīs on the other) for stating that man is subject to predestination, for God not only directs man's outer actions but also infuses man with the motives for whatever good or evil he does and the resulting rewards and punishments. Man is but a soiled, rusty mirror, which needs constant polishing to reflect the beauty of the higher world; his soul is a caged bird attempting to escape to Heaven; his heart is a double door, one leading outward to the mundane, the other toward the Inner Kingdom, the door of "inspiration and revelation." After his death, though not during his life, al-Ghazālī was accepted by the Ṣūfīs as one of them. See Islam, Ṣūfī, and Ṣūfism.

Gita Govinda, Hind. An erotic poem with an underlying theme of bhakti by the twelfth-century Bengali brahmin Jayadeva celebrating the passionate love of Krishna and Rādhā, the most beloved of the gopīs (cowgirls) who attended him. This frankly sexual work is, its devotees claim, a conversation between the individual and the Unlimited, the love of Rādhā and Krishna being the divine play (līlā), the meeting and the loving union between eternal nature and the Unlimited. The work finds its visual parallel in the erotic sculpture of the medieval temples, in which sexual love is proclaimed as a valid means to attain religious salvation.

gnosis, gnostic, Gnosticism. Gnosis is a Greek term meaning knowledge; it has also come to be a catch-all phrase for a variety of religious movements with similar themes, primarily those in which some ancient esoteric lore is believed to be transmitted through a small circle of initiates. Many forms of Gnosticism have Zoroastrian antecedents or influences. Gnosis implies the knowledge—actually the *vision*—of the Divine, which is often expressed in terms of a single deity—"God"—who is above and beyond lesser deities or powers manifested in various attributes. The school of writings attributed to the followers of the Greek resident in Egypt, Hermes Trismegistus (the first three Christian centuries), taught that God is ineffable—"Of Him no words can tell, no tongue can speak; silence alone can declare Him." Even among the Christian gnostics, though some patterned their movements after the structure of orthodox Christianity, with similar ceremonies, hierarchy, and ecclesiastical buildings, many eliminated all in such superficialities to emphasize personal experience of the Divine received under an enlightened teacher.

Gnostic knowledge of whatever form was open only to the initiate and not to the layman. The gnostic was engaged in the search for unnameable, ineffable, and supercelestial mysteries revealed only to the Thought of the Immutable. God, however, is utterly inconceivable.

In its purest form, Gnosticism is but a phase of Zoroastrianism; many of the concepts are similar. Gnostics were found all over the East in the pre-Christian period in areas that had been under Iranian rule; Zoroastrian doctrines as gnosis, in pure or adulterated form, were noted among Egyptians, Jews, Greeks, and later among Christians and Muslims. The Essenes of the second century B.C., in their *Manual of Discipline,* exhibit sound Zoroastrian dualism, worked out by the twin spirits of Truth and Perversity. Basically, in all the sects, though there are many variations and much adaptation and alteration according to the milieu, Gnosticism teaches a single, unknowable divine power, God, in His most formidable and unknowable form, beyond grasp by most men but subject to approach by initiates who have received ancient lore of great wisdom transmitted through various sages and saints. God is above everything and all, but there are a number of luminaries—angels, deities, demi-urges, emanations, spirits, and so on—who perform various functions, from the creation of matter, to incarnating certain phenomena (such as the moon or the sun), or as representatives of qualities like wisdom, justice, truth, and knowledge. Basic to gnosis are the dual antagonistic forces of good and evil battling over the world. Evil presents formidable questions: What is it? What is its nature? Why does it exist? In general, evil exists so that good can save mankind. The dualism can reach violent extremes: Matter is despised and hated as a form of evil, while the soul struggles for union with the Divine despite the chains of the world. Direct contact with the godhead may be impossible: The soul reaches out through a series of intermediaries, deities, demi-urges, or other celestial beings. To the gnostic the battle between good and evil—Light and Darkness—is at the origin of all things. In some sects, God is the creator of the dual powers; in others, he is above them—"In the beginning there existed Light and Darkness," said the Greek Basilides. "These originated from themselves and were not generated by any other principle."

The presence of so much evil often led the gnostic to identify it with the world: Matter itself becomes literally evil and must be rejected, and thus, in many gnostic movements, family and home, possessions and loyalties are to be abandoned. Such types of gnosticism had a profound effect upon the beliefs of the medieval Christian groups such as the Bulgari and the Cathari, resulting in their persecution by the orthodox. On the other side, gnosis has assumed a much more positive form among certain Ṣūfic movements, which place the emphasis on the Divine and not on the duality of good and evil, gnosis being a Way—not the only nor the best—to intimate knowledge with the Divine. Among some Ṣūfīs, gnosis serves as an example of limited rather than complete knowledge; others take it uncritically. One of the most important versions of Zoroastrianism as gnosis surfaced in the third century B.C. as Manichaeism, the brilliant and influential movement founded by the Persian Mani, who had traveled extensively in the Middle East and India. Mani, originally a Zardushti, incorporated elements of Buddhism and Christianity into his own Zoroastrianism, calling the founders of the three religions his "brothers," but stating that his doctrine was the superior. Most of the Manichaean scriptures were destroyed by enemies, not only Christians but also Buddhists and Muslims, and it is only recently that the discovery of long-lost documents in places like Chinese Turkestan has revealed some of his true teachings. See Zoroaster, Zoroastrianism.

Golden Womb, Hind. An ancient, post-Vedic ritual in which certain esteemed indigenous leaders, usually princes, warriors, or priests, were received into the Āryan caste structure as "twice born." For details, see jar-born.

gōmēz, Zor. The term is gaomaēz in the Avesta (q.v.); gōmēz in the latter Pahlavi and modern Persian. It originally meant, literally, "beef's urine"; it is prescribed in the Vidēvdāt (q.v.) and when consecrated it becomes nirang, a source of life that combats the impurity of death and other defilement; it partakes of the fecundating power of the sperm. It is a key tool in the rite of bareshnum (q.v.), a ceremony of purification. At death, the modbed or priest pours a few drops on the dying person's lips; the corpse is also rubbed with gōmēz in preparation for the funeral. See bareshnum, disposal of the dead, Zoroastrianism.

gompa, Tib. A Tibetan Buddhist monastery (the same type is found also in Bhutan and Sikkim). The term gompa means "a dwelling in solitude." Monks in a gompa gather with the primary purpose of following a spiritual path, not necessarily in common. The gompa cannot be compared to a Christian monastery. In the gompa, the wealthy buy their own quarters and will have servants; a poor monk rents his cell, and may work for others. The ranking of a lāma can depend on his family's wealth. Gompas are also colleges and accept pupils from the age of eight or nine. A student's education depends on the kind of teacher he can afford to hire. Subjects generally include philosophy and metaphysics, ritual and magic, medicine (according to Chinese and Indian methods), and the Scriptures. The lāmas are celibate.

gopī, Hind. One of the young women, daughters of cowherds, with whom the god Krishna "dallied" as a young man. (The account is found in the tenth book of the *Bhāgavata Purāṇa,* c. ninth century A.D.) The gopīs were distraught with love for the god; their love became the symbol of love of the soul for God, and this self-abandonment became central to the cult of Krishna. The openly sexual mysticism centered around Krishna helped give the bhakti movement its tremendous passionate spirituality. Each gopī felt that she alone was Krishna's beloved and that she alone experienced the divine embrace. Though each gopī had her husband and children, the gopīs in unison answered, "Thou art in all, and thou art all. By serving thee we serve all." In the ecstatic cults of the Middle Ages the erotic plays a central role: An act of disinterested love could not be found with the marriage partner, since this form of sexual union was associated primarily with the birth of children. Transfiguring ecstasy was believed more easily attainable through adulterous, abnormal, and incestuous intercourse.

Krishna's favorite among the gopīs was Rādhā, their love being celebrated in song and story, especially in the *Gīta Govinda* (q.v.). Bhaktas commonly identified themselves with Rādhā in their search for the highest bliss, on the theory that the soul must play the female in all dealings with God, the universal male. "Are we not all females before the Lord?" asked the sixteenth-century saint Mira Bai.

Symbolically, when Krishna stole the clothes of the gopīs as they bathed, he removed the artificial coverings imposed on man in his cycle of life and death. There were eight gopīs (for the purposes of this example), who were freed of the Eight Bonds (or pasa)—pity, ignorance, shame, family, custom, caste, worldy pleasure, and society—which clothe the soul (or jīva). Swami Vivekānanda (1863–1902) called Krishna's play with the gopīs "most difficult to understand" until one has "become perfectly chaste and pure"—that "most marvelous expansion of love, allegorized and expressed in that beautiful play . . . which none can understand but he who has become mad with, and drunk deep of, the cup of love. . . . Love that wants nothing, loves that does not care even for heaven, love that does not care for anything in this world or the world to come." See bhakti, Krishna.

Gotama Buddha. A variant form of Gautama Buddha (q.v.).

Govind, Govinda, Hind. One of the common names for Krishna (q.v.). Govind means cowherd; and he is the Rescuer of the Earth.

Govind Singh (1666–1708). The tenth and last Guru of the Sikhs. He reorganized the Sikh community along military lines, infusing the members with a crusading, anti-Muslim spirit, and proclaimed himself as the final Guru, establishing the Granth Sāheb (the Noble Book, the Sikh scriptures) as the eternal Guru for his people. See Sikhism.

grāmadevatā, Hind. A village deity, often feminine in nature and a manifestation of the Great Mother or Devī. The sites of the cults, which are widespread and unrelated, but which may be said to be generally expressions of worship of the universal Mother, are usually located under trees or in their vicinity. The cult figures are in most cases simple stone images of the female organ, the yoni (q.v.), which is adorned in some manner with red (powder, liquid, or paint being common) and with flowers and incense. Though stone is the standard medium, some images may be made of wood or clay or other less durable material. The cults are most prevalent in South India, among the "Dravidians" (q.v.), and are of ancient origin. While a mother deity is most often found, some grāmadevatās may be manifestations of Vishnu, Brahmā, and other male gods, or of various demons, yoginis, and other minor divinities. See Devī, Hinduism.

granthi, Hind. Knot; a knot of the ego, which ties down the ātmā (soul) and makes it feel fettered. The granthi can be loosened in meditation, and eventually, if meditation is successful, unraveled. The contemporary mystic Ananadamayee Ma (q.v.) has stated:

"So long as the knots that constitute the ego are not unraveled, even though you intend to act impersonally, you will get hurt, and this will produce a change in the expression of your eyes and face, and be apparent in your whole manner. A knot means resistance."

Granth Sāheb, Sikh. The leading scripture of the Sikhs, composed primarily by the fifth Guru, Arjun (1563–1606) shortly before his death and being issued in a final recension by Govind Singh (1666–1708), the tenth and last, who proclaimed the Granth as the Eternal Guru. The work consists of material from a number of sources, not only the Sikh Gurus (especially the first five) but also from various Hindu and Ṣūfī sources, such as those of the bhakti poet saints, the low-caste weaver Kabīr being one of the most important. The hymns are written in six languages, including Punjabi (which uses the Gurumukhi alphabet developed by the founder of the movement, Guru Nānak), and are arranged not according to the Gurus and saints who composed them but according to the thirty-one ragas or musical modes to which they are set. The Granth begins with Nānak's Jap-ji, the key to Sikh spirituality and the epitome of Sikh doctrines. The mixed origins of the Granth Sāheb make it a difficult work to interpret, for there is no Sikh priesthood to give direction to its eclectic themes. Still, it is a work of intense personal devotion, of yearning for the Eternal One. Peace, love, and serenity are the intertwining themes. The classical Indian ragas to which it is set, with their mystical, somewhat remote, but moving melodies, played on traditional instruments, are hauntingly beautiful. The Granth Sāheb is sometimes called Ādi-Granth (Initial Book) to distinguish it from the nonsacred militaristic Daśam Granth (Book of the Tenth Guru). See Jap-ji, Nānak, Sikhs.

guṇa, Hind. The three properties or aspects of prakṛti (q.v.), or primordial matter. The properties are sattva (or sattwa), rajas, and tamas. Sattva is the quality of harmony, lightness, and luminosity; consciousness is its important function. Rajas is energy and whatever produces motion. Tamas is inertia, heaviness, darkness. The guṇas constantly act and react upon each other, in a steady movement of suppression, one being dominant, for the time being, over the others. Thus, as long as the world exists, the guṇas are in a state of disturbed equilibrium.

Until the self, called the puruṣa (q.v.), can rise above the struggle of the guṇas, it cannot be free. Several means are available, the two most popular of which are yoga (q.v.) in its classical form and bhakti (q.v.).

gurav, Hind. A non-brāhmin priest who serves the lower castes in a village. Such priests are usually unlettered but nevertheless knowledgeable in rites, rituals, ceremonies, and traditional religious lore. See Hinduism.

guru, Hind. A spiritual guide and teacher, who leads a siśyā or chela (disciple or pupil) into the spiritual path, directing him, it is hoped, toward final realization. At the proper point the guru will bestow initiation (dīkṣā, q.v.) on his disciple and give him the sacred saying (mantra, q.v.) that will guide him the remainder of his life. The definitions of a guru are many: "A guru is he who, out of deep darkness, can reveal the Truth." "A guru is none other than the World Teacher" i.e., the guru, though human, is also the Divine. This is not to say that each guru actually possesses the ideal qualities and attributes to be an authentic spiritual master. Many gurus never progress along the spiritual path, and thus blocked, their pupils are also blocked unless they are fortunate enough to receive a divine grace that enables them to surpass their teacher.

There is in reality but one Guru, according to the tantrics (q.v.). The ordinary human guru is but the manifestation on the phenomenal plane of the Supreme Guru. He it is who enters into and speaks with the voice of the earthly guru at the moment of bestowing dīkṣā. The guru is not to be thought of mere man. "Guru can save the disciple from the wrath of Shiva but none can save from the wrath of guru." There is also a responsibility on the part of the siśyā: The sins of the disciple recoil upon the guru.

Traditionally the guru incarnates the highest value anyone may look for in a human being. Without a guru no one can become twice born (dvijā, q.v.), a caste Hindu. Ideally the disciple lives for twelve years with his guru; in the past, besides studying the Vedas at the foot of his master, and learning to perfection all the rites and rituals of the ancient scriptures—this orally, since the sacred texts were transmitted by word of mouth—he would also care for his cattle, but any agricultural work needed to provide food for the master and his pupils would be done by others. Theoretically such a way of life continues; in practice, training has been reduced to a few months, more often to a few hours of instruction, so that today the guru, in bestowing dīkṣā upon his disciple and in giving the mantra, can teach and give initiation only symbolically.

One retains his guru for life, for without a guru one cannot hope to attain liberation (mukti). One must seek out his guru, who will test the would-be pupil severely, even reject him at first. Sometimes this rejection is permanent, and the siśyā must continue his search until he finds the right master, who, from all accounts, will *know* that the disciple is seeking him out. Once accepted, and having passed the tests, the siśyā takes up residence with his guru, living in unquestioning obedience, regarding him as the sole and all-sufficient source of truth. It is not a question of merely assimilating doctrine and knowledge but also of undergoing a radical change of existence, transposing one's entire life to different psychic, physical, and spiritual levels.

The best guru is one who is jīvan-mukta—i.e., one who has obtained liberation before death. Thus, living on a dual level, one of the apex of a soul that enjoys the taste of the divine, the other of the common plane in which he strives to lead the siśyā's inner eye to his own level, the guru is Truth Itself. However, the guru, as the perfected being, need not teach verbally; also of spiritual value is his charisma, expressed in the term darśana (sight, vision, from which one gains spiritual benefit merely by being in the presence of a quasidivine individual). A true guru does not advertise nor look for disciples, as do some who have come to the West, or as Westerners do who believe themselves in possession of some mystic insights. The true guru exists, with his disciples, in the depths of silence, relying on voluntary contributions for sustenance. Needless to say, frauds abound, and Indians are as likely to be taken in as Westerners.

To place one's self at the foot of a guru is a psychic quest of great danger. Near the beginning of the relationship the guru often, if not invariably, demolishes the disciple's ego. The guru destroys in order to rebuild. This is an extremely hazardous encounter on all levels for the siśyā, and in the hands of an inadequate guru irreparable harm can be and has been caused. The disciple who tries to protect himself cannot continue. Full submission is demanded, for the guru can work only with completely malleable material. See ashram, Hinduism.

gurudvara, Sikh. Guru's gate, a Sikh temple. Most are in the Punjab, India, the homeland of the Sikhs. The gurudvara is also a school meeting house and resting place for travelers. The building is marked by a yellow flagpole displaying a triangular yellow flag with the Sikh symbol, two crossed swords and a dagger against a circle, symbolizing martial virtues within the eternal circle of the spiritual. There are no statues or idols in a gurudvara, the central and most precious object being a copy of the Scriptures, the Granth Sāheb (Noble Book), displayed on a charpoy (or low cot) draped with expensive rugs and fabrics. Offerings such as money or food may be placed before the book. The worshiper will approach the Granth Sāheb, which is literally the mystic personality of the Sikh Gurus, barefoot but with head covered with a turban or shawl and bow to the ground, the forehead touching the earth. See Granth Sāheb, Nānak, Sikhs.

◂H▸

ḥadīth, Isl. The total collection of the sayings, reported deeds, and even silent approvals of the Prophet Muḥammad. The Qur'ān enjoins the faithful to follow the example of the Prophet, to most Muslims infallible and sinless (cf. *Fiqh Akbar II*). Ḥadīth is supplementary to the Qur'ān, which is solely God's revelation and not the words of the Prophet, and teachings not found in it are sought in ḥadīth as an expression of the source closest to Allāh. Ḥadīth as the sayings and practice of the Prophet is tradition as a matter of record; tradition as a matter of obligation is sunna (q.v.). Attestation to the correctness of a ḥadīth is isnād (q.v.). By the ninth century A.D. the tremendous number of ḥadīth, running into the hundreds of thousands, with many obviously spurious, brought about a massive attempt to collect, sift, organize, and edit the entire known body. The best scholars in Islam were engaged in the effort. The results were a number of collections of scrupulously edited canonical ḥadīth. The six most famous are known as *The Six Genuine Ones;* that by Muḥammad ibn Isma'il al-Bukhari (A.D. 810–70), entitled *Sahih* (the "Genuine"), is the most famous, and is placed next to the Qur'ān by many Muslims, especially by the Sunnī, who were greatly influenced by the work of the Ahl al-Ḥadīth (the People of the Ḥadīth). See sunna, Sunnī.

hajj, Isl. The pilgrimage to Mecca. Hajj is the "fifth pillar" of religion. The Qur'ān (in Sura iii, 97) enjoins every Muslim capable of travel—and who can afford it—the obligation to visit Mecca at least once in his lifetime. A person who has made the pilgrimage is known as hājj. See Islam, Ka'ba, Mecca, Muḥammad.

Hakuin (A.D. 1685–1768), Buddh. One of the most famous of all Zen roshis (masters), Hakuin revitalized his own sect, Rinzai (q.v.), and reorganized the method of employing kōans (q.v.), the nonverbal puzzle, in teaching as an aid to enlightenment. Hakuin divided the teaching with kōans into five stages, from the easy "enters into the frontier gate of Zen" to the "hard to penetrate," climaxed by a sixth stage, in which the novice studies Buddhist precepts and the monastic life in the knowledge of his Zen training. Hakuin is famous for the kōan, "What is the sound of one hand clapping?" which he developed from a Chinese saying. He was also a noted poet, essayist, and painter; as artist he practiced a type of art known as zenga, or Zen painting, which has a special spiritual power, refreshing naïveté, and humor. Hakuin deprecated the easy way to salvation as evinced in the Pure Land sects and preached the incomparable power of Zen, saying that satori as he himself experienced it (at the age of twenty-four) was possible for all, which he expressed in three mystical states: the Great Doubt, the Great Enlightenment, and the Great Joy. He is credited with the development and training of some eighty Zen roshis as successors. See Zen.

al-Ḥallāj, Isl. A Ṣūfī mystic who was martyred in Baghdad in A.D. 922 for statements contrary to orthodox Islamic beliefs. His full name was al-Ḥusayn ibn Manṣūr, but he was commonly called al-Ḥallāj, the Wool Carder. He openly preached Ṣūfism not only in Iraq but also in Iran, India, and Central Asia. His was an extreme form of the doctrine of union with God. One of his best-known verses, which summarizes this teaching, says: "I am he whom I love, and he whom I love is I/We are two spirits dwelling in one body/If thou seest me, thou seest Him/And if thou seest Him, thou seest us both." Also: "Thy Spirit is mingled with my spirit, even as wine is mingled with pure water/When anything touches Thee, it touches me too, in every case Thou art I." The orthodox accused him of having identified himself with God when he said, "Anā'l-Haqq" (*I* am the Truth)—a statement that led to his arrest. He was also accused of sorcery. When he was arrested he cured the khalif and his mother of intestinal problems with the laying on of hands; however, the khalif, despite his mother's protestations, surrendered al-Ḥallāj to the will of the orthodox. Eighty of the leading lawyers of Baghdad signed a deposition saying, "His death is necessary for the peace of Islam; may his blood be upon our hands." These incidents and al-Ḥallāj's "passion"—for he was flogged in public, mutilated, crucified, hung on a gibbet, and burned—have endeared him to many Christians. The Ṣūfī poet Rumī (q.v.) was to rank al-Ḥallāj with the prophets and saints in whom God has revealed himself, among them Noah, Abraham, Jesus, and Muḥammad. See Islam, Ṣūfī.

han, Buddh. The wooden temple gong (most often a board) that is struck in Japanese Buddhist temples to mark certain hours of the day and the time for various events.

Hanafī, Isl. One of the four "rites" or legal schools of Sunnī Islam. The Hanifīs are strongest in Turkey, Pakistan, India, and parts of China, all of which had been under the domination at one time or another of various Turkish tribes, who had been converted to this form of Islam. A small branch of the Hanafīs was founded in the United States in 1967 by Hamaas Abdul Khaalis, who broke away from the Black Muslims (q.v.), considering that movement as not properly orthodox.

hanif, Isl. A monotheistic, anti-idolatrous member of a small, probably not-organized sect in Arabia, predominantly in the area of Mecca, at the time of the Prophet Muḥammad. The antecedents of the hanifs are in doubt; they may have had a long history, but little is known about them. According to the Qur'ān and to Islamic tradition they were proponents of the pure monotheism of the Prophet Ibrāhīm (Abraham), who had preceded both the Mosaic Law and Christianity. In some accounts they appear as beings anxiously in search of the truth; they also appear as celestial wanderers. The hanifs seemingly had a strong influence on Muḥammad in the period before his receiving his Qur'ānic revelations. Ṣūfī (q.v.) tradition states that the hanifs practiced meditation in a cave and that Muḥammad followed their example; it was during one such retreat that his visions began. See Islam, Muḥammad.

Han Shan (A.D. 1546–1623), Buddh. A Ch'an master, born Te Ch'ing (he is known as Kanzan in Japan, where he is very popular), who was instrumental in the revival of Ch'an during the T'ang dynasty. His name means Silly Mountain; he was a famed recluse, and with a brother hermit, San-lai, wrote a collection of poems known as the *Han-shan Shi* or *Sanrai Shi* (in Japanese, *Kanzan Shi* or *Sanrai Shi*). Han Shan was known as a madman, but his poems are highly expressive of the Ch'an appreciation of nature, as well as of the Ch'an way of life. One example:

> In rags, in rags,
> Again in rags—this is my life:
> For food I pick herbs by the roadside,
> In the moonlight I sit meditating the whole long night.
> Looking at the flowers, I forget to go home.
> This simple life I have adopted
> Ever since joining the Sangha.

Hanumān, Hind. The monkey-faced demigod, a companion to Rāma, one of the avatārs of Vishnu. Hanumān is also known as Māruti. Hanumān is seen in either of two representations: one, as Master of the Spirits, in profile, with his tail curling over his head; the other, as the perfect devotee, in full face, with his hands joined in prayer. He is one of the popular deities of northern India; his image is also found in almost all the ancient forts in the South. His father is Vāyu, the Lord of the Winds and the King of the Celestial Musicians. In some northern areas it is believed that Hanumān, by containing his semen, gained the strength to overcome otherwise insuperable obstacles. See Rāma.

ḥarām, Isl. Something forbidden, sacred, or tabooed. Part of the area outside Mecca is ḥarām—prohibited—to pilgrims; all of the city is ḥarām to non-Muslims. Medina also, and certain sanctuaries in Jerusalem and elsewhere, are ḥarām. The act of sin is described as ḥarām. The term is also applied to the women's section of a house, the usage most common to foreigners.

Hare Krishna (sect), Hind.[?] A movement founded in 1965 by the Hindu A. C. Bhaktivedanta Swami Prabhupada, who established himself as a guru after arriving in the United States. The formal name of the sect is The International Society for Krishna Consciousness, and it practices a form of bhakti (q.v.) through a limited and puritanical worship of the Dark One of the Indian populace. Hare Krishna is strongest in the Western nations but has also sent missionaries to India; their purpose has not been understood by the Indians. To orthodox Hindus Hare Krishna is an amusing but sometimes annoying aberration of traditional doctrines, as one cannot become a Hindu by conversion but by birth in the karmic cycle. The members of the sect are virtually all whites; they wear traditional Indian clothing and chant hymns in praise of the Lord Krishna. Despite criticism of their doctrine, some observers find that the sect offers a cheerful and joyous approach to the question of finding solace in a mechanistic world.

Hari, (also Hare), Hind. One of the most common names for the god Vishnu. Hari is the remover of ignorance and its effects, and takes away sorrow and gives consolation. A most popular devotion to Vishnu in his aspect as Hari is in the hymn "Hari Krishna, Hari Rām." See Vishnu.

Hari-Hara, Hind. A dual deity with the combined attributes of Siva (q.v.) for the right side of the body and Vishnu (q.v.) for the left. The cult began in the ninth century A.D. in an attempt to reconcile the growing antagonism between the great feudal lords, who worshiped Shiva and his consort Devī and the smaller landholders who followed Krishna as incarnation of Vishnu. Though the cult seemed to be simply a theological dispute among the devotees of the two great gods Shiva and Vishnu, underlying it was an intense social conflict. As social conditions changed, the cult began to wither away, and it died out after the eleventh century.

harijan. "The people of God," the name the Mahatma Gandhi (q.v.) bestowed on the so-called untouchables, the great dispossessed mass of Indians who live outside and below the system of caste (q.v.). Though Gandhi called untouchability "an ineffaceable blot that Hinduism today carries with it," and labeled the custom an evil and a curse, stating, "I think we are bound to consider every affliction in this sacred land is a proper punishment for the indelible crime we are committing," the curse still exists. Gandhi did much to bring the plight of the harijans before caste Indians, but aside from some temporary relaxation of ancient customs, the situation for harijans is still grave. Of importance for the harijans themselves is that through education and political action, they can help themselves, for no one else will aid them. Their efforts, however, have led to violence, in which, not having the weapons of their enemies, they are invariably the losers. But progress is coming slowly, and India has reached the stage, similar to other societies, where businesses, government offices, factories, universities, and social groups may have their token harijan. See caste, Hinduism.

hegira, Isl. See hijra, following.

hijra (also hegira), Isl. The Prophet Muḥammad's flight or migration (in the sense of breaking ties with his natal city) from Mecca to Medina in A.D. 622. Forced by deteriorating circumstances to leave Mecca, the Prophet and a small band of followers escaped the city at the peril of their lives. Muḥammad and his uncle Abū Bakr spent three days hiding in a cave, and then, on camels furnished by disciples, crossed the desert in seven days to Medina, then called Yathrib. The hijra marks the beginning of the Islamic calendar. Muḥammad arrived on the outskirts of Yathrib on Monday, First Rabi' 12 (September 20, 622) and entered the city itself on Friday. However, the calendar is dated from the first day of the first month of that year, corresponding to July 16, 622. See calendar, Medina, Muḥammad.

Hīnayāna Buddhism. The Lesser Way (or Little Raft) as opposed to Mahāyānist Buddhism, the Greater Way. Hīnayāna Buddhism is that followed by Sri Lanka (Ceylon) and some of the Southeast Asian countries. It emphasizes the necessity of saving knowledge and preaches the salvation as an individual responsibility, each person alone being capable of attaining it without the aid of outside agencies. The central institution of Hīnayāna is the Sangha, the celibate Brotherhood of bhikkus (q.v.) who wander about singly or in small groups begging for a livelihood and existing in the utmost simplicity. A few women may also belong to such groups. Hīnayāna stresses the Three Refuges—the Buddha, the Dhamma, and the Sangha—while Mahāyāna puts the focus on a wider path —the (various) Buddhas, the bodhisattvas (the buddhas in progress), and the Dharmakāya (i.e., the subtle body of Essence, one of the bodies of the transformed Buddha). Hīnayāna, which claims to be the only form that follows the original teaching of the Gautama Buddha, came under severe criticism from the other schools. Hīnayāna is dismissed by the Mahāyānists (especially the Chinese) as but a preparation for more complex methods, and preached to disciples of limited receptiveness. The great eighteenth-century Zen master Hakuin said the Hīnayānists "were inferior in methods of discipline and were fond of quietude; they simply had no knowledge of the noble attitudes of a bodhisattva." However, he wondered "if present-day students of Zen can equal them in the power of their insight and in the brilliance of their wisdom and virtue." An important form of Hīnayāna, with which it is often confused, is Theravāda (q.v.). See also Buddha, Buddhism, Mahāyāna.

Hinduism. The Way of the majority of the people of India, a Way that is a combination of religious belief, rites, customs, and daily practices, many of which appear overtly secular but in most cases have religious origins and sanctions. Hinduism is noted as being the only one of the major beliefs that cannot be defined, for any definition is inadequate, contradictory, and incomplete. Yet define it one must, for its influence is worldwide, its subtleties are immense and complex, and, more or less, it forms, if one includes its offshoots and daughter faiths of Buddhism, Jainism, and Sikhism, plus various schools of tantra and bhakti (which often incorporate Buddhist and Ṣūfic concepts respectively), some fifty per cent of the earth's peoples.

We will endeavor to outline (but briefly) Hinduism in various spheres—geographically, historically, doctrinally, etc.

GEOGRAPHICALLY: The members of the Hindu Way live mainly in the Indian subcontinent, in what is popularly called India, but Bharāt by the government after an ancient Āryan tribe. There are smaller numbers of Hindus, more or less following the major groups, in Nepal, Bali, Java, the island of Trinidad, the nation of Guyana, and in scatterings throughout Africa, Malaysia, the United Kingdom, the United States, and Canada.

ORIGINS: Hinduism is primordial. It always *was*. Hindu records are scanty, for time and history are irrelevant in the great cycles of the ages. Myth and fact are inextricably entwined. Historical figures blend into the gods, and the gods descend to earth. A bewildering number of semihistorical personages, shadowy and elusive, appear in the ancient epics. Are they human or divine, imaginary, literary, real? What has been added or eliminated, blended or altered by later redactors? One reaches for fact, grasps a chimera, but finds a work of unimagined beauty that puts man face to face not only with the Supreme Divinity but also with his own Immortal Self. But to pinpoint a few facts: Hinduism as it is known today is the amalgamation, fusion, melding of two major elements, one the "Dravidian" strata of prehistory, on archaic folk levels often of the most primitive, which can be traced, in informed guesses, back some five thousand years, before which all is immersed in the primordial mists; and the second, the Vedic-Āryan overlays, roughly some thirty-five hundred years in age.

What is known about the early periods, of the "Dravidian" layers, comes largely from the excavations of the cities of the Indus Valley (q.v.). Here was a civilization of unsuspected complexities and depths, highly structured and formalized, and religious in nature, centered on parallel worship of a Great Mother and a yogi-like god who is equated with the Lord Shiva (q.v.).

Cults of water, trees, the sun, snakes, animals, and other aspects of nature have also been identified, and are still powerful today, especially among the rural peoples. Another element, long lost and defying analysis and explanation, was that of a Sacred Unicorn, baffling, mysterious, male, which had an important role in Indus life, in a manner that cannot even be surmised.

The second major force, that of the Vedic Āryans who entered India from the Northwest as nomadic warriors, is relatively clear, once the various accretions and distortions are comprehended. The Āryan documents, the four Vedas (q.v.), though riddled with various non-Āryan elements from as far away as the South Pacific, give a picture of a plainly identified society and its customs and beliefs. The picture is one of a conquering, fearless—"white"—military aristocracy, worshiping a pantheon of male gods, which overran and subjugated swarms of "primitive" black savages. Since the only surviving documents were Āryan, controlled, edited, amplified, and interpreted by Āryans, it has been an Āryan view that survived over the millennia. The superficial picture is of the supremacy of the Āryan gods—Indra, Agni, Soma, Rudra, Vasyu, and so on—and the dominance of Āryan ritualism (which was centered upon the twin concepts of sacrifice, of both animals and humans, and of the sacred fire, which had to be attended to in exemplary detail and care). Yet the true picture turns out to be something else, once the scene is put into perspective. Though no pre-Āryan documents have survived, whether from the Indus or elsewhere, if there ever were any aside from the few enigmatic, undecipherable inscriptions on the Indus stamp seals (the tradition was likely oral, as was the Vedic), the epic works and scriptures, but not their themes, died out in the long twilight that followed the Āryan invasions. It was the view until the 1920s, when the Indus cities were first laid bare, among both orthodox Hindus and foreign scholars, that it was the Āryans who forged Hinduism out of their own unique psyche and its reaction to the subcontinent, and gave it their own special bent. The Āryan element is strong, but it is more like a powerful tributary joining a large, slow-moving mainstream; the waters mingle, but the mainstream remains dominant. In the case of Hinduism (and here the theme of water is crucial), the mainstream is the tremendous complex underlying stratum of pre-Āryan belief and practice, which though superficially destroyed by the Āryans, remains the true basis of Hinduism.

The Āryans eventually imposed a kind of racist slavery upon the Dravidians, the Austro-Asiatic and Mongoloid peoples, virtually all of whom were dark-skinned or yellow. The conquered remained the workers, the lower artisans, the drudges. Yet there was much intermingling, which allowed the people's beliefs to rise into the Āryan strata. One such means was sexually, by liaison or even marriage, with dark-skinned women, who would retain their own beliefs and pass them on to their children. Another means was the absorption of non-Āryan leaders—chiefs, kings, and priests—through various rites that made them "twice born"—i.e., Āryan.

THE DEVELOPMENT OF HINDUISM: The Hindu way has reached its present position after much interplay of contradictory forces, experiencing periods of tremendous growth, decline, splintering, and reassessment. Whatever the case, it consistently shows great vitality, but it often needs the perspective of history before certain movements can be understood, at least by the outsider. The growth of Hinduism might be divided into the following categories, with the understanding that dates are flexible at best, and numerous minor currents were taking place at the same time.

1. Pre-Vedic. This is the relatively unknown age whose general form, even, can only be surmised—the period of the Indus cities, the Earth Mother cult, the yogi god, and widespread animism and other forms of nature worship, including solar cults.

2. The Vedic period (roughly B.C. 1500–600). The time of the Āryans, whose lives, gods, forms of worship, wars, etc., are portrayed in the four Vedas, which are generally known as saṃhitās, or collections. The Vedic period includes a series of works called the Brāhmaṇas, which are primarily concerned with the proper celebration of ritual by the priests; the Āraṇyakas, or Forest Texts, which were composed by hermits in reaction to the ritualism and sacerdotism of the Brāhmaṇas, and the Upanishads, of which there are fourteen and which contain the "secret teachings" of the Āraṇyakas. The Upanishads contain in unorganized form much of future Hindu philosophy, and since they appeared at the close of the Vedic period, they are also known as Vedānta (the end of the Vedas).

3. The folk period (B.C. 600–A.D. 300). After the long domina-

tion by the priests there came an equally long period in which the ordinary people began to express their religious yearnings in more heartfelt terms. Personal devotion stood in opposition to priestly ritual. Popular movements, heretical to the brāhmins, arose, including Jainism and Buddhism, and the great epics appeared, among them the Mahābhārata (which contains the *Bhagavad Gītā*) and the Rāmāyaṇa, which integrate the desire for a personal god whom one can love with the loftiest concepts of Hindu speculative philosophy. It is in this age and the following one that much submerged, non-Āryan material appears in the people's epics.

4. The Purāṇic period (A.D. 300–1200). The age when a large amount of folk material was refashioned into epic form, usually focused on a particular deity, especially Vishnu, Brahmā, Shiva, and even Shakti and Krishna. Broadly based devotional movements attained great power, such as the Ālvārs (q.v.) in the South, which produced numerous saints, most often from the low castes.

5. The Muslim period (1200–1750). A continuation of the above, but with much Islamic and Ṣūfic influence: intense personal devotion, and intermingling of Hindu and Muslim, with the idea that faith, caste, and social standing were irrelevant before the majesty and love of the Divine, in which one is absorbed through one's own love and devotion.

6. The "European" period (1750 to the present). The appearance of numerous Europeans—soldiers, businessmen, and missionaries—brought both influence upon and reaction from the Hindu communities. There were few actual conversions except among the "rice" Christians or among those forced by the Portuguese in Goa, but literate and educated Hindus often felt the need for a response. Several reform movements arose, such as the Āryā Samāj (q.v.), which sought a return to a purified Vedic Hinduism, or the Brāhmo Samāj (q.v.), which adopted a Hinduism shorn of its accretions and superstitions and attained something close to Congregationalism. Many Hindus, among them Mohandas Gandhi, were taken by certain Christian teachings, such as the Sermon on the Mount, absorbing the doctrines but still rejecting Christianity. Today Hinduism faces severe challenges from the modern world; long-cherished institutions, among them caste, which form the framework of Hindu society, are threatened (it is difficult for a brāhmin and an untouchable to work side by side in

an office or factory without some kind of response, either good or bad). Education, science, nuclear power, technology, and better forms of communication put many traditional doctrines into re-examination, if not abeyance.

This entry will not discuss ritual and doctrine. See entries under ahiṁsā, Ālvārs, avatār, avidyā, *Bhagavad Gītā,* bhakti, Brahman, Buddhism, caste, dharma, dīkṣā, guru, harijan, Indra, Jainism, Kabīr, Shiva, Sikhs, Vishnu.

hinshi, Buddh. The master at a Zen temple with whom the novice does his training; roshi, the more common term, actually should be used for a higher-ranking (and often older) person.

hoama (also homa), Zor. The Iranian and Zoroastrian form of the sacred god-beverage soma. The hoama cultus dates to pre-Zoroastrian times (before B.C. 600) and shared a common origin with the use of soma by the Āryans of the Rig Vedic period about a thousand or more years earlier. Like soma, hoama is deity and drink, the nectar of the gods, the moon in plant form. Zoroastrian scriptures identify hoama as the son of the supreme God Ahura Mazdā, and eternal priest. Hoama is sacrificial victim, sacrificer, and god. It is the plant of immortality. In contemporary Parsee teaching hoama is spirit, angel, and star. In the period before Zoroaster's reformation of the ancient religion, hoama as plant was immolated along with a living animal—bull or cow—in the yasna ceremony (the blood offering being consumed by the sacred fire) and ritually partaken of by the priests and perhaps the laity. Zoroaster forbade animal sacrifices, but the use of hoama as the central part of yasna continued. According to Parsees today the identity of the original plant has been lost in the mists of time, but it is said to have grown on the sides of snow-capped mountains; they dispute R. Gordon Wasson's identification of hoama/soma as the hallucinogenic mushroom *amanita muscaria* on the basis that anything with psychotropic properties is against the Zoroastrian faith. That the original hoama, however, induced a supranormal effect is evidenced in this passage from the Yasna: "All other intoxicants are accompanied by Fury of the bloody spear, but the intoxication produced by hoama is accompanied by Truth and joy; the intoxication of hoama makes one nimble." This is not the effect of the plant used today, one of the ephedras obtained in dried form from Yazd or Kerman in Iran; the plant in this area is *ephedra distachya;* in the nineteenth century, when communications with Iran were more difficult, both *asclepias acida* and *sarcostemma viminale* were used. Whatever the plant, its twigs are soaked in water and ritually washed, pounded in a mortar to the accompaniment of various prayers, and filtered through a metal strainer wrapped with a few hairs from a bull. The pressing is done four times. Then the juice is consecrated, to be drunk by the priests during the yasna ceremony. See soma, Zoroastrianism.

Holi, Hind. A spring festival, coinciding with the full moon of the bright half of Phālguna (February–March). It is celebrated over most of India but not by every caste. Colored powder and colored water (red is dominant) are sprinkled over passers-by. Erotic, even obscene remarks may be made, lewd songs are sung, and a huge bonfire may be lighted. Holi is a relic of ancient fertility rites; the bonfire is an act performed in the past at the commencement of the agricultural year, when, in an age of adequate land, the jungle would be burned to clear the ground for planting millet and other grains. (The custom died out only recently among a jungle people, the Rāj Gonds of Adilabad.) The Holi fire has also been linked to archaic cremation rituals, in which the dead were invoked lest they harm the new crops. Holi allows a relaxing and reversal of strict traditional roles observed the rest of the year: low castes are permitted a ritualized hostility to the brāhmins, their classic oppressors, and to landlords and village headmen. Unrestricted sexual play, the eating of prohibited foods, and the reversing of power roles between man and wife help relieve the barren lives of the oppressed in country and city alike. See Hinduism.

homa, Zor. See hoama.

Hōnen (1133–1212), Buddh. Founder of the Jōdō sect of Japanese Buddhism. Hōnen caused a sharp break with other forms of Buddhism in his own country, teaching that devotion to the Amida Buddha (q.v.) through invocation of the nembutsu, a form of mantra, was superior to other religious practices. He was sent as a child to the Mount Hiei monastery near Kyotō, where he won everyone's respect for his saintliness and knowledge—"If you told him one thing, he understood ten," was a remark made about him. He then studied in China, and returned to Japan with the doctrines of Pure Land Buddhism, making it into one of the major sects, rivaled only by the Zen schools. Hōnen stated unequivocally that other forms of Buddhism were the "difficult path" and required "one's own power" for salvation; however, the nembutsu of the Pure Land sect was an "easy path." His teaching of the repetition of the mantra quickly took hold among the ordinary people, who, up to this point, had been denied the hope of attaining salvation in any form because they were forbidden the training and education to understand other Buddhist doctrines of enlightenment.

Hōnen's success as a proselytizer gained him the wrath of the Emperor. In 1207 two of Hōnen's assistants were beheaded by court order, and two of the Emperor's concubines, who had become Jōdō nuns, killed themselves. Hōnen, now in his seventies, was exiled into a remote part of the countryside, but took this opportunity to spread Pure Land doctrine among the peasants. He was eventually pardoned, and returned to Kyotō. As he lay dying a few months later, he reported to his disciples that he was surrounded by the Amida Buddha and His heavenly hosts, who were about to bear his soul off to the Western Paradise of the Pure Land. His most famous disciple was Shinran (q.v.). See Amida Buddha, Pure Land.

horse, as sacred or cult object. Because of its size and strength and its military and economic importance, the horse has played a role important to certain religions. Among the Vedic Āryans, who had a long tradition as nomadic horsemen, the horse sacrifice (aśvamedha, q.v.) was probably based on primitive fertility practices. It was an important religious and social celebration, and an affirmation of the king's domination over both his neighbors and his own people. In Shintō, an offering of a horse—ema—to the rain god was made by way of propitiation, either for rain or to stop an excess.

Hsu Yung (A.D. 1840–1959), Buddh. One of the most famous of all Ch'an masters of the recent past, he was considered the "right Dharma eye" of the present generation. He is credited with the instruction of thousands of disciples and the founding of many monasteries in China. He taught and lectured at Shanghai and other cities, and died at a monastery on the sacred Yun C'hu Mountain in Kiangsi Province, aged 119. See Ch'an.

Hui Nêng, the Sixth Patriarch (A.D. 638–713), Buddh. A leading exponent of Ch'an (Zen) Buddhism in China and the individual most responsible for turning Ch'an from a minor meditative sect of Indian origin to a major school of Buddhism in his homeland. Hui Nêng is the last of the patriarchs who began with Bodhidharma, the Indian Buddhist who is credited with the introduction of dhyāna (meditation) in China in the early sixth century. Hui Nêng is known as Wei Lang in southern China and as Enō in Japan. The famous brief autobiography by Hui Nêng, which includes many of his teachings, is corrupt, and though harmed by lacunae, is now twice the length of the original manuscript, due to much rewriting in later days.

Hui Nêng's father died when the boy was very young; the future patriarch and his mother lived in extreme poverty, supporting themselves by gathering and selling firewood. By chance, Hui Nêng met a man who told of a great monastery presided over by a great master, Hung-jen, the Fifth Patriarch, who taught his followers that if they recited nothing more than the Diamond Sūtra, it would "enable them to see into their own natures and with direct apprehension become buddhas." Hui Nêng made the long trip South to the monastery and petitioned for admission, but the Fifth Patriarch derided him as a barbarian from the North and set the boy to grinding rice, which he did for eight months. At this point, after a number of events that lead to Hui Nêng's writing a verse on a wall of the monastery, Hung-jen turned the patriarchate over to the young novice, expounding the Diamond Sūtra in such a manner that his successor immediately obtained enlightenment. Hui Nêng's verse is a landmark in the expression of Ch'an Buddhism and is often quoted. It goes:

> The mind is the Bodhi tree,
> The body is the mirror stand.
> The mirror is originally clean and pure;
> Where can it be stained by dust?

The Fifth Patriarch bestowed his robe upon Hui Nêng, but warned, "From ancient times the transmission of the Dharma has been as tenuous as a dangling thread. If you stay here, there are people who will kill you." Hui Nêng immediately went into exile, and following Hung-jen's warning, did not preach for three years. After that, he taught the primacy of the kung-an (or kōan) method to enlightenment over that of t'so-chan, or zazen (sitting). He is credited with the famous kōan, "Show me your original face before you were born." Like his master, Hung-jen, the Sixth Patriarch insisted upon the need of our seeing into our own nature through our own efforts. He said there could be no duality in Ch'an. "The Buddha Nature of which we are all in possession, and the seeing into which constitutes Ch'an is indivisible into such opposition as good and evil, eternal and temporal, material and spiritual. To see dualism in life is due to confusion of thought; the wise, the enlightened, see into the reality of things unhampered by erroneous ideas." At another time he said, "Never under any circumstances say that meditation and wisdom are different; they are one unity, not separate things. Meditation itself is the substance of wisdom; wisdom itself is the function of meditation." He told his disciple Fa-ta, who recorded many of his sayings, that the *Lotus Sūtra* (q.v.) contains all that is needed for salvation. See Ch'an, Zen.

human sacrifice, in India. Humans, as well as a large number of animals, including cows, horses, goats, bison, oxen, and sheep, have been sacrificial objects in India since the most primitive times. Human sacrifice may be divided into two major periods and forms; the earliest, sanctified by the first texts, and known as puruṣamedha; and the later period, which is intimately connected with various tantric rites.

1. Puruṣamedha. The rite is undoubtedly of pre-Āryan origin, as it is not mentioned in the Vedas but in the Brāhmaṇas and subsequent scriptures, which show much non-Āryan influence (cf. jarborn and Golden Womb). The ritual for the slaughter of a single man is based exactly on that of the aśvamedha (the horse sacrifice). The texts emphasize the healing of the sacrificer's bodily ills and not the winning of immortal life; the hymns, however, are taken from the Rig Veda and the Artharva Veda, which do not

mention human sacrifice. To some, the ritual is a mere priestly invention to fill the apparent gap in the sacrificial system that provided no place for man. On the other hand, the Yajur Veda texts recognize only a symbolic slaying of a whole host of human victims, who are set free in due course, animals being substituted. However, this point has been much debated by Western scholars on the basis of other evidence. If the human sacrifice were ever usual, every probability points to the victim having been eaten, and the very essence of the rite would lie in the tasting of the blood.

That human blood was shed in the yajña ritual is not to be denied. In building the brick altar for the fire, the pan, in which the sacrificer kept the sacred fire for a year previous, is built into the bottom layer of the bricks, and on it are placed the heads of the five victims—man, horse, ox, sheep, and goat—to impart stability, as the *Śatapatha Brāhmaṇa* clearly says. Other texts state that the head to be used is either of a kśatriya or a vaiśya, members of the warrior and tradesman castes, respectively, the victims slain by an arrow or by lightning or purchased for twenty-one beans. The head, severed from the body, was given life again by being laid on an anthill with seven holes and redeemed from Yama, the god of death, by three mantras. In other texts the four animals were allowed to go free, while the head only of the man was placed in the fire pan.

Foreign scholars have interpreted these sacrifices as being the record of the very widespread custom of slaying a human being to act as the guardian of the foundations of a building, a practice found in many countries and exemplified in ancient India, where it was considered necessary to make impregnable such strong points as walls, bastions, and city gates and to prevent dams from being swept away by flood waters. Whether the head alone or the entire body of the victim was buried in the foundations is not clear.

2. "Tantric" rituals of human sacrifice. Some tantric sects of yogis, notably the Aghorīs connected with the temple of Kāmākhyā, a form of Durgā (q.v.) in Assam, were in the past noted for their practice of human sacrifice. Records show that in 1565 alone, the temple priests (who were not brāhmins) sacrificed 140 victims on a single occasion; impressive numbers of victims died in other years, until the British forced an end to the practice

A primitive figurine of the Great Mother (or Śakti, as she is known in later Hinduism), a universal concept that is embodied in the veneration of many goddesses. This statuette was found at Mohenjo-daro, one of the great cities of the Indus Valley civilization that flourished about five millennia ago.

Mohenjo-daro (as the city is now called) was one of the twin capitals of the great Indus Valley Empire. Here and at the city of Harrapā, primitive forms of Hinduism have been found, including the veneration of a deity resembling Shiva, worship of a Great Mother (similar to Śakti), of phallic symbols, and of nature cults still popular among the Indian people.

The liṅga, or phallus, has been a common object of devotion in Hinduism since the prehistoric days of the Indus Valley cities. This liṅga, placed within the yoni, was found at Harappā, one of the twin capitals of Indus civilization. The liṅga, which is Shiva's sign, is also a symbol of the universe, and of the sun as the progenitor of worlds. The yoni, sign of the universal womb, is manifest nature. Only when the liṅga, giver of seed, is embraced by the yoni can the world become manifest.

The god Brahmā is a member of the traditic Hindu triad that includes Vishnu and Sh Brahmā is the Immense Being, the source the manifest world, creating space and ti Here he is seated on the lotus that springs fı Vishnu's navel.

The black goddess Kālī is depicted in a folk painting from Orissa standing on the lifeless white corpse of the lascivious Shiva, her sometime consort. Kālī is both destroyer and creator. She destroys evil, fear, and ignorance—though man is in dread of losing them—and is thus the Transcendent Night. Having so destroyed, passing beyond death, she brings man to the stage that is absolute joy and supreme bliss. In coition with the Lord Shiva, Kālī is active, the god passive, in the pleasurable world of creation.

Shiva in his manifestation as Natarāja, the Cosmic Dancer. It was from the god's drums that the universe was shaped, the rhythmical beat giving the form to the four types of science—yoga, vedanta (the study of metaphysics), language, and music.

The god Shiva with the Ganges falling upon his matted hair; the statue is at Rishikesh, near the upper Ganges. The sacred river falls from the roof of a cave in the Himālayas onto the god's head. Some traditions state that on the contrary, the river springs from Vishnu's toe.

Durgā, the wife of Shiva, treads underfoot the defeated buffalo fiend Mahiṣa (opposite top). The scene is a street shrine in Bengal, where images are made for popular veneration during the festival of Navarātra, "of Nine Nights." The soul of Durgā, a form of Kālī, inhabits the image during Navarātra. Unlike Kālī, Durgā's features are sweet and peaceful (the images today are copied after Indian movie stars), and the goddess is worshiped as a benevolent mother. During Navarātra, about the time of the bright side of the full moon after the autumn equinox, many goats and buffalos are sacrificed (opposite bottom), after which elaborate ceremonies are held in the temples in Durgā's honor (above). On the tenth day Durgā's images are immersed in the Ganges or another river, upon which the goddess abandons the clay figures (below).

Sarasvatī, the goddess of learning, is reflected in a mirrored room of a shrine at Rishikesh, one of Hinduism's seven sacred cities. Sarasvatī is Brahmā's wife. Her feast is celebrated during the first half of the full moon of September–October, at the same time as that of Durgā, the two goddesses being venerated in different parts of the country. Sarasvatī always carries the vina, a stringed instrument resembling the sitār.

(Top left) The six cakras. They are (from the bottom up): mūlādhāra, svādhisṭḥāna, maṇipūra, anāhata, viśuddha, and ājñā. The cakras are dynamic centers of the body, and vital to its spiritual development. They are awakened by Kuṇḍalinī, the Serpent Power.

(Top right) The yantra is the visual equi lent of the mantra, and is its soul. There are innumerable number of mantras, of which one above is the most famous. It is knc either as Sri Yantra or Sri Cakra of Devī Tripurasundarī, the Resplendent Beauty).

in 1832. One of the most notorious situations involved the Thuggees, whose history goes back to at least the fourteenth century and is probably much older. They had received a license from the goddess Kālī (q.v.) to kill demons "without shedding a drop of blood," which they did by strangling them with a square of black cloth. The sect soon progressed from eliminating demons to doing away with human beings, notably travelers, whose possessions went to the Thuggees. In their campaign to end the evils in India, the British moved against the Thuggees in 1839, appointing William Sleeman as Commissioner for the Suppression of Thuggee and Dacoitry. Sleeman painstakingly collected hard evidence against the sect, and by the time it was eliminated, some three thousand members had been convicted in court; one of the Thuggees boasted of 719 victims but lamented that he had been unable to reach his goal of 1,000 in honor of Kālī.

The goddess still claims occasional victims, especially in the rural areas, where a sacrifice comes to the attention of the police from time to time; however, many of the jungle people and the peasants on the fringes of ordinary Indian life are reluctant to cooperate with the authorities, and a number of human sacrifices go unreported and attain publicity only by accident. See aśvamedha.

◄ I ►

'ibādāt, Isl. Worship. 'Ibādāt is the abstract noun defining the attitude of the 'abd, or servant (of God); it has general and specific meanings.

1. Generally, 'ibādāt includes the various forms of worship, prayer, fasting, pilgrimage, and giving alms.

2. Specifically, 'ibādāt is ṣalāt, the rite of prayer that occurs five times daily, in full or modified forms, either individually, in a mosque or elsewhere, or congregationally. The obligation of the five daily prayers is the second Pillar of Islam. The Qur'ān (q.v.) seems to have stated only three times a day for prayer, but tradi-

tion has established five, beginning at sunset, and followed by the night, dawn, noon, and afternoon periods of prayer. The times of prayer are announced by the muezzin from the minaret of the mosque (today he may use a public-address system for the call).

Before the Muslim prays, he must be in a state of purity. To attain purity he must remove two types of uncleanliness: najāsah and ḥadath. Najāsah is dirt that may touch the body or the clothing or the place of prayer, and is chiefly matter from a person or an animal, like urine or blood. Wine also is najāsah, but milk, sweat, saliva, and tears are not najāsah. Any of the impurities are removed with water, which should be fresh and clean; when water is not available, sand or clean earth may be substituted. Each mosque has a fountain or pool, or at least a water tap, for washing in. Other types of water, from rain, a river, or the ocean, are also permissible.

If najāsah has no color, taste, or smell, it need be washed once; however, in certain cases several washings, with soap, may be required. The most serious form of najāsah comes from a dog or a pig; if such an unclean creature licks a person or drinks from a vessel or eats from a plate he uses, seven washings are required, the first with water mixed with earth, the others with plain water.

The second type of impurity, ḥadath, must also be removed from the body before prayer. Ḥadath occurs after any of the following: sleep, the passing of feces, urine, or wind; drunkenness or other "loss of mind"; touching of the sexual organs with the inside of the palm; sexual intercourse with a woman not one's wife, or even a casual accidental touching of the bare skin of any woman who is not one's mother, sister, grandmother, or aunt. Ḥadath is removed with a full ritual washing with water, an act known as wuḍū.

Wuḍū is a complicated ritual. It begins with the washing of the hands and the cleaning of the fingernails. The mouth is also rinsed and the nose emptied of mucus. The entire face is next washed and all dirt removed; the prayer at this point says, "O God, make my face white on the Day [of Judgment] when some are resurrected with white faces and others with black faces." The hands are washed up to the elbow, beginning with the right hand. The hands are wetted and part if not all of the top of the head rubbed with water, or even completely washed.

Then the ears are washed, with the index finger in the ear and the thumb behind the ear; the index finger also rubs the folds of the ear.

The feet are now washed, including the ankles; dirt from the toenails is removed. Next the du'ā', a short prayer, is said. But this elaborate ritual is not yet complete, for it should be done three times before the worshiper is in the proper state of purity. At this point the Muslim has completed both the wājib, or fard, division of wuḍū, wājib meaning "that which is necessary," and the sunnah part, which means something good but not necessary. Wājib is the intention to perform wuḍū, washing the face, washing the hands to the elbows, rubbing the head, washing the feet. Sunnah is washing only the hands, washing the mouth, brushing the teeth, cleaning the nose, rubbing or washing all the head instead of part, cleaning the ears, repeating each act three times, starting with the right before the left, saying the du'ā' for each step, and saying it at the end.

Until the worshiper has completed wuḍū, he may not touch the Qur'ān or pray. The ritual of prayer is known as ṣalāh, which must be performed only at the prescribed time of day; a ṣalāh missed may not be carried over to another period. Nor may a Muslim pray outside the appointed hours; other times should be devoted to a man's livelihood and various worldly occupations.

Rak'ah is the ritual movement of prayer (the plural is raka'āt). The worshiper must face the direction of the Ka'ba in Mecca, the qiblah (q.v.). A man must cover his body properly; a woman must cover all except her face and hands. In the mosque women pray behind a screen or curtain (but because of this requirement few women will attend the mosque except on the most necessary occasions). The ritual consists of seven movements, which are done twice at some hours, three or four times at others. The worshiper begins by standing and saying "Allāhu akbar" (God is the greatest), followed by the al-Fātiḥah, the opening verse of the Qur'ān. With the first two words the Muslim holds his hands, palms toward the holy city, the thumbs nearly touching the earlobes; with the longer verse, he either lowers his hands to his sides, or crosses them over his chest, depending on local tradition. He then adds a Qur'ānic verse of his own liking.

Next, he bends forward, says "Allāhu akbar" with his hands on his knees, and then says another brief prayer.

A second standing follows, with a simple prayer, and then the worshiper drops to his knees and places his forehead on the ground in obeisance to Allāh, conscious that the Lord Himself is aware of his acts; such obeisance may never be given a human being.

Now the Muslim sits erect on his haunches, again with a prayer. A second prostration follows, with appropriate prayers. At last he stands, saying "Allāhu akbar," says al-Fātiḥah and another verse, and repeats the entire performance either once, twice, or thrice more, as necessary. The rak'ah ends standing, with the face turned to the right and then the left in salutation to all Muslims and the angels, the recitation of the Shahādah (q.v.), and a "salaam," the phrase of peace.

On Fridays at noon in the mosque, the ritual is shortened but celebrated under the direction of an imām (q.v.), who usually gives a sermon.

Muslims are permitted, in addition to the five prayers, to observe two more optionally, one at night after sleep but before the dawn ṣalāt, and the second between dawn and the noon prayer. The cycle of prayers makes heavy demands upon the faithful, and thus there is no such observance as a "sabbath" in Islam.

Ibrāhīm, Isl. Otherwise Abraham. The most important of the series of nabis (prophets) or rasūls (messengers) of God. In the early passages of the Qur'ān references to Ibrāhīm are sketchy, but they are linked to Judaeo-Christian tradition; when he appears in later suras (chapters), the Qur'ānic view of him is at variance from that of the other faiths. Ibrāhīm is one of the "Five People of Determination." Muḥammad calls him the khalīl or Friend of God, and connected the faith he was preaching to that of his predecessor, who, since he lived before the establishment of the Mosaic Law, was neither Jew nor Christian. Ibrāhīm is also credited with the building of the Ka'ba; there is, attached to the structure, a small building that contains a stone upon which Ibrāhīm is said to have walked. Pilgrims to Mecca make a special prayer before it, asking forgiveness for sins and for faith, and ending with the plea, "Let us die as Muslims, and raise us to life as Muslims." The stone is called The Standing. See Ka'ba, Mecca, and Muḥammad.

I Ching (pron. "Yee Jing"). An ancient Chinese work, pre-Taoist and pre-Confucian, whose rudimentary forms have been traced back four millennia. The earliest versions are two separate works, which were combined, revised, and annotated; one dates to roughly B.C. 2000, the other to some three hundred years later. The present *I Ching* is believed to be the work of King Wên (c. B.C. 1150), the founder of the Chou dynasty (the work is also known as *I Chou*). The various layers of accretion and arrangement not only include primitive religious beliefs, oracular pronouncements, folklore, magic, and proverbs but also the most arcane scholarship and commentaries. Wên rearranged the sixty-four hexagrams that form the core of the *I Ching* and added the parts called the Judgments. Confucius is credited with the numerous texts known as Wings; whether he himself or his followers wrote them is a matter scholars have not fully decided; at any rate, the Sage is known to have spent much time with the book.

As the result of the extended critical and analytical commentaries and the highly skilled psychic insights into the text developed over the centuries, the *I Ching* has come to have a profound significance as a work of divination and wisdom far beyond any of its peers. It covers a broad area not quite mystical yet defying rational explanation. Its wisdom—powers, more accurately—stems to some extent on the presence of other-worldly and unseen forces, partially or fully concealed, expressed in elliptical and carefully phrased passages and phrases. Yet it is quite to the point for solving the mundane problems that beset not only every man but also every country. In Asia it played a steady advisory role in most of the nations that came under Chinese cultural and religious influence, not only Korea and Indo-China but also Japan, where until the time of the Meiji reformation in the nineteenth century, the *I Ching* influenced military tactics; it even had an indirect effect upon the training of the warrior caste until World War II. On a more vulgar level, *I Ching* readers could be found in any market or bazaar to give quick and easy solutions to the complexities of daily life. Since the *I Ching* leads one into areas that defy rational explanation, the Chinese traditionally have stated that only men of mature years are ready to learn from it; Confucius did not begin its study until late in life, expressing the opinion that he wished he had fifty years to devote to the book; as an aside, the sixteenth-century Jesuit scholars in China who concerned themselves with the *I Ching* were all later declared by Rome to be insane or heretics.

The basis of the *I Ching* is the series of sixty-four hexagrams made up of full or broken lines, each hexagram being composed of two trigrams. The origin of the trigrams and hexagrams is not known. They bear a resemblance to the underside of a tortoise shell, cracked in the sacrificial fire in the quest for omens, an ancient practice; also to a random throwing of sticks, some whole, some broken. To find the hexagram applicable to his own special interest of the moment, the questioner tosses either yarrow sticks, the preferred method, or coins, in a specified manner, building the hexagram a line at a time, starting at the bottom. Numbers six or nine, or seven or eight, are derived from the sticks or the coins; the four are sacred numbers in many cultures. Depending on the count obtained with the sticks or the coins for each line, the line is either changeable or fixed. The hexagram is then "read" in the light of the ancient texts, followed by interpretations of the accompanying commentaries. Reading is not an easy accomplishment, and demands not only maturity, knowledge, and scholarship but also great psychic insight. The texts and the commentaries state elliptically the theme of the hexagram, and infer what should be done, not what must be done. The movable lines, if any are given, are now changed, and a second hexagram is obtained, which gives a second or even new interpretation. Among the various combinations 4,096 different readings are possible, covering an extremely broad range of questions. The concept of change, implicit in the hexagrams, is crucial in Chinese thought, being a natural movement inherent in all things under Heaven. One must be ready for change, and when it is foretold, seize the moment with power, courage, and intelligence. On the other hand, there are times when one must wait patiently until events themselves change, enabling the individual then to act. The work is positive: It stresses the "superior man," the man who can lead, bear adversity, take command, go into solitude, suffer—or direct—fools, the man whose own inner resources he must constantly develop and improve. The work assumes that there is a special interdependence of objective events with the individual's life, his soul, goals, and psychic state. But *I Ching* is more than a random expression of the moment; it directs the questioner to a careful scrutiny not only of the world about him but also of his own character, attitude, and motives.

Among those sages who take the *I Ching* seriously, a copy of the book itself is kept as a sacred object, wrapped in silk or some other expensive cloth, on a shelf higher than the height of a man's head. During the "audience" with the *I Ching,* the questioner follows certain ceremonial procedures, treating it like a superior Being; incense is burned, and the questioner bows in respect. The procedure of selecting the hexagrams by tossing the sticks can take up to an hour; the entire ritual is one in which the individual allows the depths of his psyche to open up for the fullest possible reception of the ancient and salutory wisdom.

There are numerous translations of the *I Ching* in English and other European languages. The best is that prepared by sinologist Richard Wilhelm (translated from German into English by Cary F. Baynes, with a Foreword by C. G. Jung). The lectures by Hellmut Wilhelm, *Change,* are an important accompaniment to the father's original volume. John Blofeld's *I Ching* contains useful information, but his translation—often at variance with Wilhelm's—is sometimes not satisfactory. James Legge's nineteenth-century version, originally a volume in the Sacred Books of the East series, is widely reprinted but is far inferior to Wilhelm's work.

'Id, Isl. A major Islamic festival (properly, 'Id al-Fitr), celebrated for the ending of the fast of Ramaḍān (q.v.). Though it is known as the Little Festival, it is celebrated on a larger scale than the Great Festival, 'Id al-Aḍhā, which marks the offering of sacrifices by pilgrims at Mina outside of Mecca. 'Id begins when the first sliver of the new moon appears after Ramaḍān. Since the Islamic calendar is lunar, 'Id al-Fitr appears on a different date every year. See calendar, Islam.

idā, Hind. One of the three principal nādīs (q.v.) or subtle nerves of the body. The idā on the left and the pingalā on the right coil around the suṣumnā, through which arises the goddess Kuṇḍalinī (q.v.). Idā, according to tantric texts, "is of a pale color, is moonlike (candra-svarūpa), and contains nectar." The idā also symbolizes the river Gaṇgā. See tantrism.

iddhi, Buddh. A psychic or occult power possessed by a buddha or by another soul of a high spiritual development. Gautama Buddha forbade the display of such powers as dangerous, especially before the laity. See siddhi.

ijmā', Isl. Consensus or unanimous opinion, i.e., of those—jurists, theologians, and philosophers—who are thoroughly versed in the Qur'ān and Sunnah (q.v.) and who are therefore qualified to establish by inference or analogy (qiyās) precedents not definitely and explicitly laid down by the two higher authorities. Technically ijmā' is defined as "the unanimous doctrine and opinion of the recognized religious authorities at any given time."

Reliance on consensus goes back to the Qur'ān and to Tradition (Sunnah), stressing the concept that Truth is guaranteed by the community as a whole, for the individual opposing the community is a heretic. Though there may be local differences, in the long run the communal mind will not err; it becomes the seal of orthodoxy. Ijmā' depends upon its complementary relation to documentary sources. A new attitude, concept, or requirement, by its acceptance by believers, gathers the force of law and becomes truly and authentically Islamic. Thus ijmā' denotes an organic process. Though there are various schools in the Muslim world that initially may differ profoundly and deeply in the view of a particular issue, eventually ijmā' comes to dominate. Ijmā' requires stimulus and direction; it is not a haphazard development, though it most often originates with imaginative and innovative individuals, even minorities or heretics.

Yet, if there is no ijmā'—consensus—initially, how can it commence? This difficulty has been overcome by the idea of itjihad (original thinking), the controversial way to ijmā'. Itjihad (literally, striving) depends on enterprise and initiative developed in systematic but original thinking by certain highly educated scholars capable of anticipating conclusions that might result in a general consensus.

imām, Isl. A leader, especially in prayers at a mosque or other assemblage of the faithful, guiding the people in the movements as they worship. The imām faces the direction of Mecca, and the congregation is lined up shoulder to shoulder in rows behind him. Many imāms earn their position because they have made the pilgrimage (hajj) to Mecca; some may also serve as religious teachers. Among the Sunnīs (q.v.) the imām plays the role as defined above.

However, in the various sects of the Shī'a (q.v.), the imām has a totally different function, serving in a combined political-mystical leadership. Tracing the concept of the imām in this sense back to 'Ali (q.v.), the Shī'a see the imām as both sinless and absolutely infallible, not only in questions of dogma and worship but also in secular matters. Acceptance of the divine powers of the imām, for the Shī'a, is as much an article of faith as belief in Allāh and the Prophet; for some, acceptance of the imām is a sixth Pillar of Faith. The imām has had almost literal powers of life and death over his people, and it is only in the present that his authority is being challenged by some of the Shī'a faithful. He can not only order or forbid marriages, but also direct people in their choice of livelihood and expel recalcitrant members from the community, a fate of unimagined severity in a tightly structured Eastern society. Influenced by Zoroastrianism (q.v.), Persian and Afghan Shī'a sects early advanced the concept of the Hidden Imām as the epiphany of the Primeval Light, who is to come to earth to salvage mankind. A few extremist sects see the imām as an avatār of Allāh, and others as God himself, though these views are in the minority. For the majority, the imām is the divinely appointed ruler and teacher of the faithful, an infallible leader appearing in every era as a messenger of God. See Islam, Shī'a, Sunnī.

īmān, Isl. Faith, belief; it is the corollary of dīn, the practice of religion. In an early Tradition, the Prophet, in answer to a stranger who appeared at his household (actually the Angel Gabriel), defined īmān thus: "It is that thou shouldst believe in God and His angels and His books and His apostles and the Last Day, and that thou shouldst believe that no good or evil cometh but by His providence." See dīn, Islam, Muḥammad.

Indra, Hind. The Vedic god of rain and thunder, next to Agni in the pantheon. In the Rig Veda (q.v.) Indra is the great warrior, the leader of the Āryans (q.v.), who smashes the humble earthworks of the black, snub-nosed "primitives" of the land, loots the treasure houses of the "godless," and "frees the rivers" (a phrase taken to mean the breaking down of dams and levees). Indra thus seems to have been a clan chief who was deified over the centuries, accumulating the attributes of other gods. At the height of the Vedic period he was a violent, hard-drinking, Bronze Age barbarian; later on he dropped to the second rank of gods, his place ironically being taken by Krishna (q.v.), the dark enemy who haunts the Rig Veda, the berserk warrior deity of nature being replaced by the gentle trickster, erotic symbol of devotion to the Supreme. In the *Chāndogya Upaniṣad* (c. B.C. 600) the once-powerful Indra, appearing as a fumbling student of the doctrine of the Brahman, can apprehend the sophisticated teachings only with difficulty. In later Hinduism Indra becomes an aspect of Shiva (q.v.) and is subordinate to him and to Brahmā and Vishnu. The Greeks who settled in India following Alexander the Great's invasion in B.C. 326 equated Indra with their own god Dionysos. See Hinduism.

Indus Valley, civilization of. Flourishing about B.C. 2500–2000 (with the outside dates about 3500–1700), it was centered upon the cities of Mohenjo-daro on the Indus River and Harappā on the Ravi, a tributary, covering some half a million square miles, from today's Afghanistan on the west to Delhi on the east. The Indus civilization (also called Harappan, after the first city to be uncovered) completely disappeared about the time of the Aryan invasions c. B.C. 1500 and later, and was not found again until the early 1920s, and then by accident. Excavations under Sir John Marshall led to the further discovery of over 270 other sites, some of substantial size and importance, striking in the fact that during the long life span of the supposed empire there was little change and much uniformity from one end to the other; the lack of change and innovation led to the hypothesis of a regime based upon some kind of priestly rule. Evidences were found of many types of cults still active in India and in Hinduism today, among them animal worship; the cults of trees, water, and the sun; phallic worship; and especially of a Mother Goddess now equated with Shakti-Kālī (q.v.) and a male god presumed to be a forerunner of Shiva (q.v.). These discoveries led Marshall (and his successors) to agree that "taken as a whole [the Indus] religion is so characteristically Indian as hardly to be distinguishable from still living Hinduism or at least that aspect of it which is bound up with animism and the cults of Śiva and the Mother Goddess—still the two most potent forces in popular worship." The Āryan epics, the Vedas (and especially the Rig Veda, q.v.), speak of attacks upon primitive black peoples in earthworks. These were likely the inhabitants of the valley and their cities. See Āryans, Hinduism, Kālī, Shakti, Shiva.

al-Insān al-Kāmil, Isl. A Ṣūfic term meaning Perfect Man or Universal Man. The Perfect Man ("Perfected Man" would be the Hindu term) is one who has integrated human and spiritual qualities, is faultless and at the same time dynamically able to react in full conformity to the will of God in every situation, whatever the circumstances of his life, his ego having been absorbed into that of the Prophet Muḥammad. In the end the Perfect Man goes beyond the Prophet: He can meet the Divine Will in complete simplicity and in full compliance. Al-Insān al-Kāmil personifies the created universe in anticipation of the Infinite. See Ṣūfī.

Ise shrine, Shintō. The most holy center of Shintō (q.v.), located at Yamada, province of Ise in southwest Honshu, Japan. The shrine was founded in the late third century A.D., is dedicated to the sun goddess Ama-terasu (q.v.), and is the center of her cult. The cult was originally celebrated in the imperial palace; later it was transferred to a special shrine at Yamada served by the royal princes, a move that opened worship of Ama-terasu to the public rather than reserving it for the imperial family; this shift was as much political as religious, for it helped focus the devotion and loyalty of the populace on the Emperor as the descendant and heir of the Goddess, the supreme deity of all the people. Eventually the cult became so popular that in later centuries most Japanese, no matter what other religious loyalties they might have (such as to Buddhism), made the pilgrimage to the Ise shrine (and to that of the nearby shrine of Toyo-uke-hime, the Rich Food Goddess) at least once in a lifetime.

Ama-terasu's shrine, which consists of a number of wooden buildings, is located in a dense forest near the Isuzu River. A series of four fences, one within the other, encloses the central building, the shōden. Within the shōden is a mirror in which dwells the spirit of the Sun Goddess. Flanking the shōden are two small treasure houses; within the other fences are a meeting hall for the priests and numerous small shrines and pavilions for pilgrims. Only the emperor and the high priest may enter the shōden. Every twenty years the shrine undergoes a curious ritual of birth; ever since the reign of Emperor Temmu (A.D. 673–86), the entire structure, from the shōden to the fences, is rebuilt on an identical adjoining site in order to renew the symbolic youth and purity of Shintō.

When the new complex is completed and consecrated, the spirit that dwells in the mirror is led from the old shōden (which is then taken down) to the new shrine of the Rich Food Goddess to receive offerings of food; then, with its Spirit of Ama-terasu, the mirror is brought into the newly constructed shōden. The ritual is scheduled to be repeated in 1994, the sixty-first time in over twelve hundred years, but the scarcity of the special woods needed for the new buildings and the loss of skilled craftsmen lead the Japanese to fear that the current shrine cannot be replaced. See Shintō.

Ishwara, Hind. "God," the Lord, the Supreme, in an individual sense—a personal, omniscient, all-powerful, merciful being, transcendent and immanent. A certain duality, foreign to Hindu thought, arises, for individual souls are not Ishwara, are different from Ishwara. For the average man, Ishwara, as the "personal" god, may assume the form of what he can handle, what fits into his frame of reference, conditioning, and experience. Thus an abstract God is not the object of his meditation, but a special deity, such as Hanumān, Gaṇpati, or some more accessible divinity. This is not to deny the fact that the individual "knows" that his Ishwara is but one of the many attributes of the Supreme and that his own capabilities of understanding and of attaining unity are limited. In fact, with a devotion to the Ishwara, one becomes like God but not God. See also Bhagavān.

Islam. The Arabic word connotes submission to Allāh (or God). A follower of Islam is a Muslim, one who submits. Islam is the final Revelation of the Divine process that began with Adam and continued through other prophets and messengers (including Isa, or Jesus) and culminates in Muḥammad, with whom Islam was competely revealed and Allāh's plan and message fully accomplished.

A central figure is the prophet Ibrāhīm (Abraham), who is considered pre-Judaic and pre-Christian, and is credited with the founding of the city of Mecca and the re-building of the holy shrine, the Ka'ba (which had originally been constructed by angels). Though the Arabs had the constant reminder of various prophets, not only Ibrāhīm but also Nūh (Noah), Musa (Moses), and Isa (Jesus), they slid into idolatry. Only a small group of people, known as hanīfs, maintained monotheism and true devotion to Allāh. The appearance of Muḥammad in the seventh century A.D. put the final seal on the prophetic process. Muḥammad preached a strict monotheism, along with a strong emphasis on social obligations, the works of mercy, repentance of sin, and the immanence of the Last Judgment. In the beginning he could make but few conversions. It was not until his exile in Medina after A.D. 622 that his fortunes turned, and Islam began to be accepted by the Arabs of the peninsula, though not without much resistance, especially by the desert tribes. At the time of the Prophet's death in A.D. 632 plans were being made for attacks on the neighboring non-Islamic states. Within a century Islam had spread across much of the known world, from the valleys of southern France to India and the vast steppes of Asia, almost to the Great Wall of China. There seemed to be no barriers to this faith of submission to the Oneness of the Divine: Christians, Hindus, Zoroastrians, Buddhists, and animists abandoned ancestral beliefs to accept God as the Muslims preached Him. Islam not only brought a faith to these lands but also a civilization; under its aegis it produced a culture in all the forms of the arts and literature that could be rivaled but not surpassed.

Though Islam had political consequences and implications outside the scope of this entry that are still very much alive today, its theological and mystical life continued to evolve with the same vitality it had shown during its first century.

The success of Islam has generally been ascribed to the "sword." There is some slight truth to the statement, for it was often a conquering army that introduced Islam to the peoples of other lands, yet the failure of such deep-rooted faiths as Christianity to survive even underground when confronted with the fervor of Islam says much for both beliefs. Essentially Islam aims directly at the heart of man, in utmost simplicity. All a Muslim needs to know or subscribe to is the Shahādah (q.v.), the phrase that states, "There is no God but God, and Muḥammad is His prophet." Beyond that a man need go only so far as his own capabilities can bear him and his interests can lead him. However, for the average Muslim, there are certain basics, which he will subscribe to. Islamic teaching consists of two primary sections: faith and work, or creed and practice.

There is no god but God, or Allāh. He is the Creator and the Maintainer of the world and all in it. Allāh created man and all that is in the world for man's use and service. God has no partners nor offspring (as He does in the Christian doctrine of the Trinity). God is eternal, without beginning or end, self-subsistent and One in all aspects. Nothing resembles Him. Everyone and everything depends on Him, but He does not depend on anyone and is in need of nothing. Allāh is life, seeing, hearing, speaking. He is omnipotent, omniscient; He causes things according to His benevolent will.

On the other hand, man is weak, fallible, and easily goes astray. From time to time Allāh sends his messengers, the nabis (or prophets), to bring His people back to the correct way. There are twenty-five, of whom Muḥammad is the last, or "Seal," appearing at an age when God's message—Islam—would have universal application and would suit all peoples, all environments.

The Qur'ān (q.v.) is *the* sacred book, but the Tawrah (of Moses), the Zabūr (Psalms of David), and the Injīl (Gospel of Jesus) are among other scriptures recognized. The prophets received their messages through the angel Jibril; there are other heavenly beings who execute the will of Allāh. There are also evil spirits, among them as-Shaitan (Satan), and a vast horde called jinns, who may act malevolently.

The culmination of life for the Muslim is the Day of Judgment, which will take place at some unknown time, when everyone is resurrected, to be weighed and judged in the light of past deeds. Since God is most merciful and compassionate, a good deed even of the weight of an atom will be abundantly rewarded; but for the wicked, an evil deed, also of the weight of an atom, can bring eternal punishment in Hell.

The Muslim is guided in life by a group of regulations known as the Five Pillars of Islam. They are: (1) The Shahādah, or Confession of faith, already referred to. (2) The obligation of the five daily prayers; the set of prayers is called rak'ah and consists of certain prescribed body movements, prayers, and short recitations from the Qur'ān; the prayers are said at five fixed periods during the day but are forbidden during the intervening hours as those times should be devoted to worldly occupations. (3) Alms-giving (zakāt, q.v.), a major duty that is applied according to the individual's station in life and his financial circumstances. (4) Fasting during Ramaḍān; the worshiper not only abstains from all food and drink during daylight hours (defined as the time when one can distinguish black and white threads from each other), but also sexual intercourse; pregnant women, wet-nurses, travelers, and the aged are usually exempt from the conditions of Ramaḍān. (5) The pilgrimage to Mecca, which should be performed by every Muslim at least once in his lifetime; statistics show, however, that only about one in ten has the finances and the time for the arduous trip.

In short, Islam is a religion of individual responsibility. Though man has free will and alone is fully responsible for his deeds, good or evil ("No soul bears the burden of another"), there is a predetermined Divine plan for the collective benefit of all mankind. Nevertheless, each person, women as well as men, must endeavor to lead the best possible life as a Muslim. If one succeeds, he should be thankful to God; if he fails, he should not despair or be resentful. Muslims are enjoined in the Qur'ān to follow the example of the Prophet, who is considered infallible. See also, Muḥammad, Qur'ān.

'iṡmah, Isl. Infallibility of the nabis (or prophets).

isnād, Isl. The chain of attestation of ḥadīth or tradition that leads from the Prophet Muḥammad himself. The first ḥadīth existed without the supporting isnād, which probably appeared about the end of the first Islamic century.

Isnād deals not with the question of what the Prophet said (and whether it was reasonable and in character) but who said he said it, and the transmitter's credentials: Was he reliable, truthful, and so on, or was he weak, mendacious, unknown? Is the chain of attestors unbroken? Did each know the man before him in the sequence leading back to the original source? The systematic and complex study into the biographers, known as "The Science of Justification and Impugment," became complex and verbose. Transmitters were divided into various categories such as "completely trustworthy," "truthful," "weak," "mendacious," "unknown," etc. Traditionists traveled thousands of miles in search of authentification or to be able to add their own names in face-to-face meetings with the last known attestor of a certain isnād. Of the many collections of ḥadīth, six are known as "The Six Genuine Ones," being assembled by careful research from hundreds of thousands; numerous forgeries have been detected, and in some cases the forgers executed. See ḥadīth.

iṣṭa, Hind. Literally, "beloved." The object of one's supreme desire, meaning one's own chosen deity, or iṣṭa-devatā, which he worships in a manner unique from the other gods he may also worship. His iṣṭa-devatā is the one he feels closest to, though he will also acknowledge other gods, which are also manifestations of the powers of an unknowable Immensity beyond his grasp. One's mantra (q.v.) is the verbal representation of one's iṣṭa. The deity appears as a form on a lower plane but in reality is nothing but the Supreme Self beyond form.

istislām, Isl. The going to meet the Divine Will in utter compliance. In this state, one of spiritual readiness, the Muslim—more likely a Ṣūfī rather than one of the more orthodox faithful—is prepared at a moment's notice to act in even the most mundane events, for he has the capacity to move from contemplation to action without transition.

itjihad, Isl. The seed of ijmā' (q.v.)

◂ J ▸

jade, Chin. The stone has occult significance. The ancient Chinese believed that jade prevented the decay of the body after death, and ordinarily a piece of the stone was placed on each of the nine orifices of a corpse. An extreme example of this is the funeral garments of Prince Liu Sheng and his consort, Lady Tou Wan, about the late second century B.C.; both are dressed in complete suits of jade, Lady Tou's the more elaborate, being composed of 2,160 individual jade tablets of pale and muted tonalities of green and buff stitched together with gold wire. The joint tomb was found in 1968 in Hopei Province about 100 miles southwest of Peking.

Jainism. An Indian sect of great antiquity, which claims to be the primordial religion of the subcontinent, earlier than Hinduism (q.v.). Jainism contains many relics of the religion apparently practiced by the peoples of the Indus Valley (c. B.C. 3000–1700) and has developed partly influenced by, and partly in reaction to, Vedic Hinduism, and to some extent Buddhism (q.v.). Jains officially number roughly 2.8 million members in India today, but in the national census many Jains list themselves as Hindus or as a Hindu subcaste, so precise figures are impossible to obtain. Jainism, however, despite the small numbers of adherents, has had an important effect upon Hinduism, especially in the doctrine of ahiṃsā, or nonviolence.

The core concept of Jainism is the effort to free the soul from its entrapment in matter so that it may rise, in an almost literal sense, into the perfect state—nirvāṇa—in which it will enjoy the four infinities—infinite perception, knowledge, power, and bliss—for all eternity. The name of the sect is itself indicative of the struggle over imprisoning matter, for Jain (or Jaina) is derived from the Sanskrit root ji- (to conquer), or jina (conqueror).

The history of the Jains is part legend, part fact. The Jain claim that theirs is the oldest religion is supported with passages from the Vedas (q.v.), works that they otherwise ignore and even despise. Ṛṣabha, the Bull (in Hinduism he is a minor incarnation of the god Vishnu [q.v.] and represents Morality), is the original founder of the Jains, having uttered the truths by which the present cycle of time is governed. He is mentioned also in the Yasur Veda; the *Vishnu Purāṇa* and the *Bhāgavata Purāṇa* both give the story of his life, stating that he was one of the hundred sons of Nābhi (Hub of the Wheel) and his wife Meru (the axial mountain Meru is a center of Jain worship). Ṛṣabha, after raising his sons in the path of wisdom, turned the kingdom over to them and retired to a hermitage to practice austerities so fierce that he became but an "agglomeration of skin and bones." Later he visited the southern and western parts of India, traditionally Jain strongholds, preaching wisdom.

Ṛṣabha is the first of twenty-four tīrthaṅkaras (ford-makers), of whom few facts are known; the second and third are mentioned in the Yajur Veda, and the others in various Jain works. Much of the information is obviously legendary: Ṛṣabha, for example, lived 8,400,000 years and was 500 poles (a pole is 5½ yards) in height. It is not until the last two tīrthaṅkaras that we are on historical ground. Pārshva, the twenty-third, lived a century, and died 250 years before the final sage of the line, Mahāvīra (Great Hero); some scholars believe that even this part of the Jain chronology is not very trustworthy and that Mahāvīra was a disciple of his predecessor. Mahāvīra (q.v.) was, like his somewhat younger contemporary Buddha, a member of the warrior caste and born in northern Bihar. One of the two main sects of Jains believes that Mahāvīra married and had two children, the other that he was a celibate. At any rate, he left his home at the age of thirty to seek salvation, spending twelve years wandering along the Gangetic plain, until he found full enlightenment and became a kevalin (a completed soul) and a conqueror (jina). He preached for another thirty years and died at the village of Pāvā, not far from his birthplace; the village is one of the most sacred sites of pilgrimage for the Jains. At the time of his death (B.C. 527, according to the Jains; 468, in the belief of foreign scholars), the Jains (like their rivals, the Buddhists) had little influence. The Jains did not flourish until the days of the Mauryas (late fourth century B.C.), the tradition being that the young Emperor Chandragupta (c. B.C. 317–293), the grandfather of the same Ashoka who adopted Buddhism, became a Jain patron and passed the last years of his life as a Jain monk.

At this point the Jain community was hit by a major disaster, a schism, which was initiated by a famine in Bihar. The Jain leader, Bhadrabāhu, the eleventh gaṇadhara, or "supporter of the Community," as the leaders were now called, foresaw the coming of a major famine in North India. He advised the community to flee to South India, but could not obtain everyone's support. However, with a large following of monks, among them Chandragupta, he went to the Deccan in South India. When the exiles finally returned home, twenty years later, they found that the northern group had adopted a number of dubious practices, among which was the wearing of robes. The Jains were now split into two communities; the Digambaras, or sky-clad, and the Śvetāmbaras, or white-clad. (Some scholars put the schism at a later date: A.D. 80). To heighten the tragedy, Bhadrabāhu was so upset over the schism that he went into solitary retreat in the Himālayas to fast and do penance. Unfortunately, he alone of all the Jains knew the unwritten sacred works. A general council was called at Pāṭaliputra (now Patna) to try to reconstruct the sacred scriptures from the memories of the monks. However, only a partial canon could be recalled. It is known as the Aṅgas, or Limbs, of which there are eleven. Though the Digambaras and the Śvetāmbaras admit to virtually the same doctrines, some differences remain: The sky-clad do not admit the authenticity of the Aṅgas, and they retain their insistence on total nudity, at least for the monks. Also, they teach that no woman can attain salvation; thus women are not only prevented from a monastic life, the highest calling of the Jain, but also have very little role among the Digambaras. The two groups tend to prefer different areas in India, the Digambaras in the Deccan, and the Śvetāmbaras, who are the most numerous, in Gujarāt and Rajasthan. Each group writes and speaks bitterly about the other, without, however, quarreling over doctrines and other fundamentals.

JAIN DOCTRINE is centered around the basic problem of the soul struggling to free itself from the entangling fetters of matter. The Jain philosophical system is highly complex, running from what others would call the most primitive animism to the most lofty theology. The basics are easily understood and practiced by the average layman; the higher and more complex teachings, like those of all major religions, belong to the teachers, monks, and other ascetics, and philosophers. The simplest doctrine is that of the pervasiveness of life itself, even in the supposedly inanimate objects. The entire universe throbs with life. The simplest stone contains a soul, so tightly enchained by matter that it cannot escape the foot that kicks it nor even cry out in pain. Animals, fish, birds, trees, insects of all kinds, the iron on the blacksmith's anvil—all creation groans together in pain. "An infinite number of times I have been struck and beaten, split and filed," says a Jain verse; "In every kind of existence I have suffered pains which have scarcely known reprieve." Therefore the Jain stresses nonviolence, ahiṃsā (q.v.), nonkilling in an endless struggle to keep from annihilating even the most rudimentary stage of life, for all lives are but stages in a series of transmigrations caused by karma, the accumulation of debts in past lives. Each soul must be reborn one million times, though only eight in human form; even gods (who experience 400,000 rebirths) must experience a life as man. Thus daily life is an unending effort to prevent destruction of souls in whatever form.

Things are classified in five different categories, according to the number of senses they possess. The highest, with five senses, includes gods, men, the beings in hell, and the higher animals. Of these, the first three forms, plus certain animals—among them monkeys, cattle, horses, elephants, parrots, pigeons, and snakes—possess intelligence. The second classification numbers those with four senses only: touch, taste, smell, and sight, a category that includes flies, wasps, and many other large insects. The third category covers smaller insects or three-sensed beings devoid of sight and hearing; ants, fleas, and various bugs fit in here, as do moths because of their strange habit of flying into lighted lamps. The fourth category, of two-sensed creatures, with only taste and touch, includes worms, leeches, shellfish, and similar creatures. The rest of creation is placed in the fifth category, the one-sensed beings, which are further divided. Here we find vegetable bodies (including trees), earth bodies (the earth itself and all things found in the earth, such as clay, stones, minerals, and jewels);

water bodies, which run from raindrops on one hand to ponds, rivers, and seas on the other; fire bodies; and last, wind bodies, from gases to all types of winds. The *Sūtrakṛtāṅga* (*Book of Sermons*) states that earth and water, fire and wind, grass, trees, plants, and all creature that move, born of the egg, born of the womb, born of dung, born of liquids—"Know that they all seek happiness. In hurting them men hurt themselves and will be born again among them." Even a fire has its dangers: Not only is the flame, containing a fire being with a soul that may be reborn as a human being in a human body, born only to die soon, but also the fire itself kills living things. The man who puts it out "kills the fire." "Thus a wise man who understands the Law should never light a fire." "All things in the universe suffer," says the same text in another passage, so "live in striving and self-control . . . subduing anger and fear."

Self-control is necessary not only to avoid wasting life but also for one's own salvation. Enlightened self-interest—i.e., freedom from emotion, dependence on others, being neither pleased nor annoyed with life, without desires, without possessions, spurning pleasures—is to be sought. "There is no need to tell a man who sees for himself, but the wretched fool, delighting in pleasure, has no end to his miseries but spins in a whirlpool of pain." Consequently the ideal is the passionless man, who eschews the ties of love, of family, and of friends, to concentrate on his own salvation, for all lives are stages in a series of transmigrations caused by karma, as man moves upward into the highest stages, that of complete liberation, in which the jīva (the living) is rid of all its material karmic particles. Man fights alone, for there is no supreme being to aid him; all he can do is to follow the heroes, the tīrthaṅkaras. Eventually he will attain nirvāṇa.

The universe (to reduce a complicated system to a few basics) is composed of one living (jīva) and five nonliving (ajīva) substances. They are all eternal and uncreated, since the Jains do not admit to creation in any of the manners believed in by Hindus, Buddhists, Muslims, or Christians. The admixture of jīva and ajīva constitutes the world as man knows it. The jīva, to regain its natural infinitude, must separate itself entirely from the ajīva. The link between the two, a kind of elastic, metaphysical glue, is karma —not karma in the Hindu sense, but an extremely subtle matter that pours into or infiltrates the soul when worldly actions, so to speak, make an opening in it. This karma, unlike the nontangible karma of Hinduism and Buddhism, is for the Jains a literal substance, though it passes notice by the senses. After karma flows into the soul, it then creates an actual bondage, the karmic molecules settling down to form their own kind of body. At this point the soul is weighed down by its karmas; though the body will die, the assembled karmas will linger on until final liberation.

The struggle has to be relentless. First the individual must strive for self-restraint and then self-discipline, both material and spiritual, until the flow of karma is reversed and the soul begins to shed what it has accumulated. The enlightened soul will live in the world, serving humanity and no longer afflicted by the demands of good or evil. In the next stage the soul transcends the world, having dropped behind all activity, to attain the perfected state of infinite knowledge and peace.

This way is difficult, for in the early stages the individual must practice mortification and austerities, practices that not every person is prepared to undergo. Karma is burned up in the glow of austerities. Among the practices to rid the soul of karma are fasts (some to the death); reverence to superiors of whatever form; and rigid control of the senses, speech, and intellect. Confession of faults is binding on both monks and lay people. Completely purged, "the soul takes the form of a straight line, goes in a single moment without touching anything and taking no space goes upward [to a place called akasa] and there develops into its natural form, obtains perfection, enlightenment, deliverence, and final beatitude and puts an end to all misery." Thus *Uttarādhyayana Sūtra* (the *Book of Later Instructions*).

JAIN CUSTOMS AND RITES, originally distinct, have been strongly influenced by Hinduism over the centuries. The early Jains avoided a priesthood—every man was in effect his own priest—but as in the case of virtually all religious groups, a priesthood gradually came into existence; a reaction against the power of the priests (and against the increasing use of images) came in the fourteenth and fifteenth centuries. Mahāvīra had left no tradition for or against temples and iconic veneration. The Jains constructed stūpas (q.v.) and adorned them with sculptures, particularly of the tīrthaṅkaras, which, by custom, were presented nude and with downcast eyes. Veneration of these and other images, as well as ordinary domestic rites, now follow Hindu custom, such as that of pūjā (q.v.). The Jains also venerate a number of Hindu gods. Educated Jains state that "idol worship" is actually "ideal worship," the inner essences of the image being what is actually venerated. Of the Jain prayers, the invocation of the various states of the holy man (arahantas, siddhas, ācāryas, upādghyāyas, and "all the world's sādhus") is most common. Such a prayer is said four times with folded hands, to the four points of the compass. The most solemn Jain festival is that of Pajjusana, a week that climaxes the Jain year; the people fast and may live briefly like a monk ("following poṣadha"); both men and women will make a confession of sins at a monk's retreat (apāsaro) and beg forgiveness of each other, thus beginning the new year in peace and loving kindness. Other Jain practices are virtually identical to those followed by Hindus, particularly the brāhmins. The Jains observe the same regulations concerning purity and defilement, perform the same ablutions, and recite the same mantras. The ceremonies of marriage, death, and so on are similar, if not identical, depending on the type of Jain community. However, unlike Hindus, orthodox Jains take no food between sunset and sunrise, have no anniversaries in honor of the dead, putting the deceased entirely out of memory, and never put ashes on their heads, as Hindus will do, using instead various symbols—dots and lines—of sandalwood paste, which may also be drawn on neck, shoulders, and stomach.

Jain eating habits are ritually restricted. They abstain from all animal food and from many vegetables and fruits. Vegetables that grow in a bulbous shape with stalks, or roots that grow in a similar shape are forbidden; typical proscribed items would be mushrooms, onions, and eggplant, the latter a popular part of the Indian diet. In general the Jain has a fear of taking the life of some minute insect that may be found in a fruit or vegetable. The standard diet is based on rice, milk and milk products, and various types of peas. Honey is forbidden. Water is always strained before being poured to protect the life of any living creature that may be found in it. Many Jains wear a cloth mask over the mouth to avoid breathing in—and killing—insects. See ahiṃsā, Mahāvīra.

Jambudvīpa, Hind. and Buddh. An esoteric name for the continent of India. The term is translated as Rose-appletree Island, and refers to the ancient belief that India was a separate entity. The word is much used in tantric Hinduism, as well as in some forms of Buddhism, especially Tibetan.

japa, Hind. The repeated utterance or recitation of a mantra (q.v.), according to certain practices common to one's own form of devotion, such as yoga. Some teachers insist that japa be dedicated to one's own personal deity or to one's guru (q.v.); otherwise the full benefit will not be realized. The act will be returned with blessings and profit. Japa correctly performed is more than a casual act, especially in tantra (q.v.). Esoterically the two lips of the worshiper are the two causal principles—Shiva (male) and Shakti (female) —the movement of the lips being coition (maithuna), producing the "point-limit" (bindu [q.v.]), the sperm from which creation springs. The deity thus engendered is, in a way, a son of the worshiper.

Jap-ji, Sikh. The beginning of the Granth Sāheb, the holy Scriptures of the Sikhs of India. The Jap-ji was composed—or received—by Guru Nānak (1469–1538), the founder of the Sikhs, during a period of withdrawal and meditation known as the Divine Trance, which he experienced as a young man. The Jap-ji consists of a mūl-mantra, or Seed Prayer, thirty-eight verses, and a conclusion, called a śloka. The verses, formally known as pauris or rungs, contain the essence of Sikh doctrine and gave five stages through which an individual must pass in order to gain eternal bliss. These are: the Way of Duty and Action, the Way of Knowledge, the Realm of Ecstasy, the Realm of Power (where a man loses his fear of death and is freed from the round of births and rebirths), and last, the Abode of Truth (where man is merged or absorbed into the Divine Being). In the Jap-ji Nānak rejects the common quest for the Divine through pilgrimages, rituals, and ceremonies, and directs mankind to the search through the divinely appointed guru. The guru in Sikhism is the God-conscious preceptor and link between man and the Divine but not an incarnation of God. The guru's word is supremely efficacious; it is "supernal symphony" and contains the essence of the loftiest of sacred writings; it is all-pervasive and the holiest of holies. Also, in the Jap-ji man must subdue the Self within and look instead for the Divine spark; thus he will perceive the Divine Will, which governs the cosmos, Though salvation is a Sikh tenet, it is not the sole reason for man's spiritual endeavors; better still is engulfment in the Divine and the sweet contentment of this far more noble goal. See Granth Sāheb, Nānak, Sikhs.

jar-born, Hind. The term may be employed in two senses—(1) symbolic, and (2) literal—both, however, indicative of the fusion between the invading, conquering Āryans and the indigenous population of India.

1. In certain post-Vedic texts the founders of many brāhminic clan groups are said to be "born of a jar"—i.e., the mother was non-Āryan, symbolized by the jar, a receptacle often identified with the female, and the father a Vedic deity, usually the sun and sky gods Mitra and Varuṇa, a rationalizing of the fact that a white-skinned, fair-haired Āryan has entered the "black" womb of the virtually untouchable indigenous woman. Yet, at some point, the exceptional among the offspring must be legitimatized and accepted into the widening clan structure of the Āryans. Thus, out of eight commonly accepted brahminical gotras or clan structures, seven are accepted as "jar-born," though it must be noted that the accounts differ as to the names.

2. In the literal interpretation of "jar-born" the autochthone (in this case a male, a warrior, prince, or priest)—someone respected for his special talents and considered useful by the Āryans —enters a jar and in rites simulating birth, goes through dīkṣā (initiation) and emerges like a baby, "twice born"—i.e., now a member of a caste, an Āryan.

In South India, among the people loosely called "Dravidian" (q.v.), in a ceremony known as the Golden Womb, important indigenous kings were received into the Āryan fold by the brāhmins as if they were just born. The king caused a large golden bowl or jar to be fashioned by his artisans; he entered it and curled up in the fetal position. The priestly rites for pregnancy and childbirth were recited by the brāhmins, just as they did over Āryan women.

The king emerged from his womb of gold as if newly born, having shed his indigenous status, to be accepted as a kśatriya in the same gotra as the priests. Often the entire tribe or clan would be accepted along with the king but as members of the lowest castes, to serve the Āryans as peasants and artisans. The priests received the golden bowl as their fee.

This ritual, which began after the period of the Vedas, is mentioned frequently in later scriptures, especially the Purāṇas, and demonstrates how the Āryans were forced to come to terms with the non-Āryans. It is at this period, after the Vedas, that the various non-Āryan gods and goddesses, such as Vishnu, Shiva, Shakti (in all her forms), Krishna, and so on, began to assert themselves, having been carried over from the indigenous level into the Āryan structure, where they replaced or absorbed the Vedic deities.

jātaka, Buddh. A birth story, Indian in origin, centered upon Gautama Buddha, some other buddha, or another character of past ages. The primary purpose of a jātaka is to edify by entertaining. The story may focus upon a previous existence of a buddha, either as a spirit, human being, or even in animal form. The Pāli *Tripitaka* contains 547 jātakas, many of them folk tales exceedingly archaic in origin and taken over into Buddhism. Besides the Pāli texts, there are other jātakas—in Chinese, Laotian, and various other tongues. The stories are told in verse, often vivid and vigorous, with prose commentaries; the verses are considered canonical, but the narrators may take considerable latitude in their commentaries. See Buddha.

jāti, Hind. Roughly, but not quite accurately, caste (q.v.). Jāti is used as a term for subcaste, not for one of the four major castes, which are known as varna. Many jātis are confined to special professions (like metalworkers, potters, beggars, tailors, elephant wards, hunters, and so on through all the occupations), and their origins are often found in the observance of certain totems.

Jesus Christ (and Christianity) in oriental religions. First, a brief note about Jesus as He is seen in various Christian churches. In traditionally orthodox churches (Roman Catholic, the national churches of Eastern orthodoxy, and certain other oriental and

Protestant groups claiming apostolic succession) Jesus is the Son of God, the Almighty Father; He is descended from heaven, was conceived by the Holy Spirit, and was born of the Virgin Mary. Upon His death He descended into hell and after three days arose. He ascended into heaven again, where He "sits" on the right hand of God the Father. In brief, this summarizes the standard definitions found in the ancient Creeds. Certain Protestant churches and some of the early schismatic churches have differing views; some of them see Jesus as God alone and not man at the same time, while others view Him as a uniquely holy man but not divine. For a few Christians, the classical Trinity does not exist in the ancient, formal sense. However, for a Christian, Jesus is not an avatār (q.v.) in the sense that a Hindu sees a divine incarnation. For both Christian and Hindu an avatār is not "the new Adam." A Christian cannot see an avatār as "the Word made Flesh," though a Hindu may. However, in formal Hinduism, an avatār is not a human body or shape, for it is made of heavenly matter and is only a passing manifestation. Following are some diverse views of Jesus as held among Hindus, Buddhists, and Muslims.

1. In Hinduism. The view of Jesus varies according to the individual and the sect or Way followed and the sophistication and conditioning of educational levels. To some Hindus, Jesus is an avatār as other incarnations have been, no different from any of the other great sages or rishis. Jesus may also be a great guru, a mahāguru, or a mahāpuruṣa, a great teacher, and His picture or image may be found in orthodox homes along with those of Krishna, Gaṇpati, Kālī, or any other popular divinity or sage. However, other Hindus may dismiss Jesus as not being a fully realized holy man, for in Hinduism, as he gains enlightenment, the muni becomes silent. Jesus, as a perfect muni, would not have spoken, and either would have retreated into a hermitage in an isolated site or taken up a life of wandering in the manner of the traditional sannyāsi. Jesus' forty days in the desert were merely the beginning of an unfulfilled mission, not of preaching, but of attaining union with the Supreme.

2. In Buddhism. Since, strictly speaking, there is no supreme power in Buddhism, there can be no Son of God, and hence no Jesus Christ. Jesus does not enter Buddhism even on the level of the folk or village deity or spirit. Buddhists exposed to Christian

proselytizing rarely respond. An explanation might be found in the comment of the late D. T. Suzuki, a Japanese Buddhist: "Christian symbolism has much to do with the suffering of man. The crucifixion is the climax of all suffering. Buddhists also speak much about suffering, and its climax is the Buddha serenely sitting under the Bodhi tree by the river Niranja. Christ carries his suffering to the end of his earthly life, whereas Buddha puts an end to it while living and afterward goes on preaching the gospel of enlightenment until he quietly passes away under the twin Sala trees. . . . Christ hangs helpless, full of sadness on the vertically erected cross. To the oriental mind, the sight is almost unbearable. . . . The crucified Christ is a terrible sight." Another contemporary Buddhist, Fumio Masutami, states the difference philosophically. "Buddha has taught that we should depend on ourselves and the dharma as refuge, and on nothing else. In Christianity, the spirit of self-reliance and the desire for reasoning are to be abandoned; the flower of faith is to bloom through faith in Jesus. Buddhism upholds reason and urges us to develop it. Christianity denounces human reason and exhorts us to be saved by God in humble consciousness of our sin."

3. In Islam. The Muslims consider Jesus (Isa) one of the nabis or messengers of god. But they do not accept him in any sense as the Son of God. The concept that God should have issue is viewed with a feeling akin to horror. They believe that Christianity is contaminated by both the errors of Greek philosophy and the distorted views of Pauline mysticism, and that only Islam represents the true faith, being the pure teachings originally meant in both the Old and New Testaments, as interpreted by the special graces given to Muḥammad the Prophet and messenger.

4. Comment. A central objection to Christianity for both Hindus and Buddhists is the doctrine of the Body and Blood of Christ. No matter how Western theologians may define the Eucharist—which Roman Catholics as well as many other Christians take in a literal sense as the actual Body and Blood of Jesus though under the aspect of bread and wine—they are unable to restate it in terms acceptable to Hindus and Buddhists. The very thought of consuming blood and meat is abhorrent, and to partake of God's own Body and Blood is sacrilegious and nauseating be-

yond belief. The bleeding figure of the Crucified Christ, fundamentalist phrases such as "washed in the Blood of the Lamb," and so on, are extremely offensive to the East. The Cross itself, with its dangling, broken, bleeding figure—a negation of salvation to oriental minds—is the opposite of the peace symbolized in the traditional posture of Buddha and Indian saints, seated on the ground, firmly in touch with the forces of Mother Earth, completely in control of both physical and spiritual worlds. The cross signifies instability; the triangle △ formed by the Eastern holy man, stability. And the militaristic concepts of Christianity—the Army of the Lord, the Conquering Hosts, Christian soldiers, soldiers of Christ, the Jesuit superior as a "general," and so on—are offensive to nonviolent people. Also, the exploitation of the East by Christians has left an indelible mark on the consciousness of Hindus and Buddhists. And last, they are repelled by the sights, often commented upon, of an incredible, if not ludicrous, odd-colored man, in strange clothing, perspiring, speaking the local language badly if at all, asking his hearers to abandon everything they have held sacred, often for millennia—their traditional beliefs, culture, institutions, music and poetry, rites and rituals, even their families—to subscribe to a doctrine that his fellow whites barely pay lip service to. See Buddhism, Hinduism, Islam.

Jibril, Isl. The angel Gabriel, who appeared to Muḥammad during the revelations. See Islam, Muḥammad, Qur'ān.

jinn (or djinn), Isl. An invisible spirit, on the same level of creation as man but said to be of a fiery substance, a rough parallel to man but in general more prone to evil. The devil is supposed to have sprung from the same substance as that which produced jinns. They inhabit natural phenomena—in particular, the winds, hills, and wells. Muḥammad, who strongly opposed the idea of the jinn, stating that there could be no other deities but God (Allāh), still felt forced to accept them (and angels). His immediate reaction upon being spoken to by the angel Jibril (Gabriel) was that he was being fooled by malicious jinns. In early Arabia belief in jinn possession was common; one of the charges against the Prophet was that he was possessed, for he showed some of the signs, which include ejaculations, crying out, chanting of rhymed verse, and divination. See Islam.

jīva, Hind. Individual consciousness; the embodied soul. Jīva is monodic in character, conceived either as an eternal aspect of the eternal Brahman (q.v.) or as an artificial manifestation under the influence of māyā (q.v.), roughly, illusion. Jīva ceases to exist when māyā is conquered by jñāna (q.v.), or knowledge of the Supreme. Fettered by both māyā and avidyā (ignorance), jīva results in the ego-sensation. Liberation is attained by a practical realization of the oneness of the Self with the Absolute, when the person becomes jīvan-mukta, as in the case of the sage or the guru who is freed while alive. See jīvan-mukta (below); also see guru.

jīvan-mukta, Hind. The liberated soul, spared the endless rounds of birth and rebirth, attained while living in the physical world. This state is usually gained only by the advanced yogi—he is "dead in life" but "liberated in life." When he abandons his body at death his puruṣa—his Self in the most advanced stage—is completely freed of the fetters of matter. Yoga in its classic form is the only means of preparation for jīvan-mukta. See yoga.

jñāna, Hind. A form of knowledge in the higher sense—i.e., a type that leads to the Supreme. As such jñāna is a "path" to the Divine. Jñāna demands rigorous self-discipline, and here it takes on a social character, for it is the province of the upper castes who by nature and schooling can follow such a way, in contrast to the way of bhakti (q.v.), so often followed by the uneducated lower castes, which offers an ecstatic attainment of the Divine.

Ju. The Chinese term for the school of thought known in the West as Confucianism (q.v.).

◂K▸

Ka'ba, Isl. (1) The spiritual, mystical, and the holiest center of Islam. The Ka'ba is a cube of masonry, open to the sky, situated in the middle of a large square in the heart of Mecca, the most sacred city of Islam. The Ka'ba contains the sacred Black Stone, set into its southeast corner; it is the central point toward which all Muslims must pray.

The history of the Ka'ba is confused and contradictory, tradition being interlaced with myth and superstition. Some tradition states that it was built by the Prophet Ibrāhīm (q.v.), who was the great-great-grandfather of the Prophet Muḥammad. One of the fullest versions is given by Sir Richard Francis Burton (*A Personal Narrative of a Pilgrimage to el-Medinah and Meccah* [London, 1855–56]) who, as the result of his own research, established ten stages in the construction of the building, roughly as follows.

A preliminary version was found in heaven, built, in some traditions forty years, in others, two thousand years before Creation; here angels endlessly circumambulated the building singing praises to Allāh. Eventually Allāh ordered a similar house on earth for man; it was rebuilt by Adam when he was created; there are variations on the account, which need not be detailed. A third building was constructed by Adam's sons—again the versions vary—possibly of stone and mud, for the original building was taken to heaven. The accounts reach historical times with the construction of the fourth Ka'ba. It was with this building that the complicated rites of pilgrimage were introduced. In pre-Muslim days pilgrims, who were mostly pagans and not the few monotheists such as the hanifs (q.v.), circumambulated nude, going around the structure seven times counterclockwise, a practice (except for the nudity) still observed. The Ka'ba was a temple for various pagan deities, though the idea of a one God known as Allāh continued, though mixed with numerous idolatrous beliefs.

The fifth through eighth reconstructions appeared under the auspices of known historical figures, the last, according to Islamic tradition, being the Prophet himself, then in his twenty-eighth year. In the sixty-fourth Islamic year the Ka'ba, being weakened by both fire and the ravages of war, was partially pulled down and heavily restored on a grander scale by a descendant of Muḥammad's. However, his changes were unauthorized by the Islamic leaders, and in a tenth reconstruction, modifications were made to restore it to the Prophet's own version. A final building occurred sometime in the eleventh century A.D. after damage from a severe storm and flooding. Various khalifs and kings have tried to elaborate upon the Ka'ba since then but have been forbidden by the imāms and other powerful religious leaders.

Burton, who was to all intents a practicing Muslim and a Ṣūfī at the time of his visit to Mecca, described the Ka'ba as "an oblong massive structure, 18 paces in length, 14 in breadth, and from 35 to 40 feet in height." Of the famous Black Stone, he remarked, "Moslems agree that it was originally white and became black by reason of men's sins. It appeared to me a common aërolite covered with a thick shaggy coating, glossy and pitch-like worn and polished."

The Ka'ba is enclosed with a later building, the Great Sanctuary (or Harām), a vast, unroofed rectangle, the sides of which are formed by arched colonnades and nineteen arched gates embellished with colored geometrical patterns. The encircling rampart is decorated with quotations from the Qur'ān written in a flowing calligraphy. The Ka'ba itself is draped with a heavy black damask cloth ornated with gold embroidery of quotations from the Qur'ān. Each year the cloth is replaced by Egypt, the old one being either stolen in pieces by the pious or given to various pilgrims as relics. Adjoining the Ka'ba are the well of Zam Zam (q.v.), found by Ibrāhīm's wife Hajar, and another sacred stone, the maqām (literally, "The Standing") of Ibrāhīm. Muḥammad's grandfather, a tribal leader, held the concession for distributing holy water from the well. When Muḥammad occupied Mecca, he destroyed the 365 wood and stone idols and made the Ka'ba the center of the restored monotheism he preached. Ten years later he proclaimed that non-Muslims would not be allowed to make the pilgrimage to the Ka'ba, giving them four months in which to convert, after which they would be barred.

Ka'ba, Zor. (2) A marble structure in a remarkable state of preservation some five miles north of Persepolis in Iran, at Naqsh-i Rustam. It was probably built about B.C. 500. The Zoroastrians claim that this Ka'ba is the model for that at Mecca, but no firm connection has even been established. The Zoroastrian building is known as the Ka'ba-i Zardusht—i.e., Zoroaster's Ka'ba (or Shrine). It is a perfect cube, twenty-four feet square, standing in the center of an artificial lake, also square, and is about sixty feet from the base of the cliff of Hussein Kūh (Hussein's Hill), which contains the four tombs of Darius, Xerxes, Artaxerxes, and Darius II. The door of the Ka'ba faces the tomb of Darius. To the west, carved in the cliff, are two fire altars. The three sides of the Ka'ba are decorated with simulated windows. Since the rediscovery of the Ka'ba in 1821, archaeologists and historians have been baffled by the purpose of the building, for its unventilated interior could not have made a fire possible. Zoroastrians today maintain that the fire came not from burning wood but from a fabulous ruby, basing their surmise on a passage in Firdausi's epic *Shah Namah* (c. A.D. 1000) concerning a "Temple of the Ruby" standing next to a mountain in a pool of "shining waters" adjoining two fire altars; however, "shining waters" may also mean an exhalted inner mystical experience. The remains of a similar structure, with only one standing wall, can be seen at Pasargadae, the royal seat of Cyrus. See Zoroastrianism.

Kabīr, (A.D. 1440–1518). A bhakti mystic of North India, born in Benares. Accounts differ about his birth. Indian hagiographers, who put his life span at 1398–1527, state that he was found as a babe lying on a lotus leaf in an abandoned tank; he was received into the Muslim community with the appropriate rites and named Kabīr (the Great). Other sources are unable to state authoritatively whether or not he was low-caste Hindu, or a Muslim who abandoned Islam at an early age. At any rate, as a weaver by trade, he was considered of lowly origin and profession. He soon earned a reputation for mystical practices, performing miracles and preaching social equality. "None shall inquire into thy caste," he wrote; "he who shall recite the name of the Lord will be claimed by Him." He drew upon both the Vaisnavite form of Hinduism, rejecting its polytheistic doctrines and simplifying its teachings, and Ṣūfism, to preach a universal relation of God indwelling in the heart of man, attempting to show a middle way between the excesses of Hinduism and the fierce dogmatism of Islam. "Those are good horsemen who keep aloof from Veda and Qur'ān," he wrote, referring to the two basic scriptures of both sects. And: "O God, whether Allāh or Rāma, I live by Thy name." He wrote in the common tongue of the people (often quite ungrammatically) rather than in the priestly Sanskrit, for "Sanskrit is like water in a well, the language of the people is a flowing stream." His central teaching may be expressed in a passage from one of his works:

> The difference among faiths is due only to difference in names; everywhere there is yearning for the same God. Why do the Hindus and the Muslims quarrel for naught? Keep at a distance all pride and vanity, insincerity and falsehood; consider others the same as yourself; let your heart be filled with love and devotion. Then alone will your struggle be fruitful. Life is but transitory, waste not your time, but take refuge in God. He is within your own heart, so why do you fruitlessly search him out in holy places, in scriptures, in rites and ceremonials?

He believed in the mystic as ordinary man, a Ṣūfic concept. He did not follow the path of austerity or celibacy; he was twice married, had children, and worked at a common trade. During his lifetime he founded an order for monks and nuns, who served to propagate his bhakti doctrines. His teachings are known as Kabīrpanth, and his followers as panthīs. He had a profound effect upon his more famous contemporary, Guru Nānak, the founder of the Sikhs, and many of Kabīr's hymns are included in the Sikh scripture, the Granth Sāheb. At his death his Muslim and Hindu panthīs were split over the disposition of his body: burial vs. cremation. The dilemma was solved when only a bunch of flowers was found in the shroud. The Muslims established a monastery on his tomb at Mahagar near Benares, while the Hindus, who formed the larger group (now totaling over four million panthīs), have centers at Benares and Chattisgar. Phrases from his songs and aphorisms have contributed to the folk wisdom of the Indian people. Kabīr's writings, collected in the *Bījak,* have been translated into English by the nineteenth-century Bengali poet Rabindranath Tagore. See bhakti, Ṣūfī.

kāfir, Isl. A non-Muslim, or sometimes a heretical Muslim. The term may be employed in a derogatory sense.

Kailāsa, Hind. The snow-white mountain summit, mystical abode of the god Shiva (q.v.). Kailāsa plays an important part in tantric lore. It is said to be a peak of the wonderful and mysterious Meru, a Himālayan mountain sacred to tantrics. Described in tantric literature as a summerland of cool shade and lasting sunshine, musical with the song of birds, sweet with the fragrance of flowers, and resounding with the music and song of celestial singers and players, it is the paradise set aside for the devout worshipers of Shiva's symbol, the liṅga (q.v.).

Kalām Allāh, Isl. The Word of God—i.e., the Qur'ān.

Kālī, Hind. A form of the world Mother and of the female principle. She is often referred to as the goddess of destruction, especially by foreigners, who have misunderstood her many roles in Hindu life. She destroys only to re-create, and what she destroys is negative—sin and ignorance. She is equated with the eternal night, the transcendent power of time, Kālī or Mahā-Kālī, and is the consort of the god Shiva (q.v.), Kāla. Shiva as Kāla destroys the worlds, while Kālī, the feminine form, represents the energy or power of time, without which Shiva could not act.

The role of the goddess is ancient. She has been linked to the cities of the Indus Valley (q.v.), and is obviously a non-Āryan and pre-Āryan divinity. No Āryan people (the supposed conquerors of the Indus cities) has ever raised a female deity to the supreme rank that she held in the Indus and that she maintains in Hinduism today. She may have been an aboriginal deity of vegetation and agriculture. The practice of animal and human sacrifices to the goddess point to her role as a fertility divinity. Animal sacrifices are still made to Kālī, notably in temples like that at the Kalighat in Calcutta, where a goat is immolated in her honor every day. On her feast in the fall, goats and buffalos are the usual victims, along with certain types of vegetation. Human sacrifice has been banned but occasionally are reported to the authorities from remote areas.

In her iconography she is fearsome. She is presented as black, standing on the white corpse of her husband, Shiva, who is inert without her powers. Her tongue lolls, she is naked (space-clad), and she wears a garland of heads. She has four arms, for the four directions of space; one hand holds a sword, the power of destruction; another a severed head to show the living their destiny; however, a third is in an attitude of peace to remove fear; and the fourth bestows bliss. Her cult is especially powerful in Bengal and eastern India, where she is often worshiped as Durgā. Devī, Śakti, Satī, Umā, and Pārvatī are some of the names under which she also appears, usually as the consort of Shiva. Kālī is also the goddess Kuṇḍalinī, the Serpent Power, who arises from the depths of the body in tantric yoga, to pierce the thousand-petaled lotus at the top of the skull and thus bring the devotee to nirvāṇa. See Hinduism, Shiva.

Kali-yuga, Hind. The present age, the last of the four yugas (q.v.). The Kali-yuga, according to some traditions, began in B.C. 3120 on the day of Vishnu's return to heaven after his eighth incarnation (as Krishna [q.v.]). The yuga, which will last 432,000 human years (1,200 divine years), is one with a prevalence of viciousness, weakness, disease, and the general decline of all that is good. Righteousness exists only to the extent of one fourth that normally encountered in the previous yugas. The human life span has declined to a mere one hundred years, 120 if the individual leads a good life. The Kali-yuga is the age of the Buddha (q.v.), whom many Hindus regard as a malevolent avatār. The last avatār, Kalki (q.v.), the Destroyer of Sin, has yet to come. See Vishnu.

Kalki, Hind. The final avatār (q.v.) of the god Vishnu. Kalki will destroy iniquity and restore the age of righteousness, initiating a new mahā-yuga in the endlessly repeated cycle. The *Kalki Purāṇa* speaks of him as one whose body is blue, who with sword in hand will ride a white horse swift as the wind, to destroy the race of the Kali-yuga (q.v.), to inaugurate the true religion again. See kalpa.

kalpa, Hind. A kalpa is a day of Brahmā of 4,320,000,000 years. It is divided into fourteen manvantaras, which are again subdivided into seventy-one mahā-yugas, the length of each being 3,320,000 human years. The mahā-yuga (or great age) is composed of four yugas; Satya, Treta, Dvāpara, and Kali. The Satya-yuga was the golden age of righteousness, free of sin, marked by longevity, physical strength, beauty, and great stature. The world declined progressively in the following yugas; we are now in the present, the kali-yuga (q.v.), an age of sin. With the arrival of Kalki (q.v.)—yet to come—the world will be returned to a new mahā-yuga, and the ages will continue to revolve with their rising and descending races of mankind until the close of the kalpa or day of Brahmā. Then a night of dissolution of equal duration will follow, the Lord reposing in yogic sleep on the serpent Śeṣa, the Endless One, until daybreak, when the universe is created anew and the next kalpa follows.

kalwah, Isl. The practice of spiritual retreat in the solitude of an isolated cell or small hermitage or cave. Kalwah is often given Ṣūfī novices by a master; the novice may spend up to forty days from sunrise to sunset in fasting, prayer, and recitation of the Shahādah (q.v.) or the Divine Name of Allāh. See faqir, Ṣūfī.

kāma, Hind. Desire. One of the three pursuits commonly desired and followed by most men; the other two are dharma (q.v.) and artha. In other contexts kāma—as sexual desire—is one of five sins the yogi must cut off, the others being wrath, greed, fear, and sleep.

kami, Shintō. A deity or spirit. A kami can be a deity of any type, from the highest, the Sun Goddess Ama-terasu (q.v.), to the simplest spirit of a stone, tree, or waterway. Individual souls become kami after death. See Shintō.

kamma, Buddh. The Pāli spelling of karma (q.v.).

kandoma, Tib. A feminine deity in Tibetan Buddhism. See mkah hgroma.

Kannon (also Kanzeon), Buddh. The Japanese form of Kuan Yin (or Avalokiteśvara), the bodhisattva who helps lead the faithful into Amida Buddha's paradise of the Pure Land. The alternate name, Kanzeon, means "Hearing the calls of living beings," or "Hearing the calls of the suffering world." Kannon is sometimes confused with earlier deities found in Shintō (q.v.); in some references he has a thousand arms. See Avalokiteśvara, Kuan Yin, Pure Land.

Kapila, Sans. A sage and rishi, c. seventh century B.C., although many texts place him at primordial times. He was a leading member of the school that taught the ancient cosmological philosophy Sāmkhya, upon which the tenets of classical yoga (q.v.) are based. In the *Bhāgavata Purāṇa* (c. tenth century A.D.) Kapila is the fifth of twenty-four incarnations of Vishnu (q.v.). In this work he plays the role of teacher, in some instances preaching the path of devotion (bhakti, q.v.) to his mother Devahūti, advocating the awareness of the true realization of the presence of the Lord rather than the following of empty forms of devotion and rites, a brāhminical custom. "Expiatory acts are for the unintelligent," said Kapila, dismissing the priesthood; "knowledge is expiation." Rather one should practice the utterance of the Lord's name, which destroys sin completely, even an utterance meant in fun or involuntarily.

Kapila, as a non-brāhmin (though he was taken into the brāhminical structure), studied the ancient wisdom of the antigods, or asuras, and was a key figure in introducing the primordial knowledge of the earlier peoples of India into the Vedic Āryan colonizing society that came after B.C. 1500. In both the Rāmāyaṇa and Mahābhārata (see both) he is sometimes identified with Agni, the Lord of Fire; in both texts he destroys with a single glance of his flaming eye the sixty thousand sons of King Sagar who had destroyed his meditation in searching the underworld for a stolen sacrificial horse. This is clearly an act of revenge of the primordial population upon the Āryan conquerors and their practice of the horse sacrifice, aśvamedha (q.v.). See Gaṇgā.

karma. A complex concept, which is roughly summarized as "work" (and in Western minds becomes "fate"). One must work out one's karma through the actions of one's life. "A man of good deeds becomes good, a man of evil deeds becomes evil," say several Hindu texts. The word originally denoted a religious act or rite and gradually assumed other shades of meanings: action, work, past actions as producing good or evil results. Now, in a broad sense, karma implies the law of moral consequences that one performs not for personal, selfish, or ambitious reasons but in an attitude of complete detachment for impersonal reasons. That is the ideal; in practice more selfish and practical influences are present. Karma and its interpretations differ in various forms of Hinduism and in the related sects and ways. The major aspects will be considered as follows:

1. Hinduism. The present existence is shaped and determined by the deeds of a previous existence, which itself was formed by the products of an earlier existence, and so on backward, in a series of lives subject to the blind determinism of strict retribution. Thus karma is the effect of any action upon the doer, whether in a past, present, or future life. Even the gods are not spared. With this in mind, most Indian sects believe that karma works as a kind of automatic moral safeguard ensuring that the righteous move toward liberation from the cycle of birth and rebirth, while the evildoers are more and more bound to it, to their own detriment. In classical terms the series of lives is known as samsāra, or stream current; it is also compared with a vast ocean "fraught with dangers and whirlpools." Man is caught in the stream (says the *Katha-Upaniṣad*) and "Like wheat man ripens [and dies] and like grain he is born again."

The wise man distinguishes the values facing him: "What is good is different from what is pleasure" says the same Upanishad. "The sage chooses what is good, the dull-witted what is pleasurable. Those who think this world exists and the other does not fall again and again under the sway of death." Different schools teach different methods of escaping from the stream: Some teach sacrifice (yajña); others, offerings and worship (pūjā); and others, a good and moral life. Some believe that a special Grace received from the Supreme God will remove the bounds of karma. This conflict, whether one is absolved from karma by following the traditional laws, or by God's mercy, as taught by bhakti (q.v.), is one that is not resolved, one school saying "The Supreme Self can be obtained neither by verbal explanation nor by reflection nor by revelation," while the bhakti schools teach "Only he who desires Him can obtain Him; the Self reveals His own Truth," and, "He alone whom He chooses can obtain Him. The Self reveals Himself to Him."

Under the traditional laws of karma, every action produces an effect or "fruit" in the temporal world, which is related to the self (but not, however, to the *soul,* which in its deepest essence is identical with the Brahman [q.v.]). When man realizes his own true self, karma ceases for him, breaking "the endless hopping from womb to womb." Traditional masters state today that "karma is extinguished by karma"—i.e., the chain of cause and effect of past and present actions is neutralized by counteractions.

2. Jainism. For the Jains karma is something material that inundates the soul in a most unpleasant manner and ties it to the world and its attractions. Though it is a material substance it cannot be perceived by the senses; it can, however, be burned up by the proper austerities.

3. Buddhism. The Mahāyānist (q.v.) schools employ the Sanskrit term karma, and in broad outline follow the Hindu concept of the universal law of act and consequence. The Hīnayānist (q.v.), using the Pāli kamma, have divergent views. First, the Mahāyānist. Karma is a law, the working out of which cannot be escaped from. Every being inherits the karma of past lives and produces more karma, the total of which will affect future existences. But karma does not force a blind determinism upon the individual. Karma presents him with what might be called a data bank of accumulated influences; the individual has the free will to break out of the patterns that threateningly enfold him. As much as, or more than, the act is the volition that produces it. In the end, nothing but relentless striving—not prayer, sacrifice, offerings, austerities, and penances—will free the individual of the chains of karma. Within Mahāyāna the only general exception to this approach is that furnished by the Pure Land schools of Buddhism, in which faith in the Amida Buddha (q.v.) rather than one's own good works leads to salvation.

The Hīnayānist doctrine of kamma is more difficult, and one is tempted to wonder if any but the most highly educated monks comprehend it. Kamma includes not only the sphere of sentient beings but also the whole of phenomenal existence. Kamma is the reality that preserves the past, for good or evil, and evolves the future. All things are born of kamma, in change, movement, activity. Nothing is static: The world is in a continual process of becoming, with no creation and no destruction, no beginning and no end. Kamma depends on the nature of personality, the essential being not the "I" but the content. This content is never the same for any two moments. One has an illusory idea of identity but "that I am one and the same person [continually] is the result of an illusion," says the *Bodicharyāvatāra,* an early Buddhist work. Each successive "ego" is followed the next moment by another, connected by certain links. Yet nothing exists that is autonomous, for everything depends on another, and this other thing on which it depends is itself dependent. Only the individual who sees that everything originates in a cause and is able to bring about the cessation of that cause will perceive the meaning of Saddhamrma (the Way of the Buddha) and can grasp the essence of Buddhahood. At that moment he breaks the chain of kamma.

4. Sikhism. The Sikhs follow the wider Hindu beliefs in rebirth due to one's not being able to escape the bounds of karma—"Soiled by its former births the soul is black as jet," says the Granth Sāheb (q.v.). Escape comes from the twin forces of man's own efforts and God's grace. The Sikh Guru Nānak stated, "According to the seed we sow is the fruit we reap. By God's will, man must either be saved or endure new births." But life itself is an affirmation, for "Thou has acquired this human frame: This is thy opportunity to be one with God." But man cannot attain salvation alone: "There can be no peace for man so long as he thinks that of himself he can do anything. He shall wander from womb to womb in the cycle of births," but if through God's grace "a man dies to self and be born to new understanding, then the soul is free from its soiling and is not born again." See Hinduism; see also Buddhism, Jainism, Sikhism.

Kaśyapa, Hind. and Buddh. There is much confusion over this figure, who is known by two versions of the same name, Kāśyapa as well as Kaśyapa, the change in stress supposedly indicating different individuals; Mahākaśyapa and the Pāli Kassapa are but more of the same. The name Kaśyapa is an inverted magical form of the word paśyaka (seer). In Hindu tradition, Kaśyapa, the god Vision, is the universal progenitor of men, gods, and demons, all born of his thirteen wives, the daughters of Dakṣa, Ritual Skill (who in some texts is also the father of Satī, the god Shiva's wife). In the Rig Veda the Kaśyapas are mentioned briefly as a gotra or clan, obviously of primitive, non-Āryan origin; they became twice-born and brāhmins, high in caste, and prominently mentioned in the Brāhmaṇas, being a leading tribe of the (now) United Provinces and Bihār, the latter the home of Gautama Buddha. The Kaśyapas are also mentioned in both Jain and Buddhist traditions. The Jain saint Mahāvīra (q.v.) was ascribed to the Kaśyapa gotra. In certain Buddhist literature the three Buddhas preceding Gautama Śakyamuni were Kaśyapas. A Kaśyapa—which individual brother varies from version to version—sometimes known as the Uruvelā Kaśyapa, or confused with Narada, another twice-born non-Āryan (see the *Mahā Nārada Kassapa Jātaka*), is both the Gautama Buddha's immediate successor and his most prominent disciple, being himself the Master of an immense number of followers. Uruvelā Kaśyapa was one of three fire-worshiping brāhmins converted by Gautama Buddha. He is a member of the Occult Hierarchy in current Hindu occultism, and a Great One sent from Venus as a forerunner of Gautama. When King Bimbasāra was told "The Master has come," he did not know if he were to bow before Kaśyapa or Gautama Śakyamuni as the Master. When the arahats asked the Buddha the nature of Ultimate Reality, and he pointed to a bowl of flowers, only Mahākaśyapa comprehended his Master's gesture (this is traditionally the first Zen kōan). It was Mahākaśyapa who convened the first Buddhist Council after the Buddha's death. See Buddha, in Hinduism.

The Keeper of the Pass, Tao. The Keeper was one Kuan Yin-hsi (c. sixth century B.C.), a figure whose historicity is questioned. He is the coactor in a famous but doubtful incident, that of the flight of the Taoist sage Lao Tzu from his homeland into a safe haven in the West. Kuan Yin-hsi, fearful that the Sage would disappear and that his teachings would be forever lost, asked him to stop to write out the essence of his thought. This Lao Tzu did, spending three days on a brief work of five thousand characters, known as the *Lao tzu* or the *Tao Te Ching*. Kuan Yin-hsi came to be regarded as a philosopher in his own right, though nothing of his works have survived, if any had existed. However, the *Lü shih ch'un ch'iu,* a compendium (c. B.C. 240) of all knowledge that mattered, mentioned that he valued "limpidity." An earlier work, the fourth-century B.C. *Chuang tzu,* mentions him several times, and in a summary of philosophers and their thought states the essence of his thinking: "Do not take a personal point of view; let visible things be revealed spontaneously," he said. "Act like water, remain quiet like a mirror, react like an echo." He added: "Be confused like perfect freedom and silent as disinterestedness. What is shared with others is harmony; what is gotten from them is a loss. Never precede others, but always follow them." This is traditional Taoism, of the type found in the *Tao Te Ching.*

The sage Lü Yen, founder of the eighth-century A.D. esoteric cult called the Elixer of Life (Chin Tan Chiao), claimed that he derived his knowledge from Kuan Yin-hsi. See Lao Tzu, *The Secret of the Golden Flower,* Taoism.

kensho, Buddh. A Zen term that means "seeing into the self-nature." Kensho is the first experience of satori and is said to be the most important of all. See satori.

Keshab Chandra Sen (1834–84), Hind. A westernized Bengali who played an important role in the reformist Brāhmo Samāj (q.v.). He reintroduced various folk customs and practices, among them music and dance, but fought other traditions such as the legislation against the remarriage of widows. He was attracted by the supposed simplicity of Christianity and saw it as a revitalizing and strengthening support for reformed Hinduism. "Was not Jesus Christ an Asiatic?" he asked. "In fact, Christianity was founded and developed by Asiatics, and in Asia." He was also fervently interested in the Bengali saint and mystic Rāmakrishna (q.v.), whose simplicity and devoutness attracted Hindu intellectuals. Unlike many Indians who opposed the British, Keshab saw a partnership between Western science, business, industry, and techniques on one side, and on the other, Indian knowledge, meditational practices, and asceticism as taught by the ancient sages—

"the heavenly madness," he called what India had to offer. To him, the Brāhmo Samāj was the one central point on which the major religions of India—Hinduism, Islam, and Christianity—could unite in a worldwide religious brotherhood. Unfortunately, his overwhelming enthusiasm for reform, coupled with some personal indiscretions that violated his own teachings, brought about a three-way division in the Brāhmo Samāj.

khalif, Isl. The Arabic means "successor," and the term was applied to the first four Islamic leaders to follow the Prophet Muḥammad, beginning with Abū Bakr (q.v.). By the end of the first Islamic century (c. A.D. 600) the term came to have more and more of a secular connotation, and eventually could denote virtually any type of high ruler within the Arab world.

Khārijites, Isl. The term khārijī means a rebel; the plural is khawārij. The Khārijites were originally part of the Shī'a (q.v.), the party that supported 'Ali in his struggle for the khalifate, then assassinated him when he compromised. They drew their members from the borders of Arabia, Iraq, and Persia. They were noted for their intense piety and their rebelliousness; intolerance, fanaticism, and exclusivity were their hallmarks, along with puritanism and intense devotion to Allāh. They preached absolute equality of station in life and race, but felt free to kill any Muslim not a Khārijite, as well as any infidel. The movement still exists, though under different names: They are known as Ibadis or Abadis in North Africa, 'Uman and Zanzibar. They have had much influence on the Wahhābīs, a reformist, puritanical, militaristic sect very much in control in Sa'ūdī (or Saudi) Arabia. See 'Ali, Shī'a.

Khātam an-nubuwwah, Isl. The Seal of Prophecy—i.e., Muḥammad as the last of the prophets. As such, he climaxes the antecedent faiths of Judaism and Christianity, and is the Seal of the prophetic missions of Ibrāhīm, Musa, and Isa (Abraham, Moses, and Jesus), who carried out his "mandate." See Muḥammad.

khatīb, Isl. The religious leader who delivers (or reads) a sermon at noon in a mosque on Fridays in Islamic countries. He is distinct from the muezzin, who issues the call to prayer, and the imām, who leads the prayers in a mosque, though in smaller or poorer congregations one individual may serve all three functions. See Islam, mosque.

Khayyam, Umar (or Omar; also Omar-i-Kayyām), Sūfī. A minor Persian poet, born in Nashapur of Afghan parents from the Ṣūfī community at Balkh about A.D. 1015, dying, after an unusually long life, no later than 1125. Not much is known about Khayyam as a Ṣūfī, though his fame is worldwide, his fame resting upon the translation of his *Rubaiyat* by the Englishman Edward Fitzgerald in the nineteenth century. Fitzgerald, who took considerable and unwarranted liberties with the original text (which is available in differing, late manuscripts), shifting verses about, adding his own ideas, or eliminating whatever displeased him, produced a work that is the antithesis of Ṣūfism and negates the original. In fact, Fitzgerald claimed that Khayyam was not a Ṣūfī, though another good European translation, by the Frenchman Nichols and more faithful to the original, made Khayyam's Ṣūfism plain. A recent translation by the Indo-Afghan Omar Ali-Shah in collaboration with the poet Robert Graves attempts to set the damage aright, but this version lacks the flamboyance and the memorable (though incorrect) phrases of Fitzgerald's. See Ṣūfism.

khuṭba, Isl. The Friday sermon at the mosque. The Prophet Muḥammad often used the khuṭba as a means of making a formal pronouncement on faith or practice. The khuṭba, which is said by a leader called a khatīb (q.v.), can include a pronouncement or proclamation by the ruler or other high official dealing with political or military or even civic matters. The khuṭba formerly included a prayer for the sovereign; omission of the prayer was a signal for revolt by the people.

kīrtan, Hind. The rhythmical chanting or singing of devotional hymns, celebrating the names and glories of God, often accompanied by dance. The object is to induce an ecstatic state in the devotee in which he can establish direct contact with the Divine. Kīrtan may be performed by a person or a group, with musical instruments (primarily drums and cymbals). It is meant to be overheard by others so that they too may benefit. See Hinduism.

kōan, Buddh. A Zen verbal "puzzle," presented by a master to a pupil, the solution of which helps lead the latter to enlightenment through his own self-awakening gained in wrestling with and solving of the kōan. The term, pronounced kō-an, is the Japanese version of the Ch'an kung-en, originally a legal phrase for "official document" or "public case"; the kōan or kung-en came to be employed as a tool in the instruction of Ch'an and Zen students.

Traditionally the first kōan is said to have been solved by Gautama Buddha, when he puzzled over the meaning of the four sights that caused him suffering (see Buddha) while sitting under the bodhi tree near Gāya. The awakening that resulted from his meditation is evidenced in his doctrine of the Four Noble Truths (q.v.), which he followed with his doctrine of the Eightfold Path (q.v.). A second noted kōan, expressed nonverbally, was that solved by his disciple Kaśyapa (q.v.). When a group of monks asked the Buddha the meaning of Ultimate Reality, the Buddha held up a flower. With that, Kaśyapa merely smiled. This, to the Buddha, was the sign that Kaśyapa had attained enlightenment.

There are some seventeen hundred commonly employed kōans developed by the Ch'an and Zen masters, each of which may have dozens, if not hundreds of answers, depending on the individual student and the circumstances of his training. The first known popular usage of the chung-en/kōan is that introduced by Hui Nêng (q.v.), the Sixth Patriarch, with his famous Original Face question ("What was your original face before you were born?"). After that, the use of kung-en came to be widely spread among various schools of Ch'an, and the kung-en in both verbal and nonverbal forms became systematized, in groups of four, five, or six levels, according to degrees of difficulty. In Japan the kōan is preferred by the Rinzai school of Zen as the method to awakening, but it is not ignored by the Sōtō school, which places its emphasis on zazen (sitting). The kōan as it is known today is the result of a reform by the Zen master Hakuin (q.v.) in the eighteenth century, who formalized its teaching.

A few examples of kōans might suffice:

A monk asked Chao-chou, "What is the meaning of Bodhidharma's visit to China?" "The cypress tree in the courtyard," replied Bodhidharma.

A monk asked Thich Cam Thanh, "What is Buddha?" "Everything." The monk then asked, "What is the mind of Buddha?" "Nothing has been hidden." The monk again: "I don't understand." Cam Thanh replied, "You missed!"

A monk asked Baso, "What is Buddha?" Baso replied, "This mind is not Buddha."

There are no fixed answers to such kōans. The Rinzai sect, in fact, forbids the publication of formal answers because the point of the kōan is to force the pupil to discover for himself what might be "correct" in his case. The thirteenth-century Ch'an master Mu-mon (or Esai), who assembled a collection of kung-en known as *The Gateless Gate,* said, "I meant to use the kung-en as a man who picks up a piece of brick to knock at a gate, and after the gate is opened, the brick is useless and is thrown away." Despite such warnings, the kōan has an attraction that distorts its intent. The kōan to many, not only in Japan but especially in the West, seems to be nothing but a puzzle to be worked out, like a problem in mathematics or logic. Too many students take a snobbish delight in boasting of the number of kōans they have solved. However, a kōan "solved" is not a kōan solved. The kōan of another is not a kōan; a kōan is only a kōan when it is ours, and after it has had its use, it is discarded as of no value to anyone, and normally, if the student is awakened, he is not likely to boast of it. The purpose of the kōan is not to give the student so many Zen points as if in a contest, but to teach the true meaning of Buddhism—i.e., of the Eightfold Path in the light of the Four Noble Truths. Underlying the solving of the kōan is a firm grounding in Buddhism; without the foundation, there can be no proper employment of the kōan as tool. See Ch'an, mondo, Zen.

Kōbō Daishi (A.D. 774–835), Buddh. The posthumous name of the Japanese saint Kūkai. Daishi is an honorific bestowed after death, meaning Great Teacher or Great Master. See Kūkai.

Krishna (also Kṛṣṇa), Hind. The most popular of all the earthly incarnations of the god Vishnu (q.v.). Most texts, such as the *Matsya Purāṇa* and the *Varāha Purāṇa,* state that so far nine avatārs of Vishnu have appeared, Krishna being the eighth; The *Bhāgavata Purāṇa* places Krishna twentieth among twenty-four avatārs.

Krishna has appeared in a wide number of roles, the best known of which are as the charioteer god of the *Bhagavad Gītā* (q.v.) and the erotic cowherd god, the Dark One of medieval Indian bhakti, where he is the embodiment of love, the divine joy that destroys all pain. Since the medieval period Krishna has become the dominant and most erotic symbol of Indian religion and culture, the object of engulfing, self-abnegating adoration. A vast mass of complex textual material—epics, Purāṇas, poetry, and songs—has developed around the figure of the god, some of it arising from probable historical fact, but fact that is considerably distorted, developed, and intertwined with other factual material and colored by an immense accretion of legend and fable, much of it lascivious.

The derivations of the name Krishna are various. One gloss is upon the Sanskrit kṛṣ (to drag, to give pain). In this sense Krishna symbolizes the Kali Yuga, the Age of Suffering. In such a context Krishna takes away and devours the sufferings of his devotees in this descending yuga. Krishna also means "black" in the Vedas, and here, as the earliest texts state, he was the dark enemy overcome by the fair-skinned, fair-haired Āryan invaders. In this usage the non-Āryan enemies of the conquerors were identified by both the designation dāsa (servant or slave) and krishna (black); in the color distinction—varna—that was to develop into the caste structure, the dark-skinned indigenous peoples were at the bottom as slaves or helots; many were to remain as members of the śudras, the fourth caste, not always privileged to be reborn into the upper three Hindu castes.

Historically, two primary forms of the god may be distinguished—one the warrior, kśatriya, the other the low-caste cowherd. In either case he was not a member of the brāhmin caste, the priests, though the brāhmins were to employ the image of Krishna as warrior god to help enforce their domination over the peoples below them. In whatever form—dark in color—there is little doubt that Krishna originated as a pre-Āryan hero. But so numerous are his many forms that it seems impossible to distinguish the various traditions that coalesced into the dark all-god except in the broadest terms. Under brāhminical redaction and rewriting, the antihero of the Vedas became the warrior-prince of the epics, a warrior who gradually attained mystical and divine characteristics over the centuries. But during this development, another Krishna lay submerged among the populace for almost a millennium. This was the Krishna who appeared as the low-caste cowboy among a pastoral clan on the river Yamunā. This Krishna, like so many of the archaic pre-Āryan, non-Vedic beliefs, was to arise to play a major part in the Hindu pantheon along with other primitive deities like Shiva and the various forms of the Great Mother. The veneration and adoration of such deities was to surpass by far any that the Āryans had brought with them and vainly attempted to impose upon the subject masses.

DEVELOPMENT OF THE KRISHNA THEME. In c. B.C. 800 the various Krishnas began to meld into a single contradictory divine figure, a cosmic trickster who could appear as both an unscrupulous earthling or the highest divinity, no longer an enemy and villain but universally beloved, though with a touch of fear. Krishna, the archaic warrior once overpowered and smashed by the Āryan hero Indra, began to develop human attributes and a human history. Stories of his family origin, birth, and childhood appeared. At this point, from early and later texts, we can assemble a biography of the god, though a biography that is often contradictory and highly suspect, for its sources are as varied as his attributes. Incarnated at the beginning of the Kali Yuga to establish the religion of love, he was born of Devakī, sister of the tyrant King Kaṁsa, who had been warned by the astrologers that he would be slain by his own nephew. This may be a reference to the practice in certain primitive societies of the sister's son succeeding her brother as head of the family, the boy's father having only a secondary role in this situation, but being the head of his own sister's group. The King killed Devakī's first six children; the seventh, the white-skinned Bala-Rāma (another Vishnu avatār, the seventh) escaped; Krishna, the eighth child, was replaced by the daughter of a cowherd. Despite his slaughter of the innocents, Kaṁsa was himself killed later by Krishna and Bala-Rāma.

Krishna again escaped death, this time at the breast of the goddess Pūtanā, who tried to nurse him with poisonous milk. But he was to marry the goddess, an event still celebrated yearly at Vrindāvana (Brindaban), a village across the river Yamunā from Mathurā, both sites forever sacred to the god. Vrindāvana means "grove of the group goddess," apparently a reference to a forest deity; originally Pūtanā demanded a human sacrifice every year (she is now identified as the goddess of smallpox), a custom Krishna was able to avoid; in today's nuptial anniversary the goddess is represented by a tulasī plant, the sacred basil.

The story of the life of Krishna is related with minute details, beginning with his earliest years; the mischievous pranks of the child, the follies of the growing boy, and the amours of his youth are the subjects of endless wonder and delight. In the many songs and stories his dark skin has become an engaging blue and he is often dressed in yellow robes; his playing on the magic mind-beguiling flute caused all the women of Vrindāvana to fall hopelessly in love with him. These are the famed gopīs, the cowgirls who submitted in a pain of passion to the divine arrow of his love, Krishna in a myriad of forms. But this erotic cowherd is but one of many Krishnas. He also slays monsters and dragons, and appears in the Mahābhārata, after a slow start in the much-revised work, as a prince, the cousin and ally of the Pāndavas in their struggle for control.

All of these Krishnas are but part of a popular reaction to the long domination of the priestly caste. The Vedic period, with its emphasis on brāhminic ritual, the correct observance of rites and ceremonies, the great aśvamedhas (q.v.), and the propitiation rather than adoration of gods who personified the forces of nature, brought about a religious resurgence of a populace so long overshadowed by the Āryan superstructure. The movement, which had been smoldering for two centuries, was quite noticeable about B.C. 600. A small number of non-brāhmin sages, expressing the yearnings of a people fully agriculturalized and even becoming urbanized, reacted in a variety of ways. The dissident movements of Buddhism, Jainism, and Shaivism are outside this entry (but see those categories). The most powerful protest was that centered around Krishna, whose ambiguous figure became increasingly popular in the people's minds as the god of love and devotion—this among a mass that by its very nature was excluded from the worship and the ceremonies of the brāhmins. The various dark antiheroes who had plagued the Āryans a thousand years earlier in their invasion coalesced into several versions of what was to become a single though many-faceted figure, Krishna as incarnation of Vishnu.

In the Mahābhārata, originally a popular ballad that grew to epic lengths in the telling and retelling, Krishna begins as a minor figure—and possibly one who may have had some immediate factual basis—and comes to play a central role. This trickster and unscrupulous primitive from a tribe of cowherds is now a kśatriya, a warrior—*and* a divine figure. The Mahābhārata and its parallel vehicle, the Rāmayāna, which is devoted to the exploits of Krishna's white-skinned elder brother Bala-Rāma, became the expression of a religious thought and devotion for the masses, not the religious elite. With Krishna and Rāma the attitude toward God was not knowledge and the intimately perfect performance of ceremony as we see in the earlier Vedic and brahminical scriptures but that of spiritual freedom and of individual personal devotion, in which people of all castes and walks of life, women as well as men, take part in the divine worship and praise.

By the time the *Bhagavad Gītā* (q.v.) was composed, edited, tampered with to include a brāhminical sanction, and made part of the Mahābhārata, Krishna had become the highest form of divinity. Krishna is God, and God is Krishna. In the tenth book of the *Bhagavad Gītā* Krishna is not only all the gods, but the sages, too, the sacred sound ŌṂ, the Ātmān "conscious in the heart of all life," the moon, intelligence, the ocean and the Himālayas, the banyan tree, the heavenly cow, sexual desire, the Gaṇgā, the crocodile, but also "merciless death and the wealth of the wealthy," "among female virtues, fame, memory, wisdom, chastity, and sweet speech," "the deceit of the deceitful and the strength of the strong," and so on, through all the divinities of the heavens and the attributes of the mind and the objects of the earth. But we see him at his greatest when in the eleventh chapter we receive the blinding revelation of his divinity, when he reveals his supreme form—"possessing numerous mouths and eyes, glittering with divine ornaments, displaying divine signs, divinely garlanded, divinely scented, all-shaped, all-powerful, transcendent, and limitless. Were a thousand suns to explode suddenly in the sky, their brilliance would approximate the glory of the sight." Thus Krishna the All-Powerful.

KRISHNA AS BHAKTI. The Krishna movement, more popularly known as Vaishnavism (after Vishnu), produced a number of cults and sects. It was and is a laymen's movement. Its priests are not brāhmins but men and women from ordinary life, sometimes from the lowest castes, who find their Lord Krishna a total incarnation of the Supreme Being and all the attributes of divinity, not, however, so often in the Krishna of the *Bhagavad Gītā* but in the Krishna of Vrindāvana, the Krishna who was a baby like their own, who faced death from the wicked uncle, and, above all, the Krishna whose embrace of the milkmaids, the gopīs, symbolized God's love in its most intense form, the exquisite release of sexual union. This "dalliance," as the expression goes, with the 16,108 gopīs is likely a symbol of the miscegenation of the primitive black with lighter-skinned superiors, a theme celebrated in many parts of the world where two races are thrown into close and unavoidable contact. The traditional number of gopīs, 16,108, has some unexplained mystical significance, for 108 is a magic number applied in many contexts (there are 108, or 1,008 names of Shiva, and also of the Ganges, and so on). In some versions of the Krishna-gopī alliance the young women become his wives; in others they are already married to other men. Of all the young women, the most famous is Rādhā (her name means success), daughter of his adoptive father Nanda and wife of the cowherd Ayanaghosha. Rādhā and Krishna are the theme of much of the medieval and later mystico-erotic cults of India, especially in Bengal.

Rādhā was virtually unknown, though the gopīs were an early tradition, until about the twelfth century A.D., when she appeared as the embodiment of the selfless love of all the gopīs. The literature—poetry and song—is highly erotic and often detailed. The poet Vidyapati writes of "her long legs innocently bold . . . a blush on the young breasts," and Chandidāsa describes "the deliberate sensuous union of the two," the girl playing the active role, "riding her lover's outstretched body in delight, her smiling lips shine with drops of sweat. . . . She of beautiful face hotly kisses the mouth of her beloved," and so on. The passion of Rādhā and Krishna became the theme par excellence of all the bhakti poets, the couple becoming one soul in two bodies, or as some poets said, "one soul in one body." Whatever, God in His incarnation experiences an ecstasy of love—"lovers torn apart who scored the flesh with their nails." Yet, in works like Jayadeva's famous twelfth-century *Gita Govinda,* this forceful love play is but a conversation between the individual and the Unlimited, its purpose being "the dissolution of the I"—the flowering, the unfolding, and the developing awareness of the individual to the Unlimited aspect that is man himself.

Much Indian art—painting, music, temple sculpture, and literature—was influenced by Vaishnavism, whose theology could be transformed from the erotic into the highest reaches of speculative thought. Even the image of Krishna revealing himself as the Divine in the *Bhagavad Gītā* was to become the subject of numerous iconic representations whose purpose was to aid devotees to attain the same cosmic vision for themselves. On a primitive level, a bone of Krishna, who died of his own free will, still survives, being maintained in the famous Jagannāth temple of Puri, where it is contained in a huge black wooden figure flanked by two other equally imposing statues; the trio are brought through the city streets every year on a huge cart; in the past devotees threw themselves beneath its wheels in an attempt to gain immediate salvation, thus ending the cycle of birth and rebirth. The statue containing the Krishna relic is replaced every twenty years, the bone being transferred by a priest, who dies shortly afterward.

Kṛṣṇa, Hind. The Sanskrit spelling of Krishna (q.v.).

Kuan Yin, Buddh. The Chinese form of the bodhisattva Avalokiteśvara, who is the close companion of the Amida Budha (q.v.) and a prime symbol of mercy and compassion. Kuan Yin is often erroneously called a "goddess" because of the lushness of certain statues. He is clearly masculine, always being portrayed with a mustache. Moreover, a bodhisattva, a buddha in the becoming, by definition cannot be a goddess, nor even a god, for buddhas are masculine, and only incarnation as man can lead to buddhahood. In Japan, Kuan Yin is known as Kannon. See Avalokiteśvara.

Kūkai (A.D. 774–835), Buddh. The founder of the Shingon sect of Buddhism and one of its saints. Kūkai brought the Chinese tantric Chên Yen (or True Word) to Japan; it is a syncretic movement embracing Hinduism, Confucianism, Taoism, and various forms of Buddhism. It is highly esoteric in formula, relying upon "True Words" and various mystic formulas derived from mantras and passed down orally from master to disciple. Kūkai's body, in the tradition of the saint to come (cf. Zoroastrianism, the māhdis, etc.), has not decayed and awaits the Maitreya Buddha, the Buddha to come. Despite his eschewing the written word, Kūkai contributed some important works to esoteric Buddhism, among them *Indications to the Three Teachings; Memorial on the Presentation of the List of the Newly Imported Sūtras;* and *Ten Stages of Religious Consciousness; Testament,* his sayings, was assembled by a disciple. See Shingon.

Kumārī, Hind. The eternal and immaculate Virgin, divine in nature. This is the form assumed by the Divine Power otherwise called Shakti (q.v.) before the creation of the cosmos. Kumārī is the Mother of the entire universe. As virgin, Kumārī often plays a literal role in popular Hinduism. Annually young women are installed in temples in India (especially in Bengal) and Nepal as kumārīs, where they are worshiped—kumārī pūjā—for a full year as the goddess herself. In Bengal the young woman is a brāhmin virgin; however, many brāhmins consider veneration of their daughter inauspicious. The kumārī is installed with elaborate rites and is considered the goddess of learning, Sarasvatī, a form of Shakti. (In some temples Sarasvatī is held to be both the daughter and consort of Brahmā [q.v.], a god not often venerated today.)

In other locales the kumārī is selected from a lower, or the lowest caste, and is associated with tantric rites, being transformed by various ceremonies into the literal personification of Shakti. As such the kumārī must be between the ages of five and twelve. If she is older and menstruating, she is known as Ṣoḍaśī—i.e., the Girl-of-Sixteen, and is connected with Shiva. Sixteen is a perfect number, being the age of accomplishment and maturity in the human condition (one must remember the short life span in that part of the world) and the number of days building to the full moon. After sixteen, in human life as in the lunar cycle, comes the decline of faculties.

Among tantrics, tremendous psychic and spiritual energies are drawn from the discipline of kumārī-pūjā; if the devotee is ignorant and lustful, she enjoys the ceremonies in peril. In Nepal, after the year ends, the girl often continues to serve the priests, and a new virgin replaces her in the temple. In some instances of kumārī-pūjā in the past the girl was sacrificed after her year as the goddess. See Śakti, Shiva, tantra.

Kum-Bum, Tib. A Buddhist monastery at Amdo in northeastern Tibet. It is the birthplace of the reformer Tsong Khapa, founder of the Yellow Hat sect (q.v.). Kum-Bum is the site of a tree sacred to Tsong Khapa. On its leaves are the portraits of various Tibetan holy men and the mystic formula ŌṂ Mani Padme Hum (q.v.). (Kum-Bum means "hundred thousand images.") After the tree first showed its mystical character, it was wrapped in silk, and a temple, or chörten, was built around it. The early French explorer-missionaries Fathers Huc and Gabet reported seeing the tree with the inscriptions on both trunk and leaves. The tree died from lack of sun, air, and water about four hundred years ago. Two of its shoots were planted outside the chörten and are reported to be still thriving. Madame Alexandra David-Neel (q.v.), who lived at Kum-Bum before World War I, did not see anything unusual about the leaves, though there is ample evidence in both ancient chronicles and Western documents about the authenticity of the belief.

Kuṇḍalinī, Hind. The Supreme Power, otherwise Kuṇḍalinī-Śakti, in the human body. Kuṇḍalinī is aroused by the practice of tantric yoga. Sir John Woodroffe, who rescued many tantric texts from oblivion, called Kuṇḍalinī the "Serpent Power," after one of her names, Bhujangī, or Serpent. Kuṇḍalinī, the Serpent Power, is that which is coiled. Her form is that of a coiled and sleeping serpent in the lowest cakra or bodily center, at the base of the spinal column. In arising she pierces the six cakras and the Sahasrāra-Padma, the Thousand-petal Lotus. Since the arousing of the goddess in tantra involves intensely sexual practices, her worship is difficult, fraught with dangers both psychic and physical, and should not be entered upon without the supervision of a trained guru. Kuṇḍalinī is also associated with Kālī (q.v.). Some Ṣūfī brotherhoods (among them the Naqshbandi [q.v.]) have adapted Kuṇḍalinī to their own forms of meditation, a practice contrary to orthodox Islam. The goddess is often represented coiled around a liṅga (q.v.). See tantra.

kustī (also kushtī; the preferred pronunciation among the Iranians is kostī), Zor. A thin wool sash worn over the white cotton shirt, the sudreh (q.v.), by all Zardushti who have been formally received into the community. The kustī is made of seventy-two threads of lamb's wool, symbolizing the seventy-two chapters of the Yasna (q.v.). It is the "sword-belt" of the soldier in the struggle for righteousness over evil. The kustī is looped three times around the waist and is tied in four knots, two in front and two in back. The three loops signify God (Ahura Mazdā) in His aspects as Creator, Preserver, and Reconstructor; also, good thoughts, good words, and good deeds. The knots remind the wearer of the four daily duties: worship of God in self-sacrifice, loyal obedience to the tenets of Zoroaster, constant struggle against evil, and absolute confidence in God's laws and decrees. The two ends of the kustī symbolize the dual nature of the universe, form and life. The kustī also stands for the religion of Ahura-Mazdā; on the cosmic scale its counterpart is the Milky Way. The cord separates the grosser magnetic auras of the lower part of the body from the more spiritual auras of the upper part. The kustī is tied and untied, depending on circumstances, upon arising, before prayer, when bathing, before meals, and when urinating and defecating. The retying is accompanied by a number of formal prayers, which are said facing the sun (or other light, especially fire). During the funeral rites—the washing of the corpse and the procession to the Tower of Silence (q.v.)—kustīs are held between each pair of priests or mourners. See Zoroastrianism.

◄L►

Lakshmi (Sanskrit, Lakṣmī), Hind. The goddess of fortune, and the consort of the great deity Vishnu. She is also the goddess of beauty, and is thus known as Śri. Lakshmi (Fortune) is one of the rare female divinities of the Vedas (q.v.), though in a minor role. As both Fortune and Beauty she is the wife of Āditya, the solar principle, later to be incorporated into the non-Āryan Vishnu. Lakshmi as Fortune appears at the side of Vishnu in each of his divine descents. Lakshmi is a clear amalgamation of numerous local mother figures. She is a goddess of the sea in some recensions and is ocean-born, or even sprung from a sea of milk; in others she appears from a furrow in the earth made by the plow (i.e., penis; cf. liṅga [phallus] derived from lak [plow]); here her name is Sītā. Elsewhere, she is Ramā, Padmā, Mā, etc., —mā being a suffix for a mother goddess.

Lakshmi is identified with the plant goddess Tulasī (q.v.), in some versions her rival, in others herself as the wife of Krishna, the cowherd of the sacred grove Vrindāvana; her cult is likely older than Krishna's. The annual celebration of the union of Lakshmi and Krishna, ritualized as the nuptials of the plant tulasī and the sacred stone, the śalagrāma (a form of Vishnu), marks the fusion of two separate indigenous strains surviving from archaic pre-Āryan India. The goddess has no temples but is worshiped in the home. Lakshmi is an especial favorite of businessmen. See Krishna, śalagrāma, Vishnu.

lāma, Tib. A term of respect—meaning "superior" or "excellent" —applied to Tibetan monks of higher ranks. The title should be reserved for the heads of monasteries, ecclesiastical dignitaries, and aged and learned monks. (The term trapas is applied to others.) The word is correctly written blama.

Lao Tzu. The common Western name of the Chinese sage (B.C. 604–531) credited as the founder of the school of philosophy known as Taoism (tao chi). He is also the author of the book called after him, the *Lao tzu,* otherwise the *Tao Te Ching.* His name, sometimes spelled Lao-tse, means, roughly, the Old Man or the Old Boy; he was also called Lao-tan, or Old Big-ear. He was born in a village in what is now Honan. According to tradition he served as keeper of the imperial archives in the royal capital at Lo and was one of the most learned men of his time. The *Shih chi,* a first-century B.C. history, states, "Lao Tzu probably lived to over a hundred and sixty years of age—some say over two hundred—as he cultivated the way [tao] and was able to live to a great age." The same work mentions a confusion of identity with another sage of almost similar name and concludes, "The world is unable to know where the truth lay. Lao Tzu was a gentleman who lived in retirement from the world." Many contemporary scholars believe that Lao Tzu did not in fact exist; however, neither can his nonexistence be proved with any authority. Leaving aside this insoluble dispute, Lao Tzu was a noted, rather irascible scholar who kept to himself, had a famous meeting with Confucius, and in his old age, as he saw the kingdom in which he lived on the verge of collapse, he ran away from home, riding on a black ox. As he crossed the mountains into the neighboring state he was stopped by the Keeper of the Pass (probably the Han Ku Pass in Honan), who insisted that he write down his wisdom, which he did in some five thousand concise Chinese characters. (The Keeper, Kuan Yin-hsi, is credited with being the ancient source of the esoteric cult that led to *The Secret of the Golden Flower* [q.v.].) Eventually Lao Tzu returned home to spend his final years among his own people.

The work the Sage produced, the *Lao tzu,* is divided into two parts, the *Tao Ching* and the *Te Ching* (together called the *Tao Te Ching*). The actual problem of authorship is one that divides scholars; some consider it the work of a single individual, though at a later date than the Sage's time; others believe it is an anthology like many early Chinese works, for many passages are often unrelated or inconsistent, the work itself being in a constantly fluid state throughout the third century B.C., not attaining the present form, or one close to it, for another century. More than half the text consists of rhyming passages, which must have been intended to be learned by rote, the meaning being explained orally.

līlā, Hind. Literally "play," but in the religious and mystical sense, the divine sport, the movements and activities of the Supreme Being, which are free by nature and not subject to the laws of nature or man. The god Krishna, divine incarnation, playing as a child, is *the* example of līlā. However, the prime exemplar of līlā —in this case usually called rāsalīlā—is the love play of Rādhā (also an incarnation) and Krishna, which, despite its surface erotics, is entirely spiritual and supernatural.

liṅga (or liṅgam), Hind. The phallus as mystical object, the cult of which dates to remote times in India as elsewhere. Innumerable phallic icons have been unearthed in the cities of the Indus Valley (q.v.); some may be placed as early as B.C. 2500. The liṅga is associated with Shiva (q.v.) and is his symbol, thus establishing itself as pre-Āryan. The term liṅga is related to the early Sanskrit lāṇgula (plow), which is derived from an Austroasiatic root, lak (meaning both spade and penis). In Hindu philosophy of the fourth century A.D. the derivation takes a different gloss: Liṅga is the subtle body (as opposed to the gross physical body) because it is eventually merged—līyate—back into primordial matter, a concept that also stems from unknown antiquity.

The liṅga as symbol of the creative power of Shiva is the most widely venerated cult object in Saivism. The liṅga may run from formally carved or cast (often mass-produced) stone or clay to natural elliptical stones picked up from riverbeds (they are known as bāṇa-liṅgas) to larger stones, also of a natural phallic shape, and to those that are carved and polished; these may be literal or symbolic, like the various "eggs." In Shiva temples the god is usually represented in the form of the liṅga, which is frequently bathed, bedecked with flowers and garlands, covered with oil and milk, and offered rice and other foods. Often the liṅga is shown centered in a representation of the female organ, the yoni. Sannyāsis and other holy people, who are not cremated but buried, are honored with a consecrated liṅga atop the grave.

Besides the obvious representations, the liṅga takes many other forms, many esoteric. The liṅga is the universe—the earth is the womb, and space is the liṅga, erect above its pedestal, according to the *Skanda Purāṇa*. The liṅga is the Cosmic Egg, in which male and female forms are united, and a "golden egg resplendent like the sun," in the view of the sage Manu. The liṅga is the fire on the sacrificial altar, an arrow (represented with five faces to symbolize the five senses), an endless pillar of light, and so on. In Shaivite texts the liṅga is the god Himself: It is white (as he is), has three eyes and five faces, is arrayed in a tiger's skin, existed before the world, and is the origin of all things.

On a more prosaic basis, the most abject pile of stones or mud, even a mound of cow dung (since the cow is sacred), may be considered a liṅga. Liṅga shrines are found along the Indian roads, in homes and temples, and the liṅga is a personal adornment in the form of necklaces and belts, pendants and bracelets. Benares, Shiva's city, is the city of the liṅga, and contains thousands of liṅga shrines. The veneration so commonly accepted by the ordinary people has perforce drawn some defense from Hindu philosophers and intellectuals. This popular symbol standing erect in the yoni is, to the Hindu, but a sign of the divine act of creation. All children are marked with one or the other, either with the liṅga of the Giver of Wonders (Hara or Shiva), or with the sign of Devī, the Great Goddess and Resplendent One. The union of liṅga and yoni shows manifest nature, the universal energy. Pleasure dwells in the sex organ: All enjoyment, all pleasure, is the experience of divinity. From the relation of the liṅga, giver of seed, to the enveloping yoni, the whole world arises. Everything therefore bears the signature of the liṅga and the yoni—divinity under the form of all individual liṅgas entering every womb to procreate all beings. In sum, the god Shiva has stated: "He who worships the liṅga knowing it to be the First Cause, the source of consciousness, the substance of the universe, is nearer to me than any other being."

Lingāyats, Hind. A radical sect that worships the liṅga, symbol of Shiva. They were founded in the twelfth century A.D. by Bāsava (or Vṛṣabha), the brāhmin prime minister of the state of Kalyān (near modern Bombay). Bāsava, a Hindu revivalist, maintained that Hinduism had fallen from its original purity, and he wished to restore its purer tenets. He rejected caste, discarded his sacred thread, abandoned the dogma of transmigration so dear to the Hindu, and preached an uncompromising monotheism. He rejected idolatry but stated that the most appropriate symbol of the Divine was the liṅga, which he enjoined his disciples to wear as the outward symbol of their beliefs. He abandoned cremation and had his followers practice burial of their dead.

The cardinal point of Lingāyat doctrine is the unquestioned faith in the efficacy of the liṅga to bring its wearer spiritual merit. The liṅga, according to the sect, abolishes all distinctions of caste, a pariah being in no way inferior to a brāhmin. Wherever the liṅga is found, even in the most abject hut, it is considered the throne of the deity. The liṅga worn by the sect is most often made of gray soapstone found in Andhra in South India, brought to the various Lingāyat centers on foot by a special class of carriers called the Kambi Jaṅgamas. The sect does not prevent the remarriage of widows; the members are strict vegetarians, and the priests, the jaṅgamas, are usually celibate. Numbers of Lingāyats are still to be found, primarily in South India; they tend to cluster together around a maṭh (a type of ashram) headed by a jaṅgama. At death they believe that the soul is absorbed into the Divine; each devotee's liṅga is buried with the corpse.

Lion Posture, Buddh. The position in which Gautama Buddha (q.v.) lay as he was about to enter nirvāṇa (q.v.), stretched out on his right side, his head supported by his right arm. See sleep.

lobha, Buddh. Greed, one of the three roots of the evil condition of human existence. The others are dosa and moha. Through the observance of the Eightfold Path (q.v.), the Buddhist attempts to eradicate this trait, especially by a conscious effort to be actively generous and to think generously of others.

lohan, Buddh. The Chinese term for arhant, one who has attained enlightenment and perfection. Eighteen are generally recognized in China, and their images placed in temples as guardians of Buddhism. See arhant.

lokas, Buddh. The Six Worlds of rebirth or illusion. They are: heaven; the human world; the world of asuras (titanic demons), or dissension; the animal world; the world of hungry ghosts; and hell. Whatever loka we fall into is as the result of our own actions —i.e., of our past and present karma (or kamma). See kamma, karma.

lotus position, Hind. The standard posture for yoga. The yogi sits on a low or flat cushion placed on a cloth mat, which in turn may be placed on an animal skin (tiger or deer is traditional); in some cases the underlying mat is of straw. The legs are intertwined, with the left foot over the right thigh, and the right foot over the left thigh. The hands may be placed on the lap with the palms up, the left hand underneath. Some yogis prefer to extend an arm over each knee, the palms of the hands facing upward. The eyes may be completely closed, or half closed, focused on the tip of the nose, or on the spot between the eyebrows known as the Third Eye, depending on the preferred practice. The lotus position is also known as the padmāsana, which is the Sanskrit name. See yoga.

Lotus Sūtra, Buddh. The proper name is *Saddharma-Pundarīka Sūtra* (the Lotus of the True Doctrine). A second-century A.D. Indian text, it was twice translated into Chinese and became possibly the most important scripture for Chinese Buddhists. The work stresses the eternal Buddha-principle, represented in innumerable forms to work out the salvation of all suffering humanity. In the *Lotus Sūtra,* Buddha is the Eternal, Omniscient, Omnipotent, Omnipresent; the creator-destroyer, re-creator of all worlds —concepts borrowed from Hinduism and carried over into Mahāyāna Buddhism. The school known as T'ien-T'ai (Tendai in Japanese) based its teaching primarily on the Lotus, stating that it was the most complete exposition of Buddhist doctrine and that it capped all previous teachings, being the final statement. Its central thesis is that of universal salvation: Everyone and everything have within the potentiality of buddhahood. This egalitarian message had a great attraction for the thirteen-century Japanese Nichiren (q.v.), who saw himself as a messiah and Buddha. In this role he embodied two concepts of the Buddha as expressed in the *Lotus Sūtra:* the Bodhisattva of Superb Action and the Bodhisattva Ever-abused. Both prefigured his own mission, and he was an incarnation of both. Through Tendai, the teachings of the *Lotus Sūtra* still have a great appeal to the common people in Japan, as opposed to the elitism of Zen. In the twentieth century, the *Lotus Sūtra* forms the key inspiration for the altruistic, nationalistic Japanese sects, the Sōka-gakkai, Reiyō-kai, and Risshō-kōsei-kai (see all), which stress the common buddhahood within each person.

◂M▸

madrasa, Isl. A school or other educational institution for Muslims. The first madrasa was founded in Bagdad in the year A.D. 1066 (A.H. 459) by Niẓām al-Mulk, a grand vizier of the Seljūq Turks in order to defend and propagate the Sunnī form of Islam. Up to that time education had been carried on in the mosque (q.v.) and still may be in small Islamic communities. In the madrasa, students, teachers, and advanced scholars live a communal life. The curriculum of the madrasa is usually arranged on a step-by-step basis, almost standard throughout the Islamic world, though there may be some local changes in the courses. A not too untypical program of studies might begin with Arabic grammar and language, then move on to literature, arithmetic, philosophy, law, jurisprudence, theology, Qur'ānic exegesis, and Ḥadīth (the sayings and practice of the Prophet Muḥammad). See Islam.

magi (plural of magus), Zor. The magi were the priestly caste of ancient Iran, in charge of any religious ceremony of whatever sect demanded their services, but they came to dominate the practice of Zoroastrianism (q.v.) from the time of Cyrus the Great (ruled B.C. 558–530), the founder of the first Persian Empire. Scholars are divided about the proper identification of the magi, some seeing them as true inheritors of the Prophet Zoroaster, others as corruptors of his doctrines, and some seeking a balanced point of view. In the classical world of the ancient Greeks the magi were known for not burying their dead, which they left exposed to vultures and wild animals, and they regarded incestuous marriages as meritorious. They also held a dualist view of the world and of creation, according to the Greeks. These are all views unfound in early Zoroastrianism but stated in the Vidēvāt (q.v.), which leads some experts to suppose that the magi were the authors of the work. Because of the prominence of the magi in later Zoroastrianism, the Prophet himself was erroneously believed to have been a member of the caste. However, Herodotus, who never mentions Zoroaster, describes magian ceremonies in terms that show that the group had nothing in common with the Prophet. The magis' skills, supposed or real, in spells, astrology, and sorcery led to the accusation of "magic"—i.e., art peculiar to a magus but an art that again had no connection with Zoroaster. It was magi from Persia who brought offerings to the infant Jesus at Bethlehem.

Mahābhāva, Hind. The highest form of self-dedication to the Divine. Rādhā, the consort of the black folk god Krishna, is the example par excellence in this form of Vaishnavism. See Krishna.

Maharishi Mahesh Yogi. The founder of Transcendental Meditation, or TM. He is commonly called the Maharishi (Great Sage) by his Western disciples, and in India, the Mahesh Yogi. The Maharishi graduated from Allahabad University in 1942 with a degree in physics, but he immediately abandoned a professional career in favor of studying under the yogi Guru Dev. When Guru Dev died in 1953, the Maharishi retired to the Himālayas, intending on passing his life as a recluse. However, nine years later, in response to a call he felt came from above, the Maharishi left his cave and began a period of wandering, talking to small groups in villages and cities. By now he had departed from the traditional system based on the Vedas and Upanishads, and was preaching not the formal religion of Hinduism but the potentiality within everyone's nervous system. Within a few months a patron gave him a ticket to the United States; the Maharishi crossed by the Pacific route. Landing at Honolulu without baggage or introductions, by chance he met strangers who welcomed his message. In California his success was even greater. Within a short time, realizing that as an individual he could not reach everyone, he had founded an organization to train teachers who would work globally. In the 1960s he held training courses for his teachers at the sacred city of Rishikesh in the Himālayas, and later established a large ashram built along the lines of a high-rise tourist hotel. Teaching conventions were held also in various European cities and resorts. A number of subsidiary organizations have been founded, Maharishi International University (a worldwide extension service) and Students International Meditation Society, or SIMS; the latter serves as national headquarters (the address is 1015 Gayley Avenue, Los Angeles, California). See Transcendental Meditation.

Mahāśakti, Hind. The highest expression of the Supreme Divine Power, the devis or goddess Śakti (q.v.).

mahāśūnya, Hind. The Great Void. It is most often conceived of as "Empty space," a state in which space and time disappear—space left behind after the dissolution of the cosmos when the entirety of creation has disintegrated. See śūnya.

mahātmā, Hind. (and sometimes Buddh.). Great soul (mahā-ātmā), an honorific applied to an individual who has destroyed his ego and realized himself as one with the All. The title is, in too many cases, too loosely and easily applied, and sometimes means nothing more than a person with influence in religious circles.

Mahāvīra. The twenty-fourth and last tīrthaṅkara ("keeper of the fords") of the Jains (q.v.). He is popularly but erroneously called the founder of the Jains. He was an older contemporary of Gautama Buddha, living about B.C. 540–468, though the Jains themselves place the dates of his life some sixty years earlier. His true name was Vardhamāna; he was the son of Siddārtha, the chief of a warrior clan of the Jnātrikas and related through his mother to the Licchavis, both tribes living in what is now northern Bihar. Mahāvīra means the Great Hero; he is mentioned in various Buddhist documents as Nigantha Nātaputta, the "naked sage of the Jnātrika clan."

There is much myth surrounding Mahāvīra. The hard facts, if such they are, come down to roughly these: His mother, Trisalā, experienced fourteen dreams revealing that she would bear a son who would win not only reknown but also, most important of all, everlasting rest—i.e., he would be spared the endless cycle of birth and rebirth. Her dreams are often engraved around the silver treasuries in Jain temples. Siddārtha and his priests interpreted the dreams to foretell the birth of a spiritual conqueror or jina, the Lord of the three worlds and the universal Emperor of the Law. Though young Vardhamāna excelled everyone in physical beauty, strength, and courage, he was also spiritually precocious. Like a good son, he lived with his parents until their deaths; meanwhile, he married and had a daughter. (The Digambaras—the sky-clad, one of the two major Jain sects—believe that Mahāvīra followed a sterner path and did not marry.) Close to his thirtieth year he felt free of wordly ties and decided to become an ascetic. With the permission of his older brother, he left his home and family and renounced the world. He disposed of his property and joined a group of monks supported by his clan to follow a life of wandering in the common tradition of the Indian ascetic. For twelve years he wandered, never staying more than a single night in a village nor five in a town, except during the monsoons, when he would spend up to four months at a fixed retreat. "During these twelve years he meditated and walked, sinless and circumspect in thought, word, and deed," according to a Jain biographer. He was absorbed in meditation and unconscious of outward circumstances during this period.

Mahāvīra was born a jīvan-mukta—a liberated being, at birth possessing the forms of knowledge that are automatically liberating. In his wandering he acquired further forms of knowing the thoughts of all sentient beings and of omniscience. Thus, in possession of infinite and supreme knowledge and intuition, fortified by meditation and profound austerities, he was able to destroy past karmas—the accumulated debt of past actions.

With this karmic burden discharged, Mahāvīra began thirty years of preaching, starting with the warrior princes among his own kinspeople. Though he had inherited an ancient, ascetic, mystical, and philosophical tradition, it was his genius that shaped it into the community given the name of Jains—the conquerors of karma. He formed the Jains into four groups; the monks, the nuns, the laymen, and the laywomen. Some documents put the number of his disciples at fourteen thousand, headed by eleven chief leaders, others at forty-two hundred. Whatever the number, Mahāvīra holds the respect of Hindus and Buddhists today. For doctrine, customs, practices, and history, see the entry under Jains.

Mahāyāna Buddhism. One of two major schools of Buddhism, the other being Hīnayāna (the Small Vehicle); Mahāyāna is the Large Vehicle. Mahāyāna was a late development, stemming from dissatisfaction at the interpretation of the Buddha's teachings as expressed by the group that came to be called Theravāda (the Teaching of the Elders), which in turn is an important form of Hīnayāna. Mahāyāna took a marked divergence during the first and second centuries A.D. in India. Numerous outside influences affected the northernmost disciples of Buddha's Way, among them the Greek invasion in B.C. 326; the Greeks not only left small kingdoms in India, but also ambassadors to the faraway court at Pātaliputra in the heart of Buddhist country; they also gave early Buddhism an iconography of the Master based on the Greek Apollo; many Buddhas in the northwestern area of India are nothing but statues of the hellenic god. The Greeks were followed by various Iranian and central Asian groups. One of the major influences was the Zoroastrian theme of the Light.

In the earliest Buddhist literature Gautama Buddha does not speak of himself as *the* Buddha, and as used by others it means Enlightened One, Awakened One. Gautama is an arhant (q.v.), a spiritual being of the highest level. The doctrine was to change among the Mahāyānist schools: The Buddha became a Refuge. If Buddha did not exist, how could one take refuge in him? The idea of a being "unborn, unoriginated, uncreated, unformed" developed, which would offer an escape from the world of the born, originated, created, and formed. Concepts of not one buddha, Gautama Buddha, but of several, of many, began to be accepted, along with beliefs in perfected beings of various levels of spiritual development and attainment. By the second century A.D. the doctrine of the Ādi-Buddha (q.v.), the original or primordial Buddha, had been formulated, out of which came the theme of the Amida or Amitābha Buddha (q.v.), who in contrast to previous teachings, in which the individual alone was responsible for his own salvation, offered salvation by faith and in a future heaven, the Pure Land. From the Ādi-Buddha emanated other buddhas, and from them still others. The Gautama Buddha was fourth in a series of five human buddhas; after him will come the Maitreya Buddha, a type of messianic, apocalyptic figure.

By the time that Buddhism had established itself in other lands, especially China and its satellites, buddhas and other deities had multiplied to such an extent as to challenge in numbers the Hindu gods whom Gautama Buddha had opposed as superstition. One aspect of Mahāyāna Buddhism was that of the bodhisattva, the buddha-to-be, any being destined to become a Buddha in this or some future life. The multiplicity of buddhas was given authority by the Jātakas, the birth stories that recount the edifying histories of Siddārtha Gautama and other buddhas in various previous existences, as man, animal, or spirit.

Unlike Hīnayāna Buddhism, which stresses the individual's own and sole path to nirvāṇa, without the help of others, Mahāyāna offers the entire world not only salvation by knowledge but by faith and love as well. The individual is not required to renounce the world, family, and human affection immediately in order to gain salvation. In fact, Pure Land Buddhism, simply put, offers a paradise of a distinctly human tone merely on the basis of faith in Amida Buddha through the saying of the Nembutsu (q.v.). In Mahāyāna all men can become at least arahants if not bodhisattvas, and perhaps buddhas, out of love for one's fellows, though the last stage is more difficult. Once a person has attained buddhahood he can no longer be present to aid humanity. Where the Hīnayānists were lamps only to themselves, as they claimed—correctly—the Gautama Buddha taught that the Mahāyānists were to light the way for others, for the entire world if possible. In fact, say the Mahāyānists, no man lives alone, to himself and to none other; the whole creation lives as one life and shares a common karma, a common working out of fate, to which every man contributes for good or ill. See Buddha, Buddhism, Hīnayāna, Theravāda.

Mahdī, Isl. Literally the Guided One (of Allāh), an eschatological figure who originated in the earliest centuries of Islam during the upheavals in the Islamic community centered around the Prophet Muḥammad's son-in-law 'Ali, the husband of his daughter Fāṭima. After 'Ali's tragic death and the murders of his sons by Fāṭima, Muḥammad ibn al-Hannifīya, 'Ali's son by another wife, was installed as al-Mahdī, the Rightly Guided One, as ruler by a group of rebels in an uprising against the Ummayads. Muḥammad al-Mahdī disappeared (or died) in A.D. 880, but the faithful—i.e., the Shī'a—believed he was not dead but living in the mountains outside Mecca; they looked forward to his Second Coming to restore peace and justice to the world, for they believed that they had been deprived of their rights in their struggle against the Sunnī. The Mahdī became a divine personage to the people, convinced that the Islamic community had taken a wrong turn and that its leaders had brought tyranny in place of the justice promised by Allāh through His Prophet and the Qur'ān.

The Mahdī, also known as the Hidden Imām, took various forms among the many Shī'a sects, who often confused him with other saintly and messianic figures. The major sect, known as Twelvers, because they expected the Mahdī, or Hidden Imām, to be the twelfth of that number of saintly leaders, believed in the original Mahdī; others either accepted him, or found different figures on which to hang their hopes. The concept of the Mahdī, or Hidden Imām, was prevalent among all the Shī'a groups and among many Ṣūfīs, especially those who may have had some connections to Persia, where the theme of a hidden Zoroastrian saint, Prince Peshotan, had long been common. In general, all foresaw a period of decline, with much suffering and turmoil, followed by the appearance of the Mahdī. Various signs and portents would prefigure his return. Many texts were centered upon his coming. The Prophet was believed to have predicted that "a man would come out of the East who would preach in the name of the family of Muḥammad, though he is furthest of all men from them. He will hoist black flags which will begin with victory and end with unbelief. He will be followed by the discards of the Arabs, the lowest of the mawāli [non-Arab Muslims], slaves, runaways, and outcastes in remote places, whose emblem is black and whose religion is polytheism, and most of them are mutilated." But after this, the Prophet is said to have predicted "a man of my family will arise who will fill the world with justice as it is now filled with tyranny." "His justice will fill as much of the world as his authority reaches, and his successors will fill the remainder." Numerous mahdīs arose throughout Islam, in many countries. In the nineteenth century, Mahdist movements combined nationalist aspirations with chiliasm; the British had to face messianic mahdīs in Nigeria, Somalia (the famous Mad Mullah), and the Sudan, where the Mahdist state survived fourteen years until crushed by Lord Kitchener's troops. The concept of the Mahdī came to infiltrate the more orthodox Sunnī through the devotion and yearnings of the common people, for many of them saw no other way out of their abysmal living conditions. See imām, Peshotan, Shī'a, Sunnī.

Maitreya, Buddh. The Buddha who is to come, a Mahāyānist belief that states that the Gautama Buddha was but the fourth of a series of five earthly Buddhas, with the Maitreya Buddha still to appear. He is frequently mentioned in Mahāyānist works, closely resembling his predecessor but with many details different. Maitreya Buddha now awaits in supernatural form in Tuśita, the Heaven of the Satisfied, where all Buddhas (including Gautama) reside pending their appearance on earth. The area in which the doctrine of Maitreya Buddha developed was heavily influenced by Iranian invasions; the eschatological theme of the Buddha-to-come can possibly be traced to the messianic figure of the Zoroastrian's Prince Peshotan (q.v.). Maitreya, whose name is a derivative of an Indian term meaning love, is the embodiment of love and compassion (his given name is Ajita; Maitreya is his clan designation). The Pāli texts call him Metteya, and the Japanese, Miroku.

maṇḍala, Hind. The word means circle, and thus maṇḍala is a complex diagram in circular form employed for the focusing of cosmic and psychic energies. A maṇḍala may be as small as a drawing, or as large as a temple enclosure; actually, the world itself is a type of maṇḍala. The yantra (q.v.) is a form of maṇḍala, different only in that the yantra embodies but a single devatā, while the maṇḍala may enclose an infinite number. The maṇḍala is an image of the universe, a receptacle for the gods. The maṇḍala is often used as a means of concentration not only in ordinary Hinduism but also in Tantrism and Mahāyāna Buddhism. The maṇḍala, as sacred space, is a form of paradise, purified of demons. In Buddhism it is known as Diamond Land. A small maṇḍala provides the yogi with an image of the world, into which he enters psychically; the gods that inhabit the maṇḍala enter into his own body. The final *a* should not be pronounced; the first two have a short "uh" sound.

mandira, Hind. A temple where worship takes place, but a mandira is not a sacred building in the sense of a mosque, church, or synagogue. A mandira is the sanctuary of a god or goddess; usually one deity is installed in an inner room (and cared for like a living being, bathed, offered food, decorated with flowers, and incensed), and various other deities are given places inside of or around the main and lesser buildings. Generally there are daily performances of rites by priests; a lay congregation is not necessary, and the laity rarely participate in a ceremony. Some Hindus may frequent a mandira daily, others when the mood strikes, or only at festivals. The mandira is a three-dimensional, concretized form of maṇḍala (q.v.). Esoterically the mandira-maṇḍala is the "door of the god" and thus a place of passage between earth and heaven; it is the World Mountain, the womb house, and the representative of Mount Meru (q.v.), the god-haunted *axis mundi* of the Himālayas. The last vowel of mandira should be silent.

Mañjuśrī, Buddh. One of the two most important bodhisattvas, or buddhas-to-be (the other is Avalokiteśvara [q.v.]). Mañjuśrī is the symbol of wisdom; his name (in Sanskrit) means Deep Virtue or Great Fortune. In the *Lotus Sūtra,* the Buddha of the future, Maitreya, is shown seeking guidance from Mañjuśrī. Mañjuśrī is normally seen accompanying Gautama Buddha, along with Avalokiteśvara, riding upon a lion and holding the delusion-cutting sword. In Japan he is known as Monju.

mantra, Hind. A sacred saying, usually said silently (mentally). A mantra may be composed of but a single sound (Ōṃ, Śrīm, Aīm, Hrīṁ, etc.), or several syllables, or of many. The word mantra (which is pronounced with short *a*'s—m'ntruh), means "thought form." Each deity is represented by its own mantra; it is only by the correct enunciation of the correct mantra that the deity will descend to enter the body of its image, or will respond to a devotee. A mantra has great potency and is the sound form of one's ishta devata, or personal god. Name and form are inseparable. A mantra is divine power transmitted as word. Mantra represents the Supreme Being Himself in the guise of sound. Mantras are originally revealed to rishis, or seers, who pass them down to their devotees via their gurus. The disciple must keep his mantra secret and say it silently as part of his regular worship. Other mantras are openly known and commonly said; among them would be the Gāyatrī Mantra (q.v.), which forms part of the morning ritual.

Brāhmins are supposed to be the sole guardians of mantras, but mantras may also be said by others, notably doctors in curing disease (each ailment might have its special mantra), and midwives at the birth of a child. Soothsayers, astrologers, and sorcerers may use mantras mischievously and are consequently much feared for the powers they possess. See Hinduism.

Manu, Manu Smṛti, Hind. Manu, a sage of unknown antiquity, is the great Lawgiver. He is found in fourteen incarnations, which are the progenitors and lawgivers of the human race. The Rig Veda and other early texts mention him as the progenitor of mankind; in at least one he is connected to the Hindu version of the Great Deluge. The *Manu Smṛti,* credited to him, is a code of laws, dated somewhat before the second century A.D. and possibly as early as the second century B.C. It has become the canon law of Hinduism. About a quarter of the text is strictly legal; the remainder, which attempts to reassert the dominance of the brāhmins ("Let every man, according to his ability, give wealth to brāhmins, detached from the world and learned in scripture; such a giver shall attain heaven after this life"), includes much advice about daily living and contains various descriptions of life of the period, of much help to ethnologists today. Some of his prescriptions contain practical warnings, such as the statement that it is inauspicious to name girls after rivers. The *Manu Smṛti* still dominates Hindu law; such important events as the determining of an heir are based, for example, upon Manu's ruling confirming kinship by a son's officiating at his father's funeral rites, thus establishing the line of inheritance, this method being preferred to the will, which can be altered.

maqam, Isl. A very high state of Grace, in which, in the Qur'ānic phrase, "God cometh between a man and his own heart." This "station" is an integral and permanent realization of the degree of Grace, the seeker being perpetually conscious of God's being nearer to him than his innermost self.

ma'rifah (or ma'rifat), Isl. A term for Intellectual Knowledge, which is often contradictorily defined, depending on the attitude of the seeker. In some Ṣūfic mysticism, it implies theoretic under-

A saṇnyāsi, a Hindu holy man, sits in contemplation on the banks of the Ganges, Hinduism's most sacred river. The saṇnyāsi is normally a man in older years, having fulfilled his aśrama, his earlier duties in youth and as a householder.

Krishna, one of the most popular of all Hindu deities, is the embodiment of Vishnu as the Divine Joy, the Love that destroys all pain. The Vaishnavite sects see Krishna as the incarnation of the Supreme Being. Here the deity plays his flute in seducing the gopīs, the cowgirls, each of whom believes that he is her lover alone.

OM (or AUM) is the sacred symbol of the One Being, the universal sound. It is a mantra and the most sacred of sounds, representing the Divine in all of its manifestations and vibrations.

Vishnu is the pervader, the supreme cause of all, penerating all, limitless. He is commonly seen in various avatārs (q.v.). This is first of the ten most common, the Fish; the two following are the Tortoise and the Boar; the three are probably the result of a synthesis of primitive totemic cults.

A harijan, one of the "People of God," as Gandhi termed the untouchables. In the divinely ordained caste system, the untouchables are below and outside the four castes, usually live in segregated quarters, and until they gained civil and religious rights, were banned from most temples as well as certain roads and wells, being, in the eyes of the caste Hindu, polluting.

The bindi is the red "spot" worn by Hindu women. It may be a small dot, or as large as the circle as on the forehead of this yogini. The bindi has many meanings, among them the vulva, the fertility of women, the moon, and the Third Eye.

A wandering yogi reads a sacred text at the Kalighat, the most holy shrine in Calcutta. He has renounced home, family, and all worldly ties to follow a path that expectantly will bring him to freedom from the cycle of birth and rebirth.

Every morning the pious Hindu greets the break of dawn with the Gāyatrī Mantra, a prayer to the sun as deity. The prayer, which may not be said by women or men of low castes, should be recited also at midday and at sunset. The scene here is at a ghat at Benares, on the banks of the Gaṇgā.

Cows are the most venerated animals of Hinduism, being equated with the Universal Mother. (Monkeys and snakes are among other creatures that receive veneration.) Cows are usually given free run—this one is resting in the heart of Calcutta's business district.

Jain tīrthankaras line a wall outside Gwalior City in North India. The state was once a Jain stronghold, but the Jains were forced to move to other areas, especially Gujarat and the Deccan. These statues, which were damaged by the Muslims, show the tīrthankaras as Digambaras, or "Space-Clad," so liberated from material bonds that they do not own or need clothing.

A bride's hand is decorated for a North Indian wedding. Marriage, called vivaha, is one of the most solemn of all Hindu rites, as it is said to be the strongest force in preserving caste, for love marriages and intercaste and civil marriages among Hindus are rare. Usually the bride and groom do not meet before the ceremonies (though photographs may be exchanged), the marriage being arranged by parents and relatives. In place of the ring of the Western marriage, married Hindu women may wear a "collar" denoting their status or a red streak in the part of their hair.

A woman prays to a yakṣa, a spirit dwelling in a sacred banyan tree. Originally yakṣas were malevolent; now they are more beneficient, and are propitiated with offerings such as food, bits of cloth, and red-smeared stones. A sacred cobra also lives at the foot of this particular tree.

standing of the Transcendent Self (or the Divine Light), which, since it is intellectual, can only be indirect. Other sects call it "gnosis," but not Gnosis in the Christian sense, which denotes a dualism of good and evil. Ma'rifah is mystical knowledge of God along a path (tarīqah [q.v.]) leading to ecstatic union with Him or with one of His attributes, either by His indwelling in the seeker, or by the seeker's ascent to God. Ma'rifah is also "a higher plane of consciousness, in which knowledge, knower, and the Known are one."

māyā, Hind. A key philosophical, mystical, and practical concept that dominates much of Indian thought. The shorthand description that calls māyā "illusion" is beside the point. Māyā may take different forms in various schools, but all come to the broad statement that "māyā is God's creative energy"—energy that may be described for convenience as "the creative illusion of the Brahman," or "illusory appearance," but māyā is also cosmic illusion, becoming, magic, art, phenomenal existence. Māyā is thus not illusion in the sense of unreality but cosmic play, the divine līlā or sport.

Māyā, Buddh. The mother of Gautama Buddha. She was born with the moral qualities that fitted her to be the mother of a Buddha, and led a chaste and pure life from birth. Her dream of the conception of Gautama is a popular subject of Buddhist iconography: While she lay on a couch after being transported to the Himālayas, bathed and dressed as a goddess by the wives of the gods, the Buddha-to-be entered the right side of her body in the form of a white elephant. She died seven days after giving birth to Gautama —it is not fitting that the mother of a Buddha would give birth to another child. See Buddha.

Mazdayasni din, Zor. The proper name for their religion among the followers of the faith of the Prophet Zoroaster (or Zarathrustra). The term is defined as: Mazda, the Omniscient Lord, yasni, worshiping, din, faith (in the sense of revelation from God). In the Parsee Creed the faithful refer to themselves as Mazdayasni-Zaroshtis, the latter being another form of the Prophet's name. See Parsee, Zoroaster.

Mecca, Isl. The most sacred city of Islam (the second is Medina [q.v.]). Despite the fact that there is no historical evidence for the assertion that Ibrāhīm and Isma'il (Abraham and Ishmael) were ever in the city, Ibrāhīm is known by Muslims to be the founder of Mecca, an event that happened more by accident than design. He had abandoned his slave girl Hajar (Hagar) in a desolate valley, along with their son Isma'il. Hajar discovered the well Zam Zam (q.v.) and was eventually joined by a group of Yemenite nomads. This marked the beginning of Mecca as a fixed settlement.

Ibrāhīm returned to the area a number of times, and with the aid of Isma'il rebuilt the sacred temple known as the Ka'ba (q.v.), which had long been on the site. The monotheistic creed practiced by Ibrāhīm and Isma'il was followed by the Meccans for a time, but eventually they lapsed into idolatry. The Ka'ba became a pagan shrine, though a vague concept of a one god known as Allāh continued—mixed, however, with idolatrous beliefs.

Mecca, now considerably developed due to the pilgrimage trade, is situated on the Arabian Peninsula in a barren, rocky valley, forty-eight miles east of the Red Sea, on the ancient caravan route between Yemen to the south and Syria to the north. The ancient city, built of white stone and mud bricks, is today ringed with new high-rise buildings for the pilgrims, the construction of which is being financed by the bottomless funds from the Saudi oil wells. Electric lights have replaced the old candles and oil lamps; many buildings are air-conditioned. As many as a million pilgrims now fill the city every year. The most important Meccan site is still the sacred Ka'ba, the mystic cube toward which all Muslims must face when they pray. Also of significance is the well Zam Zam, and the nearby Place of Ibrāhīm; on the outskirts of Mecca, the mountains Nina and 'Arafāt are obligatory on the pilgrims' route. See hajj, Islam, Ka'ba.

Medina, Isl. Correctly, Madīnat an-Nabi, the City of the Prophet, so called because it was there that Muḥammad took up residence after his escape from enemies at Mecca; the city was originally called Yathrib. Medina is an important trading center, an oasis with fruits and dates, about three hundred miles north of Mecca. The tomb of the Prophet is at Medina; it is usually visited by pilgrims on their way home from Mecca. See hijra, Muḥammad.

Meher Baba (1894–1969). An Indian mystic, of no special sect, born Merwan Sheheriaji Irani, of Zoroastrian-Persian parents, in Poona, India. His father, the son of the keeper of a dakhmah (Tower of Silence [q.v.]) in Khooramshah, Iran, left home at the age of thirteen to become a wandering holy man, finally settling down at the age of thirty-one in Poona. Here he became engaged to a six-year-old girl from a Zoroastrian family, marrying her eight years later. The couple's second son, Merwan (the family had five boys and a girl), was, according to the astrologer at his birth, destined to be a spiritual Master. After being educated in Parsee, English, and at mission schools, Merwan entered Deccan College. During this period he encountered a famous Ṣūfī woman, Hazrat Babajan (said to have been born in 1790), and became her disciple; like the astrologer, Babajan predicted that Merwan would become a Master. In 1914, during one of their meetings, she kissed Merwan on the forehead, infusing spiritual powers of such intensity that he passed out, not recovering even partially for several days; he was not to be completely in control of his senses for years. In 1915 Merwan began to wander, temporarily putting himself under the direction of holy men of various faiths and sects. A Hindu named Upnasi Maharaj hit Merwan on the forehead with a stone in the same spot where Babajan had kissed him; this was to restore his faculties, which did not return fully until 1921. One of Merwan's masters during this period was the famous Sai Baba (q.v.).

In 1916 Merwan became manager of a theatrical company, which went as far as Lahore, but he was to return to the spiritual direction of Hazrat Babajan and others. In 1921 Upasni Maharaj passed on his disciples to Merwan, who now became known as Meher Baba (Meher meaning merciful in the Indian tongues, sun in Persian; Baba means father). From this point on, Meher Baba began to attract disciples, whom he called mandali. He now asserted his claim to be an avatār (q.v.). He established a series of ashrams that he called masts, initially at Bombay and then at other cities. He was noted as a strict disciplinarian, imposing fasts and other austerities upon his mandali; however, when his disciples broke certain rules or regulations, Baba often did penance on their behalf. In 1925 he began a year of silence, which was extended to virtually a lifetime. He communicated by writing on a slate. Despite the Silence, he was able to gain thousands of followers not only in India but also in Europe and the United States.

In 1966 he broke the Silence to communicate last messages to his mandali. He died on January 31, 1969, at the age of seventy-four, leaving behind numerous mandali devoted to continuing his work. Some have proceeded informally; others have spun off into their own Baba-inspired movements. A Baba-centered sect in San Francisco, headed by an American woman who has taken the title of murshida (an Islamic term for a spiritual leader), calls itself Sufism Reoriented; there is a Baba League in Berkeley, and Meher Baba centers in other American cities, including New York.

Meher Baba stated plainly that he was divinely sent: "There is no doubt of my being God personified," he said; also, that he was "the Christ," and that "Before me was Zoroaster, Krishna, Rama, Buddha, Jesus, and Mohammed. . . . My present Avataric Form is the last Incarnation of this cycle of time, hence my Manifestation will be the greatest." Though he was a Zoroastrian by birth, and underwent Ṣūfic and Hindu training, he did not attempt to found a new religion nor a synthesis. He said, "I am not come to establish any cult, society, or organization—now even to establish a new religion. The Religion I shall give teaches the knowledge of the One behind the many. . . . My work is to lead others to reach the goal: to live in the world and not to be of it, and to be in harmony with everything and everyone. . . . Seek refuge in me, for you are very dear to me. I will release you from all sin. Do not grieve; do not worry." His teachings and his methods of meditation (though he developed a shortened technique) were his own version of orthodox Hinduism. He was noted for various outward signs of the advanced holy man, such as astral traveling, bilocation, miracles, mind reading, and so on, though he publically eschewed such siddhis as tricks.

Mencius, a Chinese Confucian sage (c. B.C. 372–289 but the dates are uncertain). Mencius (the name is a latinization of Meng K'o) is second only to the Master himself in the Confucian tradition. Like Confucius, his father died early and he was raised by his mother, a woman of exceptional qualities and virtue. And like Confucius, he spent much of his life traveling about China in fruitless attempts to persuade sovereigns to follow sage advice instead of endlessly waging war and oppressing the peasants, finally retiring from a public role to write and teach, for his converts among the princes were few. His works, commonly called *Mencius* (though *Meng-tzŭ* is the correct term), rank along with those of Confucius.

Like the Master, Mencius taught the golden mean, for, if it is not promoted, "perverse teachings will delude the people and block the road to human-heartedness and righteousness. And when that way is blocked, beasts will devour men, and men will devour one another." His primary interests were morals and government. Religion and mystical practices played little role in his thought. He is noted for the doctrine of the Four Limbs of a Man, a central Confucian teaching. But in an abrupt break with Confucius, who saw society existing in a hierarchical structure, with the prince as Son of Heaven at the top, proceeding downward through various classes to the peasants. Mencius stated, "The people rank highest in a state, the spirits of Land and Grain come next, and the sovereign is of the least account," a doctrine he believed stemmed from the ancient Sinitic concept of a Mandate from Heaven. The Mandate was given the prince as Son of Heaven, but if he did not fulfill it honorably, his ministers first and then the people had the right and duty to dethrone him. In the eyes of Mencius, war waged unjustly by a prince (and China at the time seemed to be an endless battleground) was the worst of all sins. War teaches "the very soil beneath us to devour human flesh—a crime for which no death can atone." See Confucianism, Confucius.

Meru, Mount, Hind. A mystical, psychical point, the cosmic center that is both exterior and interior. Meru is placed in the Himālayas; whether or not such a mountain exists depends on the mind of the devotee rather than on the geographer. Meru is the *axis mundi,* the cosmic point; it furnishes the ground plan upon which Hindu (and Jain) temples are laid out. It is also the axis of the human spinal column. Meru is the center of the world lotus; around it is Jambudvīpa (q.v.), Rose-Apple Land, the ancient mystical name for India as cosmic energy form.

Mevlevis, Ṣūfī. Properly Mawlawīyas, a dervish brotherhood. See dervish.

mihrāb, Isl. The central niche of a mosque, indicating the qiblah, the direction of the holy city of Mecca. Initially, when the Prophet Muḥammad included the Jews in his message to the world, only to be rejected by them, the qiblah faced Jerusalem. He then turned to the Arabs alone, with the Ka'ba at Mecca as the qiblah. The mihrāb is always empty, but it is usually decorated with texts from the Qur'ān; often the name Allāh appears on the right side, that of Muḥammad on the left. The mihrāb is derived from the statuary niches of Christian churches and basilicas taken over by the Muslims; the empty niche symbolizes Islamic iconoclasm and the mystery of God. See Islam.

ming-ch'i, Chin. "Spirit objects" or tomb furniture interred in quantity and style fitting the deceased's station in life. At certain times in Chinese history the furnishing of tombs became so excessive that laws were passed limiting the amount of ming-ch'i to be interred.

Mira Bai (c. 1500–50, or c. 1550–1600), Hind. A Rajput princess whose husband was ruler of the state of Mewar; she left the luxurious life of the court, put on ragged clothing, and walked barefoot to Brindavan, the center of worship of the Dark God Krishna. As she made her pilgrimage she sang songs she had composed in Krishna's honor; these are works of great artistic and spiritual depths, which are still sung in North India by the ordinary people and are popular examples of bhakti. With Krishna as her celestial lover, she chanted of the ecstatic joy of a woman loved, raped, seized, consumed, pierced, abandoned, and reclaimed, distraught with Divine passion. Despite his notorious amours with the gopīs and Rādhā, Krishna is said to have found his greatest passion in Mira Bai. Hagiography of Mira Bai runs to ecstatic extremes, but once the facts are grasped, she appears as an exceptional saint, and one of the most beloved of the many found in India. See bhakti, Krishna.

mkah hgroma, Tib. Pronounced "kandoma." A feminine deity, a kind of mother goddess who bestows not only blessings but also esoteric knowledge upon devotees. Mkah hgroma is the Tibetan Buddhist equivalent of the Hindu dākinī (q.v.).

moksha, Hind. Liberation, from the stream-current of life, from the chains of karma (q.v.). (Moksha is sometimes known as mukti.) Moksha is not a negative state but one of completeness, of fullness of being, free from saṁsara, the bondage of karma, and thus from the endless round of birth, death, and rebirth. Moksha is quite foreign to Āryan concepts, and the supposition is that the non-Vedic and pre-Āryan cultures of India must have contributed to Hinduism the ideas of renunciation and asceticism leading to moksha (or mukti) and nirvāṇa, the final freedom expressed in unity in the Supreme. Moksha is gained through three ways or paths (mārga): that of knowledge (jñāna), devotion (bhakti), and ritual works (karma). While some may attain moksha at death, the goal is to achieve it well in advance, as certain yogis and the true gurus do: A guru in the fullest sense of the word should be jīvanmukta—i.e., one who has attained liberation before death. Thus moksha is the highest aim of human existence. See mukti.

mokṣa, Hind. The Sanskrit spelling of moksha, above.

mondo, Buddh. A question-answer (the literal meaning) method of teaching by Zen Buddhist masters; the Chinese term is wen-ta. The wen-ta or mondo is an early form of the kung-en or kōan, which is simplified, tighter; in practice mondo and kōan are often interexchangeable. The mondo is short, even abrupt, and seemingly illogical. An answer need not appear to reply to the question but to turn it around, or even oppose it. The Sixth Patriarch, Hui Nêng (q.v.), described what was to be the wen-ta/mondo as follows:

"If in questioning you, someone asks about being, answer with nonbeing. If he asks about nonbeing, answer with being. If he asks about the ordinary man, answer in terms of the sage. If he asks about the sage, answer in terms of the ordinary man. By this system of mutually related opposites, there arises a comprehension of the Middle Way [i.e., of Buddhism]. For every question that you are asked, respond in terms of its opposite."

Like the kōan, the mondo seeks to break through habitual thought-patterns in the student and turn his mind, to awaken the forces that will enlighten him. Mondo cannot be explained without destroying its effect: One gets the point, or one doesn't.

A mondo from the eleventh-century Chinese *Blue Rock Collection* is typical:

A pupil asked Pai-chang Huai-hai, "What is the most miraculous event in the world?" Pai-chang answered, "I sit here all by myself." The monk bowed before the master, who struck him.

Like the preceding mondo, the following contains its own explanation.

Tao-hsin asked Seng-ts'an, "What is the method of liberation?" "Who binds you?" replied the Master. "No one binds me." "Why then should you seek liberation?" See Ch'an, kōan, Zen.

mosque, Isl. The central—but not essential—place of worship for Muslims. The English word is a corruption of masjid, or place of prostration (to God). Strictly speaking a sanctuary is not considered a fundamental necessity since complete resignation and humility before Him can be shown anywhere. However, the mosque is preferred for it not only enables the Muslim to worship in community, rich and poor, high and low, standing, kneeling, and prostrating shoulder to shoulder, but it contains the fountain for washing and various aids to prayer.

The first building to be used as a mosque was the Prophet Muḥammad's home in Medina, and early mosques, aside from those Christian churches and pagan temples to be converted as mosques, followed the same plan, that of the typical Near Eastern house, a courtyard surrounded by living quarters enclosed in a wall. In the yard was a simple structure of palm trunks bearing a flat roof of palm leaves covered with mud. The quadrangle court, with a fountain, became an integral part of the fully developed mosque complex of later days. The minaret was added as an aid to calling the faithful to prayer. Regional influences have given the mosque the opportunity to develop, many structures ranking among the great architecture of the world.

The central features of the mosque, along with the minaret, are the court, the mihrāb or central niche which indicates the qiblah or direction toward the holy city of Mecca, and the minbar or pulpit, which may be permanently a part of the mosque or portable. There are no seats; the faithful stand or kneel on carpets and prayer mats. The mosque must be centered on a line with the mihrāb directed toward Mecca; thus the mihrāb of a North African mosque faces east, that of a Pakistani mihrāb west, and so on. From the beginning in Medina the mosque was a center of Islamic communal life, being a place of both divine worship and secular usages; the courtyard and attendant rooms and buildings were employed for meetings, schools, law courts, and other public purposes. In the strict Islamic countries women may not enter a mosque; in other lands they may stand in a separate section behind a curtain, or worship from a balcony with a pierced screen. See Islam.

Mother, The, Hind. The Mother is specifically the Parisian ex-socialite Mira Richard (1878–1964), although the term Mother is also applied to numerous other holy women and saints in India and elsewhere. The Mother was the partner, if not the co-avatār, of Sri Aurobindo Ghose, the Bengali mystic who retired to the French colony of Pondichéry in South India to found an ashram, where he passed the major part of his life. The Mother's life complemented Aurobindo's, and she continued his work after his death in 1950.

As a child in France, the Mother was noted for her spiritual precocity. "The Mother was inwardly above the human even in childhood," stated Aurobindo. Between the ages of eleven and twelve "a series of psychic and spiritual experiences revealed to the Mother not only the existence of God but man's possibility of uniting with Him, of realizing Him integrally in consciousness and action, of manifesting Him upon earth in a life divine." In France at the time, along with her usual education, she made an intense study of the occult. Repeated visions of a figure whom she identified as the god Krishna brought her to Pondichéry in March 1914; she was then married to the French diplomat Paul Richard, whom she left six years later in favor of a life divine with Aurobindo. She had anticipated Pondichéry as far back as 1912, for she had a vision of "the flowering of the new race, the race of the Sons of God." And in 1914 Aurobindo was, she knew, the Krishna of her dreams.

In Aurobindo she saw God descended as avatār—"Sri Aurobindo incarnated in a human body the supramental consciousness and has not only revealed to us the nature of the path to follow and the method of following it so as to arrive at the goal, but has also by his own personal realization given us the examples." In return, Aurobindo saw his partner in a similar light. "The One whom we adore as the Mother is the divine Consciousness Force that dominates all existence. . . . The Mother comes to bring down the Supramental and it is the descent which makes her manifestation possible."

In 1926 the Mother took over the administration of the small ashram founded by Aurobindo and began to build it into an international center for a new spirituality, running the institution with an iron hand. Every disciple became her personal charge; she alone could select those to be trained to become divine individuals. Each pupil accepted was expected to offer his or her material possessions to the Mother. Thus the Mother acquired a Bentley, and the ashram eventually was able to build one of the most fashionable private schools in India, a paper factory, a publishing house, a nursing home, and acquire much real estate. In the 1960s the Mother drew up first plans for the "planetary city" of Auroville, its purpose to build upon spiritual principles a center in which religion, education, the workshop, factory, home, and field would be a laboratory for a new consciousness. In 1970 UNESCO passed a resolution of support. See also Aurobindo.

muftī, Isl. A specialist in Islamic law (sharī'a), which is based upon the Qur'ān (q.v.). The muftī is as much a religious authority as legal, and under the old Turkish empire, the Grand Muftī of Constantinople was regarded as the highest religious authority and bore the title Shayk of Islam.

Muḥammad. The last of the Prophets, the last of the divine Messengers sent by Allāh—God—to warn mankind. There are three primary sources for autobiographical material. The first and most important is the Qur'ān, the sacred Book for which Muḥammad served as transmitter. The second is Ḥadīth or Tradition, which recounts all that is known of the sayings and acts of the Prophet and his companions, attested to by a chain of witnesses reaching back to the very first generations of Islam. The third is sīrah, or biographies written by historians in the second Islamic century and later; the sīrahs are based upon the two other and previous sources but present the material rearranged in chronological order. The best-known such work is the *Sīrat ar-Rasūl* by Ibn Hishām (d. A.D. 834), which is the oldest and most reliable, as it draws upon a great lost work by Ibn Isḥāq. Later sīrahs become progressively less factual and more fanciful, until the present century, when new standards of scholarship are applied. The data of the Qur'ān are limited, the Ḥadīth is profuse, and the sīrahs of later years must be treated with caution. Many millions of words, starting with Arabic and continuing through most of the languages of the world, have been written about Muḥammad; there is much exegesis, interpretation, and misinterpretation, all of which do little more than confirm the fact that for the world, Islamic or pagan, the Prophet Muḥammad is by and large a mystery, and he can be explained in no ordinary terms. Also, the individual who does not read Arabic and who is not a Muslim is likely to have difficulty in understanding Semitic patterns of thought, linguistics, and expression, and his age, with its widely differing social, cultural, and economic conditions. Even among Muslims there are varying interpretations. Muḥammad is first of all the man to whom Allāh spoke through the Angel Jibril (i.e., Gabriel) to reveal, over several decades, His final message to the world. Muḥammad is the Seal of the Prophets, the last of a long line beginning with Adam, who proclaimed God's word. To certain Islamic sects Muḥammad has become the Logos, and to others virtually an Incarnation. Some even place him dangerously close to the Godhead Itself. In any case, Muḥammad was an individual of unquestioned integrity, both moral and spiritual, chosen to be the vessel of Divine Love.

Even with the extensive exegesis and study and the weight of unimpeachable Tradition, the early dates for the Prophet's years are, in a word, imprecise. Little is known about his life before his Call. Muḥammad was born in Mecca, a small but significant trading center near the western coast of the Arabian peninsula, on the north–south caravan routes; Mecca was as well a famous spiritual center, being founded, according to pre-Islamic tradition, by the Prophet Ibrāhīm. The year of Muḥammad's birth is not clear, though it is identified as being in April in "the Year of the Elephant," so named because an Ethiopian general had made an unsuccessful attempt to attack Mecca, his forces being led by an elephant. The date is variously ascribed to the period A.D. 568–72; 570 seems to be accepted as a compromise. The name Muḥammad was given the child by his grandfather 'Abd al-Muṭṭalib, the chieftain of the Banu Hāshim clan of the Quraish tribe. "Muḥammad" was either his given name or a nickname, for it means "The Praised One." In his teens, because of his unusual probity and manners, he was called al-Amīn, which means "the Honest." He was also known for a long time as Abu'l-Qāsim, an honorific meaning "the father of al-Qāsim." The family was upper class but poor; the grandfather 'Abd al-Muṭṭalib enjoyed the honor of distributing water from the sacred well of Zam Zam to pilgrims who came to Mecca.

Muḥammad's father, 'Abd Allāh, died on a trading trip shortly before the Prophet was born, leaving the mother, Āminah, a widow. As was the custom, the infant was given to a wet nurse, a Bedouin woman named Ḥalīmah of the Banu Sa'd. At the age of four the child was returned to his ancestral home; two years later his mother died. His grandfather took over his care, but he too died two years after that. Muḥammad then passed into the care of his uncle Abū Ṭālib, a shepherd and businessman. Until he was twelve, Muḥammad tended his uncle's flocks among the Bedouins of the desert. Later Muḥammad was to remark that every prophet was a shepherd in his youth. A tradition states that during this period his cousin (called a foster brother by the Arabs) saw two angels throw Muḥammad to the ground, open up his chest, and remove a black clot from his heart, the incident being based (rightly or not) on the Qur'ānic verse, "Have we not opened thy breast and eased thee of thy burden which overwhelmed thee?" (94, 1–3). One interpretation is that Muḥammad, though still a child, had passed from misfortune to happiness, from agony of mind to faith, from ignorance to knowledge of the truth. The event touches upon the mystical cycle of the Purification of the Heart, a concept basic to Islamic mysticism.

With his desert apprenticeship behind him, a role so common to children in the Middle East, Muḥammad joined his uncle at Bostra in Syria, then part of the Byzantine (Christian) Empire. Here Muḥammad met Nestorian Christian monks, among them a certain Baḥīra, who is said to have predicted that the young man would become a prophet. (This episode is questioned by some Western scholars.) However, in his travels, Muḥammad would have crossed the lands of the Judaic prophets, among them Ibrāhīm, who plays such an important role in Islam; David, whose Zabūr or Psalms are part of Islamic belief; and the Injīl of Isa—i.e., the Evangel or Gospel of Jesus.

In his midtwenties Muḥammad entered the employ of a wealthy widow named Khadījah, on whose behalf he made at least one trading journey to Syria, during which he exhibited unusual business talents and admirable honesty. Khadījah, fifteen years his senior, proposed to Muḥammad, who was then twenty-five. The marriage, which lasted the twenty years until her death, proved to be unusually happy and successful, and in the eyes of the Meccans, added to Muḥammad's already considerable prestige and respect. When Muḥammad, at the age of forty began to experience the searing spiritual trials evoked by his Call, Khadījah showed him tremendous understanding and compassion. Meanwhile the couple had two (or three) sons, who died early, and four daughters, Zainab, Ruqaiyah, Umm Kulthūm, and Fāṭimah, the latter being the only one of his children to have children. Muḥammad also adopted an enslaved woman, Zaid ibn Ḥārithah, who was captured in a desert raid; he later freed her. Muḥammad continued to prosper financially, his virtues, business skills, and wisdom being more and more respected; yet at the same time he became increasingly introspective and contemplative. He developed the habit of retreating for days, even weeks, alone in a cave called Ḥirā' in the hills outside Mecca, where he was isolated not only from the commercial activities of daily life but also from the pagan and superstitious practices of most of his fellow Meccans. In the cave he began to speculate upon the wonders and the secrets of the Universe and upon the mysterious forces of the Divine. Though he was unlettered, having no formal education, he remained free of the idolatry of the Meccans, centered upon statues and icons of stone and wood, which he could not believe had any religious value. One of the strongest influences upon him came from the hanīfs, a small group of people who are generally labeled "mysterious." Little is known about them. According to the Qur'ān and Islamic tradition, they are the exponents of the pure monotheism of the Prophet Ibrāhīm, who had preceded both the Mosaic Law and Christianity. In some accounts they seem to be some type of spirit or celestial wanderer. They may have been Manichean Christians or converts to orthodox Christianity, like Khadījah's cousin Waraqah. They were ascetics and against idols; Islam has described itself as fulfilling the religion of the hanīfs, whose ancestral prototype was Ibrāhīm. With his increasingly inward turn, Muḥammad also began to divest himself of possessions, giving away considerable sums as alms.

The turning point of Muḥammad's life came when he was about forty. He was visited in the cave by the angel Jibril. The year was either 610 or 612. Both the Qur'ān and the Ḥadīth state that the event took place on a night in the last third of Ramaḍān, the sacred month of fasting that was commonly observed even by the pagans. While Muḥammad was asleep, a mysterious figure appeared, holding in his hand a scroll covered with signs and ordered him to read. "I do not know how to read," said Muḥammad. "Read!" said the figure again, and then a third time, winding the scroll around Muḥammad's neck. "What shall I read?" asked Muḥammad. "Read!" said the figure.

> Read in the name of your Lord Who created; Who created man from clots of blood. Read, for your Lord is most generous Who taught by the Pen; He taught man what he did not know. Man indeed trangresses if he thinks himself a law unto himself, for to your Lord all things return.

The earliest accounts state that this experience occurred under somewhat somnambulistic circumstances. The Prophet is reported to have said after narrating the incident, "Then I woke up." One of his later wives (after the death of Khadījah), 'Ā'ishah, said ambiguously, "The first revelations the Prophet said were received in true dreams, and he never dreamed but it came like the dawn of day." Thus he had either a full vision or experienced the encounter in a half-wakened state.

Muḥammad's first reaction was one of apprehension and doubt. He suspected that he may have been the victim of malicious jinns or was the subject of an illusion sent to destroy him. Feeling he might be insane or possessed, Muḥammad returned home. Khadījah took the experience at face value and gave her full support to her husband now, as she was to during the ever-increasing trials. "When I was poor she enriched me," said the Prophet, "when all the world abandoned me, she comforted me, when I was called a liar, she believed in me." At one point he went into a suicidal depression. The angel appeared again and said, "O Muḥammad, verily thou art in truth the Prophet of Allāh." With these words Muḥammad's doubts and depression ended, and the Revelations appeared on a more frequent basis, though they were to be spaced out over a period of twenty-three years and to be received not only in Mecca but also when he was in exile in Medina.

The Revelations, later collated by his disciples into chapters, or sūras, contain a variety of messages for man, from volcanic, divine exhortations to more placid, detailed passages that embody legal, social, and organizational formulas and prescriptions for all aspects of human life, from birth through adulthood to death and beyond into the reaches of Paradise or the depths of Hell. The earlier sūras are pregnant with extraordinary deep and powerful psychological content: A divine voice is crying aloud to sinning, erring mankind from the heights of heaven, taking up residence in the Prophet's heart, to offer fulfillment and love to the human soul and psyche. Even when the sūras descend to prosaic codes of society, the voice of God breaks through to warn fallible man of his duties and responsibilities. The message is one of submission to Allāh, through love, fear, through social responsibility, through common humanity, through prayer and mysticism, a message that also calls for repentance of sin, the practicing of the works of mercy, the Immanence of the Last Judgment, the mission of the previous prophets, the punishments suffered by those who reject the Divine Oneness, down to the various problems of the community, with its mundane duties, arguments, successes, and vicissitudes.

During the first three years of the Revelations Muḥammad spoke of them to only a few close relatives and intimate friends. Among them were his wife, his cousin 'Ali, his adopted son Zaid, his friend and future father-in-law Abū Bakr, and his son-in-law 'Uthmān the Umayyad. Then Jibril told him to preach openly to the Meccans. Muḥammad started with his own clan, the Hāshimites. He made few conversions. He expanded his preaching to include all the Quraishites, but was derided and mocked. He was unable even to convince his old protector and guardian, his uncle Abū Ṭālib. Because Muḥammad denounced the rich—"Your hearts are taken up with worldly gain"—he converted few of them. His chief appeal was to the downtrodden, the poor of the Meccan slums, and the slaves. Not only did he attack the upper classes—

"they believed not in the great God, they were not solicitous to feed the poor; they will burn in the fire of Hell"—he also attacked their idols, Al-Lāt, Al-'Uzzā, and Manāt, and the mysterious Hubal hidden in the Ka'ba. He also denounced the doctrine of Jesus as the Son of God—"God has taken no wife, nor has He begotten any issue."

Muḥammad's teachings were taken as a threat by the ruling classes. Their traditional polytheistic religion was being challenged and denounced, their commercial interests were undermined by his insistence on the rights of the poor and the duty of the rich to aid them, and by his condemnation of usury. Muḥammad was accused of being a magician, of being possessed by jinns, of being insane. Active and relentless persecution of the Prophet and his small group of disciples began. Yet he was to remain true to the Revelations, for they were not his sayings, his work, but God speaking through his messenger. This point must be emphasized. Non-Muslims often speak as if these doctrines were Muḥammad's, whether it was the insistence on the Oneness of God or the need for regular prayer or the manifold social regulations that he talked of. Throughout his trials Jibril commanded him to be patient.

In A.D. 620 Muḥammad experienced the famous vision known as the Night Journey (isrā') or Ascension (mi'rāj), in which he was carried from the Ka'ba at Mecca to the Temple in Jerusalem on the winged horse Burāq, under the guidance of Jibril. In the vision the Prophet ascended a ladder of light from the Temple to the foot of the heavenly throne. The sūra (17) that mentioned the event is replete with moral and practical instructions for the faithful, including the injunction to pray five times a day. Some Muslim commentators accept the Night Journey literally, others as but a vision. The Journey is commemorated every year by the faithful.

As conditions grew steadily worse for Muḥammad, and there was a rumor of a plot against his life, his thoughts turned to flight. One of his followers had made some converts at Yathrib, an oasis of some three thousand people about three hundred miles north of Mecca. These converts in turn sent envoys to the Prophet to express their fidelity. With about sixty of his own people preceding him to Yathrib, the Prophet, in the company of Abū Bakr, fled Mecca secretly and eventually reached Yathrib, soon to be known as Medina (Madīnat an-Nabi, the city of the Prophet). This flight, the hijra (or hegira), marks the beginning of the Islamic calendar (A.D. 622).

In Medina Muḥammad's mission changed radically. Though most of the Medinans soon accepted Islam, the considerable Jewish colony refused his Call as the fulfillment of the Mosaic law. A series of battles ensued, with the Jews and with various desert tribes. The concept of the holy war, the jihād, was born, the dead being promised "the enjoyment of Paradise" for having fought for Allāh. Muḥammad's armies were soon victorious everywhere; the defeated generals and princes and their troops submitted to Islam, the Jews enslaved or killed, and Muḥammad was, by March of A.D. 629, outside Mecca, "peacefully" occupying it after a series of agreements with his former enemies, who did not dare present more than a token challenge to his might. Virtually without a struggle, the Muslims were able to enter the sacred city and overturn the idols in the Ka'ba. Two years later, after more victories in the field, the Prophet proclaimed idolatry illegal in Arabia, the Ka'ba being established as the center of Islamic worship and the goal of the Muslim on pilgrimage. Feeling that death was approaching, the Prophet led a group of ninety thousand pilgrims into Mecca to perform a series of rites that are still observed by pilgrims today. Ascending Mount 'Arafāt, sanctified because it was here that Adam and Eve met, and the Prophet Ibrāhīm performed his sacrifice to God, Muḥammad preached to his people for the last time, exhorting them to remain united after his death; he emphasized the reciprocal rights of man and wife; then he restated the proscription of usury, and announced that the Islamic year would consist of twelve lunar months without solar correction. The last Revelation came to him—"Today I have made perfect that religion; I have fulfilled my Grace upon you and I am pleased that your faith should be Islam" (sūra 5.5). Three months later, on June 8 of the Julian calendar, Muḥammad died at Medina. See Islam, Ka'ba, Mecca, Qur'ān.

mukti, Hind. Liberation—i.e., from the endless round of birth and rebirth, and thus becoming one with God. Mukti, sometimes called, also, mokṣa, is due to right knowledge of Self, or intuition of Truth, which leads to liberation. The realization of mukti or its experience as a state of bliss in this life depends on the purification of the physical and vital organs, which is done through the psychomystico technique of yoga (q.v.); the reason is that mukti in an embodied state can be obtained only through the medium of the purified vehicles of mind and of prāṇa, the life force. This state of accomplishment is known as jīvan-mukta (liberation during the life span). See mokṣa.

Mūl Mantra, Sikh. The opening statement of the Jap-ji, the Sikh creed written by Guru Nānak. The Mūl Mantra ("Seed Prayer") summarizes Nānak's concept of God in a few terse Punjabi terms, which cannot be adequately translated in other languages. Versions by three respected scholars differ so widely as to seem like vaguely related works only.

By P. Lal: By the grace of the Guru! God is one, there is only one God, God is Truth, He created all things, God is without flaw, at peace with all things, Timeless and Birthless, Being of his own Being. Made known to men by the grace of the Guru! [The Meditation] Let us repeat his name. As he was in the beginning, the Truth, As he was through the Ages, the Truth, So is He now, the Truth, O Nānak, So will He be for ever and for ever.

Gurbachan Singh Talib: In the name of the One Indivisible Supreme Being, Eternal Reality, Creator Purusha [the Absolute], without fear, without rancor, Timeless Form, Unborn, Self-existent, Realized through Divine grace.

B. P. L. Bedi: The one, the parent of Sound creative, Truth is Your Name, Creator of existence and Lord of non-existence. Of beginningless Beginning and of Endless Ending, without an opposite. The embodiment of Immortality. Free from the cycle of birth and death. Self-manifested. Self-revealed, By grace of Himself. [The Meditation] Praise the One, From beginningless Beginning, truth is Your Name. From the beginning of time, truth is Your Name. Even today, truth is Your Name. Nānak says, Even to the Endless End of time, truth shall be Your Name.

See Ek Oankar, Sikhism.

muni, Hind. A term for a sage. The word is sometimes used in Buddhism—Gautama Buddha is often called Śakyamuni, the sage of the Śakya clan.

muqaddam, Isl. An assistant to a shayk (q.v.) who usually supervises a zāwiyah or Ṣūfī center on behalf of his superior; he is known to be spiritually advanced and receives members of the Ṣūfī brotherhood and conducts spiritual retreats and exercises. He carries the confidence and authority of the shayk, and his soul, in the words of a shayk, "has been purified and his inward eye opened to the Divine Light."

◂N▸

nādī, Hind. In the ordinary sense, a nerve or artery, but in Hindu tantrism, a nādī is a subtle channel of energy. Texts differ in the number, some accounts giving a total of 72,000, and others, 350,000. There are fourteen principal nādīs, of which three, idā, pingalā, and suṣumnā, are paramount. The trio are also, in a more than symbolic sense, the three major rivers of India, respectively the Gaṇgā (Ganges), Yamunā, and the Sarasvati. See tantrism.

Namadeva (A.D. 1270–1350), Hind. A Vaishnavaite mystic from Mahārāshtra. He opposed the worship of idols and the importance given mythology, such monotheistic traits making him a favorite of the Sikhs (q.v.), who included many of his abhangas (bhakti hymns) in the Granth Sāheb (q.v.). He was a tailor—i.e., of low caste, and so lived a life of poverty. His religious quest brought him to a true Dark Night of the Soul, which is marked by a burning wail of anguish in his songs, for he had to pass through experiences marked by melancholy, grief, and sorrow. Nevertheless, his faith in the Lord continued unabated, though he often felt rejected —"It is the one Lord who contains all," he sang, "O Lord, why this vain seeking for you, since you are everywhere?" In another work he asked, "Do you think I shall grow weary and go away from your presence, feeling that You would not come? The rope of my love I shall bind to your feet, to bring You to me at my pleasure. . . . I shall spread the meshes of my love and catch You alive. I shall make my heart a jail for You and shall imprison You within. Your generosity has been falsely praised, for You give only when You have taken away." See bhakti.

nāmakaraṇa, Hind. The solemn ceremony for naming a child, an extremely important occasion, usually performed on the child's first birthday. The rite includes various invocations (made to the four quarters of the universe) and prayers selected according to the child's horoscope. The ancient *Manu Smṛti* states what qualities a name must possess: "A brāhmin's name should have an auspicious meaning, a kshatriya's name should indicate strength, a vaishya's name should denote wealth, and a sudra's name should be despicable," for a person's name is one easy clue to his caste. "A brāhmin's name should have the suffix sarma [auspicious], a kshatriya's name the suffix varma [armor], a Vaishya's name the suffix gupta or datta, and a śūdra's name the suffix dāsa [servant]." Also, "Girls' names should be auspicious, easy to pronounce, and without harsh letters, of clear meaning and pleasant to the ear, denote good fortune, end with long vowels, and express blessing." See Hinduism.

namaskār, Hind. A salutation in the name of God. The palms are placed together and raised to touch the forehead, the site of the Third Eye (q.v.). Together, the hands symbolize the One Mind, or the self meeting the Self, the right hand representing the holy, or higher nature, and the left, the worldly, or lower nature.

namaste, Hind. Another term for namaskār, above.

Name, Divine. The repetition of the Name of the deity is of vital importance in many religions, Western as well as Eastern. The Jews of the pre-Diaspora could not say or write the sacrosanct Name of God, except under esoteric conditions. The vocalization of the Tetragrammaton Y H V H, the "lost word," has been unknown for some two thousand years. Y H V H had been called the shem hameforash, the explicit name, being taught to chosen disciples under tightly controlled conditions; it was "withdrawn" by the Lord Himself, and other names were substituted. The mystical sects that developed later employed various terms for the Divine as a means toward ecstasy; among these groups may be included the Merkabah or Chariot mystics, some of the medieval Hasidim who found a magical element in the mysterious power of sacred Names, various Kabbalists (such as those who engaged in the Sefirtoh, which form the "one great Name of God"). The eighteenth-century mystic, the famed Baal Shem—"Master of the Name" (of God)—attracted a great following. Christianity has laid less stress on the Name as sacred or esoteric tool, but the practice in its Eastern churches of saying the mantra known as the Jesus Prayer ("Lord Jesus Christ, have mercy on me") without cease resembles the Hindu japa (q.v.) and may have been suggested by it. In Hinduism various deities, especially the non-Vedic deities Shiva, Kālī, and Gaṇgā, are known by 108 attributes or names (1,008 in some lists). Usually upper-caste Hindus repeat the name of Shiva (or Kālī) at least 108 times during the day, and perhaps several times 108.

The Buddhists have no special cult of the name of any of the Buddhas with the exception of the Amida Buddha (q.v.) through the mantra nembutsu (q.v.), a practice especially popular in the Pure Land sects (q.v.). The Zoroastrians describe the Supreme Lord Ahura Mazdā by 101 names signifying his attributes; among them are: Worthy of Worship, Omnipotent, Omniscient, Lord of the Universe, One who can change fire into air (and air into fire), . . . air into water (etc.), Existence Itself, the One and Only Reality, One Who has ordained the Transformation from the human to the Divine. In other texts, Ahura Mazdā states, "I am the Sustainer by Name, next the Shepherd, third the All-pervading," and so on. In Islam there are Seven Divine Names and Ninety-nine Beautiful Names, the later being attributes found in the Qur'ān or in tradition; the lists are not always identical. They resemble the attributes of Ahura Mazdā, though direct influence cannot be established. The Seven Divine Names are most commonly employed. They are: Lā ilāha illa 'Llāh (There is no God but God); Allāh (God); Huwa (He); Al-Ḣaqq (the Truth); Al-Ḣayy (the Living), Al-Qayyūm (Self-sufficient); and Al-Qahhār (the Irresistible). The most important names for God are the twin titles Al-Rahmān al-Rahīm (The Compassionate, the Merciful), an invocation used at the head of all but one of the 114 chapters of the Qur'ān.

Namu Amida Butsu, Buddh. The sacred formula or prayer (actually a mantra) of the Pure Land (Shin) sect of Japanese Mahāyāna Buddhism, which is founded upon the minor second-century A.D. Indian Amida (in the original Sanskrit, Amitābha, eternal light) as a transcendental buddha. Namu means "I take refuge," and Butsu is Buddha—"I take refuge in the Amida Buddha." Repetition of the name is unusual in Buddhism; the practice in the Japanese sect most likely originated in India, where such observances are common. See also Amida, mantra, Pure Land.

Nānak, Sikh. (1) The founder of the Sikhs. Nānak is the first of the Sikh Gurus (there were ten in all). He was born in A.D. 1469 to a family of the Hindu kśatriya caste in the Panjabi village of Talwandi, not far from the ancient city of Lahore (now in Pakistan), and he died at Kartarpur, also near Lahore (but on the Indian side of the Panjabi border) in 1538. From the beginning he was spiritually precocious. To a teacher who chided him for mentioning Creation and its inner things, he replied, "There can be no beginning without the eternal sound of creativity having been learned." He rejected the thread of the twice-born, to which he was entitled as a caste Hindu, saying, "Wear not the thread spun from cotton, Wear the thread eternal. Let compassion, the essence of love Divine and universal be the Cotton." He married at fourteen and had two sons. As a young man he took care of the family buffalos for a while, then went to Sultanpur, the provincial capital, where he obtained a post as storekeeper for the governor, Daulat Khan. Here Nānak was noted for his exceptionally honest accounts and the fact that he retained only a small portion of his wages for himself, distributing the remainder to the poor in the form of provisions. It was during this period that he had an ecstatic experience while meditating in a forest and had a vision of God and received the Jap-ji, the prayers and hymns that form the basis of Sikh belief. Nānak retired from government service, gave away all he possessed to the poor, and took up the life of the wandering holy man. He was very much influenced by the saintly recluses, workingmen, and poets he encountered in his journeys, and by the tradition of bhakti or personal devotion to God that so enlivened the spiritual life of the masses of the subcontinent, not only the Hindus but also the Muslims. One of the major influences upon him was the low-caste weaver Kabīr, who drew upon both Hindu and Ṣūfī sources for his poems of devotion. Aside from the bhaktis, Nānak was not impressed by the religious life of the more orthodox, for he announced, "There is no Hindu and no Muslim," both sects in his opinion having lost the inner light. He now sought to regenerate the human race, and with various companions wandered not only throughout India but also as far afield as the Islamic countries of West Asia. He talked to holy men of whatever persuasion, drew upon their teachings as he wished, and forged his own beliefs, which were a reformed and purified type of Hinduism strongly fortified by Islamic monotheism. He rejected the worship of idols and of the Hindu pantheon, and fasting, pilgrimages, ritual, and whatever might cause disunity among men. A large number of people, mainly peasants of the Panjab, were attracted to his teachings. It is not likely that he deliberately set out to found a new sect or religion, but his saintliness had a marked effect upon those who followed him. He selected his own successor, Angad (1504–52), shortly before he died. At his death there was a gentle dispute over his body, the Hindus wishing to cremate it and the Muslims to bury it.

Nānak's teachings are simple and lack the theological sophistication and complexity of other Indian spiritual leaders. He preached the One God endlessly, a God whom one approached with loving devotion and faith, though he did not abandon certain traditional Hindu beliefs, such as that of reincarnation until the endless cycle of sin had worked itself out and one was absorbed into the Divine. He was noted for performing a series of miracles, although he denounced miracles as such (the most striking of which was his ability to speak in Panjabi and be heard in the listener's own tongue), and, along with his successor Gurus, he rejected the concept of avatār, God descended on earth to help mankind, although he had a near-divine but never formally accepted status that put him above ordinary man. The two standard accounts of his life, by Bhai Guru Das and Janma Sakhi, were written shortly after Nānak's death and contain much trustworthy material, though some of it does not meet Western critical standards. See also Kabīr, Sikhs.

Nānak, Sikh. (2) The entire group of ten Sikh Gurus is known as Nānak (see above) in the Sikh sacred writings. In Sikh doctrine, all the Gurus are one in spirit, and to look upon them as distinct would be heresy. In the Granth Sāheb (q.v.) they are indicated separately by a mystic formula that would be rendered as "The Bride of God." Thus Guru Nānak, the first of the line, would be indicated as "The First Bride," Guru Amar Das "The Third Bride," Guru Arjun "The Fifth Bride," and so on. See also Sikhism.

Nandī, Hind. The god Shiva's sacred bull, the gentle guardian of temples devoted to the deity; it is usually accompanied by his sign, the liṅga (q.v.), placed nearby. In the temples the bull is couchant, his head turned slightly; afoot he is a symbol of lust, the embodiment of the sex impulse; Shiva riding Nandī is the master of lust. Nandī's most common form is lying down inside or at the entrance to the Shiva shrine. Upon entering, devotees touch his testicles, the source of life. Despite his intimate connection with Shiva, the bull is an ancient Stone Age deity worshiped long before the god appeared to ride and conquer him. Up into the eighteenth century, human sacrifices were made to Nandī (as to Kālī, Yāma, and other archaic and demanding deities). Nandī is also known as the porter of Kailāsa (q.v.), Shiva's abode, the sacred esoteric summit where the god indulges in play. See Shiva.

naojote, Zor. See navzote.

Naqshbandīya, Isl. A vast brotherhood of Ṣūfīs (q.v.), spreading from Central Asia (it was established in Bukhara) into Turkey on the west, and on the east, across Pakistan and India to Malaysia. The Naqshbandīya trace their genealogy to the first Khalif, Abū Bakr (q.v.), a Companion of the Prophet, though Bahā al-Dīn Naqshbandī (died c. A.D. 1389) has given his name to the order. Bahā al-Dīn passed seven years at court, seven more in caring for animals, and seven as a road builder. His nickname, Naqshband, means painter, and after his death his followers were known as the Naqshbandī Chain. Naqshbandī returned to original Ṣūfī practices; his people are submerged within the Islamic milieu wherever they live, and are difficult to identify.

The name of "painter" is explained by Bahā al-Dīn's custom of drawing spiritual pictures on the heart by silent words to purify it when practicing dikhr, the reception of certain phrases, a basic exercise the order still follows. The Naqshbandīya adhere closer to orthodoxy than most brotherhoods, appealing to the elite, and forbidding unusual forms of meditation, dancing, and music. In India, where it is especially strong, the order has campaigned against Hinduizing tendencies, and has worked to purify Ṣūfism of pantheism.

However, many of the Naqshbandīya dikhr exercises are similar to those in bhakti (q.v.) and yoga cults in India. The Sacred Name (of Allāh) is led through the body in an effort to cleanse it spiritually; in other exercises it follows certain channels somewhat like those of the Hindu cakras (q.v.), the Holy Name being finally cast out, as it were, from the brain through the nostrils, to be "dashed like a bucket of water over the whole person." In a final and most difficult dikhr the Shahādah (q.v.) is conducted in its separate parts through the body, with the word Allāh being inscribed on the heart, the result being, it is reported, an intense affection for God and a complete relinquishing of the self. See Ṣūfism.

Nārāyana, Hind. One of the names for Vishnu (q.v.). The name means "Moving on the Waters," or, "He who sleeps upon the Flowing Waters," a reference to the fact that Vishnu in this form lies at rest upon the serpent Śeṣa. The term nārā (plural for waters) is not Indo-Āryan: Both the word and the god may be traced back to the Indus Valley and from there to Mesopotamia, where the god Ea or Enki sleeps in his chamber in the midst of the waters. The first two avatāras of Vishnu, the Fish and the Tortoise, are probably totems of river-dwelling tribes who were later absorbed by the Āryans, their totems being incorporated into the worship of the solar deity Vishnu, who was to accumulate so many non-Āryan attributes. Of all the names of Vishnu as the Supreme God, Nārāyana is the most venerated. The sacred mantra (q.v.) with which the devotees of Vishnu are initiated as Vaishnavites, and that they continue to repeat throughout their lives, is "Namo Nārāyaṇāya"—"All honor to the Lord Nārāyana."

Naṭarāja, Hind. The god Shiva as the lord of the dance of creation and destruction of the Universe. The cosmic dance is twofold: Shiva dances creation into existence by the sheer exuberances of his powers; in the Tāndava dance he careens down the side of the sacred mountain, drunk or insane, in a frenzy to annihilate the world, routing the half-human, half-animal creatures of the demi-cosmos, whose destruction spurs him to further madness. He may dance alone, or with his consort, variously known as Pārvatī, Umā, Satī, Kālī, or Durgā, all aspects of the creative female principle. In his cosmic dance, by means of the frenzied rhythms of his small drum, Shiva articulates a mysterious formula known as the Māheśvara Sūtra, which states the four sciences that lead directly to higher reality: They are Yoga, the comprehension and shedding of sensorial fetters to matter; Vedānta, the theory of metaphysical understanding of sensorial reality; Language as the interrelation of words or verbal signs to concepts; and Music as the perception of mathematics in relation to ideas and forms. See Shiva.

navzote (also naojote) ceremony, Zor./Par. The term means new worshiper among the Parsees of India; in Iran it is called nozad (new birth). It is an initiation rite for boys and girls between the ages of seven and fifteen but must be bestowed before puberty. In it the young person formally embraces the religion of the Prophet Zoroaster (q.v.). It is a joyous occasion, with relatives, friends, and priests in attendance to witness the saying of the Zardushti creed. The ceremony may be held either in a fire temple (q.v.) or in a home or hall. The neophyte is met at the door by a priest who waves a coconut, rice, container of water, egg, or some other object of food around his head, a common oriental custom not confined to the Zoroastrians, to remove undesirable emanations and to purify the etheric aura. Prayers, ablutions, and the taking of a sacramental drink before a fire in the presence of the priests prepare the neophyte for celestial blessings. Then comes the bestowing of the two emblems of the faith; the spotless white shirt, the sudreh, and the wool cord, the kustī (q.v. both). In addition to its usual meanings, the kustī also symbolizes a rope whereby the new Parsee descends "into the vault of his higher nature, to rediscover God's mysteries," a knowledge of which he had lost when his soul had "fallen into the flesh"—i.e., been born in a human body. This "retirement into a cave" to seek wisdom is an ancient Iranian concept associated with the Prophet himself and with the Zardushti saints. The rite concludes with a blessing and the showering of rice, raisins, and other fruitful objects on the young Parsee's head. See Zoroastrianism.

Nazir (A.D. 1735–1846). Ṣūfī poet and mystic, born in Delhi. He spent most of his life as a teacher in Mogul India; he rejected an offer from the Nawab of Oudh to be court poet, a post that would have carried a handsome stipend and much honor, preferring a simple life in a village school. Like many Indian Muslims he was heavily influenced by pantheism—a plus, in the eyes of Hindus—and thus he could, in his poetry, sing of Krishna as well as the Prophet, seeing both the Forms of the Lord and the Formless Divinity. He emphasized repetition of the Names of the Lord (q.v.), a practice common to both Ṣūfīs and Hindus (see dhikr and japa). "The meanings of all scriptures were revealed to me when I opened the book of the heart," he said, in reference to the Ṣūfī quest for the eternal within. He died at the remarkable age of 111. See Ṣūfī.

nembutsu, Buddh. The uttering of the sacred saying (mantra) of the Pure Land (Shin) sect of Japanese Buddhism, "Namu Amida Butsu" (q.v.).

neti, neti, Hind. "Not this, not this" (or, "Not this, not that"). A phrase often used by Vedāntists in which the sādhaka in search of the One Reality analyzes a physical or mental state or quality and finds that for one reason or another it lacks the character of Truth and thus must be eliminated. All that is transitory is consequently discarded. The result is that the Supreme THAT alone remains, which is the Self absorbed in the Divine Self, the Eternal Brahman (q.v.).

nibbāna, Buddh. (Pāli, from Sanskrit nirvāṇa). The Buddhist view of nibbāna is different from the Hindu, and philogically, while some Buddhists interpret the term in the Hindu manner as "dying out" or "extinction" (as of a fire), others find in it an archaic meaning of "he who is cooled"—i.e., cooled from the fever of greed, hatred, and delusion, the three principal evils in Buddhist thought. The Western interpretation of nibbāna as total extinction or annihilation was explicity denied by Buddha. However, while nibbāna does not mean extinction, neither does it mean that after death the individual exists in some manner or other. When the body ceases to function, the phenomenal personality disappears. Buddhism denies the existence of a soul at any time, whether before or after death. An Indian text of the third century B.C. states that nibbāna "is really only the inner realization of the store of impressions." Thus nibbāna is a state to be realized here and now, as well as in death. An early Buddhist brother wrote, "Illusion has utterly passed from me. Now I am cool, all fire within gone out." Buddha attained nibbāna at the beginning of his public life, and many of his disciples and followers attained it also in their lives. The third-century B.C. *Milindapañha* states that the Buddha still exists but "has passed completely away in nibbāna, so that nothing is left which could lead to the formation of another being. And so he cannot be pointed out as being here or there." The same work in a later section (probably by a different hand) describes nibbāna as "the City of Righteousness." Here the liberated man "enters the glorious city of Nibbāna, stainless and undefiled, pure and white, unaging, deathless, secure and calm and happy, and his mind is emancipated as a perfected being."

Nichiren (A.D. 1222–82), Buddh. Japanese prophet, missionary, and reformer who reacted against other forms of Buddhism in his own country, claiming they were rife with corruption, divided without reason, and followed false doctrines and impure interpretations of the Way. Nichiren's father was a fisherman, and Nichiren called himself "a son of the śudras," using the Hindu term for a low-caste person. At the age of thirty Nichiren made the *Lotus Sūtra* (q.v.), which he believed contained the final and supreme teaching of Gautama Buddha, the basis upon which to found a reform movement. Nichiren was forced to leave the monastic center at Mount Hiei near Kyotō and went directly to the people to preach the prayer Namu-myoho-renge-kyō (Adoration to the Lotus of the Perfect Truth), which he chanted to the beat of a drum, *dondon, dondon, don,* to match the rhythm of the mantra.

His sect, called by his adopted name (*nichi* means sun, and *ren,* lotus), was constantly persecuted. It was forced from the Kyotō area in 1536 when enemies from another monastic center burned twenty-one of its temples to the ground and slaughtered most of its priests, three thousand dying in the last temple to be attacked. Since then the Nichiren sect has never been a major force in the old capital, but elsewhere it has continued to be powerful, with a mass base among the ordinary people. To Nichiren, Japan was the future center of salvation. His vision was apocalyptic: He saw that in the coming of time the moral law would be achieved for all mankind in Japan, which would be the sacred center where the people of India, China, and Japan and eventually the whole world will be initiated into the mysteries of the Buddha. After World War II Nichiren's vision found expression in daughter movements, the heavily politicized and nationalistic Sōka-gakkai and Risshō kōsei-kai (q.v.). See Buddhism.

nirang, Zor. From nirui (power). A term applicable to all vehicles of spiritual force, though its primary meaning is for consecrated bull's urine. The urine, after a series of ritual prayers, becomes a container of invisible influences, being both consecrated and "magnetized." Nirang is a key substance in the rite of bareshnum (q.v.). See also, Zoroastrianism.

Nirguṇa Brahman, Hind. The Brahman, the Supreme Reality, One and undifferentiated, dynamic and static together yet above both—without form, as Pure Unqualified Being. See Brahman.

nirvāṇa, Hind. Union with the Supreme—Brahman—through mokśa, i.e., release from the cycle of birth and death and the pain, sorrow, and suffering of the human condition. Nirvāṇa is the immediate experience of the ego-less self with the blissful Brahman. The *Bhagavad Gītā* has one of the clearest expositions of nirvāṇa, calling it Brahma-nirvāṇa, i.e., union with Brahman, or extinction (of the ego) in Him. The *Gītā*'s method is by the practice of yoga (joy, peace, vision all turning inward), through which one can "come to Brahman and know nirvāṇa." The Jains and Sikhs have somewhat similar ideas expressed in their own terms; for the Buddhist view, see nibbāna.

nozad, Zor. The Persian term for the Zoroastrian ceremony of initiation called navzote (q.v.)

numbers, as esoteric and religious symbols. Certain numbers in oriental religions have mystical significance, much of which is beyond simple explanation but seems to meet some inherent need for balance and categorization. The primary numbers have self-explanatory uses: one, the symbol of unity, the Supreme, the One, Nature, etc.; two, duality or contradiction—God and man, two natures, light and dark, good and evil, male and female, truth and lie, the Self and the self, etc.; three, Trinity, triad, Tri-Mūrti, triangle (as sign of the vulva), etc. With this group might be included zero, Hinduism's śūnya, the Void, the mystical center. The numeral four expresses the concept of space and direction: the points of the compass, the Four Quarters, the corners of a building. After this, other primaries serve as neat classifications—the Five K's, the Five M's, the Five Violations, etc., the seven rishis, the seven sages, the seven brahminical clans, and so on, whether or not there be seven or some other figure, such as six or eight. Beyond this, numbers are often found in nonrational contexts, such as 84 and 108, the most commonly used. The number 84, for which no known explanation has been offered either by sages or scholars, is found, often in extremely large contexts, probably employed merely to denote the immensity of the figure—it is "known" that 84,000 holy men inhabit the slopes of the Himālayas; tantra texts state that there are 840,000,000 āsanas or yogic postures, obviously an impossible number. Yet, more simply, yogis and astrologers, in giving a horoscope, will state authoritatively that so-and-so "will live to 84," a figure too often employed to be anything but symbolic for an old age. The number 108 is the most widely employed of all mystical figures, appearing in Hinduism, Jainism, Buddhism, and Islam. The *Laṅkavatāra Sūtra,* e.g., says that anyone in misfortune should recite a certain mantra 108 times "and the evil spirits, weeping and wailing, will go off in another direction." The river Gaṇgā has 108 names (or 1,008 in some listings), and many rosaries in various religions are made of 108 bones. (The listing under 108 gives added examples.) See also śūnya.

O

ŌṂ, Hind. (and Tib.). The eternal, mystical syllable—the syllable that is the Whole. It is defined as a mantra, the Queen of all mantras. It is pronounced with a nasalized ending, halfway between *M* and *N*—roughly "omg" that drifts close to "ong." Exegesis of ŌṂ has demanded much time and energy on the part of Indian sages. Esoterically ŌṂ is composed of five parts; the guttural *A,* the labial *U,* the nasal *M,* the stop bindu, and the resonance nāda. The letters comprise a triangle that physically delineate all the possibilities of sound. Thus, since all sounds are contained within it, ŌṂ incarnates the essence of the entire universe, and is the mantra of Brahman. ŌṂ is the symbol of the three in One: the three worlds in the Soul, the three ages: time past, time present, and the eternal future. It is the three divine powers: creation, preservation, and transformation in the One Being; also, the three essences: immortality, omniscience, and joy in the One Spirit.

ŌṂ man-ni pad-me hum, Tib. Buddh. The mantra of Chenresig, the four-armed herdsman, the incarnation of the Lord Buddha in Tibet. The mantra is pronounced ŌṂ MA PAY ME HUNG (ending in a nasal). The literal translation is: "ŌṂ! The jewel in the lotus! Hum!" Ōṃ man-ni pad-me hum has manifold esoteric interpretations, the most obvious of which is tantric: The jewel in the lotus is the liṇga in the yoni. The *Mani-bhak-hbum* (History of the Mani Mantra of Chenresig) states that the mantra is "the essence of all happiness, prosperity and knowledge and the source of the great liberation." Each syllable has a specific significance. ŌṂ closes the door to rebirth among the gods; MA, to rebirth among the asuras, or titanic demons; NI, among mankind; PAY, among subhuman creatures; ME, among pretas or unhappy ghosts; and HUNG, among inhabitants of hell. Each term has a specific color corresponding to the six stages of existence.

108, as mystical number. The numerals 1 and 8 appear in various combinations in virtually all Eastern religions: 18, 81, 108, 1,008, 10,008 (even 16,108 in the case of the gopīs [q.v.]). However, 108 is the most common form. The origin of 108 (however expressed) is now lost, and insofar as is known, no seer, yogi, sadhu, or other holy person is able to explain the symbolism. However, it apparently represents three qualities: The figure 1 is the primal unity; the 0, the void, śūnya (q.v.); the balance point, the bindu (q.v.) standing between unity on one side, and on the other, the figure 8, which is the symbol of consciousness, cognition, pure awareness without content, samādhi (q.v.), etc. Eight is also an aspect of the self-nature. Whatever, 108 represents ecstatic search for the Divine through the mundane, in which man theophanizes daily tools, here the means of counting.

From the earliest ages a Hindu is aware of the figure 108. When a boy receives the sacred thread of one of the three higher castes, he is given the name of a deity to be repeated 108 times each day (often on a rosary of 108 beads). There are 108 (or 1,008) names of the Great Goddess (Shakti, Devī, Dūrga, Kālī, etc.), and the same numbers for Shiva. There are 108 pithas or sacred places of pilgrimage. In tantra there are 108 mudras or ritual gestures made with the hands in worship (some traditions list only 18), and 108 positions of the body in yoga. There are 18 in sacred classical dance.

Every day the pious brāhmin repeats the Gāyatri mantra (q.v.), an important prayer to the sun, on a rosary of 108 beads. There are 18 main gotra (roughly clan) groups of brāhmins, 18 main Purāṇas, and 18 sections of the Mahābhārata; the great war it describes was fought for 18 days between 18 legions. The *Bhagavad Gītā* has 18 chapters.

In Mahāyāna Buddhist tradition, 1,008 Buddhas are to appear, according to the Dalai Lāma (q.v.) in Jambudvīpa (Rose-Apple Land—i.e., India); four have already come, the last being Gautama Buddha, and 1,004 are still expected. The Tibetans venerate the names of 108 Indian pandits or learned men. Tibetan tradition states that there are 108 Termas (or Scriptures). In Japan, in the Buddhist ceremonies for the dead ancestors, 108 fires are kindled in welcome. Mount Hiei near Kyotō is covered with 108 Inner Shrines and 108 Outer Shrines to mark the joint alliance of the

Shintō mountain king Sanno and the Buddhist Tendai sect. In Shin and some other Japanese Buddhist sects, 108 is the number of spiritual impediments to be overcome.

Among Islamic mystics the numbers 18 and 81 "read" in the left and right palms add up to 99, the number of Beautiful Names of Allāh.

Such are a few examples. The numerals 1, 0, and 8 permeate much of Asian religious practice and belief.

See also the entry under numbers for other mystical uses of numbers.

◂P▸

padmasana, Hind. The lotus position (q.v.).

pagoda, Buddh. The Far Eastern form of the stūpa, the Buddhist memorial or shrine mound. The exact meaning of the term pagoda has not been determined by scholars, but it may be a Portuguese version of an unknown oriental word, possibly the Singhalese dāgaba (q.v.).

Pāli. The language of Hinayāna or Theravāda Buddhism. It is a derivative of Sanskrit (q.v.), the ancient liturgical priestly tongue of the Vedic Āryan peoples, and in its vulgar form was the common language of Magadha. The older Buddhist canon was written in Pāli, but it is now employed primarily for the Hinayāna; the Mahāyāna ("Greater Vehicle") rewrote portions of the canon in Sanskrit. In Pāli, Sanskrit terms like dharma and nirvāṇa become dhamma and nibbana. Pāli was the language used by Indian Buddhists in the cultural, trade, and religious penetration of Southeast Asia (i.e., "Indochina").

Parsees. See Zoroastrians.

Parsis. See Zoroastrians.

Pārvatī, Hind. One of the consorts of the Lord Shiva (q.v.). She is a gentle goddess, daughter of the axial mountain from which the terrestrial energy springs. She is all-pervading, the conscious substance of the cosmos, and the leader of the gentle elves and spirits that inhabit the world. She is equated with Śakti, the all-pervading Supreme Energy, who is also manifested as Kālī, the destructive twin of Pārvatī, also one of Shiva's consorts.

Paśupati, Hind. The god Shiva as Lord of the Animals, a concept derived in part from the Indus Valley (q.v.), where a figure believed to be a form of Shiva seated in the yogic position has been identified; he is surrounded by animals. Paśupati is also derived from the early Vedic god Rudra, the Herdsman, guardian of the earth, both the inner fire and the embodiment of ritual fire and ritual sacrifice. Rudra later came to be considered but an aspect of Shiva. As Paśupati, Shiva is the five-faced herdsman who is not only the protector of each type of animal but is also the divinity of life and the guardian of the earth, who naked wanders through the great forests.

Patañjali, Hind. The compiler and editor of the *Yoga Sūtras,* the basic statement of classical or holistic yoga. The recent opinion in India and the West, now on shaky grounds, that he is also the author of the great grammatical comment upon Pāṇini cannot be traced back beyond the tenth century A.D. The yogic Patañjali lived c. A.D. 400, the grammarian Patañjali about B.C. 200. See yoga.

Patched Robe, Isl. The wearing of patched garments is common among Sūfīs, especially the wanderers. The Robe is an outward sign of poverty and simplicity. It can be traced to the influence of Zoroastrianism, a probable source of Persian Ṣūfism, for it closely resembles in concept the Zardushti sudreh, the patched shirt worn by all adult Zardushtis to symbolize that there are no rich or poor under God. In his work about Ṣūfic orders, *Rashf al-Mahjūb* (The Revelation of the Veiled), the eleventh-century A.D. Persian mystic 'Ali al-Hujwīrī devotes a chapter to the Robe. Much of what he says is in code phrases and is intelligible primarily to Ṣūfīs (the English translation by R. A. Nicholson fails to convey the inner meanings). The Arabic term for the Robe, muraqqa', embodies a wide range of mystical interpretations, from spiritual drunkenness, the heedlessness of the Ṣūfī to the world, to the Seventh Heaven, to name but a few. The patched garment is found in a Western version in the motley garb of the court jester, who was originally a type of Sūfī in Muslim Spain. See sudreh, Sūfī, Zoroastrianism.

Peshotan, Zor. The chief disciple, a prince, of the Prophet Zoroaster, who was so holy during his lifetime that he attained immortality. Pesh-o-tan means "he who has offered his body [to his teacher]." The religious text Vohuman Yasht and other works refer to Peshotan as the future prophet of Iran. He has 51 (in some versions 151) disciples, with whom he lives in a cave-monastery on sacred Mount Alburz. The doctrine of the Secret Imām (q.v.) is likely a development of the Prince Peshotan cult. See Zoroaster, Zoroastrians.

pipal, Hind. A tree sacred throughout India and in those countries where Buddhism flourishes. In India, where the pipal is highly venerated, no true Hindu would cut or injure it, nor, in theory, lie while standing under its branches. It is par excellence the Tree of Wisdom, and it was under a pipal at Gāya that Gautama Buddha attained enlightenment; among Buddhists it is known as the bodhi tree (q.v.). Trees in general are inhabited by female spirits, the yakshas (q.v.), but the pipal, with its high-raised roots, which descend like inverted branches into the earth, is sacred to Vishnu (q.v.), while the vepu or bil is Shiva's tree. The pipal may be invested with the sacred cord of the brahmin, the same ceremonies being performed as that for the twice-born.

The tree was originally probably a totem, for certain primitive forest tribes will not eat its leaves, and in the past would not cut its wood for fuel, a prohibition that has lapsed out of necessity. The sacredness of the pipal is mentioned in the earliest epics, the Vedas, and in the Purāṇas (q.v. both).

pīr, Isl. A teacher, most likely a Ṣūfī (q.v.), often noted as a saint as well. The term is quite common in Pakistan and India.

prakṛti, Hind. Primordial matter or nature, which consists of three qualities or aspects known as guṇas, which exist in a state of equilibrium; the guṇas, briefly, are sattva (harmony), rajas (motion and whatever causes motion), and tamas (inertia, heaviness, and darkness). The theory of prakṛti is basic to yoga (q.v.), which aims at transcending it and the guṇas.

prāṇa, Hind. The vital energy of the body. It functions with mānas (mind), for both must work together.

praṇām, Hind. Obeisance to a spiritual superior or the symbol of such superiority (such as an image).

prāna pratiṣṭhā, Hind. The consecration of an image, usually for pūjā (q.v.)—i.e., worship. Before consecration the image has no value aside from the costs of its materials and workmanship; afterward, it is adored as the abode of the deity, if not his very body. Various prayers (mantras [q.v.]) are said, varying in length and solemnity, by the priest, the result being that the image is enlivened with the breath (prāna) of the god or goddess. During the rite the deity is beseeched to indwell in the idol; each arm and leg is touched by the consecrating priest and made to become an actual limb of the god. Once prāna pratiṣṭhā has been completed, the image, of whatever material, is now the deity himself, with the life-soul of the god and all five senses omnipresent. At this point the devotee can practice pūjā. Besides pūjā, which is highly ritualized, other acts of adoration are more freely enjoyed: A devotional text states, "One should engage himself in singing of Me [the deity], praising Me, dancing with My themes, imitating My exploits and acts, narrating My stories or listening to them." Some images are made the permanent home of the god; others serve as his or her home for fixed periods, usually a brief one, especially during such festivals as Durgā Pūjā, when the goddess is worshiped for three days in the form of clay images (now modeled after movie stars), which are deconsecrated (the rite of visarjana, or relinquishing) at the end of the period of celebration; the idols are normally immersed in the Ganges or other sacred waterway to dissolve. See Hinduism.

prasād, Hind. Food (sweets, fruit, rice, etc.) offered to a deity or to a living saint, sanctified because it has thereby been accepted and blessed. It is then partaken of by the devotees, or brought home to be shared by others. See Hinduism.

pūjā, Hind. The common form of ceremonial worship, performed by both the priest and the individual. Pūjā honors gods and images of various forms and types, and is celebrated on ceremonial occasions, such as anniversaries, etc. The custom probably originated among the Dravidians (q.v.) and came to replace the old Vedic sacrifices (yajña), which were performed by the priests alone and usually focused upon fire, sacrifice of animals or humans, and sometimes included the drinking of Soma (q.v.).

Normally there can be no pūjā before an image without the previous rite of prāṇa pratiṣṭhā (q.v.). The image can be composed of any of a number of materials; the Hindu scriptures list eight: stone, wood, metal, sandalwood, a picture painted on canvas or drawn on paper or in sand, or precious stones. Another category is "mental image"; the scriptures point out that the primary purpose of image worship is to direct the devotee's attention and concentration inward, and the mental image is the culminating step in meditation before one reaches the ability to worship without any image at all. Some texts also list images of gold, silver, copper, diamond, stone, sacred or sacrificial woods, iron, conch shell, brass, clay, and so on. Whatever the material, the image employed in pūjā is fashioned according to strict rules of great antiquity, and worshiped according to rarely varying formulas, depending on the aspect of the divinity.

Pūjā demands proper preparation for worship. The *Bhāgavata Purāṇa* states: "With clothes, sacred thread, jewels, garlands and fragrant paste, My devotee should decorate My form suitably and with love. With faith, My worshiper should then offer Me water to wash, sandal, flower, unbroken rice, incense, light and food of different kinds; also attentions like anointing, massage, showing of mirror and so on, and entertainments like song and dancing: these special attentions may be done on festive days and even daily." The flowers, foods (including ghee, butter, oil, milk, or water), the burning of incense and other ritualistic acts, besides propitiating the deity, all have psychological and physical effects upon the worshiper. Music and other sounds (such as the blast of the conch shell, and bells), lights, scents, gestures, and the image itself, with the ramifications of its significance, all help bring the devotee into intimate contact with the deity, thus transcending the mundane world. See Hinduism.

Purāṇa, Hind. A narrative work dealing with ancient kings, sages, heroes, and the gods. The term means literally "something that is old." There are eighteen major Purāṇas, eighteen minor, and a host of related texts, appearing in the period A.D. 300–1200. The material in the Purāṇas is called "transitional," for it supposedly originated in pre-Vedic times (a few Purāṇas are mentioned in the Vedas [q.v.]), being handed down orally from teacher to pupil, or priest to disciple. In the course of transmission the original stories, legends, and myths have been considerably altered, being shaped by the brāhmin redactors for their own purposes to illustrate themes important to the priestly caste. Nevertheless, much non-Vedic material has been retained. Two of the great Hindu epics, the Rāmāyāṇa and the Mahābhārata, are known as Purāṇas. Most of the works are concerned with the gods Shiva or Vishnu and have much to do with the growth of their cults in medieval India. The Purāṇas form a kind of *biblos* of popular Hinduism, in their synthesis of legend and myth emerging from the submerged masses to mingle with priestly teachings about ritual, theology, and philosophical speculation, all told against the background of the public and private lives of deities and kings in their wars, loves, and even sexual exploits. The Purāṇas were recited to large popular audiences, portions of them being read, chanted, or acted in temples to the accompaniment of songs and music. See Hinduism, Shiva, Vishnu.

Pure Land sect, Buddh. A school of Buddhism based on faith in the Amida Buddha (q.v.) as a form of savior (but not in the Christian sense) who will lead his devotees into a celestial paradise through the repetition of his name. The sect, which is based on Indian themes, was once dominant in China and is still important in Japan. The Pure Land—Sukhāvatī in India, and Ching-t'u in

China—is the heavenly sphere ruled over by Amida, known as Am-i-to-fo in China, aided by two great bodhisattvas, Kuan Yin and Ta Shih Chih. The doctrine of the Pure Land (originally called the White Lotus) was brought to China about A.D. 402 by Hui Yüan, a convert to Buddhism from Taoism and Confucianism; he had become absorbed in the doctrines of the greater and lesser Sukhāvatī-vyūha Sūtras, which taught the salvation by faith in Amitābha (or Amida) Buddha. Pure Land Buddhism teaches a fully developed doctrine based on the mere repetition of Amida's name (the nembutsu)—ten times is enough to gain salvation, though many members of the sect repeat it frequently. At death the faithful are transported immediately into heaven and are reborn in spiritual bodies within one of the lotuses of the sacred lake. Those of lesser virtue must await until their lotuses open; sinners have countless ages to wait. The Pure Land paradise is a "Buddha field," and not the cool nibbāna of other forms of Buddhism, which teach that salvation—i.e., from the cycle of birth and rebirth—lies within, to be attained by one's working one's way out of the karmic cycle. Pure Land themes penetrated other forms of Buddhism in China, and the Western Paradise, with Am-i-t'o-fo seated on a throne, attended by various bodhisattvas, with his lotus and peacock symbols, became a common portrayal of all forms of Buddha. Ching-t'u literature is vast, but the common theme is a single-minded focus on the Amida Buddha and prayers for rebirth in his Land. "If a man is born in that Land," says a text, "he automatically puts an end to the evils of the body, mouth and mind." In the ninth and tenth centuries in Japan, Pure Land Buddhism was propagated by monks such as Kūya and Ryōnin, who chanted the nembutsu in the streets and bazaars, gaining a following among those who felt excluded from the other sects. See nembutsu.

◂Q▸

qadar, Isl. The doctrine of the Divine Will—i.e., of Allāh's "determination" of all things: Whatever happens or comes into existence, animate or inanimate, is from Him and of Him. However, there is an unresolved duality present, for the Qur'ān teaches also that men are responsible creatures: Surah 4, 79, says, "Whatever of good happens to thee is from Allāh; whatever evil happens to thee is from thyself." Muslims are not to believe that God's deeds and acts are done without premeditation, but that they follow a predetermined plan for the collective benefit of all mankind. The Muslim must act in a moral, legal manner, and if he fails to attain his aims he should not despair or resent his fate but be thankful to Allāh.

qawwali, Sūfī. A devotional song of Indian and Pakistani ṣūfīs; it is akin to the Hindu bhajan (q.v.). A qawwali is a vocal solo, accompanied in various manners, such as by ensemble voices, handclapping, drums, harmoniums, or stringed instruments. The subjects, all sung to induce a state of ecstatic devotion, include Allāh, the Prophet Muḥammad, and mystical love.

qibla, Isl. The direction or focal point of Muslim worship, toward Mecca. Initially, perhaps as early as the time of the first revelations of the Qur'ān, Muḥammad had selected Jerusalem as the qibla; certainly it was so when he took up residence in Medina in A.D. 622. The reason for this is probably that in the early days at Mecca, the Muslims were not allowed to pray at the Ka'ba (q.v.), which at the time was a pagan shrine. Today, all Muslims, no matter where they are in relation to Mecca—east, west, north, or south—face in the direction of the sacred city as they pray. Sometime during the Medina exile, to the consternation of some of his followers, Muḥammad changed the qibla to Mecca despite its pagan connotations. In the mosque a niche called the mihrāb, before which prayers are said (though it is always empty), marks the qibla toward Mecca and the Ka'ba.

qiyās, Isl. In Muslim law (see sharī'a), analogical reasoning—i.e., concluding from a previous case the principle embodied in it that can be applied to a new case. The common, essential feature found in both cases is known as 'illa, the reason. See Islam.

Qur'ān, Isl. The sole sacred Scripture of the Muslims, revealed to the Prophet Muḥammad by the angel Jibril (Gabriel) in the seventh century A.D. To every Muslim the Qur'ān is literally the Word of God (Kalām Allāh); Muḥammad was not the author of the text but the channel through which it was transmitted to mankind. The Qur'ān is composed of 114 sūras, or chapters, of varying lengths, but arranged by an editorial committee shortly after the Prophet's death in order of length, beginning with the longest; some of the sūras are obviously compilations of shorter texts. It has been impossible to determine the exact order in which the text was received by Muḥammad, though many attempts have been made, and there are now editions that purport to give some sort of sequence.

The text was received by Muḥammad over a period of twenty-three years, beginning about A.D. 610 or 612, when he was meditating in a cave near the city of Mecca. At that time the Angel Jibril appeared to him and announced "Read!" (or "Recite!"), commanding Muḥammad, though an illiterate, to "read" the divinely sent message. Further Revelations continued over the years, some in Mecca, and many at Medina during the Prophet's exile. Initially he was frightened and skeptical, but eventually he came to accept his role in the divine transmission.

The sūras were retained in the memory of the Prophet himself and in the memories of some of his immediate disciples; however, they were also written down, beginning at an early date, the surface for the texts being pottery, skins, palm leaves, and even the shoulder blades of sheep; at Medina Muḥammad dictated the newly received sūras to secretaries. After his death in A.D. 632, his closest relative and first disciple Abū Bakr (q.v.) passed on the fragments to Zaid ibn Thābit, who headed a committee that put the text in shape. A Vulgate edition was published under the third khalif, 'Uthmān, and alternate pieces destroyed. However, owing to the fact that the kufic script in which the Qur'ān was originally written contains neither vowels nor diacritical signs, variant readings are recognized as of equal authority. Pieces of the sūras were incorporated in, or used as, prayers by the Prophet's followers during his lifetime.

The sūras themselves range from great mysticism to simple moral and ethical exhortations to instructions in methods of prayer to detailed rules and regulations for daily living. In short, the Qur'ān contains everything a Muslim needs for his religious and secular life, the two being intertwined; it is also the basis for Islamic law, and is the central text for legal studies and court use in Muslim lands.

The Qur'ān is the Eternal, Uncreated Word of God. It is an essential doctrine of Islamic orthodoxy that the Qur'ān is revealed, a Revelation made not for the elect or the priesthood but for all the faithful, of whatever race, national origin, or color. The language is Arabic, and, strictly speaking, the Qur'ān should not be read in any other tongue. As the Sacred Book of Islam revealed in Arabic (Qur'ānan 'arabiyyan), that language became forever sanctified among Muslims, and for centuries was established as well as the prime literary tongue in all Islamic lands. The Prophet himself pointed out that "We [i.e., Allāh] have revealed the Qur'ān in the Arabic tongue that you may grasp its meaning," and that is "A Book of Revelation, an Arabic Qur'ān [recital, its literal meaning] for men of understanding." Though the text may be, and is, read and used as a guide by even the simplest of believers, its ramifications are many, and normally it is studied under the direction of a teacher, with (male) children being given the Book as a first reader. Its complexity led Muḥammad himself to state in a ḥadīth (q.v.), "The Qur'ān has been revealed in seven forms. Each verse has an inner and outer meaning."

English versions (which are not sanctioned by the orthodox) have for the most part been stilted and overly literal. An acceptable translation is that by N. J. Dawood (Penguin). See also Islam, Muḥammad.

◂ R ▸

Rabī'a al-Adawīya (c. A.D. 725–801). A Ṣūfī saint, noted for extreme otherworldliness. When asked, "Where have you come from?" she replied, "From that world." "Where are you going?" "To that world." "What are you doing in this world?" "I am sorrowing." "How?" "I am eating the bread of this world and doing the work of that world."

Her interests were focused solely on "that world." She eschewed the mundane, renounced earthly ties, and refused to marry even though marriage was common among Ṣūfīs, saying, "My existence is in Allāh and I am altogether His. I am in the shadow of His command. The marriage contract must be prepared by Him, not by me." She was noted for constant weeping, which to others sounded like a morbid expression of pessimism but was actually a fear of being cut off from God. However, underneath the tears was a constant note of joy and thanksgiving. She would cry to Allāh, "Thou art my joy, firmly founded in me." Her love was known for its purity and disinterestedness, because the fear of hell and the desire for Paradise were insufficient motives. "I served Him only for love of Him and desire for Him," and, "O my Lord, if I worship Thee for fear of Hell, burn me in Hell, and if I worship Thee from hope of Paradise, exclude me from Paradise. But if I worship Thee for Thy own sake, then withhold not from me Thy eternal beauty."

The characteristic mark of her thinking was not the development of any distinctive philosophy or interpretation but the experience of the Divine and the pursuit of a way of life based on that experience. She had a great effect upon later generations of Islamic mystics. Love, she showed, was the way to the Divine Vision. She distinguished two forms: "I have loved Thee with two loves, a selfish love and a love that is worthy of Thee. As for the love which is selfish, I occupy myself therein with remembrance of Thee to the exclusion of all others. As for that which is worthy of Thee, therein Thou raisest the veil that I may see Thee." She could say: "Love of Allāh has so absorbed me that neither love nor hate of any other thing remain in my heart." To a man who boasted of not sinning since he found God, she replied, "Alas my son, your existence is a sin with which no other sin may be compared." She felt possessed, absorbed by God, saying in a poem, "In spirit, blood, bone, breath, through and through, Thou has penetrated me." See Ṣūfī.

Radhakrishnan, Sarvapalli (1888–1974), Hind. A South Indian (Telegu) brāhmin, Radhakrishnan was educated at various Protestant missionary schools, where he felt keenly the denigration of Indian systems of religion and thought. He turned to a study of the Vedānta (q.v.) and was very much attracted to the teaching of Vivekānanda (q.v.) the young swami who was preaching a neo-Hinduism based upon a purified view of the Bengali mystic Rāmakrishna (q.v.) Radhakrishnan became prominent in both academic and government affairs, and was the second President of India. His thought has been heavily influenced by Western social and religious ideas, although he denies the value of the latter and tries to reinterpret traditional Hinduism purged of its "superstitious" elements in a syncretic outlook that seeks an answer to the threats and challenges facing his own heritage. He has reinterpreted Hinduism in the light of the modern world, influenced as it is even in India by Western social liberalism, positivism, and the yearning for individual freedom. In general, he has taught that all religions are true but are primarily the local embodiment of the one universal Religion that is above and beyond all creeds, institutions, and traditions. He views Hinduism as "a Way of life," the most successful of all Ways and thus superior to all others. He states actively doctrines that in traditional Hinduism are far more passive, stressing that man to some extent participates in the nature of God, for "we are cocreators with the Divine." He even reinterprets the role of caste, which he sees as "a democracy so far as spiritual values are concerned, for it recognizes that every soul has in it something transcendent and incapable of gradations, and it places all beings on a common level regardless of distinctions of rank and status, and insists that every individual must be afforded the opportunity to manifest the unique in him." Besides *The Hindu View of Life* (1926) and numerous other works expressing his reformed Hinduism, he has done editions of the *Dhammapada* and the *Bhagavad Gītā,* both with lengthy and notable introductions and commentary.

rajas, Hind. One of the three guṇas (q.v.). Rajas is dynamic; is energy, the property of causing motion. See guṇa.

Rāja Yoga, Hind. The method of union with the supreme Ātmā or soul through control of the mental processes. It is one of four major types of yoga (q.v.).

Rāma (or Rāma-candra), Hind. The warrior-hero of the Rāmāyana, the first great epic poem of human origin in Indian literature, all others being of divine sources. Rāma is the seventh avatār of Vishnu in his solar aspect; in this sense Rāma is important in Hindu astrology. To avoid confusion with the sixth avatār, also Rāma (or Rama-with-the-ax, Paraśu-Rāma), he is known as the Charming, Rāma-candra, the Embodiment of Righteousness. His cult—actually a full-fledged religion—developed in comparatively late times, and in some places it is the dominant form of Hinduism. His chief associate, the monkey-faced demigod Hanumān, is one of the main divinities in northern India. See avatār, Hanumān, Rāmāyana, Vishnu.

Ramaḍān, Isl. The Muslim month of fasting, which is enjoined upon all the faithful. Since the Islamic calendar is lunar, Ramaḍān takes place at a different time each year. It was a holy month among the Arabs prior to the founding of Islam, and Muḥammad, as an Arab, continued it. The fast is quite strict but is observed only during the daylight hours. Between dawn and dusk a Muslim must abstain from food and drink as long as there is light enough to distinguish between a white and black thread. Some Muslims also abstain from sexual relations during Ramaḍān. The fast ends with the festival of 'Id (q.v.).

Rāmakrishna Paramahamsa (1836–86), Hind. A Bengali mystic, about whom much mythification has accreted, including elements from the life of Jesus. Rāmakrishna was born of a brāhmin family in rural Bengal, his father being the village priest. Rāmakrishna received virtually no education, but from childhood was known for the depths of his spirituality. At the age of seven he experienced his first divine ecstasy. When he was sixteen he joined his brother in Calcutta in doing priestly work for private families. In 1855 Rāmakrishna was appointed temple priest at the newly founded Kālī shrine at Dakshineswar, on the banks of the Hooghly, a branch of the Ganges. He began to experience visions of Kālī, Sītā, and other forms of the Divine Mother, as well as of Rāma, Krishna, Muḥammad, and Jesus, all of whom were God in a variety of manifestations. He easily fell into samādhi, being moved by such prosaic and diverse sights as that of a lion in a zoo or a prostitute on a street. He gained the reputation of being somewhat pāgal (mad). At the age of twenty-three his family married him to a six-year-old girl named Sāradā, who, however, did not come to live with him for another thirteen years. Meanwhile, he experimented with a range of ecstatic and devotional sects; in 1861 he joined a tantric Vaishnava group under the guidance of a brāhmin woman; he also joined in Vedānta sādhanā and a mélange of bhakti practices, including Ṣūfism. His ecstasies and samādhis became constant: "When I reached the state of continuous ecstasy, I gave up all external forms of worship," he said. Sāradā joined him in 1872, the couple, much devoted one to the other, living in continence. Three years later Keshab Sen, one of the leaders of the elitist Brāhmo Samāj, "discovered" Rāmakrishna, and Dakshineswar became a center of devotion for westernized and educated Bengalis who joined the numerous village people who crowded around Rāmakrishna. Among such new followers were the agnostic Narendranāth Datta, later known as Swami Vivekānanda (q.v.), who in 1884 placed himself under the saint's spiritual guidance. Rāmakrishna died in 1886, a simple, unsophisticated, deeply religious soul. He was regarded as a saint, and today he is considered an avatār, but, in the opinion of certain disciples, he would sooner or later have rejected the cult, due largely to Vivekānanda that grew up around his name. A number of books have been published by his disciples, both biographies of the saint and collections of his sayings; some factual and doctrinal distortion has developed. An acceptable work is Christopher Isherwood's *Rāmakrishna and His Disciples* (1965).

Rāmānuja (A.D. 1017–1137), Hind. The leading ācārya saint and theologian. His enlightenment came during a Divine vision. One day, when he was in a period of deep depression, he heard the voice of God saying, "I am the Supreme Reality, the illustrious possessor of Śri, the Divine Power; identity is in and through difference. Complete surrender to Me is the Way to liberation. Individual effort is not so necessary [as the Divine Grace]. Liberation is bound to follow after death." This vision became the core of his teaching. He was told to study under a noted guru named Mahāpurna, who initiated him into the Vedānta Order. Later Rāmānuja renounced the world—he came to be called the "prince of ascetics." He composed a number of works preaching advaita (q.v.) or nondualism; he also founded many temples. He was a leading exponent of Vaishnavism and made many converts to the following of Vishnu.

Rāma-with-the-Ax (Paraśu-Rāma), Hind. The sixth incarnation of Vishnu. He is not the Rāma of the Rāmāyana, but an earlier figure, who is credited with putting down the kingly class, the kśatryas, and re-establishing the authority of the brāhmins, reaffirming anew the concept of the monarchy dominated by the priests. That the figure of Rāma has some original basis in history is seen in the fact that on the southwestern coast of India there are non-brāhmins who claim descent from the kśatryas defeated by Paraśu-Rāma; they still have the custom of giving their daughters to the priests to serve as concubines. See avatār, Rāma-candra, Vishnu.

Rāmāyana, Hind. An epic work in twenty-four thousand couplets centered around Rāma (q.v.), a righteous king and an incarnation of Vishnu (q.v.). It is believed to be the first poetical work of purely human origin in Indian literature, being credited to Vālmīki (c. fourth century B.C.), who is known as the first poet. The Rāmāyana, like the later Mahābhārata (q.v.), had its foundation in fact, with much folklore and mythification added over the centuries. It is a Purāṇa, or one of the "transitional" texts of the post-Vedic period. Its germ likely originated about B.C. 800 and before the Buddhist period, for Rāma is not mentioned in late Vedic literature (such as the Brāhmaṇas) but does appear in various Buddhist works. Ballads about Rāma were widely sung by Vālmīki's time, especially in the courts of northern and eastern India. Vālmīki took these ballads and turned them into a long poem about the warrior king, his wife, and his companions, entitling it the Rāmāyana (The Wandering of Rāma). Five of the work's seven books are believed to be Vālmīki's; two are by other poets, and the entire work has been heavily added to and developed by unknown writers. In Vālmīki's original version, which is difficult to define precisely, since the earliest surviving manuscript dates only from the eleventh century A.D., Rāma was a noble king, and mortal; his divination came later at the hands of other scribes; about the first century B.C. he had finally attained the state of avatār, a divine incarnation. The story is highly complex. Briefly, Rāma, a warrior and wanderer in the great tradition (one might equate him to Gilgamesh and Odysseus), is faced with a series of challenges and tests, some of which involve battles with other kings, or with demons; his wife Sītā is kidnaped by a demon king and carried off in an air chariot to Ceylon; his chastity and faithfulness are tested; great battles ensue; the ending is a happy one, with Rāma restored to the throne of Ayodha, and eventually he and Sītā, after more trials, are united, not on earth but in the celestial abodes. By the time the innovators have finished the story, Rāma and Sītā are not only avatārs of Vishnu but also exemplars of all the mundane and spiritual qualities with which the cosmos is endowed. The work has special interest to historians and ethnologists, for many elements depict the social conditions of the peninsula during that period. It is involved in the conflict of the Āryans with the aborigines and the Aryanization of the latter; the monkeys and bears who were allies of Rāma were actually aborigines who bore animal names as totems, as they still do today.

The story of Rāma and Sītā, originally in Sanskrit, was later retold many times in virtually all the Indian languages, becoming a major source of Indian culture in all forms; it still furnishes Indian life with the material for folk drama, songs, village bards, and even the cinema. The Rāmāyana was brought to Indonesia by Indian emigrants and merchants in the tenth century A.D., and other versions continued to arrive over the next six centuries; Indochina and Thailand received the story in about the sixteenth century. It is as popular today in Indonesia, Southeast Asia, and Burma as it is on the mainland.

rāsa, Hind. Literally, juice or flavor (of supernatural joy tasted in ecstatic union).

rāsa līlā, Hind. Essentially, the love play of Krishna, the avatār of the god Vishnu, with the cowgirl Rādhā and the gopīs. Though rāsa līlā appears as sensual human love, it is but the symbolic representation of the union of the human soul with the Supreme, a soul in the highest type of dedication. See gopīs, Krishna.

'rasūl, Isl. Apostle or messenger, a term for Muḥammad. The word appears in the second half of the Muslim profession of faith: There is no god but God (Lā illāha la 'Llāh) and Muḥammad is His Prophet (Muḥammadun Rasūlu 'Llah). The twenty-eight nabis (prophets) are also 'rasūls. The term is also applied to the early messengers, though some nabis (among them Isaac, Jacob, and John the Baptist) may not always be 'rasūls.

Red Hat, Tib. A sect of monks, divided into various groups and schools, founded by the eighth-century Indian tantric mystic Padmasambhāva. The oldest of the Red Hat schools is the Nyingma ("ancient"). The Kagyudpas and the Karmapas are among the leading sects. The last to be founded is the Dzogschen ("great accomplishment"), divided into northern and southern schools. The Red Hat sects are rarely celibate and usually allow the drinking of beer, wine, and other forms of alcohol, a practice credited to the founder himself as a tantric. Padmasambhāva taught the Short Path (q.v.) as the way to salvation. The Red Hats commonly chant the prayer "Aum vajra guru padma siddhi hum!" (Aum, most excellent powerful teacher Padma, the miracle worker, hum!) in honor of Padmasambhāva. Celibacy is enjoined only on fully ordained monks, the gelongs; married lāmas keep families outside the monastery, but intercourse within the enclosure is proscribed.

Reiyō-kai, Buddh. One of the twentieth-century Japanese Buddhist movements based upon the teachings of the *Lotus Sūtra* (q.v.). The sect was founded in 1925 after the turmoil that followed the great earthquake that struck Japan that year, but it received its greatest impetus in the nation's wartime defeat and the consequent necessity of searching out new goals. Though Reiyō-kai puts much emphasis on the cult of ancestors, it also stresses social altruism toward the living. It goes beyond the precepts of the *Lotus Sūtra* in extending the application of its doctrines to the teaching of love and altruism not only to the four classes of Buddhism (two of monks and nuns, two of laymen and laywomen, respectively) but also to all humanity. Believing that each person is at least a potential if not an actual future Buddha, the members of Reiyō-kai do much social work without pay; Reiyō-kai has constructed new hospitals and old-age homes that it has turned over to other organizations without charge.

Ṛgveda, Ṛkveda, Hind. The Sanskrit form of Rig Veda (q.v.).

Rig Veda (also Ṛgveda, Ṛkveda), Hind. The earliest of the sacred scriptures of India and the chief of the four Vedas of the Āryans (q.v.). The Rig Veda, like its companion Vedas, was composed in an early form of Sanskrit, the sacred tongue of priestly India. The text boasts of the exploits of various warrior-gods and their deities, chief among them Indra, the heroic leader who smashed the enemy and destroyed their cities and farms, knocked down their dams, and generally devasted the land. Indra dominates the Rig Veda, with his wars, his heroic bouts of drinking the divine beverage Soma (at once both a god and a sacred intoxicant), and his gambling. Other important figures are Agni, the god of fire; Vasyu, the god of wind; Prajāpati, the god of sky; Varuṇa, the god of space. Other elements and natural events are also divinized, such as dawn as Uśā and speech as Vāk. The Vedic pantheon bears strong similarities to those of primitive Europe; for example, the Vedic sky-god Dyaus (or Dyaus-Pitar) has his parallel in the Greek Zeus, the Latin Jupiter, the Old Norse Tyr, and the old Teutonic Zyr. The Vedic Mitra has an immediate counterpart in the Iranian (Zoroastrian [q.v.]) Mithra. The pantheon is primarily but not completely masculine. Figures like the warrior Indra undoubtedly had some historic basis; likely in the telling of the stories several such figures were combined into one over the centuries, and in some cases a gradual divinization occurred. Some of the Vedic deities became aspects of the gods of the subjugated peoples—Rudra, for example, once a separate Vedic deity, later being considered an aspect of the god Shiva, by all evidence a non-Āryan deity. In later ages the Vedic gods sank to a second level, being replaced in the popular forms of the common religion by the non-Āryan Vishnu, Shiva, and Śakti, the later a widespread Earth Mother figure of tremendous importance. See Hinduism, Shiva, Vedas, Vishnu.

rinpoche, Tib. An honorific meaning "precious one" used by Tibetan Buddhists. It is a formal term in addressing a lāma (q.v.), but does not imply any special authority.

Rinzai, Buddh. One of the two major schools of Zen (the other is Sōtō). Rinzai was introduced into Japan by the monk Eisai (q.v.) in the twelfth century from China, where it was known as Lin-chi. Although sitting (zazen) is an important part of Rinzai, the emphasis is placed on sudden enlightenment gained through the "conquering" of verbal or nonverbal impasses—the unanswerable question (kōan), the nonsensical dialog (mondo), unexpected silences, paradoxes, pantomime, blows, and other techniques that are used to traumatize the monk into awareness. The Rinzai monk most often serves a long period, if not a lifetime, in the monastery, under the direct supervision of a Zen master. The monk is expected to solve a certain number of kōans, possibly fifty or more; there are no established "answers"—much depends on the relationship with the master in working out the kōan, and a lot of Rinzai teachings are secret, for much of what takes place depends on intuition rather than formal doctrines or written scriptures. See kōan, Sōtō, Zen.

rishi (Sanskrit ṛṣi), Hind. A seer. The name may be used for any holy man with special insight, but formally it is applied to a group of seers of antiquity to whom certain texts were revealed. The rishis, as seers, are those who "see" the divine law and translate it into terms of creation and knowledge. Traditionally there were Seven Rishis who were saved from destruction by means of an ark, of which the god Vishnu was the pilot in the form of the great Lawgiver, Manu (q.v.). The names of the Seven are differently given according to the text; sometimes there are as many as eight or ten. The Vedas (q.v.) were enunciated through them, and they are the source of the sacred syllables and sayings known as mantras (q.v.), all of which have been passed down orally from the mouths of the Seven.

The Seven Rishis have been traced back to the Indus Valley (q.v.) and were probably "Aryanized" by the Vedic priests and taken into the brāhmin fold for their great knowledge and wisdom. The seven leading brāhmin clan progenitors are descended from them (again, the names do not coincide in various scriptures).

In later ages, the term rishi denotes more prosaic figures, being merely human and without count. They are sometimes identified as priestly seers (brajma-ṛṣi), royal seers (rājā-ṛṣi), and divine seers (deva ṛṣi), the latter being those who now rank as gods. These rishis dwell in the sky and are the seven stars of the Great Bear; they perform the brāhminic rituals three times a day in the company of the uppercaste Hindus, the twice-born.

Risshō-kōsei-kai, Buddh. A Lotus sect of contemporary Japan, founded, like the more prominent Sōka-gakkai (q.v.), at the end of World War II in an effort to cope with the tremendous upheaval caused by the defeat the nation suffered and the challenges confronting its people. Risshō-kōsei-kai, which means Society for the Promotion of Righteousness and Neighborly Relations, now numbers several million members. It was founded by a factory woman, Naganuma Myōko, ill and unhappily married, upon the teachings of the *Lotus Sūtra* (q.v.). The sect is dedicated to the achievement of a just society based upon the common brotherhood of humanity. The realization of the integral person is stressed over the traditional cult of ancestors. Mme. Myōko stressed, "As long as a person is governed by his selfish ego, he cannot grow up." Only the humble can free themselves from this ego, for unless they do, "We are therefore not important people, and all our education counts for nothing in the eyes of Buddha. All of us are nothing."

ritöd, Tib. A meditation house. The site is normally in the wilderness, on the shore of a lake or stream, against the background of high mountains.

rnal hyorpa (pronounced naljorpa), Tib. Literally "one who has attained perfect serenity"—i.e., an ascetic with magic powers or siddhis.

roshi, Buddh. A high-ranking Zen master. See Zen.

Rudra, Hind. Initially the Vedic storm god, Rudra is also a form of Shiva. The name Rudra is of doubtful origin, and the etymologies are symbolic. The meaning may be "the red one." The god is called Rudra in the Purāṇas because he wept at birth, the word for weep being the root rud-. In other versions the name may mean "Remover of Pain," for rut is the term given to the three forms of pain (physical, emotional, and spiritual) found in the world. Rudra was eventually identified with Shiva, the unknown god of the unknown people conquered by the Āryans, to the point that Rudra became nothing more than a name for Shiva in one of his many aspects.

In the Vedas (q.v.) Rudra is the god of storms, of howling winds, and is somewhat feared, being separated from other gods in certain rituals and kept with malevolent spirits and deities. Rudra gives the sinner the tortures of hell: He is death, the demon, the cause of tears, the god that kills. He is also "auspicious," the lord of songs, of sacrifices, the sweet-scented divine healer, the most generous of gods who bestows property and welfare, not only to mankind but also to horses, cows, and sheep, the mainstay of the early Āryan economy. As a warrior, he rides his chariot bearing a thunderbolt and shooting arrows from his formidable bow.

Rudras, Hind. The divinities of the subtle world situated between the earth and the sky, otherwise known as the sphere of space. They are the principles of life, the artisans, and are the enlivening powers of all living bodies—the "working class of heaven," in comparison to the priestly and warrior deities. Their number is given as eleven in some accounts, eleven hundred in others. They are the constant companions of the god Shiva in his aspect as Rudra, above.

Rūmī, Jalāl al-Dīn (A.D. 1207–73), Ṣūfī. Rūmī was a noted Ṣūfī poet and mystic, the discoverer of the dance of the dervishes, and the founder of the Mawlawīya brotherhood. He was born at Balkh in Afghanistan, then under Persian rule. As a child and adolescent, he was noted for his many experiences of spiritual heights and his God-centered consciousness. After some sixteen years of wandering, often in caravans, he settled down in Konya, a holy city in Turkey, where he became a teacher. It was here that he developed the technique of sema, or whirling dance, after hearing the rhythms of gold-beaters at work. Some sources give a different origin to Rūmī's dancing, saying it was the enigmatic figure Shams of Tabriz (q.v.) who initiated him. Shams served as Rūmī's spiritual master for three years and then disappeared mysteriously. Some versions assert that Shams was murdered by Rūmī's students in a paroxysm of jealousy. After Shams' disappearance, or death, Rūmī entered upon a long period of mystical experiences, partly triggered by his sorrow over his loss of Shams. Many of Rūmī's best writings were done at this time. After their master's death, Rūmī's disciples, the Mawlawīya brotherhood, carried on the practice of sema, which spread to other lands. Rūmī's major works are the "collaboration" with Shams, the *Diwan Samsh Tabraiz,* and his mystical couplets, the *Mathnawi,* one of the greatest of all Ṣūfī writings. See sema, Ṣūfism.

◂ S ▸

Śabda Brahman, Hind. The eternal sound—ŌṂ—that is the first manifestation of the Supreme Reality and forms the root of all subsequent creation. The use of sound as a means to transfiguration is a type of yoga, and is popular among some groups of Sikhs (q.v.).

saddha, Hind. One who possesses the occult powers known as siddhi (q.v.).

sadguru (also satguru), Hind. A common term for a Highest Master, the guru who is believed by his followers to be an avatār. The term is much abused (a current example is the youthful Satguru Balyogeshwar Shri Sant Ji Maharaj, who was proclaimed a Highest Master at the age of eight and deposed at sixteen by his mother).

sādhaka, Hind. An individual who practices sādhana, spiritual exercises for the purpose of self-realization.

sādhana, Hind. Spiritual exercises and practice performed for the purpose of preparing oneself for self-realization. Sādhana is any form of spiritual practice, from the simplest to the most complex and sophisticated. It is best done under the guidance of a guru (q.v.); it should be practiced at fixed times, just as one takes food at regular hours. Dawn, midday, and dusk are often set as the preferable times for sādhana.

sādhu, Hind. A Hindu ascetic. The term is a general one and is employed more or less interchangeably with other types of religious who have renounced the world, such as sannyāsi, yogī, vairāgī, and fakīr. The sādhu occupies a special place in Indian society. He is the Renouncer, who has eschewed caste, social position, rank, and authority in order, by gradual stages of purification, to withdraw inward toward the ultimate reality. The search for sanctity is not thought an aberration, as in the West, but is considered the supreme achievement of the soul's own immanent power. Though many sādhus are accused of being frauds, and unquestionably many exploit the public, they are looked upon with veneration. As the seeker searching the Universal Soul in order to be absorbed in it, the sādhu, even of the highest caste, is automatically set apart from the orthodox priesthood, the entrenched brāhmins who represent the religious establishment. In the popular mind the metaphysics of renunciation are superior to the rituals of the priests. Theoretically freed of earthly attachments, the sādhu is able to attach himself as he wills, not as he is forced, to the best of the social structure. Thus the sādhu, of whatever form, is credited with much of the development of Indian culture, art, architecture, music, poetry, and literature—influencing and forming the very world he has abandoned. Such dichotomies are easily absorbed by the Indian mind.

BACKGROUND. The concept of the sādhu goes back to the earliest images of the god Shiva himself, his hair matted, his body white with ashes. The Shaivite sādhu usually wears on his forehead, drawn in ashes, sandalwood, or another soft material, the three lines of the god's trident; they may be vertical or horizontal; endless variations, depending on the sect, are possible. Shaivites may also decorate their bodies with various lines, or cover the entire torso with ashes. Most Shaivites also carry a metal trident and wear or carry rosaries of rudrākṣa beads. In the past, when there were no prohibitions against killing forest animals and the wildlife had not been depleted, many sādhus wore a leopard or tiger pelt; an animal skin, either a tiger's or an antelope's, often covered his site of meditation. Usually the sādhu's hair and beard are uncut, matted, and uncouth. Some groups of sādhus are celibate, others not; those groups of sādhus who are tantrics may share a low-caste woman among them during their rites. In general, various austerities, including fasting and mortification of the flesh, are practiced.

SHAIVITE SĀDHUS. Among the major orders or sects of Shaivites are the Daśanāmi Sannyāsīs, or Monks of the Ten Names, an order founded by the scholar Śankara, which is divided into some ten branches and scattered to the "four corners of India." The various branches admit members from all castes but are often segregated according to caste. In the Middle Ages each branch had a detachment known as Daśanāmi Nāgas (Militant Sādhus), then fully armed, in theory against the Muslims, but battles with other orders were more likely. They are no longer militant.

Various groups of yogīs may be included among the Shaivites. Some individuals and groups follow tantrism and Shaktism. The sādhus are often criticized by more orthodox Hindus for their use of forbidden items like stimulants, meat, and fish and their erotic practices. Magic is also common among them. A more respectable group of yogīs are the Gorakhnāthis (Kānphāṭa Yogīs), identifiable by the wearing of large earrings. The founder of the order, the twelfth-century Kānphāṭā, is credited with the laying out of the principles of Hatha Yoga, then a mystical, magical, sexual discipline far removed from the gymnastics the term implies now. The Aghorī Yogīs, who are now either in decline or practicing secretly, are notorious for their rites involving the dead, among which cannibalism is one. The Lingāyats (q.v.) center their worship around the adoration of the liṅga (phallus) as symbol of Shiva.

VAISNAVITE SĀDHUS. The sādhu devoted to the god Vishnu (or his incarnation Krishna) is a later development than that of the Shaivites. The first known organized Vaisnavite orders are found about the twelfth century A.D. They seem to have originated in the Ālvars (q.v.) of South India. They are commonly called vairāgīs (from viraga, detachment) and for the most part are members of the various schools of bhakti (devotion). The Vaisnavites include a large number of laymen who are attached to or centered around various maṭhs or ashrams of monks and priests. The sects do not emphasize the ascetic extremes of the Shaivites. The common identifying mark of the Vaisnavites is a white V drawn on the forehead, with an added line in either white or red in the center. Vaisnavites normally wear white and carry a rosary with beads of the tulasī or sacred basil.

Sādhus contributed greatly to the spiritual unification and development of India through their endless travels from one sacred site to another, where they repeated songs and poetry, and carried icons, paintings, and other sanctified objects. They were well known outside India: The eleventh-century Chinese voyager Ma Huan on his visit to Cochin spoke of "chokis [yogīs] who lead a life as austere as the Taoists of China but who are married." The Arab Abu-Zeyd al-Ḥassan of Syraf wrote, "The men sādhus go naked, and their long hair covers their bodies and privy parts; they let their nails grow until they become like spikes; they remove only the parts that break. They live after the manner of wandering monks; each of them wears around his neck a cord to which is attached a human skull."

Unlike the common Hindu, who is cremated at death, the sādhu is buried, usually in a sitting position; the bodies of some may be placed in a river to float downstream. The burial site invariably becomes a place of worship and pilgrimage, and in some cases an ashram may be found around it. See bhakti, disposal of the dead, Shiva, Vishnu.

Sai Baba (1) Bhakti mystic (A.D. 1856–1918). Details of his early life are speculative. He was probably born of a middle-class brāhmin family in Hyderabad, one of the princely states of India. He is said to have left home at the age of eight to follow a Muslim faqīr, and when the faqīr died, he joined a Hindu guru whom he called Venkusa. In 1872—Sai Baba was then sixteen—he appeared at a small town in western India called Shirdi. He slept under a tree; when he attempted to enter the local Hindu temple he was chased away by the caretaker, who believed the boy was a Muslim. Sai Baba then took up his abode in the local mosque, a small mud-walled building that was to be his home for nearly half a century. He sometimes said the five-times-a-day Muslim prayers, occasionally read the Qur'ān, maintained a small fire in the Parsee manner, but also recited Hindu prayers. "All that is, is Allāh," he remarked, though he was noted for his long silences. By 1900 his fame had spread, and eight years later Hindus began to revere him as a saint. Like many other Indian holy men, both Hindu and Ṣūfī, he was virtually unlettered, but he possessed widespread knowledge, which he revealed sparingly, depending on the listener. For certain people he said, "It is not necessary to have a guru. Everything is within us. What you sow is what you reap. What you give is what you get. It is all within you. Try to listen inwardly and follow the directions you get." However, he counseled other devotees on the necessity for a spiritual master. One reported: "The peculiar feature stressed by Sai Baba's example and words is the vast importance of developing this devotion on the basis of devotion to one's guru. It is seeing God in, through and as the guru, identifying guru with God." To others he said, "Stay with me and I will do the rest."

Sai Baba performed miracles and was reported to have engaged in various occult practices, such as astral traveling, bilocation, clairvoyance, and other siddhis (q.v.). However, he was quite reticent about such powers, and he used or mentioned them only when necessary to benefit a devotee. His devotees left many accounts of conversations with him and of their impressions. One will summarize the general experience. A Mrs. Manager, identified in the accounts as "a Parsi lady," said, "One noticeable difference between Sai Baba and other saints struck me. I have visited other notable saints also and have seen them in a state of trance or samādhi in which they were entirely oblivious of their body. Then I have seen them recovering consciousness of their surroundings, knowing what is in our hearts and replying to our questions. But with Sai Baba there was this one peculiar difference: He did not need to go into samādhi in order to achieve anything or to attain any higher status or knowledge. He was every moment exercising a dual consciousness, one actively utilizing the ego called Sai Baba and dealing with other egos in temporal or spiritual affairs and the other transcending all ego and abiding in the Universal Self. He was constantly manifesting the powers and features proper to both states of consciousness. . . . He was always in the all-knowing state."

Although Sai Baba died on October 15, 1918, devotees as well as people who did not know of him until years later had experiences of the saint after that date. Shortly after the saint's death, Swami B. V. Narasimhaswami collected his words and anecdotes about him in a work entitled *Sri Sai Baba's Charters and Sayings,* and also published in three volumes *Devotees' Experiences of Sai Baba.* (Both are available at the All India Sai Samaj, Madras.) A short factual biography, *The Incredible Sai Baba,* based on this material, has been written by Arthur Osborne; Orient Longmans, Ltd., is the publisher.

Sai Baba (2) A second, self-proclaimed Sai Baba (1926–) now reigns at Puttaparthi, a village not far from Madras. He claims both that he has received the soul of Sai Baba and that he is an avatār—i.e., God incarnated. Although he has attracted a tremendous number of devotees, some of whom have established shrines in his name around India, and is famed for his sanctity, many devotees of the original Sai Baba, along with a number of knowledgeable Hindus, state that he is merely a showman preying on the incredulous, his holy sayings being but a parroting of traditional religious lore and his supposed occult powers such as producing watches out of air or from a devotee's ear (such tricks have earned him the name of Siddhi Sai Baba) are worthless; his highly luxurious style of living forms a sharp contrast to the extreme simplicity of the original Sai Baba.

śakta (or shakta), Hind. A devotee of the Divine Energy, Śakti (q.v.). See also Hinduism.

Śakti (or Shakti), Hind. The eternal and Supreme Power, variously described as manifest energy, the substance of everything, the all-pervading, etc. In the Vedas (q.v.) the word means "energy." In Hindu theology Śakti is a term for the manifestation of the creative principle. However, the concept of Śakti is derived from the hoary past and brāhminized in later centuries. The concept of the supreme power as female, a mother, a womb, a vulva is not found in the pre-eminently patriarchal scriptures of the Āryans (q.v.) but arises, to be made respectable by the higher castes, from the submerged prehistoric mother cults of the earliest peoples of the subcontinent. Today Śakti has been connected with, is identical to, the power of the gods Shiva, Vishnu, or Brahmā, the great Hindu triad. From the most ancient scriptural times Śakti, under a variety of names, is intimately linked to Shiva, the Lord of Sleep (and his various guises, especially Rudra). Shiva is helpless without the fecundating divine energy, Śakti. The two, coupled in sexual union, are the two inseparable forces that impregnate the universe with life in all its forms. Without Śakti, Shiva is merely the Void. "He has no visible form," the *Liṅga-arcana Tantra* states. "What can be expected from the worship of nothingness?" Shiva (or Rudra), thus a corpse, cannot be worshiped without Śakti. The Goddess is the source of all, the universal Creator. Śakti does not need even Shiva; as eternal Virgin (Kumāri) she does not depend on any one, any power, for she is the One Itself as Power. See Hinduism; also see Durgā, Kālī, Kumāri, Shiva.

Śākyamuni Buddha. One of the names for Gautama Buddha, commonly the Buddha. Śākya is the gotra or clan to which he belonged, and muni means sage—the Sage of the Śakyas. See Buddha.

śalagrāma, Hind. A small "stone," actually an ammonite, a fossil genus of marine cephalopod, which is considered by brāhmins to be a natural representation of the god Vishnu (q.v.); it plays an important role in the worship of brāhmins, being a living, earthly form of the deity. The śalagrāma is mentioned as far back as the Artharva Veda (c. B.C. 1000), where it is written that any brāhmin's house that does not contain the śalagrāma is to be considered as impure as a cemetery (an abomination, since the twice-born are cremated), and the food prepared in the house as unclean as a dog's vomit.

Śalagrāmas are found in the Gundak River in Nepal. They are black or dark-colored, round or oval, striated, umbilicated, and ornamented with natural arborizations or treelike markings. The most sought-after are perforated in one or more places by worms: The god Vishnu has entered the stone in the shape of a serpent. The number of perforations and the curves of the striations signify various forms of Vishnu—e.g., a śalagrāma with one perforation and four spiral curves resembling the footprint of a cow and a wreath of flowers contains Lakshmi Nārāyaṇa, symbolizing the female and the male aspects of the god. A stone bordering on violet represents a vindictive avatār such as Narasinga, which only the bravest brāhmin would possess, for this is Vishnu as the ferocious, fearful Man-lion.

The śalagrāma is kept in the home, wrapped in cloth; it is frequently bathed and perfumed and in hot weather may be exposed with water dripping upon it from a jar; its bath water is highly prized and is drunk for its sin-destroying qualities. The śalagrāma is paired with the tulasī plant (a type of basil), the symbol of Vishnu's favorite mistress. The god's wife Lakshmi, jealous of his attentions to Tulasī, changed her into a plant; the god then took the form of the śalagrāma; the yearly nuptials of plant and stone are celebrated in some areas. When a person is dying, a śalagrāma is placed near or on the chest, and leaves of the tulasī are scattered about the body. After the death and cremation of the owner of a śalagrāma, it becomes the property of his chosen son.

The śalagrāma is a yantra (q.v.)—i.e., a visual representation of mantra or prayer, here to Vishnu. Though the stone is Vishnu in visual form, it is also a linga, the Shiva phallus, and a type of the Cosmic Egg (q.v.). It partakes of the essence of all the other deities, and through it pūjā (individual worship) may be offered to any or all of them. See tulasī; also see Krishna, Vishnu.

salām, Isl. Peace. The word is central in ritual greetings, in the sense that it is bestowed by Allah upon his "slaves."

as-salamu 'alaikum, Isl. "Peace be on you," which is said upon greeting and leaving, at the end of the daily prayers, and notably at the end of the funeral prayer.

samādhi, Hind. (The term may also be used in Jainism and Buddhism, including Zen.) The eighth and highest stage of yogic concentration, following dhyāna (deep meditation). Samādhi means, literally, "concentration"—i.e., of the soul within the soul; also, a solution or completion—samādhana, which signifies the perfect resolution of form, formlessness, manifested being, and nonbeing. It is the state of pure isolation in which all sense of personal identity ceases. In some forms (there are several) the individual exists in complete detachment from both the self and from the godhead. The *Bhagavad Gītā* (q.v.) states that samādhi is "seeing the self as abiding in all things and all things in the self." Union with the Supreme is often a goal in some types of yoga, but not always. The classical system of yoga does not necessarily postulate a godhead, and in Buddhism the concept of God in any form is either proscribed or ignored. In this sense samādhi is not union or divine knowledge but a "state." Exteriorly, samādhi resembles a trance, but it is emphatically not a hypnotic state, as some critics charge. Ordinarily samādhi requires the full progression of yogic techniques (or something similar, such as Zen), but a few saints, such as Rāmakrishna and Anandamayee Ma (see both), easily slipped into the highest stage in a fraction of a second as the result of some fragmentary exterior impulse. Rāmakrishna's samādhi has been described as a state in which there is consciousness of nothing but timeless consciousness itself—"the wholly ineffable experience." See yoga.

Sāma Veda, Hind. One of the four Vedas (q.v.). The Sāma Veda is a collection of hymns, which are chanted; it follows the Rig Veda (q.v.) in date of composition.

saṃhitā, Hind. The term means a collection, being generally applied to collections of hymns and similar texts, mantras, charms, and magic formulas. In a specific sense it refers to the four Vedas (q.v.).

saṃsāra, Hind. The cycle of life in the world through a continued series of births, deaths, and rebirths. This chain, which invokes so much suffering, is the result of karma, the accumulated "debts" arising from ignorance, sin, and bad acts and actions.

saṁskāra, Hind. Literally, purification, consecration; the term has three major meanings:

1. Impressions, dispositions, or psychic traces remaining in the mind after an experience. Whatever is done consciously or unconsciously leaves a saṁskāra, whether from the current life or a past birth. Saṁskāras represent the root impressions received from all one's past experiences in all lives, molding present character, and indirectly controlling one's acts and thoughts, even though those of the past have been forgotten. Nothing in the past is eradicated or lost: Each impression in turn produces states similar to itself. Thus actual states cause saṁskāras, and saṁskāras cause actual states.

2. A rite performed with the aid of mantras, prayers, and other efficacious aids intended to restore something to its original pure state. In this sense a saṁskāra can purify a temple or image or a ritual object.

3. Purification rites for the various stages in the life of a brāhmin, among them the first eating of rice, the name day, the bestowing of the sacred thread, marriage, and death. In this sense saṁskāras approximate—roughly but not precisely—the sacraments of the Christian churches (the two words are cognate).

sandhi, Hind. The "junction of time" at sunrise or sunset, which are considered by yogīs to be especially efficacious periods for meditation, when the mind is calm and refreshed and in a sattvic (roughly, harmonious, pure, and luminous) state.

Sangha, Buddh. The Buddhist Brotherhood, the third of the Three Gems (or the Three Refuges), which include the Buddha and the Dharma (the Buddhist Way). The five Hindus converted by the Lord Buddha at Sarnath became the nucleus of the Sangha. The term originally meant assembly, and was used in North India in this sense at the time of Buddha.

śaṅka, Hind. A conch shell, used in religious ceremonies. Its function has been traced back to the non-Āryan, non-Vedic, non-Indus peoples of primitive and early India. The conch is a symbol of various gods, among them Vishnu, Indra, and Yama. In the hands of the greatest of these, Vishnu, the conch is a symbol of the origin of existence, its multiple spiral evolving from a single point into ever-increasing spheres. Its deep sound signifies the primeval sound of creation, the sacred mantra ŌṂ (or AUM).

sannyāsa, Hind. Renunciation. This is the last of the four āśramas (q.v.), the stage of life when a man (or sometimes woman) leaves family (now grown) and renounces caste, social position, worldly affairs, livelihood, or career—whatever one might be attached to—to surrender oneself in the final search for the Divine. See sannyāsi below.

sannyāsi (or sannyāsin), Hind. One who has renounced his life as an ordinary citizen—i.e., (in most cases) that of the householder. This break with mundane ties brings freedom of a type otherwise impossible, for the sannyāsi is the liberated man, the Renouncer par excellence, the holy wanderer with no goal, no obligations but to seek eternal salvation. In Indian life the Renouncer is not an outcaste, nor an oddity, but an examplar of society at its best, more often admired and envied than wondered at. Though he has eschewed caste, or may be of the lowest castes, the sannyāsi is above the brāhmin, the epitome of caste, in his new role.

Some sannyāsis function individually; others join various orders. A rite of passage (now simplified) may be entered upon, in which, with appropriate ceremonies, the future sannyāsi retreats into a cave or hut, undergoes purificatory rituals, and is reborn into his new status; the ritual may involve an imitation of the fetal position, with a ceremonial expulsion from the womb.

The sannyāsi is freed from the necessity of earning a living or of any kind of self-support; he is now dependent upon society for food, shelter, and other sustenance; in return, to a certain extent, society depends upon the spiritual benefits gained by his sannyāsa. Some sannyāsis wander from village to village, or through the forests and jungles and along the rivers and to various sacred sites. Others may withdraw completely into a jungle or mountain hermitage either alone or in company with others.

Sanskrit, Ind. The priestly and classical language of Hindus, and the ancestor of the tongues used by Buddhists (see Pāli) and Jains in their sacred writings. Sanskrit is a prominent member of the vast family of Indo-European languages, and the parent of many of the languages of northern India, among them Hindi, Urdu, Bengali, Maharathi, Panjabi, etc., all of which have many loan words from numerous other sources. Classical priestly Sanskrit, which contains a number of loan words from non-Sanskritic tongues, infiltrated the Dravidian and other languages of South India, which have different origins, and has affected, through its offshoots (especially Pāli), the languages of Southeast Asia (Indochina) and Indonesia, which were once subject to Indian cultural, religious, and economic influence. The pre-Indian form of Sanskrit is not known; the earliest scriptures, the Vedas, and many of the subsequent texts were not committed to writing but were memorized by the priests. A long line of brāhmin grammarians was climaxed by Panini (c. fourth century B.C.) and the second-century B.C. Patañjali (not to be confused with the author of the *Yoga-Sūtras*), who firmly fixed the principles of Sanskrit grammar in highly condensed rules, but with logic and clarity. According to the most recent Indian census, Sanskrit is still the mother tongue of several thousand people. It is not only required for the practicing brāhmin priest (who may not always understand it), but also is often a subject of study by Buddhist scholars abroad, especially in Tibet and Japan, for many Mahāyānist texts were composed in Sanskrit.

Since sound and the word are sacred (the mantra is a prime example) and speech is a goddess, Vac (in some texts she is the wife of the god Brahmā, in others of the sage-deity Kaśyapa), the well-trained priest recites the Veda with precisely the same intonation, rhythm, and pronunciation that his forefathers did three thousand years ago. See brāhmins, Vedas.

Sarmad, a seventeenth-century Ṣūfī mystic. Daniel (later Hazrat Saeed) Sarmad was born of Jewish parents, probably in Palestine; he became a merchant, trading successfully in Armenia, Persia, and India, but he finally gave up the secular life to search out the Divine Truth, a decision he made in Patna in eastern India. He converted to Islam after a long search, then passed beyond into Ṣūfism but went naked like a Hindu sādhu. He became a tutor for prince Dārā Shikōh, oldest son of Shāh Jahān (the builder of the Taj Mahal), teaching the prince the Upanishads and the *Bhagavad*

Gītā, both Hindu scriptures, for Sarmad, like many Indian Ṣūfīs and bhaktas, took the best of both Islam and Hinduism. Though he preached that the only true mosque or true temple was within, he spent much of his time at the popular mosque, the Yamma Masjid in (old) Delhi. In 1658 Shāh Jahān's third son, the notorious Aurangzīb, imprisoned his father, murdered Dārā, and the next year initiated a purge of non-Muslims. Among the victims were the ninth Sikh Guru, Teg Bahadur, the Hindu saint Lal Bahadur, and Sarmad, the latter being executed for "violation of Qur'ānic law," the major accusation being that of going naked in public, a sin against Islamic teaching. Sarmad was beheaded outside the mosque. He left behind a collection of 321 quatrains, the *Rubāiyat Sarmad,* in Persian. His cult is now popular, and his tomb, on the site of his martyrdom, is a famous center of pilgrimage and is the site of an annual urs (festival) held to commemorate his memory.

śastra (or shastra), Hind. An authoritative treatise, especially religious, scientific, or medical. The term is applied to the sacred, authorative Hindu scriptures.

satguru, Hind. See sadguru.

satī (anglicized as suttee), Hind. The ritual burning of a widow on her husband's funeral pyre. The self-immolation is said to be "voluntary," and no doubt it was (and is) in many cases, but all too often the widow was forced upon the flames by relatives and clan, sometimes in a drugged state, and either tied hand and foot, or else the pyre was set in a deep pit from which the woman could not escape. Satī may be traced back to primitive human sacrifices and fertility rites among the early inhabitants of the Indian peninsula, and developed for a number of reasons after the Āryan invasion, especially among the warrior caste (kśatyrias). The word itself means "faithfulness." The custom came to have religious sanction, no matter what the practical reasons. In a story, found in many versions, and often quoted by the priests in extenuation of the rite, the god Shiva married the daughter of King Daksa; the new bride's name was Satī (Faithfulness). Anguished because her father had opposed the union, Satī killed herself. While Shiva wandered the heavens distraught with sorrow, the body of his wife over his shoulder, Daksa followed, hacking the corpse to pieces with his discus (the places where the parts of the body fell, like the Kalighat in Calcutta, are especially sacred shrines; Satī is equated with Kālī). Thus satī is but the rite of faithfulness to the husband, though to accept brāhminical explanations, one has to set reason and logic aside.

Originally the custom was practiced only among the frontier warrior peoples of the Northwest, including Kashmir. Satī is mentioned, though casually, in Hindu scriptures about B.C. 300, and six hundred years later it seems to be widespread among the brāhmins, who had previously opposed it, for to kill a brāhmin (or his wife) is the gravest of all sins. Satī became common, even among the lowest classes, there being adequate examples of the rite among weavers, barbers, and masons. Cases are recorded, aside from those of single burnings, of rājās being followed by all their wives, sixty-four in one case, eighty-four in another, four hundred and seven hundred in still other attested satīs. Even today cases are reported in the provinces but denied officially. The Muslims attempted to stamp out satī, and the British, aided by a number of Hindu reformers in the nineteenth century, virtually eradicated the practice during their reign.

Though the custom horrifies the foreigner, and many Hindus as well, it must be considered in the light of vastly different social, economic, historical, and religious perspectives. The lot of the widow (who often has her head shaved and is relegated to a degrading position even by her own in-laws) is a sorry and miserable one, for under Hindu law she has no rights; her food and support are due solely to the generosity of her sons, especially the first-born. From birth, in an orthodox Hindu milieu, the woman is virtually an outcaste; even if she is of one of the three upper castes, she is not entitled to the sacred thread, a prerequisite for salvation; in fact, she cannot even hope to attain salvation until she is reborn a male and can work out her karmic bonds and as a man attain final liberation. By sacrificing herself on her husband's pyre she automatically cuts the karmic cycle and wins eternal merit. The eighteenth-century Jesuit missionary Roberto di Nobili witnessed satī and was moved by the ecstatic devotion by which young widows consummated their lives on their husband's crematory fires. Satī does not require women with young children to immolate themselves; in such cases it is definitely discouraged, as it would leave numbers of orphans to be cared for by the husband's family.

The rite itself is one of unsurpassed interest, up to the final act. The satī herself was an object of the highest veneration and honor. As the ceremony was to begin, the impressions of her hands made with turmeric paste were imprinted on the walls of houses. A grand procession to the accompaniment of music led her to the river or tank to bathe. She put on fresh clothing, and all the insignia of married bliss (called saubhāgya)—her red paste (kumkum) for the dot (bindi [q.v.]) on her forehead, her mirror, comb, betel leaves, and so on. Her ornaments were distributed to her friends and relations as sacred mementos. Then she would take her leave of each person. Often people would entrust messages to her to carry to deceased relatives in heaven. Ascending the funeral pyre, the widow would place her husband's head on her lap, and the flames were lighted. Normally the widow was burned on the same fire as her husband; if there were several widows, the practice differed, sometimes the favorite wife getting the honor of dying with the husband's body, the others receiving separate fires. Often, petty jealousies having been resolved in satī, all the wives would go together. Women who ran away at the last minute were regarded as untouchables and were not accepted back by their castes and families. In a few cases of women rescued by Europeans, the foreigners often married them to keep them from the alternative fates to death. In instances where the husband's body is buried, as among low-caste people and certain Shaivites, the wives have been buried alive with the same ritual as for cremation. See Hinduism, karma.

satori (Chinese, tun wu), Buddh. The sudden illumination or enlightenment received in Zen (or Ch'an) Buddhism. Satori has been much discussed and analyzed, but the consensus is that satori characterized either mentally or emotionally is not satori, for the experience is beyond communication and explanation. Satori, however, is an experience that is repeated, bringing further maturity to the practitioner; the first experience, known as kensho, is said to be the most important. To Zen practitioners satori is not samādhi (q.v.) but a stage beyond; to Zen Buddhists samādhi is nothing more than the unification of consciousness, while satori is an awakening from such a state. Satori is said to come abruptly and momentarily; if the experience or sensation persists, it is not satori; such is the teaching in the Lin-chi and Rinzai schools. However, the Tsao Tsung and Sōtō schools accept a more gradually developing awareness. Whatever the school, in China and Japan the practitioner experiences all and is embraced by and is identical with the Great Tao. The Chinese master Han Shan said that after the "work" of purifying the shadows of our habitual thinking and flowing thoughts, "If suddenly the surging thoughts stop, one clearly sees that his self-mind is originally pure, genuine, vast, illuminating, perfect and devoid of objects." Such, he says, is "wu" (or satori). This view of seeing into the self-nature is about as close to a description of satori as any Ch'an or Zen practitioner is ever likely to give. See Ch'an, Zen.

satsang, Hind. The company of saints, sages, and other seekers after Truth, either in actual physical assembly (as at an ashram [q.v.]) or in the sense of reading the holy scriptures or the lives or words of saints. Satsang is also a religious meeting. In any sense, it implies being in the presence of the Divine.

sattva, Hind. The most positive of the three guṇas, and the one that must transcend the others lest they manifest their (negative) qualities. Sattva is the property of harmony, lightness, and luminosity. See guṇa.

satyāgraha, Hind. Literally, "holding onto truth." The term satyāgraha was coined by Gandhi (q.v.) to describe the type of resistance he was attempting to practice in South Africa against the British Government. Satyāgraha is both political and moral, and involves not only nonco-operation and civil disobedience as weapons against a superior force but also the spiritual regeneration of the practitioner. Love, not hate for the opponent, a prime requisite. Fasting must be done in a religious spirit, not against an enemy but against "a loved one, not to extract rights but to reform him." Satyāgraha is not passive nor an acceptance of evil. It requires a positive, cheerful "co-operative resistance" aimed at dissolving not an antagonist but antagonisms. One must be ready to co-operate with the opponent but not to submit. "Nonviolence in its dynamic conditions does not mean weak submission to the will of the evildoer, but it means putting our whole soul against the will of the tyrant." Gandhi was insistent that satyāgraha not be an excuse for cowardice; he stated that if forced, he would choose violence to cowardly nonviolence, but for the brave, nonviolence is the best of all ways, and "infinitely superior to violence." See ahiṃsā, Gandhi.

Second Coming. The theme of the return of the god, prophet, saint, or seer is common to many religions. In Hinduism, the Lord Vishnu will appear as Kalki at the end of the age of strife, riding a white horse and holding a sword blazing like a comet, to punish evildoers and to establish a golden age; he will destroy the world, and a new one will arise out of the ruins. In Buddhism, the Lord Buddha will return as the Maitreya Buddha. Zoroastrianism expects the return of Peshotan, the first and most faithful disciple of the Prophet. Various Islamic sects, especially the Shī'as, await the Māhdi or the Hidden Imām, in much the same apocalyptic spirit. Christianity expects the Second Coming of the Lord Jesus, again with the knowledge that the sinful will be punished and the righteous rewarded in a Golden Age. See Vishnu, Kalki, Maitreya Buddha, Peshotan, Māhdi, Imām, Jesus.

Secret of the Golden Flower, The (the T'ai Chin Hua Tsung Chih). A Chinese mystical work discovered by the German Sinologist Richard Wilhelm, to whom the West is indebted for knowledge of the book. Wilhelm found the book (retitled *The Art of Prolonging Human Life* or *Ch'ang Shêng Shu* by the latest publisher) in printed form in Peking in 1920. However, it had been transmitted orally for a long time, probably until the seventeenth century, when an edition printed from wooden blocks appeared; another edition was published in the eighteenth century.

The oral tradition dates back to the eighth century A.D., to the religion of the Golden Elixir of Life (Chin Tan Chiao); the founder is said to have been a Taoist adept, Lü Yen (also called Lü Tung-pin, or Lü the Guest of the Cavern), who is known as one of the eight immortals. The sect, though openly tolerated at first, was always esoteric and secret and became more so as its members were accused of political intrigue, some fifteen thousand being murdered by the Manchus in 1891. Lü himself attributed the origin of his knowledge to the legendary Kuan Yin-hsi, the Keeper of the Pass (q.v.), for whom Lao Tzu wrote out a summary of his knowledge (the *Lao tzu,* or *Tao Te Ching*). A number of ideas in Lü's system are derived from Lao Tzu. By the time of Lü Yen Taoism had accumulated a distracting accretion of magical and alchemical practices, and his movement was one of reform and purification. Though the sources of *The Secret of the Golden Flower* are primarily Taoist, Wilhelm found certain points that coincide with the mysticism of the Zoroastrians of Persia (mainly in the concept of Light as a force); there are also, he believed, Mahāyāna Buddhist influences, and even some from Nestorian Christianity, which had a foothold in China in the eighth century.

The work itself, apparently simple, is actually a highly complex, sophisticated manual of meditation; part of it is quite literal (sitting, breathing, posture, fixing of the heart, etc.) to develop "Circulation of the Light" in order to attain readiness for "the Far Journey." Parenthetically it must be said that the Westerner is likely to be enthralled by the immediate charm of the work, and then to be frustrated if he or she tries to follow it, for it requires a human guide, much time for study and meditation and mystical development, plus an understanding of Taoism and other esoteric oriental practices. Lü Yen states the goal immediately in unfamiliar terms: "That which exists through itself is called Tao," Tao being translated as Meaning by Wilhelm. "Tao has neither name nor force. It is the one essence, the one primordial spirit. Essence and life cannot be seen. It is contained in the Light of Heaven. The Light of Heaven cannot be seen. It is contained in the two eyes." Lü explains, "The Golden Flower is the Light," though it is merely an image, for "It is the true power of the transcendent Great *One,*" adding, "The Great *One* is the term given to that which has nothing above it. The secret of the magic of life consists in using action in order to achieve nonaction. One must not wish to leave out the steps between and penetrate directly. The maxim handed down to us is to take in hand the work on the essence." The Far Journey leads to "The land that is nowhere," for "that is the true home." The theme of "nonaction in action" is basic to the work, for Lü states, "Nonaction prevents a man from becoming entangled in form and image (substantially). Action in nonaction prevents a man from sinking into numbing emptiness and a dead nothingness." The conclusion of the work depends heavily upon Buddhist concepts, notably those of "emptiness, delusion and the center." Lü relates Taoism to it: "The expression 'to produce emptiness' contains the whole work of completing life and essence," the goal being the finding of the spiritual Elixir in order to pass from death to life. This spiritual Elixir "means forever tarrying in purposelessness. The deepest secret in our teaching, the secret of the bath, is confined to the work of making the heart empty. Therewith the heart is set at rest." Of the ultimate truth attained by his adepts, Lü warns, "Keep it secret and hold to it strictly."

The Secret of the Golden Flower, translated by Richard Wilhelm from the Chinese into German, and by Cary F. Baynes from German into English, is available in several editions. See also Lao Tzu, Taoism.

Selsabil, Isl. A fountain in Paradise that gives ginger-flavored water; it is mentioned in Sura 76 of the Qur'ān. Selsabil is a symbol of the Pure Water of the Divine.

sema, Ṣūfī. The dance of the "Whirling Dervishes," developed by the Persian mystical poet Rūmī. See dervish, Rūmī.

Seven Means, Buddh. A way to liberation. The devotee rides a "horse" of the Seven Means to attain enlightenment by the practice of contemplation, selecting the proper teaching, effort, joy, freshness of thought, meditation, and indifference to the world. See Buddhism.

Shahādah, Isl. The Muslim confession of Faith, "Lā ilāhā illa 'Llāh, Muḥammadun rasūlu 'Llāh." (There is no god but God, and Muḥammad is the Apostle of God.) The Shahādah is the first of the Five Pillars of Islam and is the fundamental statement of belief. It is sufficient for a person who decides to accept Islam merely to utter the Shahādah and be received as a Muslim, with all the rights and obligations that membership in the Islamic community denotes. Belief is first of all in the heart; the Shahādah is the out-

'reparatory to prayer, a Muslim nust wash according to a prescribed ritual. Face, hands, and eet should be carefully cleansed vith water; if water is lacking, hen desert sand may be used. 'he impurities to be removed re called hadīth, and the ritual f purification is known as wuḍū.

Shi'ite Muslims at Benares, India, celebrate the festival of Muharram in honor of ʿAlī, Muhammad's cousin and son-in-law. ʿAlī was the disputed fourth khalif, or righteous leader, and the quarrels over his succession split the Islamic world into two major sections, the Sunnī and the Shi'a.

At the great Jama Masjid in old Delhi, an Indian Muslim performs the raka'h (or movement) of submission in the afternoon prayers (the salāt al'asr). As he says prescriptions of praise to Allāh, he touches his forehead to the earth; both hands as well as the toes of both feet and the knees must also touch the ground. He then raises the upper part of his torso to a sitting position; his two hands are placed on his knees.

Shi'a Muslims observe the noon prayers at a mosque in Isfahan. The fivefold daily iteration of prayer is called salāt. The kneeling man has just touched his head to the ground in submission to Allāh; now he is saying prayers for mercy and divine protection. The other figures have completed the various raka'āt, or movements (there are seven in all) and are saying prayers known as takbīrs.

Islam means submission, and the Muslim is o who submits. Here, in the most symbolic of gestures, an Iranian Muslim touches his fo head to the ground to signify that before Al he is nothing but the dust of the earth.

Sai Baba, Indian mystic and saint, is seen in the only known photograph. He is seated near the tiny mud-walled mosque that served as his home for nearly half a century. Here he said both Muslim and Hindu prayers, and kept a fire in the Parsee tradition.

ie famed Selim mosque in Damascus shows e standard architectural features of Islamic ildings—the domed roof and the minars, minarets, from which the daily prayers are nounced.

'kh guru. Like all orthodox Sikhs, the guru rs the full beard and long hair (hidden by urban) of the traditional Indian holy man. his right wrist are the Sikh bangles. Since man is a holy wanderer, he carries his essions in the metal pot, which he also for washing and cooking.

Guru Nānak, the founder of the Sikhs, accepts the repentance of the faquir Wāli Kundhāri, who rolled a stone down a hill in an attempt to kill the saint and his companions, the Muslim Brother Mardana (at the left, with his rubab), and the Hindu Brother Bāla (at the right). Nānak's handprint can be seen on the stone, which rolled to a stop an arm's length away. Bāla is credited with writing down virtually every one of Nānak's deeds and sayings.

The Golden Temple, or Darbār Sāheb, is the center of Sikhism. It is located at the pool of Amritsar (in the city of the same name), on a site where Guru Nānak miraculously made water appear in a dry tank. Amritsar (the Pool of Nectar) was built by Rām Dās, the fourth Sikh Guru in 1579; the temple was completed by his son and successor Arjun, and rebuilt, with its marble façades and gold dome, by Ranjit Singh, the great Sikh war-leader, in the nineteenth century. A copy of the Sikh scripture, the Granth Sāheb, is kept in the temple sanctuary as the last Guru. Around the tank are shelters for pilgrims.

Designs in colored chalk are stenciled outside homes in Bombay to mark the festival of Nowrōz Patētī, the Parsee New Year. The swastika, a sign of good luck, is a sun symbol. Nowrōz Patētī begins at sunset of the previous night according to the ancient Iranian calendar. It is a time of repentance, in which the faithful make an "audit" of the past year, and resolutions for the coming one. Offenses are pardoned, ties of friendship renewed, and every heart is filled with love and joy. After dressing in new clothes and attending the fire temple in honor of Nowrōz Patētī, Parsees visit relatives and friends, to feast and to join hands in a rite called hamma-i-join (simply, hand joining) to wish each other a happy New Year.

ward expression of such belief. The Shahādah is chanted five times a day from the minarets of mosques, is the essential formula of all prayers, is said at marriage, is whispered into a baby's ear at birth, and is the last sound a dying person hears. See Islam.

shaik, Isl. See shaykh.

Shakti. See Śakti.

shaman. A mystic, either male or female, who engages in ecstasy through various techniques, either esoteric or literal, such as mastery over fire, astral travels and flight, descent into the underworld, disappearance into the sky, etc. The word shaman comes via the Russian from the Tungusic šaman. Not every ecstatic can be considered a shaman. The definition offered by Mircea Eliade (cf. *Shamanism,* Princeton University Press [1964]), here condensed, succinctly summarizes the shaman. "The shaman is also a magician and medicine man; he is believed to cure, like all doctors, and to perform miracles of the fakir type, like all magicians, whether primitive or modern. But beyond this he is a psychopomp, and he may also be priest, mystic, and poet. Shamanism in the strict sense is pre-eminently a religious phenomenon of Siberia and Central Asia. Through this whole region in which the ecstatic experience is considered the religious experience par excellence, the shaman, and he alone, is the great master of ecstasy. A first definition of this complex phenomenon, and perhaps the least hazardous, will be: Shamanism—*technique of ecstasy.* Generally shamanism coexists with other forms of magic and religion."

A different point of view, that of the anthropologist, is expressed by Margaret Mead (cf. *Sex and Temperament in Three Primitive Societies,* William Morrow [1935]): "The aborigines of Siberia dignified the nervously unstable individual into the shaman, whose utterances were believed to be supernaturally inspired and were a law to his more nervously stable fellow-tribesmen. Such an extreme case as this, where a whole people bows down before the word of an individual whom we would classify as insane, seems clear enough to us. The Siberians have imaginatively and from the point of view of our society unjustifiably, elevated an abnormal person into a socially important one. They have built upon a human deviation that we would disallow, or if it became troublesome, imprison." Thus, in Mead's opinion, deviation or abnormalcy is institutionalized.

The primitive Tibetan religion Bön (q.v.) has strong affinities to shamanism as defined by Eliade. Mystical ascents, such as by a steed, by ladders, ropes, etc., or descents, again by ladders or ropes, have parallels in such disparate elements as Muḥammad's ascent to paradise by the steed Burāq and the Zoroastrian girdle, the kustī, which symbolizes a descent by rope into a mystical cave. Whether or not these are remnants of earlier shamanistic beliefs cannot be determined now, but they probably come from primitive levels of the different religions that have been overlaid with more rational and elevating doctrines. Zoroastrianism has been charged with shamanism by the Swedish scholar H. S. Nyberg (*Die Religionen des Alten Iran,* Leipzig [1938]; German translation from the Swedish), who places Zoroaster (q.v.) firmly among the shamans, stating that the Prophet held the hereditary office of witch doctor and medicine man in the tribes of his area of Asia and was "shaman-in-chief." Other scholars do not accept this extremist point of view.

Shams of Tabriz (also Shams al-Dīn Tabriz, or Tabraiz), Ṣūfī. A mysterious figure, possibly "celestial," who initiated the Persian poet Jalāl al-Dīn Rūmī (thirteenth century A.D.) into the art of mystical dancing; as a result, Rūmī is credited with the founding of the Mawlawīya brotherhood of dervishes. Shams was also Rūmī's teacher. "Truly I say you are my teacher, my disciple, my pain and my cure, light in my heart and my God," said Rūmī, a phrase that—incorrectly—has been taken to mean that the disciple put Shams in place of Allāh. Shams—an "emissary from an unknown world"—stayed with Rūmī for three years, then disappeared, leaving no traces except for what he had deposited in Rūmī's mind and soul in the form of esoteric teaching. This Rūmī wrote out in the third of his great works, *Diwan Shamsh Tabraiz* (The Diwan [Secret Account] of Shams of Tabriz). Part of the *Diwan* consists of conversations between the two mystics, in which one or the other (or both) pass into transcendental ecstasy as the result of some saying or explanation. Other sections center on secret meetings of dervishes, with illustrative stories, anecdotes, and fables. In short, the *Diwan* is esoteric, initiatory, and technical, and like most Ṣūfic works is all too capable of misinterpretation by the uninitiated. See Rūmī, Ṣūfī.

sharī'a, Isl. Islamic law, which is nothing other than religious law. The term sharī'a originally meant "the path [or road] leading to the water"—i.e., a way to the original source of life. The verb shara'a is literally "to mark out a clear road to the water."

From the earliest period in Islam, sharī'a, as the "highway of good life," has connoted not only the spiritual but also all other aspects of man's existence, mental and physical, and above all, legal. Not only personal behavior but also juridical and social transactions are included in sharī'a, integrating the spiritual and the legal into a harmonious whole. The correlate of sharī'a is dīn (q.v.), the literal sense of which is submission or following.

The concept of law based on religious principles began in the first Islamic century (A.D. 700s), on the principle of Allāh—God —as the sovereign and the "Ordainer whose Will is Law." With the Qur'ān as his primary source and the Prophet Muḥammad as the most perfect commentator, man must discover, formulate, and execute that Will. During the time of the first four khalifs (q.v.), when Islamic society was still in a primitive, almost tribal form, administration of the government and the act of legislation were virtually founded on the same regulations and principles, being the joint work of the community or its elder members. When the khalifate was established at Damascus and became secularized, a separate body of jurisprudence began to develop, based in part on the Qur'ān and Sunnah (tradition), in part on the practice of local customs. However, the religious leaders at Medina (q.v.) began their own construction of Muslim law, which eventually, adjusting to local and regional needs, developed into sharī'a, law, and became the common law of Islamic governments from the end of the first Islamic century to the present.

Essentially, Islamic law is a secular application of religious principles. A law student in a Muslim country begins his schooling with a sound study of the Qur'ān. Actions, deriving from Qur'ānic principles, are ethically classified into five categories: obligatory, recommended, permissible or indifferent, reprehensible, and forbidden. Sharī'a is of a different type from Western jurisprudence, either Napoleonic or Anglo-Saxon. In it there is great leeway and understanding of the agent's "heart" (i.e., of his faith, intention, and will). His religious and moral states are considered in all circumstances. Most actions are examined in the light of a general principle known as the law of resoluteness ('azima) and relaxation (rukhsa). Such latitude of interpretation, one must note, lends itself both to leniency and compassion on one side, and to opportunities for false witnesses and corruption on the other.

Since, on the Day of Judgment, man is accountable to God in every thought, word, and deed, law cannot be an abstract entity, to be followed in relative purity and abstraction. It is an inquiry into the Will of Allāh: What does He want, and how is one to obey His Will? Theoretically, in court, men do not confront each other in a face-to-face opposition in an adversary attempt to arrive at abstract justice and truth but to resolve their differences in the light of God's Will. Sharī'a, as the embodiment of the unity and the ideology of Islam, sets the standard for human society. Thus law is not a convention of social jurisprudence but an obligation to obey a religious commandment.

shaykh (also shaik; sheik is incorrect), Isl. A spiritual master and teacher, with absolute authority over a Ṣūfī brotherhood in mundane and religious affairs alike. Equivalent words are pīr or murshīd in Iran, Pakistan, and India; the North African Arabic term muqaddam denotes a shaykh's deputy bearing his full powers. The disciples are known as murīds; other terms, depending on the area, may be faqīr, darwīsh, ikhwān (or khwān, brother), or aṣhāb (companion). Ṣūfism emphasizes the necessity of a spiritual guide. The famed al-Gazālī stated:

"The way of the faith is obscure, but the devil's ways are many and obvious, and he who has no shaykh to guide him will be led by the devil into his ways. Therefore the disciple must cling to his shaykh as a blind man on the edge of a river clings to his leader, confiding himself to him entirely, opposing him in no matter whatever, and binding himself to follow him absolutely. Let him know that the advantage he gains from the error of his shaykh, if he should err, is greater than the advantage he gains from his own rightness, if he should be right."

The center in which the shaykh resides and teaches is known as zāwiya (or zāwiyah), ribāṭ in the Arabic countries; khānkāh in Iran, Pakistan, and India; and tekke in Turkey. See Ṣūfī.

Shī'a, Isl. A major movement of Islam, second only to the more orthodox Sunnīs. The Shī'a, who include a vast number of sects, developed from an early controversy over the role of 'Ali, Muḥammad's cousin and son-in-law, the fourth khalif (see 'Ali for details of the schism). Sunnī scholars assert that the original break was purely political. Whatever the cause, the tragic fate of the house of 'Ali had tremendous appeal to the peoples of Iran (Persia), Iraq, Afghanistan, and western India (including present-day Pakistan). It might be noted that these areas were formerly Zoroastrian and Manichaean, and that many of the earlier doctrines have survived under a layer of Islam. The influences of the religion of Ahura Mazdā, as well as Manichaeism, are yet to be fully explored. Many themes related to Zoroastrianism are readily apparent in Shī'ism, among them that of the Hidden Imām (q.v.), the mysterious figure who will return as a kind of savior or redeemer; the Imām strongly resembles Prince Peshotan (q.v.), who plays a similar role in Zoroastrianism.

Shī'ism is divided into numerous subsects, many of which rely upon the Imām and other mystical figures for inspiration and leadership. Where Sunnī Islam is centered solely on Muḥammad as the culmination of Prophethood, the Shī'a go beyond to the imāms as sacred and esoteric leaders who work as agents of divine illumination and intervention. These imāms, usually sinless, are mediators between God and mankind. Some Shī'a sects count seven imāms only, others twelve. In most sects the seventh, or the twelfth, imām, the Hidden Imām, is still to come.

Broad generalizations are unfortunate but inescapable. Sunnī Islam may be described as more legalistic, scholastic, and formalistic, its doctrines being more easily codified and rationalized; its structure is more hierarchical. On the other hand, Shī'a Islam runs more to the spontaneous and emotional. Shī'ism, though descended from the Prophet Muḥammad, shows an even more intense devotion to the tragic house of 'Ali; the massacres of 'Ali, and his sons Ḥasan and Ḥusayn, are celebrated yearly with much pageantry, emotion, and mystical release, this among peoples whose daily lives are an epiphany of suffering and hopes for redemption.

Among the more notable Shī'a sects are the Twelver Shī'a, the largest, who believe that their last Imām, Muḥammad (b. A.D. 873), disappeared mysteriously but will return; the Ismā'īlīs (also called "Seveners" because that is the number of their imāms), who exhibit strong Zoroastrian influences; and the Hurifis, who have built an esoteric doctrine out of the letters and numbers of the alphabet. The Druses, found primarily in Lebanon, where they have been politically powerful, are a branch of the more orthodox Shī'as; they, too, await the return of a leader. The Persian movement founded by the Bāb (q.v.) arose in reaction to the power of the Shī'a mullahs of the Shakhī sect and their exploitation of the masses; Bābism was driven from Persia, becoming the movement known as Bahá'í, with many adherents in the United States.

Shin, Buddh. The Japanese term for the Pure Land form of Buddhism. It is based on veneration of the Amida Buddha (q.v.), and it practices the chant known as nembutsu (q.v.) as a means to salvation. See Pure Land.

Shingon, Buddh. A Japanese form of esoteric Buddhism, much favored by the nobility in feudal times. Shingon, derived from the Chinese tantric sect Chên Yen (or True Word), was brought to Japan by Kūkai, then aged thirty-two, in A.D. 806. Kūkai, a member of an aristocratic family that had been reduced to disgrace, was raised in a Japanese Confucian college, but then became a Buddhist monk at Mount Hiei. In an effort to find a unified Buddhism in place of the scattered forms encountered around Mount Hiei, he went to China to study, where he encountered Mantrayāna practices, a late form of Mahāyāna that emphasized the mystical use of mantras or prayer syllables. Unlike other types of Buddhism, which were based upon the Gautama Buddha either solely or as one of several buddhas, Kūkai's Shingon saw everything manifested in the Mahā-Vairocana Buddha (in Japanese, Dainichi), whose body comprises the entire cosmos, unlimited, without beginning or end, where mind and matter are inseparable —"two but not two." The Vairocana Buddha is the Illuminator, the essence of the universe in Shingon (he also plays a role in the Tendai sect as the Dharma Kāya, the self-being, self-existent Truth Body of the Buddha).

As a form of esoteric Buddhism, Shingon puts its emphasis on the transmission of the secrets of the cosmos by the word, the mantra, passed on orally from master to disciple. The inner knowledge is not written in books, where the uninitiate can read it. However, a great emphasis is placed on the use of painting so that the obscurities of the esoteric can be better understood. Kūkai himself was an excellent artist and an art patron. He stated: "The various attitudes and mudrās of the holy images all have their sources in Buddha's love, and one can attain buddhahood at sight of them. Thus the secrets of the sūtras and commentaries can be depicted in art, and the essential truths of esoteric teaching are all set forth in them. . . . Art is what reveals to us the state of perfection."

Shingon was seriously challenged by the Zen sects, but even today it is still one of the major forms of Japanese Buddhism, and has had much influence on Shintō (q.v.). See Kūkai.

Shinran (A.D. 1173–1263), Buddh. A disciple of Hōnen (q.v.), the founder of the Pure Land sect (q.v.) of Buddhism in Japan. Shinran went farther than his master in reducing Buddhism of complex forms, saying that scriptures and spiritual exercises were irrelevant. What counted was faith in the Amida Buddha, which could be expressed in the nembutsu (q.v.), the invocation of Amida—even a single sincere saying of the prayer was sufficient, rather than the ten Hōnen had predicated for salvation. Shinran's version of Hōnen's reform was known as Jōdō-Shinshu (The True Sect of the Pure Land); it became the most popular and largest Buddhist sect in Japan, and is still powerful. Shinran rejected celibacy (he had been a Buddhist priest) and monastic robes to follow an ordinary family life. He discouraged worship or veneration of other buddhas, even Gautama Buddha, who, he said, was but an instrument for the transmission of the true faith. Because he took a wife, Shinran was exiled into a remote area, where he lived as a social outcaste, but actively proselytizing among the common people in his fugitive existence. See Amida Buddha, Hōnen, Pure Land.

Shintō. The traditional, primordial Japanese religion. Shintō means literally "the way of the gods," but the term was not applied until the sixth century A.D., when it was necessary to distinguish the ancient faith from encroaching Buddhism. Originally Shintō was a crude and vibrant polytheism, without written records or written literature, with no codified laws, no traditions of philosophical inquiry, and only a rough experience in the arts and sciences. The primitive belief stated that all perceptible objects were in some way alive, inhabited by either good or evil spirits. The first chronicles to be composed speak of waterways, vegetation, and stones that could talk; however, to label this a simple animism falsifies the point. The much-celebrated Japanese appreciation of nature—an unusual rock, a twisted tree, a few scattered leaves, an expanse of white sand highlighted by a fringe of pines, snow falling gently in the distance—can certainly be traced back to early Shintō. The vivification of the inanimate and the vegetative is more than superstition. Later the original nature deities were developed into a complex, institutional religion, with a priesthood, shrines, and monasteries, all embodying the cult of the Emperor (and the nation) as the son of the great Sun Goddess Ama-terasu-ō-mi-kami (literally, Heavenly Shining Great Deity).

The earliest accounts of Shintō are found in various Chinese chronicles of the eighth century A.D. and later, which mention three different types of "priests," one a group later called the Imibe, whose responsibility was to ensure the ritual purity of people and objects connected with religious rites. (Purity and the fear and avoidance of pollution were early features of Shintō, and continue to be basic to the present; what is repulsive is not so much a violation of the moral law but of rite and ceremony.) A second group, the Nakatomi family, who had the power of communicating with the gods on behalf of the ruler, performed the liturgies and the ceremonies. The third group was the Urabe, who were diviners; they employed traditional methods of their age to seek out on behalf of the ruler either anticipation or interpretation of events. These three groups, sometimes called "corporations" in translation, had the exclusive privilege of dealing directly with the gods. There was also a priestly caste, men who lived as laymen (usually as state officials) who discharged various religious duties. They had no special training or background other than the maintenance of a prescribed level of ritual purity attained by bathing, fasting, and related practices.

The history of Shintō falls into four major stages, the first being the archaic, which runs from the prehistoric age to the introduction of Buddhism into Japan in A.D. 552. Much of this early period can only be surmised, for not only was there no special name for the ancient system of belief, but also no scriptures or other documents except what was passed on by oral tradition, and very little archaeological evidence. What has survived are some great burial mounds of the princes, numerous haniwa (figures of clay possibly meant as substitutions for early human sacrifices), many clay models of shrines (and of houses), a few mirrors, bells, and other implements. The earliest Shintō teachings, as reported by the Chinese, pictured the universe as being neither friendly nor hostile; divinity was manifest in everything, and there was belief in the concept of the soul, which existed in two parts; One, nigi-mitama, was mild-mannered, cheerful, and linked with health and prosperity; the other, ara-mitama, was the opposite, sometimes associated with evil, and was adventurous and impetuous. The soul was a substance, a pale ball of fire that might be discerned in the darkness after death. Sometimes the soul remained nearby. In any event, it became a spirit, divinity, or god known as kami, a term that was used for anything divine, no matter of what stature. The chronicles indicate that there were no standard sets of beliefs, for the indigenous religion comprised a number of varied cults in different parts of the archipelago and among different tribes and clans.

It is not until the second phase, when Shintō and Buddhism met head on, that more precise information is known about the local cults. However, at this time, the indigenous faith was being interpreted in terms of Chinese thought and culture and was heavily influenced by foreign ideas, not only Buddhist but Confucianist as well; and both Chinese and Koreans were flocking to Japan in large numbers, bringing monks and mystics along with businessmen, soldiers, and numerous craftsmen, who imposed not only alien ways but also alien religious concepts upon the Japanese. Buddhism swallowed Shintō whole, to become the islands' dominant religious power. Shintō had no philosophy to support itself, and no organization. It could awaken to its own consciousness only many centuries later after its contact with Buddhism, and only then learn to express itself. In the first centuries of the Buddhist invasion, Shintō deities were identified with Buddhist gods and doctrines, and buddhas were eventually established in the Shintō shrines themselves. The Buddhists could now claim that Shintō was but a primitive form of Buddhism. Even the Emperor, who owed direct allegiance to the Sun Goddess at the shrine of Ise (q.v.), was forced to compromise with Buddhism.

This assault on Shintō lasted through the ninth century. Shintō then went into a further decline, largely political in cause, due to the hostility of the shōguns ("throne field marshals"), the military dictators who opposed the royal family. During the great feudal period, the twelfth through the mid-nineteenth centuries, when the shōguns ruled, the Emperor's person remained sanctified. Under the feudal Tokugawa rule (1600–1867), Shintō was combined with Confucian beliefs to assert the role of the Emperor as a form of divine father of his nation, reaffirming his descent in an unbroken line from divine ancestors traceable back to the Sun Goddess Ama-terasu.

The revival of Shintō came in 1868, when some of the samurai Tokugawa, aided by a few court nobles and wealthy merchants, shifted their allegiance from the shōguns to the Emperor, forcing the resignation of the current and last dictator, Yoshinobu. With the Emperor as the fixed point of worship and of political authority, both the state and Shintōism, in a religiopolitical dialectic, strengthened each other, while forcing Buddhism into a minor role. It was the latter's turn to be persecuted. Shintō was now the official embodiment of the national spirit of Japan, a role it maintained until Emperor Hirohito publically renounced his divinity in his New Year's message of 1946. However, the average believing Shintōist saw this gesture as having little significance except to appease the occupying enemy.

DOCTRINE AND PRACTICES. Reflecting an undeveloped civilization, Shintō did not possess sacred scriptures (nor epics or folklore) in written form until the introduction of Chinese script in the very early eighth century A.D. Up to this time almost everything had been transmitted orally. The few exceptions were some provincial records c. A.D. 403, the "Constitution" (604) of the Buddhist Emperor Shotoku Taishi ("Sage-virtue"), which promotes

Buddhism, some commentaries on the Buddhist scriptures from the same period, the code of laws of the Omi (the royal clan), and some short documents on stone and bronze. Virtually all of this material is Buddhist, of Chinese origin or inspiration, and not Shintō. In 712 the ancient mythological and historical traditions of Japan were compiled into the *Kojiki* (Record of Ancient Things) and the *Nihon-shoki* (Chronicles of Japan, also called the *Nihongi*), the latter work being written in Chinese; in fact, both were written, or compiled, under mainland influence, and whatever either work says about Japan must be considered in the light of its Chinese (and Korean) influences. Also, both works were produced to strengthen the rule of the reigning clans of Yamoto in southeastern Japan and to glorify the ruling family and its ancestors.

The *Nihon-shoki* combines two independent themes, entwining them into a single strand. One, clearly of Chinese origin, is cosmogonic, and delineates the creation of Heaven and Earth from an egg-shaped chaotic mass, the sky coming from the finer parts and the Earth from the coarser. The second theme, a theogonic account, which strongly resembles Polynesian legends of the creation, tells of the birth of gods—seven generations in all, ending with the two who are the central figures in Shintō, Izangi and his wife Izanami, the male who invites and the female who invites. Ordered by the celestial deities, they descended to earth to produce the terrestrial world, beginning with the islands of Japan, then the forms of nature, the waters, winds, mountains, fields, food, fire, and mist, culminating in the rulers of the world, chief of whom was the Sun Goddess Ama-terasu-ō-mi-kami, who produced the rice fields, the canals to irrigate them, and who organized the rituals, especially those dealing with purity. From her eventually came the ruling family of Japan.

The *Kojiki* version, somewhat different, states that, standing on the "floating bridge of Heaven" (possibly a rainbow), Izangi and Izanami stirred the formless mass with a jeweled spear (taken to be a phallic symbol), from the point of which the mass dropped to form an island. The two gods descended to earth to be married; they procreated the eight other islands of Japan, and a series of deities, among them Ama-terasu. Her grandson, Ninigi-no-Mikoto, received from her the symbols of the Empire, the mirror, sword, and jewels still used as the royal insignia. In B.C. 660, states the *Kojiki* anachronistically, one of his descendants, Jimmu-Tenno, the first human Emperor (his name means "Emperor of the Godly Warriors"), led his tribe into Yamato to found the first ruling dynasty. This founding of the Japanese Empire—on February 11, B.C. 660 (actually sometime in the seventh century A.D.)—places the mundane squarely in the center of the cosmic.

The scriptures contain a mixture of Chinese elements and primitive and even shamanistic characteristics—e.g., when the brother of the Sun Goddess insulted her, one such denigrating act was the flaying of a "heavenly piebald colt," an ancient shamanistic practice in which the shaman dons the skin and dances in it. There are references in the Chronicles to phallic worship, and there are numerous records of festivals and ceremonies of phallic gods; phallic stones have been found in ancient sites, and even today such stones are set up on the edges of rice fields to encourage fertility.

Early in the tenth century A.D. a large number of religious and state rituals were written down; the most famous of these collections is the *Engishiki* (Ceremonies of Engi), containing fifty volumes; its eighth book, the *Norito,* contains twenty-seven basic liturgical texts still in use. Though these texts were meant to contain the most ancient prayers and petitions to the gods, they were probably composed about the seventh century, and were heavily rewritten by the editors in being committed to written form. They have been criticized by foreign experts (cf. G. B. Sansom, *Japan, A Short Cultural History*) for being "rather poorly articulated" and of having, as a chief characteristic of style, a "solemn pleonasm as in the phrase, 'in the myriad ways of the tides of the raging sea and the myriad meeting places of the tides of the myriad sea paths.'" (The Japanese, in Roman characters, reads, "Ara-shio no shio no yaoji no yashioji no shio no yaoai.") It may be, however, that such faults are due to the fact that we are now reading what was meant to be chanted, words that have been filtered through at least two other alien cultures, Chinese-Buddhist and Western, seriously distorting the original in its optimistic world of spirits and nature, celebrating the beauties of life and the bounty of the divine.

Whatever, the gods are everywhere. The Sun Goddess and her

retinue are not the only deities in the cosmic sphere; there are also countless spirits (the actual number differs), called, like even the highest divinities, kami, a word originally meaning "upper." The kami include deities such as those of the moon, the storm, the sea, fire, food, and rice, to name but a few; there are also many minor kami, among them even some for the parts of a house—the door, kitchen, hearth, privy, and so on. New kami are added from time to time; twelve Emperors are also honored as deities, along with some statesmen and generals.

Worship of the gods involves varied rites, among them offerings of rice and sake (rice wine); sacrifices of animals and humans have long since been abandoned, and in the rituals of offering horses and clothing to the gods, effigies are now used. Worship may take place in a private home (the ancient site), or originate in the home and be completed in a shrine, the miya (ya [house] with the honorific mi-). Japan is profuse with miya, which in most cases have not evolved much beyond that of the ancient type of house; they are most often nothing but simple wooden buildings consisting of a prayer hall and a central hall. Originally, in the most primitive times, worship seemed to have been conducted in the open before whatever rocks, trees, or bodies of water, or even the sun, contained the presence of the god. Today worship is conducted by the priest inside the miya, with the devotees standing outside. Much secrecy surrounds Shintō. The members do not see the cult object of the shrine, which is hidden by a curtain. The god-body, the shintai, resides in the object, which may be a mirror, sword, or even a pillow; even in public processions the object is concealed. Originally worship consisted of obeisance, various offerings, prayer, and petitions. Later there developed the gohei, an object consisting of strips of cloth attached to a stick and placed upon the altar; the gohei came to be considered as sanctified in itself and to contain the deity mystically descended. Gohei may be taken home by the faithful. A similar object, the nusa, made of strips of paper and hemp fiber tied to a straw rope, all cut in a prescribed manner, may be hung from the ceiling in a house. Both gohei and nusa confer a special sanctity upon whatever place they may be enshrined.

Some Shintō shrines claim certain animals as "messengers." At the great holy mountain of Hiei, near Kyoto, this honor belongs to the monkey; caged monkeys are seen at the Shintō shrines there, and under the eaves of buildings are carved monkeys. The fox, a symbol of the god of agriculture, Inari ("Rice Man"), is also kept at temples, either alive, or as a statue. Such animals may be the relics of an ancient totemic cult.

After the restoration of the Emperor in 1868 (the Meiji Restoration), Shintō became the official state cult. Although it had always been able to survive in the court, where it played a psychologically important role in keeping alive belief in the Emperor as the intermediary between the people and the ancestral gods, Shintō took on new life when the shōguns were forced into the background and the power of Buddhism was broken. The princely emphasis on Shintō has gradually divorced the cult from many of its primitive sources, turning it into an official system of rites and ceremonies, many borrowed from Buddhism. Even much Shintō philosophy has been taken from its rival. Efforts have been made to separate the two faiths, but they tend to meld together despite the most rigorous attempts at purification. Today a number of minor Shintō cults have developed, partly in reaction to the Buddhist elements in Shintō. They stress different aspects of Shintō and other religions, some trying to return to ancient sources, others uniting nationalistic concepts. Some sects preach a single God, others a trinity, while still others, influenced by Zen (q.v.), now emphasize such practices as yoga and faith healing. Attempts by the government census office to separate Shintōists from Buddhists have failed, for the majority of Japanese claim allegiance to both Ways.

Shiva (or Śiva), Hind. One of the major gods of Hinduism and the center of numerous devotional cults, the Shaivites. Shiva is one of the triad that includes Brahmā and Vishnu (see both), and his worship, under many names, is primary in Hinduism. Of his past, little is known except by conjecture. He was not one of the gods of the conquering Āryans of the Vedas (q.v.), though Rudra, a member of the Vedic pantheon, became identified as another aspect of Shiva, but belongs to the earliest strata of prehistoric India, gradually being assimilated into the brāhminical structure. In the fullest sense he is a deity of the people, of the common fold, at first excluded from the aristocratic Āryan conquerors. Representations of a god who appears identical to Shiva have been found in the cities of the Indus Valley (q.v.), especially in stamp seals, where he is shown three-faced and seated in the lotus position of meditation, surrounded by animals, wearing what may be a headdress of horns. In these small representations he appears lean and ascetic, his body marked with painted stripes and his arms extended over his knees.

Because the horns of his headdress resemble those of a buffalo, he has been linked with the buffalo god later known as Mhasobā, the deity of primitive pastoral tribes who, though most commonly found in the South, wandered all over the subcontinent. The buffalo god was in conflict with an Earth Mother, the goddess of rival food-gathering (agricultural) people; eventually the two are found linked as male and female, the forerunners, it is presumed, of the Shiva and Shakti (or Shiva-Pārvatī, Shiva-Durgā, etc.) of more historic times. Shiva is also the god of various goblins and demons, minor deities inherited from primitive ages, and is closely identified with various animals, not only his famous bull Nandī (a bull alone is another motif of the Indus stamp seals) but also a sacred cobra and the elephant god Gaṇpati or Gaṇeśa, his son; he is sometimes clad in a tiger skin or is accompanied by a deer. All of these animals are possibly totemic remnants that have coalesced around the god. Over the millennia innumerable local gods have become absorbed into his more powerful cult or have been identified as aspects of him. He has 1,008 names (108 in some recensions), which are but manifestations of his accreted powers, thus leading to one of his names as Mahādeva or Maheśvara (the Great God).

In the Vedas (q.v.) the word śiva means auspicious and is employed only to describe the Vedic deity Rudra, the epithet later replacing the name of Rudra, with whom Shiva was identified. By the time of the post-Vedic period (after A.D. 300, Shiva appears frequently in the various scriptures, especially the Purāṇas and Āgamas (see both). He stands fully in his own right, the beliefs of the common people having been absorbed by brāhminism and given an orthodox stamp of approval. There are six Shaivite Purāṇas alone; the majority of the others contain a number of stories about Shiva. Certain of the Purāṇas read as if they were summaries in the brāhminical Sanskrit of traditional beliefs expressed in a fuller form in the popular languages. A "Dravidian" (q.v.) tongue is the supposed origin of these stories, many of which are even now passed on orally or in the sacred literature of the Shaivite sects and still have escaped study by both Hindu and foreign scholars.

More than any other aspect of Hinduism, Shaivism stresses yoga as a method that forms a basis of spiritual progress and the attainment of liberation, for it embodies, it has been noted, "the strange and profound teachings of the most ancient cosmology," teachings still followed by many of the ordinary, unheard peoples of the subcontinent. See Hinduism; also see Indus Valley, Shakti.

Short Path, Tib. A direct method of attaining liberation in the present life instead of experiencing the long round of births and rebirths. Tibetan Buddhists say it is a way "to attain Buddhahood in one life, in one body." It is a most hazardous path, like scaling a Himālayan peak straight up the face rather than following the natural trails and paths to the summit. Failure can mean a spiritual fall to the status of a demon. The Short Path is considered in part to be pre-Buddhist, drawing upon the teachings of the hoary past from central and northern Asia. For the insider, there are probably shamanistic aspects. The Path is bound only by the sketchiest of disciplinary rules, and the adept experiments as he will, even in fear and trepidation at his own courage in the ascent. A brief initiation from a guru, who gives the adept a mantra (q.v.) and some general directions, is all the training normally encountered.

The general framework includes three broad principles: (1) to look and examine; (2) to think and meditate; (3) to practice what has been learned and to realize. Some gurus offer another version in three stages: the first, in two parts, consists of a study of the nature, origin, end, and the causes upon which they depend, of things, and the study of various doctrines; the second stage, thinking and meditating upon what has been learned with introspective meditation; and the third stage, understanding and realization of the earlier stages. Whatever the method, the adept must withdraw from the world and live within a certain area, often enclosed, such as a cave or a house with high exterior walls around its courtyard. For the advanced mystic the physical barrier or border is psychic rather than literal. In most cases the adept sees no one directly, giving interviews through a screen or door; his meals are left on his threshold by his servant. Some mystics live in complete darkness, their light being the luminosity produced by their ascetic practices. Most adepts enter such strict seclusion for a short period, perhaps only a month; a few for life. A common term is three years, three months, and three days.

shruti, Hind. The anglicized spelling of śruti (q.v.).

siddhi, Hind. Literally "perfection," siddhi is an occult power gained through the mastery of the higher stages of yoga (q.v.). The siddha, the person who has the power of siddhi, possesses eight magic powers, according to classical yoga. These are: (1) atomization (the yogi becomes "atomic"); (2) levitation (the yogi is not bound by gravity); (3) magnification (the yogi can become any height he desires); (4) extension (the yogi can touch the moon with his fingertip); (5) efficacy (the yogi can pass through solid matter); (6) mastery (the yogi has control of the elements and is not controlled by them); (7) sovereignty (the yogi is master of all production and arrangement of material things); and (8) the capacity to will (the yogi can make all elements do as he wishes).

In more specific terms, the yogi is not only able to control all his bodily functions (even the nonvoluntary ones, like pulse, digestion, and breath), but also can read minds, engage in astral traveling, walk on water, bilocate, predict the future, make objects move without touching them, and so on. These immense powers are not used by the more responsible class of yogis, who state that siddhis are distractions, not aids, in the upward ascent of the self to the Self. Others find them valuable tools in dealing with the public. Scientific experiments under controlled conditions, in New Delhi, Bombay, the Menninger Clinic at Topeka, and elsewhere, have determined that yogis do indeed possess certain siddhis, notably those concerned with bodily functions, such as heart rate, body temperature, and the ability to put the mind into a state defying interpretation by instruments. However, some "yogis" are reduced to such "siddhis" as pulling watches from a disciple's ear, mysteriously filling jars with Ganges water, and making scents appear; the man known as Siddhi Sai Baba (cf. Sai Baba [2]) is such a person. See yoga.

Sikhs, Sikhism. A syncretist religious movement founded in the Panjab in western India by Guru Nānak (1469–1538), based in part upon the bhakti sects of the Hindus (especially that of the bhakti mystic Kabīr) and partly upon Ṣūfism. Nānak sought to winnow out the excesses of Hinduism, and heavily influenced by the monotheism of Islam, concentrated on an understanding of the One God whose Being is beyond understanding and knowing but whose glory is manifest in His creation. His followers are known as Sikhs, the term being derived from the Sanskrit siśya (disciple), and follow not only Nānak but also nine succeeding Gurus as teacher-leaders and the last Guru, the sacred scripture called the Granth Sāheb.

Nānak was born of fairly well-off parents of the kśatriya (warrior) caste of Hindus, near the city of Lahore in the Panjab. There are many accounts of his life, stressing his unusual piety even from childhood. Part of the material is of doubtful value, and the accuracy of some events is now impossible to establish. After an ecstatic vision while meditating in a forest, during which he had a vision of God receiving the Japji with the seed prayer (Mūl Mantra) that forms the basis of Sikh belief, Nānak gave away to the poor all that he possessed and took up the life of a wandering holy man. Nānak taught that there was only one God, and opposed the idolatry of Hinduism. He rejected the caste system, and much of Hindu social and religious belief, including that of avatār, or divine descent, though at Baghdad he announced, "I have appeared in this age to indicate the way unto men. I reject all sects and only know one God whom I recognize on the earth, in the heavens and in all directions." His teaching was simple and direct, and in the tradition of the intense personal devotion of both the Hindu bhaktis and the Ṣūfīs. This utter simplicity and directness attracted a large following, especially among the Panjabis. Six months before he died, Nānak chose as his successor a disciple rather than one of his own sons. This was Lena (1504–52), whose name Nānak changed to Aṅgad, which means "part of his own self." This move established the mystical descent of the Sikh Gurus as divine or nearly so, though the Hindu concept of avatār as God incarnate on earth to aid mankind was a doctrine that the Gurus rejected.

The Granth Sāheb states that through Aṅgad, "Nānak himself reigns as Guru," and the entire line of leaders referred to themselves as Nānak, "as one lamp lit from another." The official formula is "All ten Gurus are revelations of one light and one form." Aṅgad assembled Nānak's various prayers and other texts; these were composed in Panjabi and written in a script called Gurumukhi ("from the Guru's mouth"), which he had devised from the traditional Sanskrit Devanagari. Gurumukhi is still the standard alphabet for Sikhs and Panjabis. Aṅgad also established centers for disseminating Nānak's teachings. The third Guru, Amar Dās (1479–1574), was elected at the age of seventy-three; he adapted Hindu festivals and rituals for the Sikhs, and further lessened the bonds of caste by establishing the free common kitchen (called the langar). His son-in-law Rām Dās (1534–81) was chosen Guru in 1574. He is noted for establishing the Golden Temple (Harimandira or Darbār Sāheb) at the Pond of Amritsar; the city was named Rāmdāspur after him, but eventually came to be known as Amritsar and is the central Sikh shrine. Rām Dās was a friend of the eclectically religious Akbar, Emperor of central India. From Rām Dās onward the line of succession went directly through the Guru's sons, his youngest, Arjun (1563–1606), assuming the leadership of the community at the age of eighteen. Guru Arjun stands as one of the greatest of the ten. He assembled and edited the vast collection of writings the Sikhs were using in their worship, not only Nānak's but also many others, including those of the weaver Kabīr, the shoemaker Ravidās, the barber Saina, and others of various castes, plus some Muslims. The collection, the Granth Sāheb (Noble Book), sometimes Ādi-Granth (First Book), included works not only in Gurumukhi but also in five other languages; it was published in 1604. Arjun's numerous proselytizing and organizing activities plus his aggressive attitudes toward Muslims led him into conflict with the Mogul Emperor Jahangir, a repressive and intolerant ruler who had murdered the noted Islamic theologian Abū'l Fazl in 1602. Jahangir had Arjun tortured to death in Lahore in 1606. At this point, with the accession of Arjun's son Har Govind (1595–1645), the guruship was to pass directly through the male line of descent. And the Sikhs, in reaction to the attempts to repress them, became a militant, crusading, anti-Muslim brotherhood. Though he was only eleven when he became Guru, Har Govind organized his people into an army. Armed clashes with the Muslims in India now became a matter of course, the Sikhs becoming noted for their military skills and foolhardy, almost insane bravery in battle. To symbolize the two aspects of his leadership, spiritual (faqīrī) and secular (amīrī), the Guru was now to wear two swords.

The next two Gurus also assumed the leadership at early ages. Har Rāi (1630–61) was only fifteen when he became Guru; his major contribution was military, and he was involved with severe clashes with the Mogul Aurangzeb. Har Krishan (1656–64) became Guru at the age of five and tragically died at eight, his promise unfulfilled. The leadership of the Sikhs now passed to Tegh Bahādur (1621–75), who inherited the endless wars with the Moguls. He was captured by Aurangzeb's forces and beheaded at Delhi, leaving young Govind Singh (1666–1708), then only nine, to assume guruship. Govind Singh was the tenth Guru, and after Nānak, the most famous. He was highly educated in secular, martial, and religious arts. Govind Singh revised or reformed Sikh rites and announced the great step that ended the line of Gurus and made the Granth Sāheb the Supreme Guru, the eternal Guru in whom all authority was inherent for all times in the future. Henceforth, also, a majority decision by the representatives of the entire community (the Panth) was binding on everyone.

Govind Singh's innovations were wide-ranging and unusual. He effected the final separation of the Sikhs from both Hindus and Muslims in a special rite on the Hindu New Year's Day of 1699 when he initiated his five closest favorite disciples, the Panj Pyārās (the Five Beloved Ones), and in turn was initiated by them. All drank sweetened water (amṛt) stirred by a double-edged dagger from the same communal bowl. This destroyed the last vestiges of caste among the Sikhs (those assembled were a brāhmin, a kśatriya, and three low-caste men), since it was not lawful for orthodox Hindus of different castes to drink from the same vessel without incurring pollution. Thus both caste and social distinctions were formally abolished. The rite also included the taking of new names: The suffix Singh (lion) was obligatory for all Sikhs (women are called Kaur [princess]), and the adoption of the five K's—unshorn hair and beard (keś), a comb in the hair (kaṅgh), a steel bangle on the right wrist (karā), short drawers (kacch), and a sword (kirpān). Hair was to be worn uncut (it is tied in a knot on the top of the head and covered with a turban); unshorn hair put the Sikhs into the category of Indian holy men such as sādhus and sannyāsis. This was one of the four rules of conduct (rahat), the others being prohibitions against alcohol and tobacco, against meat slaughtered in certain forbidden methods, and against sexual relations with Muslim women.

Sikhs who adhere to the Five K's and the four rules of conduct are known as khālsā (pure). Theirs is the ideal of the warrior-saint, fearless in battle for the protection of the community and devoted to God—mystics ready to fight like lions. Govind Singh's own writings, the *Daśam Granth* (Book of the Tenth Guru), is primarily an exhortation to saintly battle, drawn upon the great Hindu epics and the Purāṇas, with their stories of great wars, war-gods, and noble heroes. "When all other means have failed, it is righteous to draw the sword," said Govind Singh. "Light your understanding as a lamp and sweep away the filth of timidity." As the epitome of the warrior mystic himself, he had succeeded in effecting the final transformation of the peaceful farmers of the Panjab—"training the sparrow to hunt the hawk," in his famous phrase, "and one man to fight a legion." But not all the people of the Panjab were ready to go to such extremes. Those who followed the teachings of the Granth Sāheb without accepting either the casteless proscriptions of the initiation rite or the Five K's are not considered fully Sikhs, being known as Sahajdhāris (or Easy-goers), as opposed to the Keśadhāris (or Hair Wearers). And though caste had been regularly rejected—"Let no man be proud of his caste," says the Granth Sāheb, "One God created all men; All men were molded of the same clay; The Great Potter hath merely varied the shapes of them"—caste still remains among Sikhs of all types, though in a less precise form. And Hindu rites and rituals, gods and religious concepts have either never been fully extirpated, or have returned in the centuries since Govind Singh's death.

DOCTRINES. Ideally, Sikhism teaches and preaches a strong monotheism. "There is one God, Eternal Truth is his name," said Nānak in his famous Japji, the basic formula of Sikh beliefs. In the oneness of God is the fellowship of man. All the Gurus declare that the aim and end of life is not to attain a heavenly abode but to develop the Essence that is in man and thus merge himself in God. God is described as both personal (sagun) and absolute (nirgun).

Unlike the Hindu doctrine of avatār, God does not incarnate himself, not even in the Gurus, sanctified as they nearly were. "He lives in everything, He dwells in every heart. Yet He is not merged with anything. He is separate, He lives in all, yet is ever distinct. He abides with thee, too. As fragrance dwells in a flower or reflection in a mirror, so does God dwell inside everything; seek Him therefore in the heart."

The Sikh scriptures constantly emphasize that the repetition of the Name is the first step in spiritual progress and an invaluable intermediary. "He is the Indescribable, the Formless One," a concept found in the bhaktis whether Hindu or Ṣūfī. Tulasī Dās had said, "The Name acts as an interpreter between the material and immaterial forms of the deity and is a guide and interpreter to both." The Sikh Scriptures say, "Remember God and banish neglect of Him from thy heart. Accursed [is] the life of him in the world who breathes without uttering the Name." "He who is dyed with God's praises never loves the world and loses his life in the game. To realize Him is very simple. Make thy body the field, good works the seed, irrigate with God's name. Make the heart the cultivator. God will germinate in thy heart and thou shalt thus obtain the dignity and reward of Nirvan."

In Nirvan (or nirvāṇa), a concept borrowed directly from orthodox Hinduism, the light of the soul is merged with the light of God. The traditional Hindu belief in rebirth until past misdeeds and evil acts are purified through countless transmigrations is basic, but to it is joined the Muslim concept of God's absolute domination. "According to the seed we sow is the fruit we reap. By the will of God, O Nānak, man must either be saved or endure new births," etc. Nirvāṇa comes when "through the grace of the Guru a man dies to self and is born to new understanding, then the soul is free from its soiling and is not born again." A number of Hindu deities appear in the Granth Sāheb, among them Brahmā, Vishnu, and Shiva, but their role is only to serve and bear witness to the Formless and Transcendent One.

See also Amritsar, Granth Sāheb, Nānak. Many of the Sikh scriptures have been collected and published in *Selections from the Sacred Writings of the Sikhs,* UNESCO (1960), though some of the translations bear signs of European concepts and influences.

sirāh, (also sīrat) Isl. A biography of the Prophet Muḥammad. The first sirāhs date from the second Islamic century and are based upon previously written (but lost) material, verbal accounts, and the Qur'ān. The earlier sirāhs are the most reliable, the latter being embellished with much fanciful narrative and speculation. See Muḥammad.

Sīrat-ar-Rasūl, Isl. A famous ninth-century A.D. biography of Muḥammad by Ibn Hisham (d. A.D. 834), the oldest and known as the best of the early hagiographical accounts. It draws upon a great lost work, widely known, of Ibn Ishaq. See Muḥammad.

Śiva, Hind. The Sanskrit form of the more common Shiva (q.v.).

Six Doctrines, The, Tib. A Buddhist treatise concerning the practical application of various forms of yoga. Much of the work deals with the practices dealt with in the *Bardo Thödol* (q.v.).

Six Pāramitās, Buddh. These are methods of attaining enlightenment, and are, respectively, charity, discipline, patience or endurance, zeal and progress, meditation, and wisdom. They conform roughly to the eight steps of traditional Indian yoga (q.v.), modified for conditions in other countries, especially China, where these steps were popular.

Six Tattvic Centers, Hind. A group of dynamic, mystical focal points (also called cakras), ascending from the pelvic area to the forehead, which are aroused during tantric meditation. See cakras.

sleep, position during. In both Buddhism and Islam, virtually the same position during sleep is recommended on the basis that it was practiced by the founder (i.e., Gautama Buddha and Muḥammad). The Buddhists call the position the Lion Posture—that followed by the Lord Buddha as he prepared to enter nirvāṇa—lying on the right side, with the head resting on the right hand. Captain Sir Richard Francis Burton describes the Islamic custom as follows: "Sleeping like the Prophet, namely, in early night (when prayer hour is distant), with 'Iftirash,' or lying at length with the right cheek on the palm of the dexter hand; and near dawn with 'Ittaka,' i.e., propping the head upon the hand, with the arm resting upon the elbow." In both sects the faithful are enjoined to follow the custom of the founder.

smirti, Hind. The anglicized spelling of smṛti (q.v.).

smṛti, Hind. The type of Hindu text that is not revealed (śruti [q.v.]) but "recollected"—i.e., texts that have a human rather than divine origin. Smṛti depends on śruti, which is earlier and superior. The smṛti period begins roughly about B.C. 600 and continues to the present, comprising all religious works that recognize the Vedas (q.v.) as final authority. Among such classic examples would be the Rāmāyaṇa, the Mahābhārata, and the Purāṇas. Smṛti is fallible because the intermediary who transmits the divine truth to the world is fallible. Smṛti is divided into six categories, known as the six Vedāṇgas, or Limbs of the Vedas. They are: kalpa (ceremonies), śiksā (phonetics), chandas (prosody), vyākaraṇa (grammar), nirukta (etymology), and jyotiṣa (astronomy). See Hinduism.

snake and the rope, Hind. A common image in Indian philosophy, that of a rope being mistaken for a serpent in dim light, the one idea being superimposed over the other, this being an example of māyā or illusion. Under such circumstances, in the dim light of ignorance, man takes the manifested, illusionary world to be real.

Sōka-gakkai, Buddh. A Japanese sect founded upon the teachings of the *Lotus Sūtra* (q.v.) and the Buddhist saint Nichiren (q.v.). Sōka-gakkai means Society for the Creation of Values. It arose out of the need to adjust to the problems caused by Japan's losing World War II. The founder, Toda, stated that whether men wished to recognize the fact or not, all nations and all social classes are now mutually dependent on each other; and every person has the identical responsibility: to be a bodhisattva (a buddha to be) for the salvation not only of his fellow but also for the world. Defeated and humiliated in a world war, Japan now has the role of waging a struggle for world peace and happiness, a struggle realized by the "wonderful truth of the *Lotus Sūtra*."

From a few hundred followers, Sōka-gakkai has grown to well over five million, with tens of thousands of converts every year. The sect is militantly missionary, and, fired with the example of Nichiren, who suffered much persecution for his beliefs, its members are willing to endure hardship and hard work in order to help every person attain his own Buddha-self.

Soma, Hind. A Vedic god, plant offering, and beverage. In the Vedic texts the sacred, deified substance Soma is paired with Agni (q.v.), fire, the devouring principle. Both are major divinities in the early stages of Hinduism but dropped to a lower rank after the emergence of Vishnu, Shiva, Shakti, and Krishna in later centuries. In the Rig Veda more hymns—120—are addressed to Soma in his various forms than to any other figure. Soma is that which is offered, is food, the food of the universe, the drink that leads to immortality, a beverage, the beverage of the gods, the divine nectar, is semen, the essence of life, is the Moon. In the Rig Veda the doughty warrior-god Indra quaffs hug quantities of Soma both for his uproarious pleasure and for the strength it gives him in slaughtering his enemies.

In the Vedic period this divine substance was consumed by the priests in ceremonies similar to those practiced in Iran, where it was known as hoama (q.v.). Soma produced a state that raised man to union with the divine, a state that, from the texts (read in a contemporary context), was clearly psychotropic. The priests, the only ones privileged to partake of Soma, linked it to the heavenly forces emanating from the Sun, who was also a god. "Soma is your share, accompanied by the rays that are His in common with the Sun," says the Rig Veda, and "Purify yourself with this stream with which thou [Soma] has made the sun to shine," etc. As a sacred drink soma possessed powers of a wonderful and awesome nature; as the food of the gods it had the character of sanctity; the deities' most beloved nourishment raised man to a vibrant state of divine ecstasy.

From the texts it appeared that soma was a plant that grew in the mountains alone; it was leafless, branchless, and had a heavy stalk. It was prepared by crushing the stem; the juice was mixed with ghee, milk, or yogurt. Soma was the equal of gold in color, or a morning yellow, or the color of fire, the red of the morning, and so on. Whatever the plant was, it was an unusual one. As the Āryans moved farther from the lowlands of the mountains in northwestern India into the burning plains of India, it became increasingly difficult to obtain the substance that was turned into soma. At some point the priesthood seemed to have decided on a separation of soma into its ritual consumption and its psychotropic effects. Other, nonhallucinogenic plants were substituted in the rituals for soma, and at the same time the priests turned to a psychospiritual technique that, followed to its end, produced another form of mind-elevating experience. The technique was yoga and the end was samādhi, union with the Divine Self.

The history of soma and its substitutes was of no interest among Hindus, and it was not until the early nineteenth century, when Europeans were beginning to study the sacred books of the East, that the question of its identity came up. The search for the original substance became almost an obsession with some foreign scholars, and various suggestions for the Vedic soma were made —*cannibis indica* or its derivative hashish, Afghan grapes, honey, mead, wine, hops, different types of palms, beer, and various plants. Meanwhile, the brāhmins who still celebrated Soma used such substitutes as plants from the ephedrine, asclepias, and sarcostemma families, to name the most popular. An apparent solution to the question has come recently through the inspired investigations of the American mycolophile R. Gordon Wasson, who identifies soma as the psychotropic *amanita muscaria,* the fly agaric, which he calls the "divine mushroom of immortality." The fly agaric is large, about the size of a man's hand, with a thick stem and a brilliant red or yellow cap usually flecked with white knobs. When crushed it gives a juice that runs in color from yellow to red. The fly agaric matches every possible description found in the Vedas and other early scriptures. Wasson believes that reference to stream (see above) fits the practice of drinking a priest's urine after he had consumed soma, for its hallucinogenic effects would still be present. In some rites soma was given to a bull—Soma is also a sacred bull in the texts—and the bull's urine consumed, a rite similar to the practices today where both a cow's urine and feces are still partaken of in certain ceremonies of purification. See Āryans, cow, hoama, Hinduism, Indus Valley.

Sŏn, Buddh. The Korean form of Ch'an (or Zen). Buddhism entered Korea, which was long under Chinese influence, about the sixth century A.D., from China. Shamanism was then a dominant Korean religion, along with a popular faith resembling the Japanese Shintō (q.v.). Sŏn received steady support from Ch'an masters, with many Chinese monks visiting the peninsula, and Koreans studying in China. Sŏn was also influenced by the Chinese cult of the Amida Buddha (q.v.) and the salvationist doctrines of the Pure Land; the various beliefs, including Confucianism, eventually merged within Sŏn, making it widespread. See Ch'an.

Sōtō, Buddh. One of the two main Zen sects today, the other being Rinzai (q.v.). Sōtō is derived from the Ch'an school called Ts'ao-tung, which was developed in the ninth century A.D. by Chinese monks from the Indian methods introduced two hundred years earlier by the Indian Buddhist Bodhidharma (q.v.). Sōtō's primary concept is the oneness of the Absolute and the relative-phenomenal. Sōtō's basic method is sitting—known as zazen (q.v.); this is considered to be an "Indian" form of meditation in search of enlightenment, for this is the method practiced by Gautama Buddha himself. Rinzai favors the kōan (q.v.) and a sudden rather than growing awareness. The Japanese monk Dōgen (q.v.), on an exploratory voyage to China to search out a more authentic Buddhism than the degenerating form practiced in his own country, returned home with the practices and teachings of Ts'ao-tung. Dōgen, as the chief architect of Sōtō, stressed the immediacy of the present—the need of "acting like the Buddha" now rather than trying to become like him in the future. In his great work *Shōbōgenzō* (Treasury of the Eye of the True Doctrine), he states:

"Without looking forward to tomorrow every moment you must think only of this day and this hour. Because tomorrow is difficult and unfixed and difficult to know, you must think of following the Buddhist way while you live today." He adds: "You must concentrate on Zen practice without wasting time, thinking that there is only this day and hour. After that it becomes truly easy. You must forget about the good and bad of your nature, the strength or weakness of your power." Also: "If life comes, this is life. If death comes, this is death. There is no reason for your being under their control. Don't put any hope in them. This life and death are the life of the Buddha. If you try to throw them away in denial, you lose the life of the Buddha. . . . The so-called past is the top of the heart; the present is the top of the fist; and the future is the back of the brain." His disciple Bankei confirms this theme in other words: "You are primarily Buddhas; you are not going to be Buddhas for the first time. There is not an iota of a thing to be called error in your inborn mind. If you have the least desire to be better than you actually are, if you hurry up to the slightest degree in search of something, you are already going against the Unborn." See Zen.

śrāddha (not to be confused with śraddhā, a term for faith), Hind. A commemorative funeral rite celebrated between eight and thirty days after the deceased has been cremated. The higher the caste, the shorter the period, for defilement has been incurred by association with the dead, and brāhmins are more easily purified than members of lower castes. The rites of śrāddha may take as long as three days, though the tendency now, especially in the cities and among the better educated, is for a simpler ceremony. The son of the deceased is the central celebrant. Some ashes or a bone of the deceased should be present; statues, especially of Krishna, are often installed in the ceremonial room or yard. A number of brāhmins is always invited; the priests receive presents, often of great value, in the name of the deceased in exchange for prayers and their good will. Much food is offered, for śrāddha is done for all the ancestors, and they must be fed. Members of other castes also may attend the ceremonies and partake of the feasting, and even beggars from the streets may be fed at the end of śrāddha. The poorest and lowest castes can afford only a simple ceremony (but always there has to be a brāhmin in attendance), but for the well-to-do, śrāddha can equal a wedding in ostentation and may cost hundreds of thousands of rupees, for it is an event of great social as well as religious importance.

śruti, Hind. "What is heard"—i.e., the eternal truth "heard" by the sages and transmitted by them through the means of sacred texts. Śruti is both eternal and impersonal—received and reproduced, as it were, as an echo of the Divine Word. Śruti is carried on by oral transmission, sound being of the utmost importance, because while a word has a single meaning, it also has many manifestations due to accent, pitch, intonation, and so on. Correct transmission, to the exact pitch and stress, can be done only verbally; in effect, śruti texts (many of which have not been written down until comparatively recent times) are like three-thousand-year-old tapes of ancient documents, perfect to tone, pitch, syllable, and rhythm. Unfortunately, while sound is impeccable, the meaning of the content has often been lost or distorted. The four Vedas, and the documents associated with them, the Brāhmaṇas, Āraṇyakas, and Upanishads (q.v. all), are śruti. Later texts are smṛti—i.e., "recollected." Śruti is infallible, unlike the fallible smṛti. It is the eternal authority in all matters of religious truth and practice. However, not all Hindus accept the ancient texts as śruti; those who do are called āstikas (believers), while those who reject the infallibility of the texts are nāstikas (unbelievers). See Hinduism.

stūpa, Buddh. As the primary symbol of Buddhism—and its holy of holies—the stūpa, a mound that takes many forms, was not known in Buddhism itself until the time of the third-century B.C. Indian Emperor Ashoka (q.v.), who is credited with the construction of 84,000 in his realm (84 is a mystical number). However, previous to the age of Gautama Buddha (sixth century B.C.), similar structures of varying sizes and shapes had been long common. In its primitive and simplest form, the stūpa is a hemispherical burial mound; on a large scale it marked the grave of princes, and in smaller sizes, of holy men. Some stūpalike structures were stones and were venerated as phallic symbols of the Hindu god Shiva; others were dedicated to primitive deities of the aboriginal people of India. Today, the Koli fishermen at Karle on the Mahārāshtrian coast still worship Buddhist stūpas as the goddess Yamāī (a form of the Great Mother); the structure is daubed with red clay, a symbol of blood; newborn children are shown the stūpa, and yearly a goat is sacrificed to Yamāī. These are all practices of the most primitive type. Other such survivals even on the most sophisticated level include circumambulation around a stūpa counterclockwise, following the course of the sun in the Indian and tropical latitudes. On the Deccan plateau a group of megalithic monuments in the form of stūpas is described as small-scale predecessors of the later Buddhist stūpa. One type of monument, near Poona, is known as dhātugarbha (relic womb).

As a shrine, the stūpa takes precedence before all other Buddhist structures. Originally it seemed to have stood alone, with the devotees living around it in temporary buildings according to the simplest forms of the Way. Later formal monasteries were built as Buddhism became more and more worldly. The complexes became exceedingly elaborate, with many buildings for the residences of the monks, houses, halls, cloisters, and storerooms surrounded by gardens with lotus pools, fruit trees, fan palms, banyans, and pipals.

The original meaning of the term stūpa was topknot, and the stūpas resembled Gautama Buddha's own topknot, as artists and architects believed it to have been. The term then came to signify vertex, peak, and finally mound, in the sense that it denoted the burial site of the remains of the Buddha. By tradition there were eight stūpas. In this sense, or when built over the remains of other buddhas or holy men, the stūpa was known as sharīra. From the Ashokan period onward, rulers and the wealthy felt the need not only to enlarge the old stūpas but also to construct new ones. Many stūpas in India and Indonesia (an Indian colony) were encased in a succession of stone coverings; since it was considered a sacrilege to destroy a stūpa, even one in bad condition, the intervening space between the old structure and the new exterior was filled with earth and rubble. As the concept of the stūpa progressed eastward to other Buddhist lands, the shape changed, becoming more and more elongated, until it reached the tall, narrow form now known as the pagoda. Confusion of the basic, rather flattish stūpa form with that of the tower is evident. In China pagodas sometimes reached elaborate sizes, being built of bricks and stone, with much attention paid to roofs and decorations. The tiers of roofs, whether square or polygonal, all extended from a central circular column symbolic of the axis of the world. In Japan the pagoda is usually of wood and of unsurpassed delicacy, with decorations confined to the use of certain colors rather than scenes from the life of the Buddha.

ESOTERIC DESCRIPTION. In its most basic form the stūpa has a circular base (medhi) from which rises a massive hemispherical dome, symbol of either the Cosmic Egg (anda, egg) or the womb (garbha). Upon the slightly flattened top of the dome is a square stone railing. From the center of the dome rises a mast supporting three circular umbrellas, one above the other. Each stūpa contains relics (or should); some have many. The relics are considered seeds (bīja) of the sacred, and are placed within a series of containers, the most valuable, which is stūpa-shaped, inside the others.

Esoterically the stūpa is a maṇḍala, an image of the metaphysical world-diagram. In India the stūpa is the sacred world mountain Sumeru, and, as well, the Tree of Enlightenment. As maṇḍala, the stūpa radiates toward the four (or eight) points of the compass. It is the eight-petaled lotus and the Wheel of Buddha, the cakravartin (q.v.), the Universal Emperor. The stūpa not only contains the body of the Buddha (as relic) but it is also the Body of the Most Enlightened One. The stūpa is the Buddha in nirvāṇa and so is itself a symbol of nirvāṇa. Decorations on the sides, winding upward, show the ascent of the individual soul to Enlightenment. The cosmogram of the stūpa contains the five elements: The cube of the base is earth; the dome, water; the cone, fire; the umbrella bowl or disk, air; and the finial, ether. Circumambulation is a march toward the center, not only of the world but also of oneself. See also Buddha, Buddhism, dāgaba, maṇḍala.

sudreh (also sadarah, sedrah, sudrah, sudre), Zor. The short-sleeved muslin V-necked shirt that must be worn next to their skin by all Zardushti, men, women, and young people who have passed through the navzote ceremony (q.v.). The sudreh is a symbol of faith in Ahura Mazdā, the Omniscient Lord. The sudreh is spotless white and is made of small pieces of cloth to signify that even the poorest person can make one up of patches. The normal clothing of one's own milieu (traditional or Westernized Iranian or Indian) is worn over it. A wool belt, the kustī (q.v.), is tied around the waist of the sudreh and is of the utmost importance.

The symbolism of the sudreh is complex. It is a sign of innocence, but, above all, a symbol of the Zardushti faith. It is "the garment of the good mind," the outward sign of inward grace, and is the armor against Satan. A small pocket on the bosom, the giroban (or gire-ban), has a dual significance: to remind the

Zardushti that one's inner faith should be a source of encouragement, and to symbolize "a pocket to collect meritorious deeds." The giroban is also known as the kisse i kirfe ("the purse of righteousness"), indicating that one must not only fill his pocket with money but also with good deeds. The giroban is a constant reminder that when the Zardushti stands before God at the Last Judgment, the pocket must be well filled. When a Zardushti wants to reassure someone of his sincerity, he places his hand in the giroban.

The sudreh has an obvious connection with the Patched Robe (or Shirt) of the Ṣūfīs (q.v. both). The eleventh-century Persian Sūfī Ali al Hujwīrī devotes a chapter to the Robe in his *Kash al-Maṅjūb* (The Revelation of the Veiled). See Zoroastrianism.

Ṣūfī, Ṣūfism. The term Ṣūfī is usually defined as "a Moslem mystic," a most limited and dubious explanation; the origins of the word are unknown, though the commonly accepted derivation is from sūf (wool), because of the white robes that Ṣūfīs wore in contrast to the luxurious and worldly garments of the Ummayad and 'Abbasid courts of Syria and Iraq. Similarly, the robes are said to be in imitation of those of early Christian monks of the Middle East. In either case, the coarse material of the Ṣūfī's clothing was a sign of asceticism and renunciation. Other etymologies, from later periods, state that Ṣūfī is derived from the root ṣafā (to be pure), or from ṣuffa (the raised platform in the Prophet Muḥammad's mosque in Medina where poorer people used to sit in devotion). Some contemporary authors believed the word originates in the Greek sophós (knowledge). Only the first explanation has any validity, and all are doubtful.

The origins of the practice of Ṣūfism are also unknown. Just as the Gautama Buddha (q.v.) is said to be the first Zen practitioner, so is the Prophet Muḥammad said to be the first Ṣūfī. Some believe that Ṣūfism is an ancient doctrine, of pre-Islamic origin, which coincidentally found Islam the shell and frame within which to function. Other views express the opinion that Ṣūfism arose several generations after Muḥammad; the word Ṣūfism itself did not appear until 1821, in a German work (in the form of Scufismus); Ṣūfī was not employed until some two centuries after the death of the Prophet. Earlier names for the type of mystics later to be called Ṣūfīs were The Kindred, The Recluses, The Virtuous, The Folk, and The Near Ones, all expressive of the apartness of such mystics.

Whatever the origins and the date, there are certain traditions that connect Ṣūfism of certain types with some of the tenets of Zoroastrianism (q.v.), the religion of the Ahura Mazdā, the Omniscient Lord of Iran and its colonies. Certainly Ṣūfism has been strong in the areas once ruled by the various far-flung Persian (Archaemenid and Sassanian) empires, all of which eventually succumbed to Islam; Persia itself has been a Ṣūfī center par excellence.

Zoroastrians themselves state unhesitatingly that Ṣūfism is derived from their faith, though one suspects that the affirmation is more on instinct and desire than provable fact. But the reasons are interesting. When Islam overran the Persian Empire in the seventh century A.D., those Zoroastrians who did not withdraw to the area of Yazd in the province of Pars or migrate out of the country, were converted, willingly or not, to Islam. It is apparent that many Zardushti, especially the priesthood, accepted Islam only on the surface, retaining a number of their own beliefs, which they practiced secretly or in a disguised form. The distinctness of Islam in Persia, either as Ṣūfism or as the Shī'a (q.v.), seems ample proof. Though the Muslims overcame the religion of Ahura Mazdā, those in Persia were influenced by the older doctrines, which refused to die gracefully.

Scholars of this century, notably Henry Corbin and Muhammad Mu'in, have confirmed the long-held belief of the Parsees and other Zardushtis that many Persian Ṣūfic practices were but a code form of Zoroastrianism; knowledgeable Zardushti have stated that the original Ṣūfīs were the Magi (q.v.). Under Islamic rule, what had been open practice was forced underground. Secret lodges or "halls" were formed, where the esoteric lore of the past was rephrased. The ancient mystical teachings became the "wine" of Ṣūfī poetry; divine ecstasy was intoxication with that wine; the teacher was the "wine bearer." Ṣūfī songs and poetry took a sensuous, erotic turn: God became "the Beloved," and meeting with the Beloved was but union with Ahura Mazdā. The Divine Names of Ahura Mazdā found their parallel in the Divine Names of Allāh. Other poetic images abound: The bird in the cage was the soul striving for release from the bonds of the world; the Old One, or the Ancient One, was the Ṣūfic Perfect Man.

Mu'in has noted that many of the Persian Ṣūfī poets have disclaimed Islam (but one must take such disclaimers with caution). Aṭṭār (q.v.), the author of *The Parliament of the Birds,* wrote "We are the eternal Mazdeans, we are not Muslims." Sana'i sang that Mazdeans and Ṣūfīs are the same people, professing the one mystical religion of love. Mawlawi and Hafiz are among the many others he establishes as showing Zardushti strains in their poems. In another area, some of the teachings of Jesus, especially in the Gospel of St. John, seem, to those with Ṣūfic experience, to be true Ṣūfī statements.

THE WAY. Ṣūfism is essentially a search for the Way (Arab, Ṭarīqah), a Way that is both a seeking out of divine ecstasy and submission to the Divine almost to the point of annihilation, and a protest against the juridical formulation and the worldliness of the Arab courts and the practices of the merchant. Mystic love is stressed to the exclusion of everything else, though the Ṣūfī is also completely aware of the world about him. There is no such thing as an "impractical" Ṣūfī. The Ṣūfī is expected to earn his living, often at a manual trade—tentmaking and sandalmaking were common livelihoods of the past, but there were also lawyers who were Ṣūfīs. Usually the Ṣūfī is married and has children; there are some few exceptions who are celibate recluses. Though some rare individuals may make the search alone, the ordinary man (or woman) is a member of a brotherhood under the guidance of a master, variously called shaykh, faqīrī, darwīsh, or ikhwān. Some brotherhoods are but local or regional in scope; others are international, especially in the area of Persia, Afghanistan, Pakistan, and India. A Ṣūfī brotherhood, of whatever size, has no purpose but to teach Ṣūfic doctrines. It may ebb and flow, and pass out of existence once it has lived its useful life, but others will arise in turn.

Essentially, Ṣūfism is a folk movement, with its base among the poor, the proletariat, and the dispossessed; princes and the wealthy who become Ṣūfīs give up their possessions, or at least set them aside to follow the simple life. The forms of Ṣūfism vary across the Islamic world, running from a purity acceptable to the strict orthodox Muslim to an embodiment of shamanistic and magical practices, including self-mutilation, the handling of snakes, levitation, bilocation, astral traveling, and other occult and esoteric performances. Some brotherhoods have traditionally used music and dancing to help induce ecstatic states; drugs are sometimes taken; yet many eschew all extraneous aids to meditation and ecstasy aside from prayer and techniques of breathing.

DOCTRINE. Ṣūfī doctrine is esoteric and inner. It cannot be assembled in neat and cogent systems of the type developed in orthodox Islam. Ṣūfism is "a secret garden. . . . He who tastes, knows." Among Ṣūfīs two individuals might hear the same teaching yet receive, accept, and employ it in entirely different manners according to their respective spiritual advancement. Doctrines cannot be codified, synthesized, or systematized. Philosophical argument has no place: The subject slips away, for Ṣūfic teaching escapes analysis. Although there are numerous Ṣūfic writings, from poems to elaborate expositions, much of it is beyond comprehension to the outsider, and even seems banal in its employment of mundane eroticism, lists of numbers and letters, puns, and comic characters. Such material has no value unless read—and the Ṣūfī do not encourage reading—under the direction of a master, who can lead the pupil to a transcending of his own soul, in a Ṣūfī's phrase, of "letting one's Spirit rise above oneself."

The impossibility of communicating the mystical transport is a keynote of Ṣūfism, as of other esoteric Ways. Mystical truth exists for the individual, and for no one else. It cannot be conceptualized. The Persian Ṣūfī al-Gazālī (q.v.), one of the few members of an Eastern religion to leave a spiritual autobiography, has written briefly of his search for divine ecstasy, which probably states as succinctly as anyone can, what mystical ascent is.

"The science of the Ṣūfīs aims at detaching the heart from all that is not Allāh, and at giving to it the sole occupation the meditation of the Divine Being," wrote al-Gazālī. He states that he studied certain works in order to understand what can be learned by reading, "Then I recognized that what pertains most exclusively to their method is just what no study can grasp, but only [mystical] transport, ecstasy and the transformation of the soul. How great, for example, is the difference between knowing the definitions of health, of satiety, with their causes and conditions, and being really healthy or filled. How different to know of what drunkenness consists—as being a state occasioned by a vapor that rises from the stomach—and *being* drunk effectively. Without doubt the drunken man knows neither the definition of drunkenness nor what makes it interesting for science. . . . Similarly there is a difference between knowing the nature of abstinence, and *being* abstinent or having one's soul detached from the world. Thus I had learned what words could teach about Ṣūfism, but what remained could be learned neither by study nor through hearing from a teacher but solely by abandoning one's self to ecstasy and leading a pious life."

Al-Gazālī spent months trying to free himself from the multitude of binds that fettered him, and the temptations that surrounded him on every side. At Baghdad he fell ill of a paralysis, obviously of psychic origin, that paralyzed his tongue. At last he abandoned himself to Allāh. "He answered, as He answers the wretch who invokes Him." At this point al-Gazālī distributed his possessions and left his family, to go to Syria, where he spent two years in seclusion, following Ṣūfī practices in conquering his desires and training himself to purify his soul, in order "to make my character perfect, to prepare the heart for meditating on Allāh." But, though he wanted to live in solitude, "the vicissitudes of the times, the affairs of the family, the need for subsistence, changed in some respects my primitive resolve, and interfered with my plans for a purely solitary life." However, there were some advances. "I had never yet found myself completely in ecstasy save in a few single hours. Nevertheless, I kept the hope of attaining this state. Every time that accidents led me astray, I sought to return, and in this situation I spent ten years. During this solitary state things were revealed to me which is impossible either to describe or to point out. I recognized for certain that the Ṣūfīs are assuredly walking in the Way of Allāh. Both in their acts and in their inaction, whether internal or external, they are illumined by the Light which proceeds from the prophetic source. The first condition for a Ṣūfī is to purge his heart entirely of all that is not Allāh. The next key of the contemplative life consists in the humble prayers which escape from the fervent soul, and in the meditations of God in which the heart is swallowed up entirely. But in reality this is only the beginning of the Ṣūfī life, the end of Ṣūfism being total absorption in Allāh. The intuitions and all that precede are, so to speak, only the threshold for those who enter. From the beginning, revelations take place in so flagrant a shape that the Ṣūfīs see before them, while wide awake, the angels and the souls of the prophets. They hear their voices and obtain their favors." The key sentence follows. "Then the transport rises from the perception of forms and figures to a degree which escapes all expression, and which no man may seek to give an account of without his words involving sin."

Al-Gazālī then states the difficulties of verbalizing the experience:

"Whosoever has not had the experience of [mystical] transport knows nothing but the name of the true nature of prophetism. He may meanwhile be sure of its existence, both by experience and by what he hears the Ṣūfīs say. As there are men endowed only with the sensitive faculty who reject what is offered them in the way of objects of the pure understanding, so there are intellectual men who reject and avoid the things perceived by the prophetic faculty. A blind man can understand nothing of colors, except by what he has learned from hearing others and from hearsay. Yet Allāh has brought prophetism near to men in giving them all a state analogous to it in its principle characteristics. The state is sleep. If you were to tell a man who was himself without experience of such a phenomenon that there are people who at times swoon away so as to resemble dead men and who while dreaming still perceive things that are hidden, he would deny it. Nevertheless, his arguments would be refuted by actual experience. Just as the comprehension is a stage in human life in which the eye opens to discern various intellectual objects not understood by sensation, so in the prophetic the sight is illumined by a light which uncovers hidden things and objects which the intellect fails to reach. The chief properties of prophetism are perceptible only during the transport, and by those only who embrace the Ṣūfī Way. The prophet is endowed with qualities to which you possess nothing analogous, and which consequently you cannot possibly comprehend. How should you know their true nature, since one knows only what one can comprehend? But the [mystical] transport which one attains by the Ṣūfī method is like an immediate perception, just as if one touched the objects with one's hand."

The Qur'ān is the standard book for Ṣūfīs, though it may be read in an esoteric sense, often heretical to the orthodox. Ṣūfīs have no sacred city, though many make the pilgrimage to Mecca, and revere it as much as any other Muslim; still others see the Holy City as within and eschew outward manifestations of piety, such as the hajj (q.v.). While Ṣūfīs may attend a mosque, they also may not. Usually Ṣūfīs are attached to, or centered around, a meeting place, the zāwiyah (q.v.), under the guidance of a shaykh (q.v.) or other religious leader.

sunna (or sunnah), Isl. Literally, "the trodden path." The term was employed by the pre-Islamic Arabs to denote the model behavior of the tribal forefathers. Sunna is one of the four principles of Islamic law, referring to the words and deeds of the Prophet Muḥammad; the other principles are the Qur'ān, ijmā' (the consent of the community) and qiyās (analogy) (q.v. all). Briefly, in other words, sunna is the Path of God Himself as seen in the Qur'ān, the way of the pre-Islamic forefathers, the sunna of the Prophet and the Companions, and the sunna expressed by each generation as it lives with the sunna of previous generations. Sunna is thus not only verbalized through ḥadīth (tradition of the Prophet) and formalized in commentary and jurisprudence, but is also nonverbal, being expressed as a Way of life.

Sunna is tradition seen as a matter of obligation. The degree to which the Muslim feels bound by sunna may be seen in this quotation from the great al-Gazālī, writing in the eleventh century A.D.

"Know that the key of happiness is following the sunna and imitating God's Apostle in all his goings out and comings in, in his movements and times of quiescence, even in the manner of his eating, his deportment, his sleep and his speech." The faithful must not only follow the Prophet in matters of religious observance, but also, "You must sit while putting on trousers and stand while putting on a turban: You must begin with the right foot when putting on your sandals, and eat with your right hand; when cutting your nails you must begin with the forefinger of the right hand and finish with its thumb; in the foot you must begin with the little toe of the right foot and finish with the little toe of the left. It is the same in all your movements and times of quiescence. Muḥammad ben Aslam refused to eat a melon because the manner in which God's Apostle ate it had not been transmitted to him."

Sunna is a subject of much study and controversy, among both

Islamic scholars and divines and Western students of Islam; there is considerable dispute over the finer points. Much of sunna is not accepted by the various sects of the Shī'a. See Islam, Muḥammad, Shī'a, Sunnī.

Sunnī, Isl. A member of the majority group of Muslims, who consider themselves the "orthodox." They follow the sunna (see above) of the Prophet and of tradition. The other important grouping, which has numerous divisions, is the Shī'a. During the short, controversial reign of the fourth khalif, 'Ali, the Prophet's son-in-law, the Islamic world found itself in two major camps, depending on whether the Muslim follow the Path of the Prophet and the Companions—sunna—or remained a loyal follower of 'Ali. The first party is known as the Sunnīs, a term still used. Shī'a, the opposition, now includes a wide range of subsects, not always in agreement with each other; their political differences with the Sunnī have also become theological. The Sunnīs, who place a heavy emphasis on law, codes, and dogma, view Muḥammad as the culmination of a series of prophets beginning with Adam. The Shī'a usually (depending on the sect) see him in the same light, but add the doctrine of the imām (to the Sunnī, the imām is only a leader of prayers) as an agent of the Divine throughout the ages; some few Shī'a also raise Muḥammad to a part of the Godhead. The Sunnī have stressed the historic khalifate, which the Shī'a reject in favor of the emotionally charged question of 'Alī as the righteous khalif. Among the Sunnī the latter khalifs and other leaders of the community have had no spiritual powers; in fact, each of the faithful is entitled to a share in the communal approach, though he must in the end be part of the consensus. The Shī'a, on the other hand, place great significance in the individual religious experience and see their imāms and other leaders (among them the various mahdīs who have appeared at the head of the faithful in various ages and countries) as special incarnations of the divine powers. Sunnī Islam is more legalistic and formalistic, and has contributed the majority of scholars and judges. See 'Alī, Islam, Shī'a, sunna.

śūnya (or śūna), Hind. The void; also the excessive and the swollen. In India more than any other land, numbers play a mystical role par excellence. Such numbers include one, three, seven, 84, 108, etc., but of all, the number and symbol 0—Zero—is the most important, being expressed in the concept of śūnya, the void. Zero, the void, is the transition point between opposites, symbolizing the true balance within divergent tendencies. It is the All and the None, the matrix of positive and negative, of generation and destruction. Metaphysically, 0 is nirvāṇa, the state in which all karma—the fruit of ignorance—is burned out in the Void, śūnya. This psychic state of balance, the metaphysical void of 0, was picked up from India by the Arabs, and, completely desacralized, was transmitted to the West, where, ritualized as both 0 and decimal point, it replaced the duodecimal system of ancient Rome, revolutionizing European mathematics and eventually forming the central point of the computer, by which American man was able to land on the sacred Hindu deity, the Moon. See numbers.

suttee, Hind. See sati.

Suzuki, Daisetz Teitaro (1870–1966). Japanese Zen adept and scholar, one of the leading contemporary spokesmen for the Rinzai school of Zen, which in later life he advocated to the almost total exclusion of Sōtō. Suzuki preferred sudden enlightenment through the kōan as taught in Rinzai to the gradual mystical development based on Sōtō's zazen techniques of sitting in meditation. After completing college and university studies, Suzuki entered zazen practices and is said to have "understood the Way of Buddhahood," meaning that he had gained satori, or enlightenment. Shortly after this experience he went to Chicago, where he stayed for eleven years, climaxing his American studies with a trip to Europe, after which he returned to Japan to take up university work. From 1936 to 1964 he lived in the United States, usually close to various universities, teaching, lecturing, and writing; his work runs to some one hundred books.

His belief in the primacy of Rinzai's kōan method over Sōtō's zazen may be stated in this summary of his thought on "Sudden and Gradual Enlightenment": "To speak of suddenness or gradualness implies time, but enlightenment experience is not in the category of time; enlightenment is timeless. Gradual means time; sudden means no time. Enlightenment itself is beyond time. All experience is related. There is nothing that is not related in our experience, since our experience comes through the senses which we recognize by their relatedness. How can we who are finite, come to the realization of infinity? Thus we have to make a sudden leaping experience in order to gain sudden enlightenment. To leap, in terms of space, is leaping; in terms of time, it is not. This is sudden enlightenment. We must leap from finity to infinity and then we shall know what we are."

◄T►

takbīr, Isl. The invocation Allāhu Akbar (God is the Greatest). See Allāhu Akbar.

tamas, Hind. One of the three guṇas. Tamas is a negative quality, inertia, heaviness, darkness, and produces delusion. See guṇa.

tantra, Hind. A non-Vedic form of yogic practices leading to divine ecstasy through certain rites that emphasize the erotic and forbidden. Tantra, also known as Kuṇḍalinī-yoga, is centered upon Shakti, the divine female power, the active, fecundating, and productive force of the universe; this power is worshiped by the sādhakas, the male practitioners, through the śaktis (named after the goddess) who are her earthly incarnation in the tantric ceremony. Where traditional Indian (and Hindu) spirituality emphasizes a stripping away of physical, emotional, and tactile pleasures, as well as a negation of the mundane world, tantra cultivates and makes use of them. In place of liberation through renunciation, tantra teaches liberation through bhoga (enjoyment).

The origins of tantra are unknown, but they clearly are related to primitive fertility practices found not only in India but also in other parts of the world. Tantra was probably celebrated in India in the Harappā civilization of the Indus Valley previous to B.C. 2500. Long practiced by the lower castes and tribal peoples, what was to be called tantra had a sudden emergence about the sixth century A.D., affecting not only a receptive Buddhism and Jainism but also even the priestly and conservative brāhminism. It was especially strong in the areas that had least been affected by the Āryans, such as South India, Bengal, and the Himālayan areas including Tibet. To varying degrees tantra touched virtually all of Indian culture, especially art, architecture, and literature, with much influence on the devotional movement known as bhakti. Tantric texts proliferated in all the Indian religions. As a highly erotic discipline, tantra found an expression in the sensual sculpture of the Indian temples, an art form that combined devotion and sex in a manner that has much puzzled foreigners and even many Indians. But within the context of tantra, which envisions the coupling of male and female as union with the Divine and the ecstatic bliss of orgasm indicative of the total release of the soul in the godhead, the erotic is but a means to the eternal Brahman. Even the sexual control in some forms of tantra that redirects the semen and vaginal juices back into the sādhaka and śakti respectively is but another form of this nirvāṇic bliss.

The core of tantra is the feminine, generative, reproductive principle Shakti, without which the world would not function. Shakti incarnates the Divine Woman and Mother, the mystery of creation and of Being, of everything that is, that incomprehensibly becomes and dies and is reborn, according to a commentator. In tantric doctrine Shakti is One with the eternal Brahman. Shakti is the Ānanda-rūpiṇi Devī, the goddess by whom the Brahman expresses itself. Brahman (neuter) is manifested in the forms of all the devas and devīs, the deities of all types and sexes, and in the worshiper himself. Its form is that of the universe and of all things and beings therein.

The power of Brahman as Shakti is found within man in the figure of the goddess Kuṇḍalinī, the famed Serpent Power, who lies coiled and sleeping in the lowest cakra or bodily center, the mūlādhāra, at the base of the spinal column. Kuṇḍalinī is awakened and aroused by certain yogas, the chief of which is tantra, and ascends through the six mystical centers, the cakras, to pierce the Sahasrāra-padma, the Thousand-petal Lotus. From the mūlādhāra, the seat of Shakti, Kuṇḍalinī has risen to the Sahasrāra-padma, the seat of the god Shiva, to unite both. This mystical coition is expressed by tantric rites, which may be either literal, vāmacāra (the left-hand way), or symbolic, dakṣinācāra (the right-hand way).

THE RITES. The ceremonies that waken Kuṇḍalinī are diverse and complex, and vary from one school to another. The sādhaka follows the eight stages of classical yoga (q.v.), but in his own manner. There are certain āsanas or postures that are peculiar to tantra alone, in which skulls, the funeral pyre, and a corpse respectively form the seat of the sādhaka. Many magic ritual objects, including paintings, yantras, and mantras, are employed. Siddhis, or occult tricks, which are looked down upon in classical yoga, are much practiced. Many are definitely objected to—a tantric sādhaka, in his search to unite the male and female principles, can make both the penis and testes disappear in the pubic arch so that the body has the appearance of a woman's. Another rite (of many outside classical practice) may be mentioned as an example. In a form of sitting known as śavāsana, the sādhaka sits astride the back of a corpse (its head is pointed to the north). The sādhaka draws a yantra on the skull, says mantras, and performs rites of pūjā on it. The corpse is chosen as being a pure form of organized matter, since it is free from sin or desire. The goddess materializes by means of the corpse and enters and possesses it. At the conclusion of a successful rite (it is not always a success), it is said that the head of the corpse turns around and, facing the sādhaka, speaks, asking that he name his request, which may be spiritual or worldly advancement, as he wishes. Only the hero (or vīra) attempts śavāsana, as it is accompanied by many terrors. However, the conquest of fear and the attainment of indifference are the goals of the tantric yogi. The cremation ground is much favored because that is where the desire body and its passions are consumed, the outer burning being no burning at all.

The higher stages of tantra encompass the employment of five forbidden things: madya (wine), māṃsa (meat), maṭsya (fish), mudrā (a type of parched grain), and maithuna (sexual union). These are known as the pañcamakāras or Five M's. The vāmacārīs employ them literally; the dakṣinacārīs, symbolically. Each makāra has profound and endless mystical and esoteric meaning. To take but a few: Wine is the Divine Dynamism of Shakti, the meat the Divine Substance of Shiva; the fish represents not only the sacred rivers Gaṇgā and Yamunā but also the currents of breath, expiration, and inspiration, and so on; mudrā is the knowledge of the luminous Ātman, the Self; and maithuna is the bliss enjoyed with the Ātman (i.e., Brahman) in the Thousand-petal Lotus. Each makāra enjoys profound elaboration. In the right-hand path, substitutions are made as follows: coconut water or milk for wine; salt, ginger, sesamum, wheat, or garlic for meat; eggplant, radish or water chestnut for fish; paddy, rice, or wheat for mudrā; and lastly, an offering of flowers or a joining of certain flowers in dedication, or the gesture of the hands for maithuna.

THE LEFT-HAND WAY IN PRACTICE. The sādhakas will likely perform their rites during a woman's menstruation, since the blood's ovum and estrogens contain energizing powers that are both invigorating and sedating. The right-hand way prefers certain days on the dark fortnight of the moon after the woman's period. The tantrics meet in a circle in the presence of a guru; in some cases each sādhaka has his śakti; in others there is but a single woman to be shared. The tantric circle is laid out as a type of yantra, according to the rites of that particular group, and becomes a sacred ground, a cosmic center. The sādhaka is purified through various mantras and pūjās, as is the śakti's body. She is anointed and massaged with sweet-smelling oils from head to foot, with special attention to the pudenda. A dot, the bindu, is painted on her forehead to symbolize the Third Eye, and a red line—the line of Kuṇḍalinī's ascent—is drawn from the genital area up her body to the bindu. The śakti is now literally the Goddess herself. The various rites then begin, with the step-by-step consuming of each of the Five M's, the seat being a consecrated mat of kusa (or kāśa) grass covered with an animal skin or a wool cloth. The preferred light is a castor oil lamp, which gives a violent flame believed to stimulate the sex organs; the śakti may be loosely wrapped in thin purplish or violet silk. During the rites the sādhaka sits in a traditional āsana such as the lotus position, with the śakti astride him. Ideally they reach the point of orgasmic release without seminal discharge, the vital sexual fluids being retained and reabsorbed. If ejaculation occurs, the sādhaka has the power to draw his semen back into his penis.

As in the case of other Eastern disciplines today (cf. the Zoroastrians), tantra is sometimes formulated in contemporary terms. After tantric sexual union, the bodies of sādhaka and śakti are surrounded by an "electromagnetic radiation field," an egg-shaped nimbus extending two to three feet on all sides. It is said to resemble a fetal sac (the Golden Embryo) or the Brahmāṇḍa (the Cosmic Egg).

DIFFICULTIES OF TANTRA. This form of yoga has been much misunderstood, not only in the West but among many Indians as well. For some, especially Europeans with little comprehension of Indian mystical practices, it had become a means of sexual experimentation and release rather than a yogic discipline, and much psychological damage has been done, especially to the women who fall victim to self-styled tantric gurus. In India, where there is now much sexual repression, charlatans have also employed tantra for nefarious purposes. The tantric texts—as well as the most regarded masters—all stress the need for proper training, dedication, self-control, and supervision by a guru.

A few tantric texts are available in English (most are in Sanskrit, Tibetan, Bengali, and various Indian tongues and often in manuscript). The most noteworthy are those collected and edited by Sir John Woodroffe in collaboration with various tantric scholars. Recommended are: *The Serpent Power, Introduction to Tantra Śastra, Hymn to Kālī, Śakti and Śākta, Kularnava Tantra,* and *The Garland of Letters.* The publisher is Ganesh & Co., Madras 17, India. So-called tantric works by the Theosophists (q.v.) are not to be taken seriously. See Brahman, Śakti, yoga.

Taoism. A school of thought, essentially mystical in nature, founded, according to tradition, by the Chinese sage Lao Tzu (B.C. 604–531). The central core of Taoism is found in the book that bears his name, the *Lao tzu.* However, contemporary scholars see little evidence to establish the Sage as a historical figure, and believe that the book is a compilation from several sources, reaching a near-final form about the middle of the second century B.C. The fourth-century B.C. sage Chuang Tzu, whose historicity is not in question, is the second most important source of Taoist doctrines. The Chinese term for Taoism is tao chi (the school of the way). Though Tao (which will be capitalized in this sense) is taken by the Taoists as essentially metaphysical, eternal, all-pervading, inexhaustible, fathomless, the source of all things, the tao (not capitalized) of Confucius is ethical in sense and deals with a way of life and with daily philosophical and moral problems.

The central fact of Tao is that it cannot be defined, for the *Lao tzu* states that "The way that can be spoken of is not the constant way." And: "The way is forever nameless." Also: "The way conceals itself in being nameless." Consequently the term Tao is but a name used for lack of something better. Yet there have been numerous attempts to grasp its essence. Chuang Tzu observes, "Tao cannot be conveyed by either words or silence. In that state which is neither speech nor silence its transcendental nature may be apprehended," a mood that parallels that of Hindu metaphysics. The *Lao tzu* states, "If the Tao could be comprised in words, it would not be the unchangeable Tao." Yet in the effort to name the unnameable, Tao has often been described, by the Chinese themselves and by others. Often there are no precise translations for the Chinese ideograms, though their equivalents may range from the abstract First Principle to Primal Source to a mystical Cosmic Mother, depending on the frame of interpretation. Westerners may refer to Tao as "God," but this is the most erroneous of all interpretations. Thus the American Sinologist James R. Ware can state that Lao Tzu, Chuang Tzu, and Lieh Tzu (another Taoist of doubtful historical value) are "extremist advocates of the case for God." The great English Sinologist Arthur Waley says that the Tao "meant 'the way the Universe works'—and ultimately something very like God, in the more abstract and philosophical sense of that term," a connection not recognized by Chinese scholars familiar with Western concepts. The historian Arnold Toynbee even reduced Tao to "the line of least resistance," a kind of Chinese laissez-faire in which the search for markets was replaced by "a way which was the truth and the life," again a most questionable interpretation.

What does Taoism say of itself? The *Chuang tzu* is not concerned with a definition, for what IS (in the form of itself) is Tao. However, the *Lao tzu* says this (in the Waley translation): "Tao is real, is faithful, yet does nothing and has no form. Can be handed down, yet can not be passed from hand to hand, can be got but cannot be seen. It is its own trunk, its own root." Elsewhere the work says, "one need not peep through his window to see Tao, Tao is not there. The further one goes away from himself the less he knows."

The *Lao tzu* says, "Great Tao is like a boat that drifts; it can go this way, it can go that," a sentiment echoed by Chuang Tzu, who said, "I myself have traversed it this way and that; yet still know only where it begins. I have roamed at will through its stupendous spaces. I know how to get to them, but I do not know where they will end."

The sensible middle way of the Taoists' rivals, the Confucians, with their emphasis on goodness or human-heartedness, and righteousness or morality, was an affront to the Taoists. They saw man and the universe, all living life, as a unit; the Confucians fitted everything into a hierarchy, with each part connected and responsible to those above and below. For the Confucian, human society and civilization were an earthly mirror of the cosmic tao. But this arranging of society, no matter how perfect, was, to the Taoists, a crime against the natural order of the universe. Before the Confucians came, man, as Chuang Tzu said, was in a state of pure simplicity, without knowledge, free from desires and of a natural virtue. "The nature of people was what it ought to be." Then the sagely men, the Confucians, appeared, "limping and wheeling about in human-heartedness, pressing along and standing on tiptoe in the doing of righteousness." The Confucians went to excesses in their ceremonies and destroyed the natural law in hacking up materials (both clay and jade are among those mentioned) to make their sacrificial vessels and their objects of culture, leisure, and commerce. The result was that "men began to be separated from one another." The answer to the chaos caused by "order" was, as the *Lao tzu* said,

> Banish wisdom, discard knowledge,
> And the people will be benefited a hundredfold.
> Banish human-heartedness, discard morality,
> And the people will be dutiful and compassionate.
> Banish skill, discard profit,
> And thieves and robbers will disappear.
> . . .
> Give them Simplicity to look at,
> the Uncarved Block to hold
> Give them selflessness and fewness of desires.

The Taoists believed that the Confucians lost Tao, substituting power for it, their two major qualities of human-heartedness and morality, which were lost in turn, being replaced merely by ritual. "Now ritual is the mere husk of loyalty and promise-keeping and is indeed the first step toward brawling." This Confucian middle way, a self-styled mainstream, the Way of the Mean that seeks a harmony for all—the prosperity of each bringing the prosperity of all, and the general prosperity bringing the prosperity of the individual—is, in our contemporary term, a team enterprise. It is in effect, to the Taoists, a totalitarian state, with the sage philosophers instructing every man, especially the ruler, from a vantaged position, on the fulfillment of duties and on rites and honors. Confucianism is the modern era to perfection, building roads, founding towns, establishing markets, making laws and regulations for the "betterment" of the people. But Taoism is a counterculture, an alternate culture. The material world has no relevance for the Taoist, for Tao is "the very progenitor of all things in the world. In it sharpness is blunted, all tangles untied, all glare tempered, all dust smoothed. It is like a pool that never dries." "Only he that rids himself forever of desire can see the Secret Essences." The Taoist goes by himself, without schools, hierarchy, adepts, disciples. "I will leave you and enter the gate of the Unending, to enjoy myself in the fields of the illimitable. I will blend my light with that of the sun and moon, and will endure while heaven and earth endure. If men agree with my views, I will be unconscious of it; if they keep far apart from them, I will be unconscious of it; they may all die, and I will abide alone."

The Taoist's heart must be free from all desire, and he must travel through desolate wilds.

> For to the south there is a place called the Land Where Tê Rules. Its people are ignorant and unspoiled, negligent of their own interest, and of few desires. They know how to make, but do not know how to hoard. They give but seek no return. The subtleties of decorum, the solemnities of ritual are alike unknown to them. They live and move thoughtlessly and at random, yet every step they take tallies with the Great Plan. They are ready to enjoy life while it lasts, are ready to be put away when death comes. I would have you leave your kingdom and its ways, take Tao as your guide and travel to this land.

The Tao man lives on another wavelength: "I am as serene as the ocean, as mobile as the wind." However, he also says of himself, "My mind is that of an idiot, so dull! Vulgar people are clear, I alone am depressed, vulgar people are alert." And when the multitude has more than enough to fill its wants, the Tao man is in want. When the multitude is happy and engaging in feats, the Tao man alone is inactive. When the Confucian strives for a similar way of life, the Taoists accuse him of sham, both the hermit who hides away conscious of his own superiority—"the man in whose eyes the world is always wrong"—and the sage who would set the world in order or put others above himself out of a false sense of modesty. For the Taoist, "To remain detached from all outside things is the climax of oneness. To have in oneself no contraries is the climax of purity."

In the *Chuang tzu* the Tao man assumes a more positive guide. Here he is the Supreme Man, the True Man, the Man of Supreme Inward Power. "His soul is intact." "The great bushlands are ablaze, but he feels no heat, the River and the Han stream are frozen over, but he feels no cold. Fierce winds break the hills, winds rock the ocean, but he is not startled. He can climb high and not stagger, go through water and not get wet, go through fire and not be scorched." (This kind of symbolism, taken literally, later led to the disastrous results in the anti-European Boxer Rebellion in the late nineteenth century, when the leaders felt themselves immune to bullets.) The Superior Man is one of the accretions to the pre-Confucian layers of the *I Ching* (q.v.), the great book of divination, and reflects a growth of Chinese thought from the primitive to more sophisticated stages of development. But here the Superior Man is a creature of a different sort, much more practical, as the Confucians would have him, and able to absorb adversity or direct a war or receive honors with equal aplomb—in short, the ideal of the Way of the Mean.

Unlike the Confucians, the Taoists practiced yoga on a rather large scale, though the literature is vague and many of the terms are now beyond comprehension. The practice goes back to very early times. Lao Tzu was reported sitting "so utterly motionless that one could not believe a human being was there at all . . . stark and lifeless as a withered tree." The *Chuang tzu* gives the case of a man named Ch'i who went into an ecstatic trance (or possibly into what the Hindus know as samādhi); Ch'i was sitting against a low table when "He looked up to heaven and his breath died down. Without a sound he seemed to lose his partnership of soul and body." His disciple Yen Ch'eng thought Ch'i's body "like a sapless tree" and "his mind like dead ashes," adding, "At this moment the person leaning against the table is not the person who was leaning against it before." Ch'i replied, "When you saw me just now, my self was gone clean away." In another section of the *Chuang tzu,* an adept named Pu-liang Yi is described as going through progressively higher stages, passing beyond the world, beyond created things, and lastly beyond life. "After that he could be Morning Light, then Solitariness, then free from time. Then he entered into neither death-nor-birth, where the destroyer of life does not die, and the producer of birth is not born. As governor of things, he escorted and greeted them all, destroyed and perfected them all. The name is Active Tranquillity. It means 'to achieve after action.' "

A common term for this inner voyage was yu (to wander or to travel). The Confucians used it in the sense of wandering from court to court. But for the Taoists it meant an esoteric journey. "He whose sightseeing is inward can find in himself all he needs. Such is the highest form of traveling, while it is a poor sort of journey that depends upon outside things." Hu-chi'iu Tzu said, "The greatest traveler does not know where he is going, the greatest sightseer does not know what he is looking at. His travels do not take him to one part of creation more than another; his sightseeing is not directed to one sight rather than another.

Some later Taoist yoga, like some Hindu yoga, emphasizes the withholding or withdrawal of semen, the vital force. Taoist yoga, yang-shêng (nurturing life), falls into four branches. The branch concerned with sexual practices is called The Secrets of the Chamber, which enabled the Yellow Ancestor to enjoy twelve hundred concubines without depleting his strength. The other branches resemble Hindu yoga also, being breath control, physical exercises, and diet. The nineteenth-century work *Hsin Ming Pa Cheuh Ming Chih* (Secrets of Cultivating Essential Nature and Eternal Life) by the Taoist alchemist Chao Pi Ch'en (b. 1860) makes such conservation the central core of his yogic teaching. The work states that each breath, in and out, shakes the field of the mystical elixir that flows into the testicles; if the liquid of the elixir follows its earthly course, it will produce offspring. But if properly controlled and reversed under the guidance of an enlightened master, this liquid "will contribute to the production of the golden elixir." However, *Secret of the Golden Flower,* the product of a long yogic tradition going back to the eighth century A.D., if not earlier, ignores this aspect completely, and more sanely concentrates on the transfiguration of the idea of the person in order to return to the undivided One, Tao. These various forms of yoga are the disciplines of highly skilled adepts, the masters, sages, and their disciples; the lower strata of society turned such beliefs into the employment of talismen, charms and spells, magic mirrors, pencils, and other implements, and spiritism and devil possession, death spells, and rainmaking through mediums, shamans, and witches.

Tao underwent extensive changes due to its influence by Buddhism, which was imported into China in the first century A.D. Indian Buddhist concepts were expressed in Taoist terms, and many ideas in both sects seemed to be identical. "Push far enough toward the Void, hold fast to Quietness," said the *Lao tzu,* "What has submitted to Fate has become part of the always-so. To know the always-so is to be enlightened. And: "It was always and of itself so." Under the pressures of a Buddhism that was highly structured, Taoism began to change from a free, anarchistic, personalist Way to a formal cultus. The hermitages of the independent, isolated sages gave way to complex monasteries, with systems of rites and rituals. The simplicity of Lao Tzu and Chuang Tzu grew into an involved mythology. In fact, Lao Tzu became one of a Trinity that also included the Heavenly King of the Primal Beginning and the Jade Emperor. The Heavenly King gave birth to the Holy Mother of All Creation, their son being the Emperor. About the second century A.D. Taoism had reached the point where it resembled nothing less than a church in the Western sense, with a high priest (the Master of Heaven), who was the earthly regent of the Jade Emperor, living in the Dragon and Tiger mountains. Deities grew apace, and the pantheon included Eight Immortals, who, like other saints, had attained immortality by eating certain drugs. By this time Taoism's great object of scorn, the pedantic, upright, lecturing-the-world Confucius, had been accepted into the heavenly assemblage. Meanwhile, amid the magic, the selling of secret formulas, the miracles, the charms and the amulets, small groups of adepts, now in monasteries, still tried to remain pure in the Tao of Lao Tzu. See also Confucius, Lao Tzu, *Secret of the Golden Flower*.

taqlid, Isl. The simple acceptance of authority and tradition in religion. Taqlid, to the less orthodox, is seen as uncritical veneration.

Tashi Lāma, Buddh. The second-highest Lāma of Tibet, surpassed in religious and secular power only by the Dalai Lāma (q.v.). The two Lāmas represented dual tendencies in Tibet in the past, the Dalai Lāma being exploited by the British in their own interests, and the Tashi Lāma by the Chinese. The Tashi Lāma is considered a tulku or avatār of the bodhisattva Wodmagmed (the Indian Amitābha [q.v.]), "He of the Boundless Light." Much without his consent, and probably without his knowledge, the Tashi Lāma plays an important role in the doctrines of the Theosophists, who state that he has sent messengers—the Occult Brotherhood—to guide them; the Theosophists do not consider the present Tashi Lāma authentic and claim the line ended with the Lāma who passed into nirvāṇa in 1937. The present Lāma, who is now in China, they say, is merely a Communist puppet without spiritual qualifications; the sect today awaits the tulku of the true Lāma, the child who will inherit his soul, they believe, having been born in 1970. See Theosophy.

Tathāgata, Buddh. A term frequently used by Gautama Buddha in reference to himself. The origin is unknown, and it may have had a pre-Buddhist usage. It can be roughly (but not accurately) translated as He-who-has-thus-attained, He-who-has-thus-come, or He-who-has-thus-gone. In general, it is employed in the sense of meaning that the Tathāgata cannot be discovered—i.e., known empirically—not only during life but also after death. The widely read *Vajracchedikā Sūtra* (Diamond-cutter Sutra) states that if anyone were to say that "the Tathāgata goes or comes, or stands or sits, or lies down" does not understand the Buddha's teaching, because "the word Tathāgata means one who does not go anywhere, and does not come from anywhere; and therefore is called the Tathāgata [or Truly Come], holy and fully enlightened." Various other texts and glosses do not shed any better light on the term. See Buddha.

tekke, Isl. The Turkish name for a zāwiyah (q.v.), a prayer hall or meeting place of a Ṣūfī brotherhood. The dervish dance, the sema (q.v.), was practiced in five special tekkes until banned by the Ataturk government. See dervish.

Theosophy. An occultist, synthetic religion, drawing upon all faiths but originating in an esoteric form of Buddhism; however, its doctrines are primarily a free adaptation of Hinduism. The Theosophical Society (as it came to be called) is the basic vehicle for theosophic ideas.

The Society was founded in New York in 1875 by Madame Helena Petrovna Blavatsky (1831–91), a Russian-born spiritualist, in company with an American, Colonel H. S. Olcott, her partner in numerous occult and spiritualist performances; another American, W. Q. Judge; and thirteen other interested people. The Society was established on the thesis that there is an Ageless Wisdom, the thread of which can be traced through all cultures and mythologies, through religion, philosophy, and science. Headquarters were transferred to Bombay in 1879, and were permanently established in the town of Adyar (now a suburb of Madras) four years later. The Society today has national centers in some sixty countries, but is barred from Marxist nations with the exception of Yugoslavia.

The prime mover of the Society was Madame Blavatsky (see separate entry). She stated that she had been selected by an incarnated Buddha, the fourteenth-century Tibetan Tsong-Kha-pa, who chose her as the link between a group of enlightened souls, the Adept Brothers, and the Western World, Tsong-Kha-pa having enjoined his Arhats, his most spiritual disciples, to make "an attempt to enlighten the world, including the 'white barbarians,' every century at a specified period." Madame Blavatsky herself stated, "The Buddha left the regions of the Western Paradise to incarnate himself in Tsong-Kha-pa in consequence of the great degradation into which his secret doctrines had fallen."

Madame Blavatsky, who is known as H.P.B. among Theosophists, revealed that the world was now under the guidance of the Adept Brothers, two of whom, known as the Mahatma Morya and the Mahatma Koot Hoomi (respectively Mahatma M. and Mahatma K.H. in Theosophical literature), were jīvanmuktas (liberated souls); like all the Adept Brothers they had crossed saṁsāra, "the ocean of births and deaths"; as jīvanmuktas they remained "in incarnation to help the world on its upward path." Also, the Adepts were "highly evolved men, living men, for whom H.P.B. was agent and from whom she received a mandate to establish a nucleus of occultism in the West."

The mahatmas communicated with H.P.B. by esoteric means, their letters—messages and instructions—being impressed or precipitated into the inner layer of rice paper by some unknown, occult process. In some cases the letters answer questions that had been asked only a few minutes earlier by Society members. The correspondence is now in the British Museum; it has been published as *The Mahatma Letters to A. P. Sinnett,* transcribed and edited by A. T. Barker.

With these credentials, and these sources of direction and support, H.P.B. brought the Society to the attention of a Western elite disenchanted with Christianity and open to new ideas, especially from the East. Olcott (1832–1907) was named the first president of the Society, to be followed by the dynamic Annie Besant (1847–1933), an Englishwoman who renounced her citizenship and became an Indian, joining the freedom movement against the British and being elected president of the Indian National Congress in 1918. It was during this period that the Society functioned with its greatest élan.

However, despite regular growth, the Society has been marked by a number of schisms and divisions. W. Q. Judge (1851–96) left in 1895 due to a difference of opinion with his colleagues and formed a separate Theosophical Organization. At least three other schismatic groups may be counted: There are separate Theosophical Societies in Pasadena and in Unterlengenhardt, Germany, and the United Lodge of Theosophists in Los Angeles (with several foreign branches). A major schism was led by Dr. Rudolf Steiner of Germany, who, after an argument with Annie Besant, formed the Anthroposophical Society in 1912. Attempts at reunification are in progress, but are so far unsuccessful.

DOCTRINES. The teachings of the Theosophical Society are based upon certain basic texts—esoteric lore received from the Adept Brothers and given H.P.B.—that have been transcribed and written down for publication. The key works are H.P.B.'s *The Secret Doctrine, Isis Unveiled,* and *The Key to Theosophy,* and *The Mahatma Letters to A. P. Sinnett.* There was much rephrasing of basic themes during the earliest years; three fundamental "objects" were at last established; they are the core of all Theosophical doctrine, no matter how esoteric. They are:

> First Object: To form a nucleus of the Universal Brotherhood of Humanity, without distinction of race, creed, sex, caste, or color.
>
> Second Object: To encourage the study of Comparative Religion, Philosophy, and Science.
>
> Third Object: To investigate unexplained laws of Nature and the powers latent in man.

These deceptively simple objects hide a highly elaborate occult theory of the Divine and man. To summarize some of the cogent doctrines of Theosophy:

There is "ONE LIFE, eternal, invisible, yet omnipresent, without beginning or end," said H.P.B. in 1888 in *The Secret Doctrine,* "the one self-existing Reality." Basic is the concept of "The fundamental identity of all Souls with the Universal Over-Soul, the latter being itself an aspect of the Unknown Root; and the obligatory pilgrimage for every Soul—a spark of the former—through the Cycle of Incarnation, or Necessity, in accordance with Cyclic and Karmic law, during the whole term." In this view man is actually identical with the Universal Oversoul, which is an aspect of the Unknown Root. However, despite this identity of every soul with the Over Soul, the One Divine Consciousness, every individual is embarked on a pilgrimage and is governed by the law of karma, of action and reaction, cause and effect. By the process of reincarnation, each one is evolving in an ever-increasing spiral toward a state of complete unfoldment. Man is a god in the becoming, a miniature universe; he is a microcosm of the Macrocosm, his potentialities beyond his own imagining. All are links in an endless chain of existence with no apparent beginning and no apparent end.

Both *The Secret Doctrine* and *The Mahatma Letters* state the idea of a Septenary Law: From the One emanate seven primordial rays. There are seven basic forces in nature, seven principles or differentiations of matter that form seven planes of existence; corresponding to these are seven states of consciousness. The Septenary Law is also manifest in man, in whom the seven rays are reflected. Man is described as saptaparna, a seven-leafed lotus. Each petal is a principle, which must be fully unfolded in order to come to the flowering of the perfect man.

One of the most important aspects of the Septenary Law is the concept of seven Root-races, each with its own seven subraces. Each Root-race is said to be a phase of human unfoldment in which a new sense is developed and a new level of consciousness. These seven Root-races bear a striking resemblance to certain Jain beliefs about the souls of various stages of animate and inanimate matter. The first Root-race has only the sense of hearing, and the second added the sense of touch; together they were a stage in the comprehension of sensation and perception. The third Root-race, known as the Lemurian, which evolved eighteen million years ago, produced man's bony skeleton, and the development of speech and sight, the beginning of mentality, emotion, and the separation of the sexes. The fourth Root-race, the Atlantean, is marked by the development of the lower mind and the sense of taste. The fifth Root-race, the Aryan or Indo-European, which arose in Central Asia, has seen the awakening of the higher mind and the sense of smell. Man is now in the fifth subrace of this race. The sixth Root-race will develop intuition and clairvoyance; the seventh, the faculty of direct perception and clairaudience.

At a time when it seemed the white man's destiny to colonize the brown-, black-, yellow-, and red-skinned areas of the world, the Root-race thesis was accepted at face value. However, it has come back to plague the Theosophists. To the early members (as to most Europeans) it was a fact of easily verifiable observation that nonwhites were inferior. "Take any savage of the lowest type," said Annie Besant in a lecture, "the aborigines of Australia, the Veddhas of Ceylon, the hairy men of Borneo—these are scarcely human, yet they are human: their language . . . is little better than the language of an ape that some have learned to reproduce. Try to realize him mentally and morally; he has practically no mind and no morals, only the germs of them."

To the credit of some modern Theosophists, they have tried to face up squarely to past mistakes ("We have committed some very grave and hurtful errors in our interpretation of the very mysterious subject of root-races," a leading member, Helen V. Zahara, stated in 1970), while others lay the blame on a misunderstanding of Theosophy of outside critics. Yet a racist attitude continues through the doctrine, and cannot be expunged from the standard texts without doing harm to basic tenets. Since the First Object stresses the Universal Brotherhood of Humanity, one asks, "Who are the members of this common fraternity?" "The white race must be the first to stretch out the hand of fellowship to the dark nations, to call the poor despised 'nigger' brother," said the Mahatma K.H. to A. P. Sinnett, giving the views of the Adepts. "If Theosophists say . . . the lower classes and the inferior races . . . cannot concern us and must manage as they can, what becomes of our fine profession of benevolence, philanthropy, reform, etc?"

It became part of the Society's goal to save such races. In India at the time, and in fact in virtually every nation, the concept of racial and social brotherhood was a dim prospect, and the Theosophists' stand a daring one. In 1894 Olcott went so far as to establish a school at Adyar for untouchable children (four others have since been founded), a move that went against the ingrained beliefs of most caste Hindus.

OCCULTISM. Not only did H.P.B. believe in the secret Wisdom of the ages, which was not apparent to the eyes of men, she also believed that there was a path to that Wisdom. Also, there is a secret code of conduct—a way of life—that enables one to travel the path to that Wisdom and make it one's own. She herself stated that as the result of her spiritual development in former lives, she had acquired the occult power known in Tibet as Tulku (as she called it), through which she could temporarily but deliberately and self-consciously remove her own Egoic consciousness and permit the influence of a far greater Individual, the Buddha, to act through her. She realized that occult powers were not for every Theosophist, and she formed an inner circle, the Esoteric Section, under her personal direction, teaching the Ageless Wisdom by "the study of practical Occultism or Raja Yoga." H.P.B.'s methods were undoubtedly successful, for the German philosopher Hermann Keyserling, a hostile critic, who wrote at length in unflattering terms about Adyar, stated in 1919, "As to Annie Besant, there is one thing of which I am certain: This woman controls her being from a centre which, to my knowledge, only very few men have ever attained to. . . . Mrs. Besant controls herself—her powers, her thoughts, her feelings, her volitions—so perfectly that she seems to be capable of greater achievements than men of greater gifts." He discussed the question of occult powers with C. W. Leadbetter (1847–1934), another leading Theosophist. "There is no doubt that both of them are honest, and both assert that they possess possibilities of experience, some of which are known under abnormal conditions, most of which, however, are totally unknown: Both of them declare that they have acquired these powers in course of practice."

The Society's centennial (in 1975) brought an expectation that the last true Tashi Lama (the current lama in their view is a Chinese puppet), who died in 1937, would be incarnated in the West to be the successful messenger of the Occult Brotherhood who carry out the mandate of Tsong-Kha-pa. Such a lama, if incarnated, must be sought out and tested before his acceptance, a process requiring a number of years.

Theravāda Buddhism. A form of Buddhism that arose early among the Buddha's disciples. The term means "the Teaching of the Elders" and refers to the group who maintained that they alone possessed the true doctrines and disciplines, while others were either too rigid or too lax in their interpretation. Theravāda, which is a form of Hīnayāna (q.v.), has kept the Buddhist scriptures in Pāli, rather than the Sanskrit and other languages employed by the other major group of schools, the Mahāyāna. While it is a truism that almost any one statement about Buddhism can be contradicted by another equally valid statement, and that identical doctrines can be shared by hostile schools, some Theravādin beliefs might be stated: They believe that the Gautama Buddha is a man like any other, but that he differed in the state of his understanding and intuition into things as they are, into the secrets of life and sorrow, and final release, nibbana (or nirvāṇa in other schools).

Theravādins state flatly, "Buddhism has nothing to do with religious mysticism or with dreams and ecstasies, visions and trances, which other religions [among them various forms of Mahāyāna] regard as affording supernatural powers." They also say that belief in a permanent self or soul is a pernicious error; such beliefs are but the result of longing for a deathless life and will naturally produce attachment to life and breed a craving for pleasure and an egotism not only on earth but also in "heaven." See Buddhism, Hīnayāna, Mahāyāna.

thich, Buddh. A term taken by Vietnamese Thien (Zen) monks, as in the cases of the famous medieval masters Thich Cam Cam and Thich Tri Boa, and the contemporary Thich Nhat Hanh. Thich is an abbreviated form of Thich-Ca, the Vietnamese for Śakya, the family name of Gautama Buddha. See Thien, Zen.

Thien, Buddh. The Indochinese form of Zen (Ch'an) Buddhism. Buddhism was introduced into the northern part of the Southeast Asian peninsula into the area then called Giao Chau (the nineteenth-century Tonkin, later North Vietnam) about the second century A.D. by land from China and by sea from India. The country at that time was a stopping-off point for commercial trade between the two great lands, and was under Chinese hegemony. Tao and Confucianism were the dominant sects, with much animism among the village people. Thien Buddhism soon dominated other forms of Buddhism but developed into various sects and subsects according to indigenous influences. Meanwhile, the southern section of the peninsula took up Theravāda or Hīnayāna forms of Buddhism, which have always been in a minority (in 1963 a united Buddhist church was formed out of Thien—Mahāyānist—and Theravāda sects). Thien as practiced by masters and monks takes a purified form, differing from other religions by not being conditioned by any set of beliefs. Only the search to attain, to penetrate, to see in order to attain satori (q.v.) has any reality. Right living—right eating and drinking—and the right techniques—right breathing, concentration, and meditation—form the basis of Thien, as they do other forms of Zen.

Village Buddhism is a combination of Thien and Amidist or

Pure Land beliefs, with some Confucianism and animism intermixed. These practices have affected even a large number of the Thien monasteries.

Among leading Thien saints and masters are the King-monk Tran Thai Tong, the author of the *Thien Tong Chi Nam* (Guide to Zen); Tue Trung Thuong Si, a warrior-hero who routed the Mongols and later retired into solitude to found a Thien sect purified of Confucianism; and Truc Lam, an imperial counselor who also became a monk.

THIEN TEACHING. The masses of Vietnamese people practice a mixture of Confucianism, Taoism, and Thien Buddhism. The villages engage in a certain amount of Thien against a background of more orthodox Buddhism, especially in its Pure Land form. Each village has a common house (dinh) and a pagoda (chua); in the former, with its relics of animism, the titular god of the village is maintained and worshiped; the pagoda houses a statue of Buddha, which is cared for by the local monks. In the past, at the other end of the social structure, Thien monks played a vital role in the nation's affairs. In the ninth and tenth centuries A.D. they served as imperial counselors and helped train Vietnamese leaders capable of resisting the Chinese and building their own empire, employing Confucianism for practical matters and Thien for a powerful inner life. It was not uncommon for an Emperor to seek to give up all: "Well aware of the impermanence of glory that has affected monarchs in the past, I have come to seek nothing but the path to Buddhahood," Tran Thai Tong told Truc Lam, who replied, "The Buddha is not in the mountain but in your very mind. When your mind is calm and clear, Buddha appears. When your Majesty discovers the right nature of the mind, then you may attain Buddhahood immediately and do not have to go far to seek it."

Tran Thai Tong stated the precepts of Thien by saying in his *Guide to Zen,* "Buddhahood recognizes no South or North, and everyone, whether ignorant or intelligent, has his share of ability to scrutinize the problem of birth and death in the most-crystal-clear fashion, which is the doctrine of Buddha." He added: "On the other hand, the doctrine of St. Confucius bears the heavy responsibility of preserving the balance of discipline for future generations. The Sixth Patriarch [q.v.] said: 'There exists no difference between Buddha and the St. Confucius.' This shows that the doctrine of Buddha needs Confucianism for its perpetuation in the future." See Buddhism, Ch'an, Zen.

Third Eye, Hind. and others. A mystical center or cakra (q.v.) situated between and slightly above the normal eyes. It is otherwise known as the ajña cakra, and is the last of the six that are awakened by the goddess Kuṇḍalinī in meditation. The Third Eye contains the mystic mantra ŌṂ (q.v.), and is the spot through which the soul leaves the body in samādhi, the highest stages of meditation, and in death. The bindi (q.v.) worn by Indian women and by some men symbolizes the Third Eye, though it does not mean in fact that the individual possesses the occult powers often associated with it.

Three Baskets, Buddh. The *Tripiṭaka,* the Buddhist canon of basic scriptures. See *Tripiṭaka.*

T'ien-T'ai, Buddh. A Mahāyānist school, syncretist in character and distinctly Chinese in development and form, based upon a North Indian or Central Asian scripture, the *Saddharmapuṇḍarika Sūtra* (Lotus of the Wonderful Law). The name of the sect is derived from the monastery of its founder, T'ien-t'ai (Heavenly Terrace) Mountain in Chekian Province. The scholar who shaped T'ien-t'ai was the Grand Master Chih-k'ai, or Chih-i (A.D. 538–97), who spent his life in studying and interpreting the Sutra for his disciples. Combining the intellectualism of the South (from which he came) with the meditative practices of the North (where his own teacher lived), Chih-k'ai decided that the two approaches were as similar as the two wings of a bird. His central teaching in a highly complex system may be stated as the Principle of the Perfectly Harmonious Threefold Truth: Emptiness (all things, all dharmas are without content), Temporariness (all exists but for a while), and the Mean (all things are only a combination of Emptiness and Temporariness). The three are intimately involved, working upon each other somewhat in the manner of Hinduism's three guṇas (q.v.), each depending upon the other. Chih-k'ai also taught that all things have the Buddha-nature within them and thus all are to attain salvation, a philosophy of One-in-All and All-in-One, poetically expressed by the phrase "Every color, every fragrance is none other than the Middle Path." Chih-k'ai's disciples stated that the Lotus teaching is the most complete of all Buddhist doctrines. See Buddhism, Mahāyāna.

tilak, Hind. An alternate term for the bindi (q.v.), the red mark that Hindu women and some Hindu men wear on their foreheads.

tīrtha, Hind. A place of pilgrimage, though the English translation is held by Hindus to be far too limited. A tīrtha may be an actual sacred "place," but also a sacred river, mountain, forest, or even region, though in the latter case the term kṣetra is more properly applied. A tīrtha is a place where God dwells and where He reveals Himself. The word originally meant a river ford, and the common phrase tīrtha-yātrā (to go on pilgrimage) literally means "undertaking journey to river fords." Tīrtha may also be taken metaphorically: For example, a yogi may physically stay put but through meditation go on pilgrimage to the Seven Shrines, shrine in this sense implying a certain quality such as "truth." One might add that tīrtha-yātrā is valueless if the pilgrim has not led a moral and upright life.

tīrthaṅkara, Jain. Literally "keeper of the fords." One of the legendary Jain leaders or sages, of which there are twenty-four, the last being Mahāvīra, the only one with some historical credibility. See Jain, Mahāvīra.

TM. The common term for Transcendental Meditation (q.v.).

Tooth, Holy (or Sacred), Buddh. The Lord Gautama Buddha's tooth, enshrined in Kandy, Sri Lanka. For details, see Buddha, relics.

tortoise, as mystical symbol. The tortoise is a maṇḍala of the Divine in certain cultures; in others its significance is solely evil, or implies danger or black magic. Among the Chinese, the creature is both revered and feared. In the *I Ching* (q.v.), the magic tortoise is "a creature possessed of such supernatural powers that it lives on air and needs no earthly nourishment" (Hexagram 27). The image of letting the magic tortoise go "means that a man fitted by nature and position to live freely and independently renounces this self-reliance and instead looks with envy and discontent at others who are outwardly in better circumstances. But such base envy only arouses derision and contempt in those others. This has bad results." In ancient China the tortoise shell was employed as a form of oracle, its heating in a fire and subsequent cracking of the undershell developing patterns that may be said to foreshadow the trigrams and hexagrams of the *I Ching*. However, among other Chinese the tortoise was known as an animal of the worst character and its representation avoided.

Farther afield, among the Fans of Africa, men in their prime never eat tortoise for fear of losing their vigor and speed; the old men do so freely; having lost strength and fleetness of foot, they fear no harm from the flesh of such a lumbering animal. In Tanna, in the New Hebrides, in the days of cannibalism recently past, the tortoise was an alternative to human flesh, and some clans could eat tortoise meat only, its consumption being observed with rites equal in profundity to those for that of human flesh.

In India the tortoise holds a most sacred place. The creature is an incarnation of Vishnu (q.v.)—his second, following the Fish; the Tortoise is a form he took to recover some of the things lost in the Great Deluge, the accounts of which in part strikingly resemble Genesis 7 and 8. In another context, the *Mārkaṇḍeya Purāṇa* describes the continent of India resting permanently upon the back of this tortoise, Vishnu himself. The tortoise of the *I Ching* and that of primal Indian belief are most certainly expressions of primitive totemic worship.

As a maṇḍala or mystic circle the tortoise becomes a complex symbol. The late Dr. Sohran Ardeshir Eruchshaw Jamshedji Sola Hakim has described the tortoise maṇḍala as follows:

"The water-dwelling tortoise, with its round shell and limbs, head and tail withdrawn, represents the dormant circular universe suspended in boundless space. Putting out its head is the first point of creation, and by extending the tail, forms the first line bisecting the circle into hemispheres. The head, with the lower limbs extended, forms the triangle within the circle. The four limbs, the square; with the head, the pentagon; and with the tail protruding, the hexagon within the circle, the symbol of the fully manifested universe, swimming in space."

In Ch'an Buddhism the symbolism takes a different form. The six senses of man are equated to the six vulnerable parts (head, tail, the four legs) of the black tortoise, which shrink into the shell when the creature is attacked, these senses disappearing in the practice of meditation in the Ch'an hall, when nothing can disturb the mind. The simile is common in Buddhist scriptures to advise the human being to shut the Six Gates of the senses so as to be detached from external surroundings. See Ch'an, Zen; also see maṇḍala and yantra for related concepts.

Tower of Silence, Zor. (The correct name is dakhmah.) A sacred enclosure used by both Iranian and Indian Zoroastrians (Parsees) to dispose of the dead. The tower is prohibited to everyone except the priests in charge. The tower should be located in an isolated area, where birds (normally vultures) are present in number. Usually a hill or mountain is chosen as the site, but if the dakhmah is to be built on a plain, a high plinth will be laid as foundation. Before building commences, a "maṇḍala" (q.v.) of the shape is traced on the ground with metal spikes and cord. This pattern is filled with earth, and construction commences. The ceremony of dedication contains prayers of apology to the Archangel of Earth for defilement of the land with a tower for the dead. If construction of a dakhmah is not feasible, a small enclosure, open at the top, is erected.

In the remote past bodies were left in the open to be disposed of by animals and birds. Today, primarily vultures enter the towers, which must be open to the sky. The rite is euphemized as "exposure to the sun"; funerals are held only during daylight hours, on the theory that since mankind receives certain vital currents from the sun, they should be gratefully returned. Under the high period of Zoroastrianism, each worshiper of Ahura Mazdā, the Omniscient Lord, built his own dakhmah during his lifetime for his own death; these were known as dakhmah-i tan bah tan (dakhmah for a single body). The large towers, of the type presently in use, are known as dakhmah-i lashkari (dakhmah for soldiers) and became common after the Muslim invasion of the seventh century, when there was much slaughter of Zoroastrians.

Each tower has a series of niches: one set for men, another for women, and a third for children. Large towers may have as many as 450 niches, though with the small population of Parsees today they are rarely in full use. After the bones have been picked clean —the vultures require about twenty minutes—the bones are put in a paved central pit, where they eventually crumble to dust and are carried by rainwater to four deep subterranean wells. Bones may be used as fertilizer, but no tombs can be erected on the basis that using ground otherwise needed for crops is a sin. The method of disposing of corpses is an ancient one but is much criticized by non-Parsees and even by some less traditional-minded members of the sect. See Disposal of the Dead, Zoroastrians.

Transcendental Meditation (commonly called TM). A form of meditation derived from yogic principles (many of which have been discarded along the way) by the Indian Maharishi Mahesh Yogi, in 1958, after much thought and experimentation. The movement, according to its leaders, numbers in the hundreds of thousands; it is based in the United States, but has branches throughout Europe and a large ashram in Rishikesh, India. TM is "not a religion, a philosophy, or a way of life," spokesmen say, but "a simple and effortless technique for expanding consciousness [offering] access to an unlimited reservoir of energy and 'creative intelligence' that lies at the source of thought within the deepest layers of the psyche." TM has eliminated the five early aṇgas or stages of yoga (q.v.), calling them "esoteric," to begin immediately with "meditation," the sixth, according to classical yoga; āsanas (q.v.), the ethical codes of yoga's first two stages, and the need for a special room or other place in which to practice are eschewed. TM is stated to be easily learned and practiced by everyone. The goal is the experience of pure consciousness.

METHOD. The basic "tool" of TM is the mantra (q.v.), which is said repeatedly. The mantra is given by the TM teacher at the first meeting. Here, in a brief ceremony, the teacher receives from the student flowers and fruit, and a white handkerchief; some Sanskrit prayers are recited, the mantra bestowed (it is to be kept secret by the student), and instructions in meditation given. The student along with other beginners returns for three days more of instruction and discussion. After this initiatory period, the student is required to practice alone for two periods a day for fifteen to twenty minutes each time. Four check-up sessions are required. A substantial fee is charged, its size depending to some extent on the student's status in life.

The mantra, as the heart of TM, is said repeatedly. Extraneous thoughts, which in classical yoga (and other meditative practices such as Zen) must be emphatically excluded, are, in TM, accepted as a part of the process, being considered a kind of cathartic agent similar in purpose to the dream. TM teachers and most students claim great success with the method, and can cite numerous examples of individuals surmounting anxieties, neuroses, and psychosomatic conditions, plus gaining better physical health. However, there is much criticism of TM, especially on the part of those who follow more orthodox paths of Eastern disciplines, who charge that TM appeals to individuals who want "instant enlightenment" without the preliminary basic training, which is considered necessary to proper spiritual growth. See Maharishi Mahesh Yogi.

trapas, Tib. A lower-ranking Tibetan Buddhist monk. One of the higher ranks is a lāma (q.v.), a term often misapplied to Tibetan monks in general.

Trimūrti, Hind. The triad of the three major gods, Brahmā, Vishnu, and Shiva, three aspects of the Supreme—the One God in three forms, manifestations of the one Primeval Spirit, the Lord adored by all, the one undecaying Brahman; the Trimūrti are masculine, but Brahman is neuter. The theme is largely artificial in concept and is one by which the brāhminical theologians of the late post-Vedic period attempted to absorb and make use of the two popular non-Vedic deities, Vishnu and Shiva, in order to prevent their arising cults from undermining the Vedic Brahmā. The attempt had little effect upon the popular religions of the non-brāhmins, Vaisnavism, Shaivism, and Shaktism, which became the dominant forms of public worship and devotion. The Trimūrti is notably absent in most works by Hindu philosophers, even among the brāhmins; it is rarely worshiped except by some members of the priestly caste, and commands virtually no temples or cult.

In the Trimūrti, Brahmā is seen as the Creator, Vishnu the Preserver and Shiva the Destroyer (in order for Brahmā to create again). The *Vishnu Purāṇa* concisely states the doctrine: "The Lord God, though one without a second, assumes the three forms respectively of Brahmā, Vishnu, and Shiva for creation, preservation, and dissolution of the world." The *Padma Purāṇa* says, "Brahmā, Vishnu, and Shiva, though three in form, are one entity. No difference between the three exists except with respect to attributes." Both texts, though Vaisnavite, are brāhminical, the priests favoring Vishnu over Shiva. The Trimūrti, artificial as it is, has had a great appeal to Westerners, especially missionaries and theologians, who see in it a form of the Christian Trinity. The French Indic scholar Alain Daniélou (to take one literate out of many illiterate examples) sees Shiva as the Progenitor, the Father; Vishnu as avatār, the Redeemer and God incarnate, his descent as Krishna resembling the birth of Jesus; and Brahmā as a type of the Holy Ghost, the link between the Father and the Son, proceeding from both. However, he makes the interesting point that "It might not be difficult to find a historical link between the Trinity and the trimūrti. Hindu philosophical conceptions were known in Greece and the Middle East before and after the beginning of the Christian Era. It may, however, be noted that, whereas the Trinity is presented in Scholastic philosophy as a mystery, it is a fundamental definition of Hindu religious philosophy."

Despite the fact that seemingly nothing can be higher than the Trimūrti as the expression of the Brahman, devotees of the Shiva's son, the elephant-headed god Gaṇpati (or Ganesha), place him above it as the supreme deity. See Brahmā, Brahman, Gaṇpati, Shakti, Shiva, Vishnu.

Tripiṭaka, Buddh. The Three Baskets, the Buddhist canon, consisting of the basic documents collected, collated, and edited (and sometimes expanded) by Buddha's disciples. Scholars disagree on the dates of the works involved. Some believe that the Tripiṭaka achieved near-final form within a century of Buddha's death, others that it represents a slow accumulation and editing. However, some parts of the collection are the actual words of the Buddha himself, more or less changed. Much of the original Tripiṭaka, especially the Mahāyānist versions, has been lost, surviving only in translations in other tongues (Chinese and Tibetan, for example). The most complete Tripiṭaka, of the Theravāda school, was produced in Ceylon in about A.D. 80 in Pāli, the Buddhist liturgical tongue. The work is so complex, running some seventy times the size of the Christian Bible, that it is impossible for any one individual to master it.

The Tripiṭaka covers a wide range of material: Some of the texts are ancient, being in an archaic form of Pāli; others date from more recent periods. Not only do they report sermons and sayings of the Buddha and many incidents in his life (some obviously fanciful), but they also include numerous directives for living, parables, fables, proverbs, aphorisms, songs, and stories, many of great literary, artistic, cultural, and sociological value. The Baskets are: Conduct (Vinaya), Discourses (Sutta), and Supplementary Doctrines (Abdhidhamma). The *Vinaya Piṭaka* is mainly codes of disciplines for the men and women who entered the Sangha, the Buddhist Brotherhood. The *Sutta Piṭaka,* by far the most interesting and significant, contains discourses, dialogues, numerous talks, conferences and sermons of Buddha and his followers. Much of what Buddha said was taken down, according to the text itself, by his favorite disciple Ānanada. The style is clearly indicative of direct preaching to the public, and the material includes parables, allegories, stories, and poetic matter, with much repetition for emphasis. In this Basket are also many works called Jātakas, accounts of the lives of other Buddhas, and the famous *Dhammapada,* a concise collection of Buddha's sayings. The *Abdhidhamma Piṭaka* is a highly complex later collection of seven works dealing with Buddhist metaphysics, psychology (one section lists and defines over three hundred different human types), answers to common questions brought up by the faithful, and refutations of unorthodox teachings.

tulasī (also tulsi), Hind. A sacred plant of the basil family (*ocynum sanctum*). Tulasī was one of Vishnu's paramours; in jealousy his wife Lakshmi turned her into a plant, and the god became the śalagrāma stone (q.v.) to keep her company. (In some versions of the tulasī story, Lakshmi and Tulasī are but different names for the same goddess; some ethnologists see both as archaic forms of an Earth Mother deity.)

The plant grows up to three feet in height. It is kept at temples and at the homes of brāhmins, usually planted on a small mound of sandy soil, called the brinda-van (or some variation of the name Vrindāvana, the sacred grove of Krishna). It may also be planted in a vrindāvana pedestal, a type of horned altar also found at some archaic sites in the Middle East. The daily circumambulation of the plant is a meritorious act, and its leaves are believed capable of purifying the soul and the body; the highly aromatic leaves are taken as a digestive after meals. During an individual's last hours the plant and a śalagrāma are placed in the death room; a bit of tulasī root is inserted in the mouth; leaves are scattered about the face, eyes, ears, and chest; and the dying one is sprinkled head to foot with water from a tulasī twig. A tulasī branch given a distressed person will avert present troubles. Yearly, at the sacred Krishna shrine of Vrindāvana and elsewhere, the śalagrāma and tulasī are married to each other, often with elaborate and costly rites, both being personifications of their respective deities and so venerated. See Krishna, Lakshmi, śalagrāma, Vishnu; also see vegetation.

tulku, Buddh. A Tibetan term (actually spelled bsprul-sku) meaning "one who is divinely incarnated"—e.g., the Dalai Lāma (q.v.), who is the tulku or avatār of the bodhisattva Chenrezig, the Tibetan form of the Indian Avalokiteśvara.

tumo, Tib. The word signifies heat or warmth. Tumo is the art of keeping warm without a fire even in the dead of winter. It is a skill of the naljorpa (q.v.), who wears only a cotton robe or may even be naked. Tumo, in the sense of heat or light, is applicable to mystics only. There are several types of tumo. In esoteric tumo the adept is able to stay warm whatever the depths of snow or ice or the ferocity of the winds. Tumo is gained after certain secret initiatory rites, followed by rigorous training in meditation at altitudes over ten thousand feet. As a test of the naljorpa's mastery of tumo, his body is covered with wet "sheets" dipped in water obtained from an ice-covered lake. Sitting in meditation at night, the naljorpa dries the sheets by the heat of his body. Forty sheets so dried is said to be an acceptable number. Esoteric tumo is the spontaneous result of peculiar raptures that envelop the mystic in the "soft, warm mantle of the gods." In mystic tumo, the adept experiences "paradisiac bliss" though still in this world. Mystically, tumo is the subtle flame that heats the generative fluid until its energies overflow into the channels of the rtsas (identified with the nādis of Hinduism), the veins, arteries, and nerve channels.

tun wu, Buddh. The Ch'an (Chinese) term for satori (q.v.). The term may be shortened to wu alone.

◄U►

'Ulamā', Isl. The continuing line of Muslim divines who interpreted the Qur'ān and the Sunna and proclaimed sharī'a (Islamic law). The 'Ulamā' are primarily the protectors of orthodoxy, not only serving as guides to the past but also controlling most education in the light of their own spiritual and intellectual ideals. This rigidity and concern with formalistic aspects of Islam brought conflicts on one hand from secular rulers who tried to control them, and on the other, from the folk movements, in particular the Ṣūfīs (q.v.), which often disregarded the 'Ulamā'. Though their conservative attitudes have led to much intellectual stagnation within the vast Muslim world, particularly in the secular sciences, their great power gave tremendous cohesiveness, especially through the development of sharī'a. Because of the social changes within Islam in recent centuries, the 'Ulamā' have been forced to confine themselves to formulas of belief and creed based on the past, and to proclaim fatwās (authoritative legal opinions) based on external jurisprudential matters.

umma muslima, Isl. The Community of the Faithful, the concept of a universal brotherhood on the basis of submission (islam) to Allāh—i.e., God—faith being substituted for the old blood-ties and tribal loyalties of the primitive Arab clans. Such was Muḥammad's vision, which came into being. But faith and belief alone are only the grounding; the Community also is based upon the principles of humanitarianism, egalitarianism, social and economic justice, righteousness, and solidarity. Though the umma muslima was originally constructed from the neighboring Arabic tribes of the Peninsula, it soon included great numbers of non-Arabs, who quickly outnumbered the Arabs themselves. "Umma" may also apply to non-Islamic groups, such as the Christians (in the religious sense) and the Franks (in a political sense).

Upaniṣads, Hind. A collection of speculative treatises, of which 108 are said to be still extant (108 is a mystical number). The term upaniṣad means sitting next to, or under (a teacher); also, "secret teaching." The Upaniṣads, composed roughly in the period B.C. 800–600, are part of the vast corpus of Vedic scriptures known as śruti (what is heard), and come at the end of the collection; hence they are also referred to as Vedānta (q.v.), the end of the Vedas. The Upaniṣads mark a shift in emphasis and interests from the heroic, sacrificial hymns and magical formulas of the four Vedas and probe the themes already foreshadowed in less esoteric terms—the sacred interior cosmos of both the universe and man—the Eternal Brahman, the ground of all Realities, and the Ātman, the self or soul, the ground of the thinker himself. Some Hindu scholars claim that the Upaniṣads had a profound influence upon Gautama Buddha, but against this, one must also consider the horror with which many brāhmins hold him. However, the Upaniṣads do correspond in a number of broad aspects to the doctrines that later developed in Mahāyāna Buddhism. See Ātman, Brahman, Buddhism, Vedas.

Upanishad. See Upaniṣads.

upāsaka, Buddh. A lay disciple (male) who follows certain basic rules otherwise observed primarily by Buddhist monks, especially the Eight Moral Precepts, fasts at certain times, and perhaps practices of meditation.

upāsikā, Buddh. The feminine form of upāsaka, above.

V

vairāgya, Hind. Freedom from desire; dispassion; detachment from the world. There are two forms of vairāgya; aparā (lower), denoting detachment from the objects of pleasure, and parā (higher), denoting detachment from the guṇas or nature as such in its primordial condition. Vairāgya is conceived as a fire, since the individual in such a state experiences a burning agony in the least contact with worldly things or sense objects.

Vaisnavism, Vaisnavite, Hind. The cult of the god Vishnu (or a member of the sect); Vaisnavism is popularly expressed in the adoration of the god Krishna, an incarnation of Vishnu. See Krishna, Vishnu.

Veda, Hind. The word means knowledge. There are four Vedas, dating from the earliest period of known Indian scriptures; the Rig Veda (or Ṛgveda), a collection of praises in the form of hymns; the Ṣāma Veda, also a collection of hymns; the Yajur Veda, a collection of sacrificial formulas; and the Atharva Veda, a collection of charms and magic formulas. They are known together as Saṃhitās (Collections). The Vedas are śruti, which means what is heard, their text being delivered to mankind through the seers as the sound of eternal truth. The texts, developed over a long period, possibly beginning before the Āryans, whose scriptures they are, arrived in India in the period c. B.C. 1500 (B.C. 1700–1200 according to some scholars). Some contain references to geographical sites in Afghanistan, and many refer to sites on the Indus plain and eastward, either being late compositions or later insertions. The texts were passed down orally, being handed on from one generation of priests to another, syllable perfect in intonation and rhythm from memory and by rote. An error in recital led to punishment and penances; in effect, to hear a Vedic passage today is to hear the oral equivalent of a tape recording over three thousand years old. It was forbidden to write down the text, but about the fourteenth century A.D. at least part of the Vedas had been transcribed, and later editions were prepared, some under the auspices of European scholars who feared the loss of such valuable material at the hands, ears, and mouths of priests who often did not understand the sacred texts and were increasingly likely to make errors.

English translations, as in the case of much oriental literature, are stilted and hampered by a concentration on philology rather than meaning. Portions of the Vedas, especially of the Rig Veda, now enjoy adequate renderings in foreign tongues, but the entire text is still a guarded province of scholarship. See Hinduism, Rig Veda.

Vedānta, Hind. Literally the concluding portion of the Vedas (q.v.). This includes the Brāhmaṇas, Āranyakas, and Upaniṣads, which are all developments and elucidation of the Vedas; the Vedas are śruti (what is heard) a term that includes early Vedānta. However, in theory, all literature derived from or dependent upon the Vedas are Vedānta, even the most contemporary. There are numerous schools of Vedānta, but all contain the kernel of Vedic thought—that beneath the outward, shadowy, changing appearance of the universe, expressed as māyā (briefly, illusion and ignorance), there is an essential, unchanging Reality, which it calls Brahman or the Ātman, the Godhead. The one impersonal Brahman may take an infinite number of aspects, personal and impersonal, but its essential unity is stressed. The central subject matter of the Vedāntas is knowledge of the Supreme, this knowledge being that which will unite the individual with the universal Godhead. Modern expressions of Vedānta may be found in the life and teachings of the Bengali saint Rāmakrishna and the society founded in his name by his chief disciple, Vivekānanda, and in the West, the California group inspired by the Rāmakrishna Mission, of which Aldous Huxley, Gerald Heard, Christopher Isherwood, and Swami Prabhavananda were the chief exponents with their thesis of "The Perennial Philosophy," which they saw as the universal religion of man.

vegetation, sacred. The cult of trees and plants is primordial, especially in Hinduism, which in turn has affected Buddhism. Since the Hindu's temple and altar are the world, everything within the universe is sacred; what grows, more so. Animistic beliefs are included side by side with the highest philosophical and religious speculation, and are often expressed mystically and esoterically. The tree deity is found in the stamp seals of the Indus Valley (q.v.). Sacred groves, homes of mother goddesses, abound, and some types of trees have attained major standing. Plants such as the tulasī, a type of basil, are equally important. One of the leading trees in both Hinduism and Buddhism is the pipal (*ficus religiosa*), the bodhi tree (q.v.) under which Gautama Buddha attained enlightenment. The pipal is the object of universal worship throughout India. The spirits that inhabit trees are the yakshas, feminine deities; male figures never appear in such a connection. Veneration of the tree is a symbol of Shaktism, the cult of the Great Mother; the first duty of a śakta (q.v.) upon arising is to offer a short mantra in honor of her cult, a veneration that is non- and pre-Āryan. There are said to be seven sacred trees, but the list varies from one accounting to another; however, the pipal is always included. The vepu or margosa, also called the bil (*melia azadirachta*), is included in most listings; it is sacred to Shiva, and its trefoil leaves form an important part of daily worship, particularly in Bengal. The vepu, as a male, may be married to the pipal in brāhminical rites lasting several days; in some areas a plantain or banyan may play the masculine role. See bodhi tree, pipal, and tulasī; for parallel archaic concepts, see also animals, numbers, sleep.

Vendidad, Zor. "The Law against the Demons." Vendidad is the incorrect title for Vidēvdāt (q.v.), the last major portion of the Avesta, the Zoroastrian scriptures.

vibhūti, Hind. (1) An outer expression of inner Reality, manifested in the One Supreme Form revealed in all objects of the senses. (2) The supernormal powers acquired by a yogi in his ascent through the eight stages toward perfection. Vibhūtis are realized through the purification of the mind, and thus all vibhūtis are fundamentally mental.

Vidēvdāt (sometimes known as the Vendidad), Zor. The third of the three major sections of the Avesta, the sacred scriptures of the followers of the Prophet Zoroaster. The work, which is in twenty-two chapters, is written in ungrammatical and poor Zend and is not easily comprehensible, even by members of the faith. An immense part of it is concerned with ritualistic and legalistic problems, especially the disposal of corpses, sanitary codes, the observance of contracts, ritual uncleanliness and the rites of purification, protection of animals, penalties for illegal conduct, and various offenses, many of which involve contamination of both the living and of the earth and buildings by corpses and carcasses. Many prescriptions are formulated in terms of a dialog, almost a catechism, between Ahura Mazdā, the Omniscient God, and His Prophet Zoroaster. See Avesta.

vihāra, Buddh. Literally an abode, but in Buddhist usage a monastery for bhikkhus (monks), which would contain not only huts or cells but also classrooms, libraries, and halls for communal worship and meetings, plus whatever other facilities are needed for ordinary living. The area of eastern India where Buddha lived later had so many vihāras that the state is still called Bihar.

visarjana, Hind. The ritual of "relinquishing"—i.e., of deconsecration of an image that has previously been infused with the life-soul of a deity by prānā pratiṣṭha (roughly the establishment of the sacred breath) at a festival. In visarjana the god is thanked for having dwelled among the devotees and is requested to return again when the festival is next celebrated. In many cases the image is destroyed—e.g., by immersion (as in the case of a clay figure) in a river, often the Ganges, where it melts away and is carried off by the sacred waters to the ocean. See Hinduism.

Vishnu (Sanskrit, Vṣṇu), Hind. One of the Trimūrti (q.v.), the three great gods of Hinduism (the others being Brahmā and Shiva). Like Shiva, Vishnu has his antecedents in the hoary past before the Āryan arrival, and the deity we know today is an amalgamation of various traditions. Vishnu was more easily absorbed into the Vedic Āryan pantheon than Shiva; there are traces of

Vishnu in various forms in the early Upaniṣads (possibly as later insertions after B.C. 600), but the fullness of the deity does not appear until the following centuries, in the Mahābhārata, the *Bhagavad Gītā,* and the Purāṇas, where Vishnu himself takes his final form and the doctrine of the avatār is stated in detail.

Vishnu appears as a majestic figure, the Godhead at peace, propitious, anthropomorphic. A solar and cosmic deity, he is god of the ocean and of the luminous sky, the protector and sustainer of the world. He is known as the All-Pervader, being the cohesive, centripetal constructive power of the universe, as contrasted to the dark, dispersive, destructive power of Shiva. The origin of Vishnu's name is in doubt, some glosses being found in roots signifying a pervading or entering power, others indicating a phallic origin. Whatever the source, he is seen as the universal intellect, the cosmic vision, the inner cause by which things exist, the symbol of eternal life binding the universe together.

Two main themes may be distinguished in the pre-Āryan cults that coalesced into that of Vishnu, along with the minor themes such as those of the various avatārs that became interwoven in the grandeur of the deity. One is the cult of Vāsudeva, an ancient hero of the Vrishni tribe, which claimed descent from the Yadus, the tribe of the antihero and erotic cowherd Krishna, later to become an avatār of Vishnu. The other is Nārāyaṇa, a cosmic deity of unknown origins; today he is synonymous with Vishnu, lying on the coiled serpent Śesa floating on the primeval waters, the resting place of the worlds. The Āryan priests, the brāhmins, identified Vāsudeva and Nārāyaṇa with the Vedic cosmic solar deity Vishnu.

Having pervaded—manifested—the world, Vishnu rules it as guide and ruler, saving it in times of stress and trouble. This is the concept of avatār, the Supreme incarnated on earth to rescue man and beast. The several Vishnu Purāṇas give various conflicting lists, running from ten (the most popular figure) to twenty-two to thirty-nine. In the list of ten, the first three incarnations, the Fish, Tortoise, and Boar, appear to have totemic origins. The most popular incarnations are those of Krishna and Buddha; both had widespread appeal among the common people, but contradictory uses for the brāhmins: Krishna was turned to priestly purposes, while Buddha was considered an enemy. The final incarnation, Kalki, is yet to come.

Krishna became the erotic, sensuous deity of the populist Vaisnavite movement, with its expression of bhakti (devotion) in opposition to the ritualism of the brāhmins, which separated them from the people. The Mahābhārata, and the *Bhagavad Gītā,* the later edited and distorted from its original form by the priests, and the Purāṇas established the god as a popular deity with brāhminical sanction. The *Vishnu Purāṇa* shows the direction taken by the priests to maintain their own superiority and sanctification: "He who pleases Vishnu obtains all terrestrial enjoyments, heaven, final liberation, and in a word, all his wishes find gratification with whom Vishnu is pleased. How is he to be rendered complaisant? The supreme Vishnu is propitiated by a man who observes the institution of caste, order and purificatory practices [all of which are controlled by the brāhmins]; no other path is the way to please him. . . . [Vishnu] is propitiated by him who follows the duties prescribed by his caste . . . who is diligent in the service of the gods, brāhmins and religious preceptors." The same message to the lower castes had already been stated in the *Bhagavad Gītā.* On the other hand, the brāhmins had been unable to control or absorb the kśatriya (warrior caste) Gautama Buddha, so immediately popular in his rejection of Vedic sacerdotalism and ritualism. When the Buddha became in the people's mind an avatār of the Lord Vishnu, the priests could do little but denigrate him as the embodiment of delusion.

In the *Bhāgavata Purāṇa,* where Buddha is the twenty-first avatār, the vision of a destructive, murderous incarnation is seen, somewhat confused with Kalki, the avatār to come. The brāhmins have taken this theme, along with other texts, and have developed it into philosophical and theological refutation of what they had seen as threatening and pernicious doctrines, destructive to their interests. The Buddha preached—or will preach, for some are not sure that he has actually appeared—pure atheism to mankind and even lead the gods themselves into sin and error. The śudras, the lowest caste, will wear red cloth, a color fitting only for brāhmins, and will acquire knowledge, even that of the Vedas. The brāhmins will not fulfill the duties of their calling and will not observe the rules concerning defilement and purity. Caste will disappear, and children will not obey their parents. Kings will act vilely, and universal disorder will prevail. The land will lose its fertility; little rain will fall; cows will be dry of milk, and the little they give will not be fit for making ghee. Today most brāhmins agree that this Buddha has already appeared, for his age had marked the end of Vedic domination and the ritual sacrifices they had practiced.

Viśnanātha, Hind. A name for Shiva as presiding deity of the sacred city of Benares (q.v.). The term denotes the Lord of the universe who is One with the Supreme.

Vivekānanda (1863–1902), Hind. A Bengali intellectual, born Narendranāth Datta in Calcutta. He was educated in English schools in his own city. Although an agnostic, he joined the reformist Brāhmo Samāj (q.v.) and was introduced to the Bengali mystic Rāmakrishna, to whom he soon attached himself as a disciple. When the saint died in 1886, Swami Vivekānanda took sannyāsa (spiritual withdrawal) and with some disciples spent six years on pilgrimage in India. In 1893 he attended the Parliament of Religions in Chicago and was taken up by an American following; he increased his Western flock of disciples in London, where he spent much time. Back in India in 1897, he made a triumphal tour of Colombo (Sri Lanka), Madras, and Calcutta. In the same year he organized the Rāmakrishna Mission, which was to be highly successful in promulgating Vivekānanda's version of the saint's teachings. A second trip to the United States and England brought more fame and success. He died at Belur, Bengal, at the math or ashram he had founded there in 1898. His teachings were a streamlined, modernized Vedānta, rejecting past superstitions and reactionary tendencies, with a layer of Western social reform. However, some of his ideas show a morbidity unacceptable to positive-thinking foreigners. He was a fervent devotee of Kālī, and saw life in terms of her negative aspects. "There are some who scoff at the existence of Kālī," he said. "Who can say that God does not manifest Himself as Evil as well as Good? But only the Hindu dares to worship him in the evil." He also said, "I worship the terrible! It is a mistake to hold that with all men pleasure is the motive. Quite as many are born to seek after pain. Let us worship the Terror for Its own sake. . . . How few have dared to worship

Death, or Kālī! Let us worship Death!" Like others of the neo-Hindu revival, he saw Hinduism and India as the world Savior, and that, as a disciple reported, "the East must come to the West, not as sycophant, not as servant, but as Guru and teacher."

One of the Swami's early and most important converts was the Irishwoman Margaret E. Noble, who followed him from London to India in 1898. He called her Nivedita (the Dedicated One), the name by which she has been known since. Nivedita became his biographer, the collector of his sayings, and the editor of his writings; her own works are a reflection of Vivekānanda's ideas. The Rāmakrishna Mission is a paragon of unselfish devotion and hard work on behalf of the Indian poor, transcending caste and racial barriers. The group maintains a number of centers outside India, including one in New York. Orthodox Hindus find the Mission's version of Hinduism inauthentic and too Westernized. See Rāmakrishna.

Vṣṇu, Hind. The Sanskrit spelling of the more common Vishnu, (q.v.).

◂ W ▸

Wen Shu, Buddh. The Chinese name of the bodhisattva Mañjuśrī (q.v.).

Woodroffe, Sir John George (1865–1936). Editor and translator of a number of important tantric texts. An English barrister, educated at Oxford, and a member of the Inner Temple, 1889, Woodroffe went to Calcutta to practice his profession in 1890. He soon rose to be a professor at the University of Calcutta and a judge of the city's High Court, a post he held from 1904 to 1922, as well as serving as Officiating Chief High Justice of Bengal. Upon his retirement from the Indian court, he was reader in Indian law at Oxford until 1930. But more important than his impressive legal career was the work Sir John did as a scholar in tantra (q.v.), finding and rescuing obscure texts and translating and editing them, either alone or with the aid of Indian experts. His researches form the basis for the larger part of current tantric studies and popular books, in both the Indian languages and in English. The tantras which form the basis of much of the present age of Kali Yuga (q.v.) were deliberately ignored, misunderstood, or defamed by the West until Sir John began his series of publications. With a masterly command of tantra Sir John evinced an inner affinity for it which for a westerner seems unique. Possibly his most important work is *The Serpent Power,* a translation with commentary of two previously untranslated, unpublished manuscripts dealing with the goddess Kuṇḍalinī (q.v.). Others of his publications include *The Garland of Letters, The Greatness of Śiva, Mahá Mâyâ, Principles of Tantra* (ed.), *Shakti and Shakta, The Wave of Bliss,* and *Tantra of the Great Liberation.* His work was originally published under the name Arthur Avalon: on later editions his own name is used.

World Community of Islam in the West. The formal name of the Black Muslim movement, which had previously been known as the Nation of Islam. See Black Muslims.

◂ Y ▸

yaga (also yagna, yagnam), Hind. See yajña, below.

yajña, Hind. The Vedic ritual of sacrifice. (It is also called yaga, yagna, and yagnam.) Vedic religion was mainly one of sacrifices, carefully observed down to the most minute gesture and intonation of phrase. Fire was the central means and instrument of sacrifice, with four kinds of victims: horse, cow, elephant, or man. In the earliest period, the horse was the standard sacrificial object; this was the aśvedmedha (q.v.). The sacred books deal regularly with yajña blood sacrifices. Originally they were simple but grew to incredible proportions as the number of victims increased, making wearying demands upon the tribal economy, though their purpose was in part the increase of cattle and food and a prosperous life for the people, as well as propitiation of the gods.

Under the Buddhist reaction to brāhminism, blood sacrifices gradually died out. Cost prohibited their resurrection except in the most unusual circumstances. Today pūjā—nonbloody sacrifice and worship on a small scale, either individual or by a priest hired for the occasion—is the ordinary method, though simple, abbreviated, nonsacrificial forms of yajña are celebrated among the brāhmins. The sacrifice of goats, fowl, and buffalo in various temples and on certain festivals is held by non-brāhmins in honor of the goddess Kālī or her alter ego, Durgā, etc.

Attempts have been made to restore the practice of yajña in the modern age. A long yajña costing millions of rupees was celebrated by the Hindu merchants of Karachi during the world depression of the 1930s. In 1975, after the failure of an earlier attempt, what its participants stated would probably be the last true yajña was held in Kerala in South India in the remote village of Panjal by the Namputiri Brahmins, who claim to be the only people now capable of performing the ancient, complicated rites. The traditional fireplace in the form of the sacred bird Garuḍa was built; and all measurements of the structures were made in multiples or divisibles of the yajamana (the one who performs the rites) when he stands upright with his arms raised in a posture of supplication. Two white horses were tethered at the eastern side of the yagasala, the central sacrificial building, but were not slaughtered; no metallic implements or vessels were used; and "soma," in this case a leafless creeper called *carcosterma brevistigma W & A* (see Soma), was drunk. Because neither horses nor cows (nor elephants nor humans) can any longer be sacrificed, goats were to be substituted. However, the public protest that this was an act of hiṃsā (violence) almost brought a cancellation of the ceremonies. In the end, the celebrants of the last yajña of all had to be satisfied with clay figurines of animals.

Yajur Veda, Hind. The third of the collection of ancient texts called the Vedas (q.v.). The Yajur Veda consists of sacrificial formulas performed by the priesthood.

yaksha, Hind. A local spirit, sometimes male but more often female, worshiped in a site such as a grove or a tree. The essentials are a stone tablet or altar located near or under a sacred tree. The yaksha may reside in the tree. The cult has been traced back to the Indus Valley, where stamp seals showing a nature spirit in a tree have been found. The cult was and is one of devotion (or bhakti) and finds its counterparts in Buddhism and Jainism. See bhakti, Indus.

Yama, Hind. The Lord of Death, originally a solar deity who was the first of immortals to choose a mortal destiny. He gave up immortality in order to conquer death and lead the mortal world after him; thus he is the First Ancestor and the King of Ancestors (cf. the Yellow Ancestor, the Chinese equivalent). Yama drinks the sacred substance soma, in the Rig Veda, and carouses with the gods and departed souls alike in his own palace, where the deceased will once again look upon the sun. In later texts he came to have a fearful aspect, being variously described as ugly and ill-shaped, of dark green complexion with glowing red eyes. He carries a noose, a rod, perhaps an ax, sword, and dagger as well. He may ride upon a black buffalo, or appear as one. To the virtuous he takes a different guise: The Mahābhārata describes him as "splendid like the Sun, of faultless blackness, beautiful, with red eyes," though he can still inspire dread. The *Padma Purāṇa* states that he resembles Vishnu, "with four arms, a dark complexion. His eyes resemble open lotuses. . . . His sacred brāhminical thread is of gold. His face is charming, smiling. He wears a crown, earrings, and a garland of wild flowers." His messengers may be equally as ugly and as wrathful as their master. Yama's palace is guarded by two four-eyed dogs; this detail, along with many others in the descriptions, of the god and his assembly hall, and the methods of judgment of the good and the sinner, are remarkably close to that of the Zoroastrian god of death, Yima. See four-eyed dog, Yima.

yama, Hind. The first of the eight stages of yoga (q.v.).

yantra, Hind. Yantra is the visual form of mantra (q.v.), a prayer. A tantric text states, "Yantra has mantra as its soul. The deity is the soul of the mantra. The difference between mantra and deity is similar to that between a body and its soul." Though two-dimensional, yantras are conceived of as having depth and full dimension. Yantras may be drawn or painted on any material, out of any substance. However, the human body is often called by tantrics "the best of all yantras." There is no parallel for the term in English, but yantra may be summarized as a two-dimensional diagram in which visualized energies are concentrated, or simply, "a field of energy." With its mantra, a yantra is a complex of stored imagery of sight and sound and psychic and mystical content. Many yantras seem like nothing more than an interwoven complex of geometrical designs centered upon a point (bindu). Triangles, sign of the female sexual organ, the yoni, may predominate, enclosing the bindu, the dot, which symbolizes the energizing, fecundating drop of semen. The whole may be enclosed by a square, signifying the cosmic dynamics and the four corners of the universe. Yantras are thus worshiped as containing the divine presence. The yantra is often understandably confused with a maṇḍala; the first is appropriate to a specific devata only, while a maṇḍala implies any devata.

yaosdāthregar, Zor. The highest level of Zoroastrian (or Parsee) priest. The sacerdotal class or caste among the Zoroastrians is hereditary. Only a priest's son may become a priest, though not all do so. The Zoroastrian caste structure, which once resembled that of the Hindus, has fallen into desuetude except for the highest, that of the priesthood, the lower three castes being merged into the laity in general.

There are four steps in attaining the priesthood. The first is that of navar (meaning a navigator), based on the concept that a priest's outlook must be unworldly (minoivinashni) and that he must "sail out to the other shore" in the boat of a dedicated life. In this initiatory step the sacerdotal neophyte passes through two ten-day periods in seclusion, sleeping on the floor or ground of the fire temple outbuildings, not touching defiling objects, and living in austerity and prayer. After these periods are completed, two priests begin a seven-day period of prayer and preparation on behalf of the initiate. On the final day, the initiate is taken into the temple itself (the dād-gāh, the fourth or ordinary level of such temples) to be tested in his knowledge and proficiency in the Yasna (q.v.), which is at once a sacred work and the system of rites and ceremonies. He spends three more days in isolation, eating one meal a day, at noon. On the fourth day he is escorted home in procession, now entitled to the rank of erward (roughly, "the reverend"), meaning he is proficient in sacred recitals.

The next stage is somewhat similar. The young ordinand must read from the Vidēvdāt (q.v.), and be able to recite by rote any of the seventy-two chapters of the Yasna and the Visperad. He is now a marāteb (master).

The final stage is that in which the candidate becomes a full priest (yaosdāthregar). The ceremony is known as narag din, and requires nine hours, starting at midnight, without a stop in the performance of the rite nor in the chanting and saying of prayers and hymns before the sacred fire. The mature yaosdāthregar may now perform all the varied duties of a Zoroastrian priest and can enter the innermost sanctum of the atāsh-beherām, the highest rank of fire temple. The title yaosdāthregar means sanctifier or "conductor of reunion with God." The new priest can now counsel the faithful and prepare amulets, celebrate the sacraments, and practice other spiritual rites on behalf of his people.

The priest is not paid, but his family and his community assure his livelihood and well-being. He receives cash offerings of moderate amounts from the laity for performing rites on their behalf. A priest by his circumscribed existence, not being supposed to mix freely in crowds under profane conditions (the theater, parties, in traveling, etc.), must set a sterling example for the faithful, not only in prayer and deportment, but even in maintaining himself physically clean and attuned. He must exhibit, without showing off, his absorption in spiritual activities. Because the life is financially unrewarding and confining as well, there is now a shortage of yaosdāthregars, especially among the Parsees, who, as one of the most enlightened and progressive groups in India, are subject to many secular and material influences. See bareshnum, fire temple, Parsee, Zoroastrianism.

Yasna, Zor. One of the three major sections of the Avesta, the Zoroastrian scripture, being a collection of rites and rituals used in the liturgy. The Yasna contains seventy-two chapters, and is dated from the time of Zoroaster; it includes hymns, the Gāthās, in a very early form of Zend, which were probably written by the Prophet himself. See Avesta, Zoroaster.

Yellow Ancestor (or Yellow Emperor; ancestor is Arthur Waley's version, and probably more apt). Huang Ti, a legendary Chinese ruler known primarily from a lost work, the *Book of the Yellow Ancestor,* which survives in quotations in Taoist works and in anecdotes, especially in *Chuang Tzu* (q.v.). Huang Ti is known as the forefather of God, but he is also in an endless quest for God, according to the *Chuang Tzu.* He has a definitely Taoist caste, but is blamed for having separated Earth from Heaven, thus destroying the Primal Unity, the substanceless image of Tao (q.v.), which pre-existed Huang Ti himself. The Ancestor is a rather late arrival in Chinese thought, but since he is an Emperor, and a divinity of sorts, he had to be inserted somewhere into the known list of rulers; the only place where he could safely fit without conflicting with assured historical personalities was before the sage kings (the chiefs of various clans, c. twenty-fourth to twelfth centuries B.C.), so he appears third in the list that begins with Fu Hsi, the Conqueror of Animals, and Shen Nung, the Divine Husbandman, roughly in the century ending with B.C. 2599.

Yellow Hat, Tib. Otherwise the Ge-lugs-pa ("Those who have virtuous customs"), a reformed sect of Tibetan monks founded by Tsong Khapa about A.D. 1400. In doctrines and liturgy the Yellow Hats do not differ much from the earlier Red Hats (q.v.), except that the Yellow Hats are celibate, do not drink alcohol, and in general eschew the excesses of the older sects.

Yima, Zor. The King of the Dead, the same figure as the Hindu Lord of Death, Yama. Iranian texts speak of the vara of King Yima, the vara being a huge rectangular palace or assembly hall into which neither death nor cold could penetrate until someone sinned. To save his people from general punishment, Yima took death upon himself, thus becoming the first man and the progenitor of the human race, as is Yama in the Rig Veda. Until he became mortal, Yima ruled in a form of a Golden Age, where there was neither cold nor heat, famine, drought, illness, old age, nor death. In ancient Iran, Yima was "sunlike" and "having the royal glance of the sun." However, he was denounced by the Prophet Zoroaster; nevertheless, Yima survived in later Pahlavi texts, where he is described as living in an earthly paradise underground, from which he appears every thousand years along with the elect he has chosen to accompany him. In the last days he will repeople the earth, stricken and devasted by the sins of mankind. See Yama.

yin and yang, Tao. (and Conf.). The ancient Chinese principle of polarity of negative and positive. Yin, the receptive female principle, represents the moon, darkness, quiescence, the negative, and the left. Yang, the creative male, is the sun, light, motion, the positive, the right. Yin turns inward and is interior activity, while yang radiates in all directions, like the solar flames.

The concept of yin and yang is ancient, being found in the (presumably but not likely eleventh-century B.C.) *Shih Ching* and *Chou Li* (or *Chou I*), both credited to the early Chou dynasty and collated and edited by Confucius. The latter work states, "The Great One separated and became Heaven and Earth. It revolved and became the dual forces. It changed and became the four seasons. It was distributed and became the breathing [ch'i]." Thus, in both works, they are the two primal forces and were analogized to the weather, the months of the year, rites and rituals, musical instruments, the points of the compass, and to personal attributes. In the work bearing his own name, Lao Tzu tells Confucius he had journeyed "to the World's Beginning." There "the mind is darkened by what it learns and cannot understand; the lips are sealed and cannot speak." But "I saw yin, the Female Energy in its motionless grandeur; I saw yang, the Male Energy rampant in the fiery vigor. The motionless grandeur came up out of the earth; the fiery vigor burst out from heaven. The two penetrated one another, were inextricably blended, and from their union the things of the world were born." In other early Taoist works, the *Lieh-tzŭ* and the *Huai Nan-tzŭ,* yin and yang play a basic role. In them yin, clouded and heavy, sank and fell to become earth, while the pure light substance of yang rose to become the air of the heavens. Yin and yang produce, variously, life (ming) and essence (hsing). The late Taoist work *The Secret of the Golden Flower* draws upon a development of the concept. The individual contains a central monad, which at the moment of conception splits into life and essence, superindividual principles. In the personal bodily existence of the individual they are represented by two other polarities, a p'o soul and a hun soul, which are in conflict during the person's life, each striving for mastery. At death they separate and go different ways, the p's sinking to earth as a ghost being and the hun rising to become shên, a revealing spirit or god, which in time may return to Tao, the undivided Great One.

In the *I Ching* yin and yang are known as the Two Ch'i, the Breaths of Heaven and Earth. They are also identified as the negative and positive forces of the Ridgepole of the Universe (T'ai Chi), the primal monad in which yin and yang are shown intertwined.

The original meaning of yin was probably sunless, and of yang, sunny. The northern side of a mountain is yin, and the southern, yang. However, in a valley, yang is the north or bright side, yin the south or dark side. And in the most ancient usages, yin, the feminine, took precedence over yang. Yin contained the character for cloud and was the overshadowing, but implicit in it also was the image of life-giving water as a dispenser of nourishment. The character for yang shows a yak tail or pennant fluttering in the sun; as something gleaming in the light it became the symbol of the power of command. See Confucianism, *I Ching,* Lao Tzu, Tao.

yoga, Hind. (also Jain. and Buddh.). A technique of physical and spiritual training by which the bodily and psychic energies are controlled, unified, and directed in order to attain the individual's liberation from the fetters of the world. The term yoga is derived from the Sanskrit root yug- (or yuj-), to unite, join; it is cognate with the English yoke. It means simply the liberating union of the self with the Self.

Yoga may be divided into two basic types: one, classical or

holistic yoga, as taught in the aphorisms of Patañjali, the *Yoga-Sūtras;* the other, a broad group of what can be best defined as "people's yoga," or "folk yoga." Classical yoga is a soundly based, deeply reasoned philosophical system and is known as one of the six schools of Indian philosophy. Nonclassical yoga encompasses a wide variety of diffuse and not so easily categorized forms, some of which are but fragments of holistic yoga; others are tantra (q.v.), and still others are parallel systems, such as the various Buddhist yogas. Over eighty schools of yoga are known from the millennium preceding Christianity, with some twenty subdivisions. Traditionally, there are four major categories; mantra yoga (based on the repetition of certain prayers), layā yoga (which involves the vibrations of sounds at different levels), haṭha yoga (biological development of the body with the control of the mind secondary), and rāja yoga (which stresses the taming of the mind as a stage toward union in the divine). Other important forms are bhakti yoga and jñāna yoga (the yogas of devotion and of knowledge, respectively). The Buddhists have been especially profuse in their schools, with the Chinese Ch'an-Na and the Japanese Zen becoming, perhaps, yoga in its purest forms. The elastic use of the term yoga in the *Bhagavad Gītā* has helped create some of the numerous schools; in that work we find yogas of action, renunciation, meditation, and knowledge. Tantric yoga has clear pre-Vedic origins and still contains elements of fertility rites. Considerable confusion has been caused by the many divisions, and fragments of holistic yoga have become the mainstay of many, in India as well as in the West. Miracles, mysticism, spiritualism, occultism, expectations of the arousing of the Kuṇḍalinī (the famed Serpent Power), of immediate liberation, or of visions of one's personal deity (Īśvawara) are a few of the claims of certain schools.

Classical yoga is the doctrine outlined by the sage Patañjali (q.v.) about A.D. 400 in his *Yoga-Sūtras* (q.v.), in which he established a basic code systematized from traditional sources, schools, modes, and practices of some antiquity, roughly the period before B.C. 600–400. References to yoga are found, though not precisely stated in detail, in the Vedas, Brāhmaṇas, Āraṇyakas, and the earlier Upaniṣads, suggesting that there were already several schools of yoga. A direct reference to the techniques of yoga occurs in the *Maitrāyaṇī Upaniṣad*. The concept of controlling the respiratory system and the discipline of the prāṇa (the life force) come from this period. The idea that liberation could be gained not by yajña (ritual sacrifice), mantra (prayer), or tantra (briefly described as devotional practices of a highly sexual content) but by an intense self-endeavor developed during these centuries.

BACKGROUND. However, before this, yoga had already had a long though obscure history of gestation and development. Yogic forms can be tentatively identified from about B.C. 2000, if not earlier, in the cities of the Indus Valley (q.v.), where stamp seals of a figure, believed to be an archetype of the god Shiva (or his son and guru Kārttikeya), is seen seated in the well-known lotus position of meditation; Shiva is in some aspects the patron of yogis and ascetics. Some small stone statues also show what appear to be yogis in meditative postures. All the images are male. Women do not appear in a yogic context but as various Mother figures symbolic of the Divine Energy, which is female. A single example has been found of a "yogini," a woman used by the men in tantric rites—so identified by the tantric scholar Ajit Mookerjee. In this context the woman is in effect a ritual tool employed by males in the search for ecstasy and liberation.

Anthropologists trace much in yogic practice to early rites of tribal medicine men, the outsiders of the Vedic world, whose techniques of the control of the breath and contorted bodily postures became so important in classical yoga. Other yogas maintained the primitive austerities such as excessive and prolonged fasts, and exposure to extremes of climate, sexual sublimation on the one hand or orgiastic rites on the other. Classical yoga proscribes fasts and austerities, and while favoring celibacy tries to maintain a "balanced" view of connubial sex. Some practices among the fringe yogas, especially the sexual, were sublimated by means of mystical interpretation of once literal observances. Where rites associated with magic, sorcery, and fertility practices might demand ceremonial and literal use of female accomplices—what came to be called the "left-hand way"—the "right-hand way" placed everything on a symbolic plane. One text asks rhetorically, "Why do I need an outer woman? I have an Inner Woman [Kuṇḍalinī] within myself." Kuṇḍalinī when aroused shines like "millions of lightning bolts" in the inner cosmos of the seeker's body. Many elements similar to shamanistic beliefs and practices can be found in the nonclassical yogas: They include astral traveling, bilocation, mystical ascents, and so on.

That even much of orthodox yoga had primitive sources among the pre-Āryan peoples can be seen in the many references to non-Vedic and non-brahminical deities, and esoteric and mystical concepts, such as the pre-eminence of the feminine power—variously described as Shakti, Kuṇḍalinī, and others—which is needed not only to initiate the process of release but even to attain the final culmination of liberation through the Third Eye, the Thousand-petal Lotus, or whatever the symbol might be. Holistic yoga tried to keep such imagery as such, without letting it become literal. While brāhminism was absorbing or employing popular yoga for its own purposes and uses, so were Buddhism and Jainism. In the latter two cases it is difficult to state in what forms and under what circumstances the Jains and Buddhists were influenced by folk yogic practices, whether by adoption or by absorption of converts who continued their own methods of āsanas, breathing and meditation, or, as is likely, something of both.

Actual techniques—the technology—were passed down orally from one generation to another by initiates, whether brāhminical or of the people. In the Vedic cycle of scriptures, yoga was a brāhminical institution, being the province of a male, leisurely, often parasitical social group, whose primary functions and interests were ritual observances observed with great scrupulosity, along with an obsessive attention to physical functions, such as avoiding proscribed foods, elimination of excreta according to proper ritual, the control of sexual desires, and even sleeping in the proper position. The obsession with purity, whether of ritual or of the self, and the concomitant fears of contamination, helped bring about concentration of the individual upon his inner cosmos, this at a time of great social changes, when brāhminical institutions were being challenged by the Buddhists, the Jains, and the popular devotional movements.

Since no other Āryan groups, with the possible exception of the early Zoroastrians of Persia, have produced a record of practices similar to the techniques of yoga, it can be inferred that yoga was adopted from the indigenous peoples by the Āryan brāhmins in response to some inherent psychic, spiritual, and bodily need. One suggestion (see the author's *Cities of the Sacred Unicorn*) is that the ritualized ecstasies induced by the sacred substance soma (hoama [q.v.] in Iran) were replaced by similar but not identical mind-blowing techniques of meditation learned from the pre-Āryan population. Certainly the Soma of the Rig Veda, god, plant, and sacred substance, is not the soma of later centuries, the first having apparent hallucinogenic properties, the latter none. If the original sources of soma dried up, as happened as the Āryans moved farther from the Northwest, where it was plentiful, to the great Indus and Gangetic plains, where there was none, was it not possible that physical and psychic techniques might induce what the chemistry of a plant had previously? Certainly anyone who has seen a master yogi in samādhi can appreciate that this is a state far beyond any artificially arrived at.

Classical yoga and tantric yoga, though sharing many techniques and much vocabulary and imagery and probably a common origin, show many divergencies; they might be said to stand at opposite poles of the yogic axis. Much of what appears identical is merely on the surface. In classical yoga, after the long initiatory period of training under a master, the guru, no one else need exist in the solipsist world of the yogi. His preoccupation is a shedding not only of material impediments but also of psychic hindrances—memories, the residue of dreams and impressions, desires, fears, yearnings—in order to attain liberation. On the other hand, ecstasy as much as liberation appears to be the goal in tantrism, much of which stems from primordial fertility rites, with a rowdy, bawdy, sensual enjoyment of forbidden food, drink, drugs, and sex, all ritualized. Broadly speaking, tantra, which might also be called village yoga or people's yoga—yoga practiced among peasants, agriculturalists, laborers, non-brāhminical priests, and including women—has a communal aspect, often being enjoyed in groups (the cakra or circle), upon fixed occasions (perhaps monthly), with the help of numerous aids to ecstasy, not only the forbidden items but also incense, unguents, paint, powders, drawings, statues, and nature itself; in some cases in the past sacrifices of animals and humans were included. Tantra attains the fullness of ecstasy within the divine embrace of Kuṇḍalinī or the goddess Shakti, their powers being manifest not only in the exterior world but also the sādhaka's interior cosmos. The various other yogas, which may be said to represent and inhabit the crowded middle ground, emphasize one aspect or another of the vast yogic cosmogony.

CLASSICAL YOGA: THE PHILOSOPHICAL BACKGROUND. Patañjali's yoga, which is the standard—and only—recognized text, stems from the philosophical school known as Sāṃkhya (or Sāṇkhya). Sāṃkhya is the work of several sages, the most famous of which was Kapila, whose chronology is unknown. Sāṃkhya, briefly, posits a dualist philosophy, which involves a struggle between the self and matter. Sāṃkhya teaches the complete independence and freedom of the self based on the confidence that the individual mind is able through its own powers to transcend the suffering caused by matter, illusions, and supernatural agencies. Only knowledge can bring liberation. However, this is not knowledge for its own sake, as in the West where objective Truth is valued, but the knowledge that brings final release. Without this goal, everything—study, work, meditation, whatever—is valueless.

The central character in the drama of liberation is puruṣa (the Self, the soul). Puruṣa may also be said to be the unchanging principle of intelligence, Pure Consciousness, the individual and spiritual self, without subject-object relations, without change, and outside causal connection. Such consciousness is entirely self-luminous. However, puruṣa (usually identified as masculine in Hinduism) is fettered by the chains of māyā (briefly illusion).

The ground against which puruṣa operates is prakṛti (nature or Primordial Matter). Prakṛti, the principal of empirical reality, comprises the objective world outside man, as well as the inner sphere of human experience and activity. Prakṛti consists of three aspects or qualities known as the guṇas, which are balanced in a rough equilibrium that is consistently shifting and in which one may dominate over the others, depending on the strength and weaknesses of each. The guṇas are: satva, or sattwa (the quality of harmony, purity, and luminosity), rajas (motion, passion, unrest, or whatever causes unrest and attachment), and tamas (inertia, heaviness, darkness, unknowing, torpor, and sleep).

The three guṇas continually act and react upon each other. So long as the world exists they are always in a state of disturbed equilibrium, their interaction causing the evolutionary process. But prakṛti does not evolve by itself single and alone but through its proximity to the unchanging puruṣa. It would remain unconscious but for the illumination received from the light of the puruṣa, which is inactive but *seems* active and ever-changing because of the changing empirical body. Puruṣa and prakṛti become intertwined, to the detriment of the former. The central question now becomes clear: how to separate puruṣa, the unchanging principle of conciousness, from prakṛti, the material universe. Sāṃkhya taught that it was knowledge—right knowledge, intellectually and theoretically conceived and applied—that brings separation of the puruṣa from prakṛti. But Patañjali read Sāṃkhya in a deeper, broader, and more liberating sense. Liberation comes not only from right knowledge but also from yoga. Yoga occurs in two forms. The first and ultimate yoga—union—is of the self with the True Self. This is attained by the means of achieving that union, the practice of yoga, which he succinctly states to be "the concentration which restricts the fluctuations [of the guṇas in prakṛti]. Freed from them the Self attains to self-expression." The result is that "the seer stands in his own nature."

In Patañjali's codification of many centuries of experimentation and achievement, there are eight stages, or "Limbs," all of which are necessary to liberation. *All,* not some, as in other yogas, must be followed and mastered. They are known as the Eightfold Path of Discipline, or Aṣṭāṅga Yoga. They are:

1. Yama. Abstention from injury through thought, word, or deed (i.e., ahimsā [q.v.]), from falsehood, stealing, passions and lust, and avarice.

2. Niyama. Self-improvement, which means external and internal cleanliness, contentment, simplicity of life, study, and devotion to the Supreme.

3. Āsana. The term means posture, or sitting, and in the yogic sense, the various postures used to discipline the body, as well as those during which contemplation is practiced.

4. Prāṇāyāma. Control of the life force, best exemplified by the "breath," which is regulated in its inhalation, retention, and exhalation.

5. Pratyāhāra. Control and restraint of the senses, which must be checked from speeding outward haphazardly and directed inward.

6. Dhāraṇā. Fixing the mind on the object of meditation, like the end of the nose, a spot placed on the wall, or the midpoint between the eyebrows, or on a more abstract object—e.g., the lotus of the heart or one's personal deity.

7. Dhyāna. Meditation; the undisturbed flow of thought around the object of meditation, steadfast without a break.

8. Samādhi. The term means contemplation. Samādhi is the ultimate step in yoga. Here the mind is completely absorbed in the object of meditation, becoming one with it. This is the state in which the fetters to the external world are broken and through which the seer has to pass before attaining liberation. Samādhi is of two kinds: one in which the former consciousness of the object persists, and the second in which it is transcended and there is not even consciousness of the object of meditation. Both forms have been divided again into several categories of highly technical complexities.

The first five Limbs are called external aids to yoga, while the three following are the internal aids. Some schools of yoga follow only the third through the fifth, while others plunge recklessly into the last three on the theory that if the tree flourishes, the seed must already have been planted.

Yoga of the Eightfold Path demands the presence of a guru for interpretation of the texts, not only Patañjali's but also the various commentaries and related works, and especially for practical instruction in the techniques—how to sit and breathe. The technology, which has been passed down orally, is not found in any books about yoga, and the seeker who goes off on his own will, without fail, lack a suitable basis for his work. The yogi's life changes radically. He should follow certain regulations concerning cleanliness, living quarters, meditation site, food, and sex. Simplicity and purity are stressed. The yamas and niyamas must be observed with care. The advanced yogi should not be distracted by the various supernormal powers—such as astral traveling, clairvoyance, bilocation, levitation, etc.—that come in the latter stages, for these are distractions from the final goal, the absorption of the self in the Self. See guru.

yoni, Hind. The vulva. The yoni as sacred symbol plays an important role in various forms of Hinduism, especially tantra (q.v.). It is often depicted abstractly with the liṅga (q.v.) as the combined sign of the generative powers of the Divine. In three-dimensional form the yoni may be manifested as a stone circle, or as a square or pedestal, in the later case with the liṅga arising from it. On a flat surface (paper, cloth, wood, etc.) it is often triangular, with the bindu (point) within it as the symbol of the cosmic sperm. See bindi, bindu, liṅga, yantra.

yuga, Hind. An "age" or measurement of time on a cosmic scale. The yuga is a quarter of a mahā-yuga, which in turn is but part of the manvantara, which is part of the kalpa (q.v. for details of the esoteric calendar).

Yün-mên Wên-yen (the Japanese call him Ummon monyen) (d. A.D. 949), Buddh. A leading and radical Ch'an master, known best for his enigmatic questions and sayings, which stressed the simplicity and directness of Ch'an. He said, for example, "In walking, just walk; in sitting, just sit. Above all, don't wobble." When one of his disciples asked him the ultimate secret of Buddhism, he replied, "Dumpling!" In another exchange he disposed of the Enlightened Man thus: Disciple: "What is the Pure-Body of the Dharma?" Yün-mên: "The hedgerow." Disciple: "What is the behavior of the one who thus understands?" Yün-mên: "He is a golden-haired lion." In Ch'an (and Zen) symbolism the golden-haired lion signifies "virility, sincerity, whole-heartedness; he is divinely human; he is not a manifestation but Reality itself, for he has nothing behind him, he is the 'whole truth,'" as Lin-chi I-hsüan (d. 867) said in his *Analects*. See Ch'an and Zen.

Z

zakāt, Isl. The Third Pillar of Islam, the tithe or alms-giving decreed by the Prophet Muḥammad in the second year of the hijra, to be given by all Muslims (except women, children, the poor, and the aged) for the welfare of the Community. It is normally paid once a year. Zakāt is to be distinguished from sadaqāt (charity), which is voluntary. Originally zakāt was intended primarily for the poor or for communal purposes, but now it is more often employed for the upkeep of mosques and shrines, for religious instruction, and for charitable services. Theologically what a man owns is held through the community; it is his duty to return part of what he has gained or earned. Private property connotes private beneficence, and social responsibility is enjoined upon all adult males. Zakāt, in many Muslim lands, is now more voluntary than obligatory; however, in the past (as in certain still-strict Islamic nations), the following rate was in effect, depending, of course, on the Muslim's possession and income: 2½ per cent of annual revenue in money and merchandise if their value is at least twelve pounds sterling; for the farmer, ten per cent on a farm or orchard, but five per cent if he must use irrigation; on income from mines, twenty per cent of the annual product; the rate on cattle depends on the type and size of herds. At the end of Ramaḍān (q.v.) the Muslim must pay five pounds of "corn" or another grain, or its equivalent in money. Non-Muslims living in a Muslim land are not subject to zakāt but must pay a poll tax. See Islam.

Zam Zam (or Zem Zem), Isl. The sacred well of Hajar, the slave girl of the Prophet Ibrāhīm (q.v.), whom he abandoned in Mecca with his son by her, the young Ismā'īl. The prophet left the woman and child with nothing more than some dates and a jug of water. After the water had been drunk, Hajar searched for more, traveling between the hills of Safa and Marwah seven times (a route repeated today by the pilgrim to Mecca) until she discovered the well called Zam Zam. The derivation of the name is unknown, being variously ascribed to a call in the wilderness to a Persian word for a deity of light; Sir Richard Francis Burton, who visited Mecca in 1853, states authoritatively, after mentioning many possibilities, that no one source can be definitely ascertained. The water is always drunk by pilgrims, who also pour it on their heads and bodies and even wash in it. The taste has been described as bitter, brackish, or tart; Burton thought it "much resembling a tea-spoonful of Epsom salts in a large tumbler of tepid water . . . exceedingly 'heavy' to the taste."

The well is enclosed in a large, square building, the interior of which is ornamented with marbles of various colors. The very pious believe that Zam Zam's water not only causes sins to fall from the spirit "like dust," but also to heal disease. Burton remarks that the water is transmitted to distant regions in glazed earthern jars (metal containers are used today). "Religious men break their Ramdan fast with it, apply it to their eyes to brighten vision, and imbibe a few drops at the hour of death, when Satan stands by holding a bowl of purest water, the price of the departing soul. . . . The copious supply of the well is considered . . . miraculous; in distant countries it facilitates the pronunciation of Arabic to the student; and everywhere the nauseous draught is highly meritorious in a religious point of view." Many pilgrims will dip a corner of their ihrām (pilgrimage) robe in the water for eventual use as a shroud.

The story of Hajar (or Hagar) is also told in a slightly different manner in Genesis 21. See Ibrāhīm, Islam, Ka'ba, Mecca.

Zarathustra. The name preferred by Parsees for the ancient Persian Prophet Zoroaster (the Western version inherited from the Greeks). The name is derived from zara (golden), thush (shining), stra (star)—so-called because the Prophet "actually illumined the place where he was born with his divine effulgent aura." Thus a modern Parsee scholar, Dastur Kurshed S. Dabu. The Prophet's followers are properly known as Zardushtis, also Zarathoshtis. But see Zoroaster.

zāwiyah, Isl. Literally "corner" or "nook," a zāwiyah is the regular meeting place of a Ṣūfī brotherhood. It can be a building of any size, from a single room to a mosque complex with various outbuildings. See Ṣūfism.

zazen (or za-zen), Buddh. The method of sitting in Zen meditation and the practice and results of such meditation. The purpose of zazen is dhyāna (final enlightenment). The pupil practices zazen under a roshi (master), who selects apt candidates, supervises their meditation, and gives them counseling. In the long hours of sitting the pupil is likely to doze off; an elder of the monastery will whack him with a fist, sandal, slipper, or stick. The practice of zazen was favored by the great Zen innovator Dōgen (A.D. 1200–53), who taught that the gradual lifelong realization attained by sitting in meditation without any thought of spiritual gain or of any thought in mind is preferable to the sudden enlightenment produced by the kōan method.

Zem Zem, Isl. See Zam Zam.

Zen, Buddh. A Japanese school of Mahāyānist Buddhism derived from the Chinese meditative schools called Ch'an (q.v.), both names being nothing more than mispronunciations of the original Sanskrit dhyāna (meditation). Zen is one of the most important and influential forms of Buddhism and is the one best known in the West, its import far outweighing the actual number of adepts. Briefly, Zen aims to induce the direct, mystical experience of Reality—to reveal the Buddha within—through a nurturing of the inner experience. Though Zen masters often deride scriptures, verbal instruction, rite, ritual and the written word itself, it has still developed an extensive literature and a number of formalized practices. In short, Zen attempts to break through the bonds imposed by words and concepts in one of two primary methods: (1) zazen, or sitting in meditation on a regular, formulated basis under the direction of competent authority in order to attain gradual awakening, or (2) reaching enlightenment through the employment of a verbal jolt, the kōan—an enigma or puzzle that forces the student's mind outside normal thought processes in order to gain instant enlightenment. Abstractly two parallel or even contradictory methods, in practice zazen and kōan may coincide or overlap. The kōan, which offers immediate success—instant ecstatic gratification, one might say (which is a reason why it is so attractive to Westerners)—may in actuality require years to solve. Ordinarily a young monk can spend a long novitiate in the monastery in meditation trying to break through the limits of the puzzle, to produce an "answer" by which his master will realize that the pupil is enlightened. All too often the pupil may fail his first kōan or two and be given others. Instruction does not end with the solving of the initial kōan; it is the monk's own decision to continue with his life in Zen. In whatever method, zazen or kōan, a competent master is required for proper training. And in either case there is always a long period of hard work required.

The two schools of Zen are Rinzai, which favors the kōan, and Sōtō, which employs the zazen method. Though Ch'an had been introduced into Japan several times previous to the twelfth century A.D., it wasn't until Eisai (A.D. 1141–1215), a Japanese scholar monk, studied with the Lin-chi school of Ch'an in China and returned to his homeland to establish a Zen school that this form of Buddhism was able to establish a proper hold. Lin-chi was transliterated as Rinzai. One of Eisai's much younger disciples, Dōgen (A.D. 1200–53), eventually questioned the kōan method, broke with Rinzai, and established the other great form of Chinese Ch'an, Ts'ao-tung, in Japan, Sōtō, stressing the importance of zazen—sitting in meditation, without any thought of acquisition or attainment or any specific problem (as in the kōan) in mind. Other forms of Ch'an introduced into Japan flourished temporarily, but either faded away or were absorbed into Rinzai and Sōtō.

Zen has had a vast influence on Japanese culture and life. Zen monasteries, often based upon Chinese models, are noted for their great aesthetic appeal, discipline, order, quiet, and cleanliness. The life of the monk is disciplined but not rigorous; austerities of the type once practiced by Gautama Buddha in his search for Enlightenment (and still followed by Indian holy men) are unknown. Among the first to take up Zen seriously were many of the warrior class, the samurai. They developed kendō, the art of the sword, and judo, the art of aggressive self-defense, as forms of Zen. Tea, introduced from China, used both to keep the monks awake during meditation and medicinally, became the basis of a ritual of simple beauty, the tea ceremony (cha-no-yu). Flower arranging, gardening, art, literature, and the drama (the Nō play) were among the things enlivened with the inner spirit of Zen. See Buddha, Ch'an, kōan, zazen.

Zoroaster, Zoroastrians, Zoroastrianism. The ancient Iranian prophet Zoroaster is the founder and central human figure in the religion called after him. This entry will be divided into (1) the Prophet and his life; (2) the faithful, better called Zardushti; and (3) the major tenets of Zoroastrianism.

The dates of the Prophet's life cannot be precisely determined: B.C. 626–551 are credible figures; some Western scholars put the date of his birth at B.C. 660. However, the Zardushti, on the basis of a misreading of the ancient Greeks and Romans (among them Herodotus and Pliny), who knew of the Prophet, emphatically set "6000 to 7000 as the approximate period," though they may qualify the statement by admitting that there is considerable dispute as to when Zoroaster preached his message. Considering the state of civilization at this primitive period, the seventh millennium B.C. is an improbability, as the Avesta, the work in which Zoroaster sets out his teachings, predicates a society of considerable advancement, with a royal court far above that of the tribal chief. Yet all Zardushti sources are united on an extremely early date. Where the Prophet was born is another question. Zardushtis may place his birthplace at the ancient city of Rei (or Rae), not far from Teheran; others somewhere in the vicinity of Lake Urumiah in Azerbaijan in western Iran (a site given some credence by Western scholars); Phages in Media is a third possibility.

Scholars' views of Zoroaster have run to extremes, from those who see him as a shaman to those who describe him merely as an agrarian reformer in a primitive pastoral society. The view expressed by Nietzsche (*Also Sprach Zarathustra*) to express his doctrine of the superman, of the Prophet as magician, astrologer, and quack is a travesty and need not be considered here. Most scholars place Zoroaster squarely in the tradition of the prophetic reformer. His followers—and theirs is the view that must be accepted, leaving aside the corrective and tidying efforts of the non-Zardushtis—see him as a divinely appointed instructor, thoroughly human and real, who suffered at the hands of Evil, a force, which like Good or Truth, is created by Ahura Mazdā, the Omniscient

Lord. Both Evil and Truth work ultimately for Righteousness. Evil is created to test man, as the Prophet said in the Yasnah, a section of the Avesta directly attributable to him. It was the Prophet's mission to triumph over Evil through Righteousness.

THE TESTING OF THE PROPHET. Much folklore surrounds the figure of Zoroaster. He is, for example, said to be the only person ever to be born with a smile, the aura of which spread all over the town of Rae. Terrorists, aware of his sanctity as a young boy, attempted to murder him on several occasions, but a series of divine miracles saved his life. A fire into which he was thrust was extinguished without human interference; herds of horses and cattle did not trample upon him though he was placed in their path; wolves were unable to open their jaws in attacking him; an assassin's dagger was deflected, and so on.

There is no doubt, however, that he spent a long period of meditation (ten years in some versions, fifteen in others), retreating into a cave in a mountain at the age of fifteen. At the end of his retreat he experienced a heavenly vision of Ahura Mazdā, the Supreme Lord. "I acknowledge Thee as holy beneficent, O Wise Lord," he chanted in his meditative poems, the Yasnahs, which he wrote during this period. He was given the divine message of Purity, Uprighteousness, and Truth, the three standards of Zardushti life.

Returning to the world, he began to preach that "Righteousness is the best good" (Ashem vohū vahishtem astī). He was attempting, not to found a new religion, but to purify the ancient one, Mazdayasni, "the religion of Mazdā" the Omniscient and Supreme God, into which he had been initiated, and to re-establish it over the Daevayasni, the religion of Satan as a mighty destroyer. Zoroaster's mission to purify the ancient doctrines and to assert the pre-eminence of the One True God met with stiff opposition and even persecution, for he was preaching in a time of social change, when the old settled pastoral communities were threatened by marauding, nomadic tribal societies that murdered and plundered. He wandered through Iran, Afghanistan, and Turanistan without gaining much of a hearing, passing ten years on the road as a kind of dervish. (Some of the locales, especially in Azerbaijan, can still be identified.) He experienced visions during this period, seven in all, which showed him the mysteries of heaven.

From various divine beings, angels, and personified abstractions, he received commands and injunctions to pass on to mankind. They taught the doctrine of purity of the body as well as of the soul, and enjoined the care of animals, especially the cow and the dog (q.v.); they emphasized the necessity of keeping the earth, fire, and water undefiled; one of the important commands was that of civil reform. Other ethical tenets included an abhorrence of falsehood, and the universal obligation to speak the truth. His ecstatic experiences included a revelation of the future, which included the resurrection of the dead and the afterlife. But while in these excursions into the supernatural world, he was warned of a spiritual enemy, Angra Mainyu or Ahriman, the devil. From the dazzling splendor of heaven Zoroaster caught sight of the darkness, filth, stench, and torment of the Worst World.

This led him into a period of temptation in which Ahriman sought unsuccessfully to get Zoroaster to renounce the Good Religion of the worshipers of Mazdā.

In his preaching Zoroaster divided the world into two basic groups, the followers of Truth and the Followers of the Lie, the two Spirits, Asha and Druj, that divide the universe between them. Good and Evil, God and the devil, are in constant warfare with each other. How is the conflict to be resolved? Man is a free agent, Zoroaster taught, and man is to solve the problem by electing right and choosing goodness, as the Prophet himself was doing. The reward will be joys eternal at the resurrection "when the dead shall rise up, the quick be made immortal, and the world, as desired, made perfect."

During this initial period of preaching the Prophet made only one convert, his cousin Maidhyoi-Maonha. Then Zoroaster was called by King Vishtaspa, the last paramount chief of the Chrosmian confederacy before it was overthrown by Cyrus, the founder of the Achaemenid Empire. Vishtaspa asked to hear the tenets of Zoroaster's teaching, but then demanded physical proof. Among other miracles, the Prophet displayed heavenly fire that could not be extinguished but that would not burn anyone who touched it. The King accepted Zoroaster as a Prophet, and gave him a house, arousing the anger of the court magicians. They placed the tools of magic under the Prophet's bed—hair, human bones, the heads of animals, excreta, and other matter used in casting spells. Zoroaster was placed in prison. Upon curing the King's horse after the magicians failed (the animal's legs were withdrawn into its body—the Prophet released each leg upon the promise of the King and Queen and the royal children to follow his teachings) Zoroaster was released and restored to power. The King now followed a program of spreading the revived faith, including the building of fire temples.

Zoroaster's death came during the holy wars that arose as the result of his preaching. Many of the people of Iran, mainly polytheistic, who worshiped various gods of nature and temperament and practiced ritual slaughter, rejected his doctrines. The Prophet was attacked from behind while praying at a fire temple; as he fell he cast his prayer beads at his assailant, a Turanian soldier, who dropped dead at his feet. In Zoroastrian doctrine Zoroaster cast aside his physical body when his work was done in order to return to the Lord Whose messenger he was. He left behind six children: three boys and three girls; his progeny are a matter of dispute among foreign scholars. His work did not die, being carried on by his disciples, Peshotan (q.v.) being the chief of them. See Avesta, and Zoroastrians and Zoroastrianism, below.

ZOROASTRIANS. The followers of the Prophet Zoroaster and his doctrines. For the purpose of this entry they will be divided into two groups: (1) those in Iran who survived the Muslim invasion and (2) those who migrated to India.

Both groups are known under various names, including Zoroastrian. The Iranis are likely to be called Fārsīs after the province of Fars or Pars. Gabar, or guebre, also used, is a common but incorrect, even derogatory term. The group in India is known as Parsees (or Parsis), after Pars. Either group may be called Zardushtis, after one of the versions of the Prophet's name, Zardusht. Bab-Dīnān, another term, means "those of the Good Religion"—i.e., Zoroastrians, a term that in Iran encompasses all members of the faith but in India only the laity. Zardushtīān, also, is common in Iran.

Up to the time of the Muslims the Zoroastrians formed the major religious group in ancient Persia (or Iran) and in many of the territories under Iranian rule. Under the Achaemenid and Sassanian Emperors (among them Cyrus, Cambyses, Darius, Xerxes, Artaxerxes I, and Artaxerxes II) the Empire was extended as far as India in the East to Africa (Egypt, Lybia, and Abyssinia) in the West; southern Russia and part of Greece were other boundaries; thus a major portion of the ancient world fell under Iranian—and Zoroastrian—influences. Zoroastrian doctrines had a marked effect upon many of the peoples under the Iranians: The mystery religions of Egypt and Greece, the many forms of Gnosticism (q.v.), Marcionism, Mithraism, and Manichaeism are but a few that show profound traces of Zardushti tenets. Also, one must list the Jews of the Babylonian exile, the primitive Christians, and Islam, especially in the form known as Ṣūfism (q.v.).

About the beginning of the Christian era, Zoroastrianism experienced increasing challenges from other religions; Hellenistic ideas invaded the faith, which was belatedly made the official religion of the Iranian (Sassanid) Empire in A.D. 226. Christianity and its heresies, along with Manichaeism (which relegated Zoroaster to a rank of "brother" with Buddha and Jesus—Mani, a Persian, was the fulfillment of all three), presented formidable threats. In the early seventh century A.D. Islam became the major challenge, invading, conquering, and converting the far-flung lands of the former Persian empires. A decisive battle in Mesopotamia in A.D. 635 brought the end of the Sassanids and the decline of the religion of Ahura Mazdā. Though the Muslims theoretically practiced tolerance, the Zardushtis felt oppressed; there was much unrest and active rebellion in the province of Fars, which had the positive effect of producing a Zoroastrian revival, as much a result of nationalism as of religion. Some important religious works stem from this period, among them the Dēnkart (q.v.), a kind of Zardushti encyclopedia of what the faithful feared would be lost under the Muslims. Beleaguered on all sides, the Zardushti also found expression in works like the *Shkand Gumanik Vichār* (Decisive Solution of Doubts), a defense of the faith of Ahura Mazdā against Judaism, Christianity, and Islam.

Many Zardushti preferred to emigrate rather than remain under the Muslims, some going to China, others to India, in both cases to areas where there were already Iranian settlements, notably of traders. In China the Zoroastrians flourished for many centuries; an Arab traveler noted fire temples in China in A.D. 905, but later the Zardushti were absorbed into the Chinese mass and disappeared from history. A small group of Zardushtis, meanwhile, had retreated to central Fars, to Yazd, southeast of Isfahan; those who remained in their own land existed under considerable handicaps, for in A.D. 820 the Muslim governor of Fars ordered the burning of all Zoroastrian documents; however, not everything was lost, some works being successfully hidden, others being spared by enlightened and sympathetic Arabs, who were proud of their own scholarship. The two groups of Zardushti survivors will now be considered.

1. The Zoroastrians of Iran. The Zoroastrians are centered around the town of Yazd (or Yezd). The survivors of this once-great religion now number some twelve thousand to twenty thousand, the higher figure being more likely, with most in the area of Yazd, and smaller groups in Kerman, Teheran, and elsewhere. Irani Zoroastrians still immigrate to India.

The Fārsīs suffered many disabilities until the end of the nineteenth century. They lived in seclusion to avoid irritating their Muslim rulers, could wear clothing of yellow, gray, or brown only, were not allowed to use eyeglasses or umbrellas, could not patronize the public baths or ride vehicles, live in houses with upper stories, engage in trade (they were mainly farmers and agriculturalists), or wear white stockings. In the 1890s, as the result of efforts by the Society for the Amelioration of the Zoroastrians in Persia (founded in Bombay by Parsees in 1854), many of the restrictions were legally removed, though in practice prejudice remained.

Despite the years of separation, Fārsī and Parsee customs, rites, and rituals are almost identical, except that those celebrated in Iran are often simpler, and may be influenced by Islam. Education of the youth has been meager compared to that in Bombay, which resembles the English system fortified by a variety of Zoroastrian subjects. The Fārsīs employ charms and amulets to a greater degree than the Parsees. Ceremonies such as the initiatory rite of kustī are rarely practiced, the sacred thread merely being adopted by the young person somewhere between the ages of seven and fifteen without a celebration, as soon as the necessary prayers can be mastered. The wearing of the sudreh (the consecrated, symbolic shirt) is uncommon at Yazd.

However, the various rites and observances dealing with purity and defilement by unclean matter are usually observed almost to the same degree as in India. Marriages among children in their early teens and even younger are common; the practice has been banned in the Indian community. Again, the rites in Iran are simpler than among the Parsees. The Irani Zardushti usually celebrate the marriage with only the men present; the bride and her attendants sit out of sight but not out of hearing. The bride is dressed in green silk and veiled from head to foot.

Funeral rites are virtually identical, extreme conservatism being observed in following the ancient prescriptions laid down in the Avesta. Yazd retains several dakhmahs or Towers of Silence for the disposal of the dead, located well outside the city. One is known as Dakhman-i Jamshid (Tower of Jamshid) and is of unknown antiquity; a tower erected by Indian Parsees c. 1854 is ordinarily employed. Farther away is an ancient ruined tower, Dakhman-i Kuhnah (Old Dakhmah), used for exposing the bodies of the still-born or abortive children and of suicides and those who have died other violent deaths. There are some neighboring dakhmahs, on a smaller scale, erected primarily as memorials by various Fārsīs.

2. The Parsees of India. There are now about 120,000 descendants of the early Zoroastrian immigrants to India, most living in the Bombay area; some counts set the figure closer to 100,000. Parsee means someone from Pars—i.e., Persia. Both the early history of the Parsees and some of their doctrine are in dispute. Care must be taken in reading material either by a Parsee or a non-Parsee scholar, for the Parsees, much influenced by Hinduism, Islam, and Christianity, have a tendency to edit and rewrite their own heritage, and the non-Parsee all too often reads into Parseeism what he himself wants it to be. Parsee immigration into India apparently began during the time of the great Sassanian Empire (A.D. 226–635), when small colonies of traders and merchants were established along the western coastline. After the Muslims overran Persia in the seventh century and began to convert the already weakened and increasingly superstitious Zoroastrian population to Islam, a large group immigrated to India. The exact date is a matter of argument; it has been set variously from 636 to as late as A.D. 936. However, Parsee tradition places the first fixed settlement of refugees at Sanjan in 716. One of the conditions imposed by the local rājā was that the immigrants never try to proselytize

among the Indians themselves, a condition that the Parsees have always faithfully observed; even the child of a mixed marriage will not be received as a Parsee. A second major group of refugees came to India during Timur's invasion of Persia at the end of the fourteenth century.

The Parsees progressed rapidly during this period, being engaged in agriculture, weaving, carpentry, ship building, coastal trade, general business, and all crafts except those that had to do with fire (such as blacksmithing), for fire was sacred and could be handled only by the priests. The Parsees' major center shifted to Surat in Gujarāt; it was here that they became deeply involved with the British, as merchants and as intermediaries with the Indian community. When the British shifted their center of activities to Bombay in 1668, the Parsees followed. Today they are a small but prosperous community, highly educated, philanthropic, and socially conscious, playing a beneficial role in Indian life far beyond their numbers.

Parsee belief, custom, and worship is derived from Zoroastrianism, though for a long time they lost contact with their homeland. In their emigration, the Avesta and other sacred scriptures disappeared, and though the community maintained as much of the outward signs of Zoroastrianism as it could remember, such as the fire temples and the towers of silence, there were no guides to any point of religion that might be in question. To solve this problem, priestly missions, twenty-two in all, were sent to Iran between 1478 and 1773 to ask questions; the replies and the inquiries were collected in a work called the *Rivāyat,* which deals with matters of faith, ritual, and law. The sixteenth-century Mogul Emperor Akbar (q.v.) attempted to found a syncretistic religion with elements of Zoroastrianism, including the fire ceremonies, but it did not survive his death. The Persian Zoroastrian mystics who remained in India produced a number of minor works, of little value, along universalist and allegoristic lines. They also served as instructors for the Parsees. It was not until the French scholar Anquetil-Duperron began to live among the Parsees at Surat and question them about their beliefs that the Parsees themselves returned to their own study of their sacred works. The work of other European scholars also then enabled the Parsees to rediscover and comprehend much of their past. In the next century Parseeism underwent a reform. Hindu and Islamic accretions were noted and when possible removed, the leakage by conversion to Christianity was slowed, though today, as Parsee leaders complain, all three faiths still have too much influence upon the community. The entire structure of Parsee life was re-examined in the light of contemporary conditions. Bigamy was ended, women were allowed an education, the priesthood was declared no longer a hereditary privilege, and laymen were enabled to perform certain sacred functions. The community initiated a program of aid to its impoverished brethren in Persia. Social services, such as hospitals, orphanages, and charitable organizations, were established. The return to original sources, and the modernizing movements were not entirely beneficial to the community as a whole. The Parsees were soon divided over basic issues into reformists and conservatists, a split that has been deepened today by the rejection of younger Parsees of ancient rituals and rites, such as exposing the dead in the Towers of Silence.

Zoroastrian beliefs and customs are in general better observed in Bombay than in Yazd, for the original remnant has been much subject to persecution by the Muslims. However, in the attempt in the mid-seventeenth century A.D. to establish correct texts of the scriptures and the proper performance of rites and ceremonies, the Parsees became involved in a question of the calendar. Because of variances in adjusting the calendar to the solar year, the Parsees found themselves at odds with the Irani Zoroastrians, whose own calendar was also not accurate. The Parsees split into the Kādmi (from kādimi [ancient]), who followed what they thought to be the restored traditional practice, and the non-reforming Shahenshai, the majority. In 1906 a group of the Kādmi raised the question of when to begin the New Year and were forced to break away; they are known as the Fassāli (from fassāl [season]). Both the Kādmi and Fassāli now suffer a shortage of priests.

The Parsees themselves state that they are a declining community. Restrictions against marrying outside their own group, a declining birth rate, problems caused by much inbreeding, and emigration abroad all are weakening the Parsees. Their long-term survival is much discussed.

ZOROASTRIANISM is a complex religion and often is not much understood, either by the faithful or by the many Western scholars who have attempted to unravel its mysteries. The faithful, of whom the Parsees are the largest group, tend to leave the complexities to the priests, but carefully follow the prescribed prayers and observe the celebrations; special attention is paid to the ethical aspect of Zoroastrianism. How great the priests' own understanding is, is a mystery, for true scholars among them are rare, and much of the doctrine is highly esoteric, its origins, development, and interpretation lost in antiquity. In India, Hindu tenets, especially that of reincarnation, are accepted by some leading Parsees as part of Zoroastrianism but denied by others.

Western scholars, many of whom have been extremely fascinated by Zoroastrianism, often tend to interpret it in terms of their own disciplines and interests; to take but two easy examples, H. S. Nyberg (*Die Religionen des alten Iran* [Leipzig, 1938]) refers to the Prophet himself as a "psychopomp"—i.e., a form of shaman (q.v.), an interpretation also subscribed to by Mircea Eliade (*Shamanism* [Princeton University Press, 1964]), while the English expert R. C. Zaehner (*The Dawn and Twilight of Zoroastrianism* [New York: Putnam, 1961]) can put the high period of the faith in terms of "catholic Zoroastrianism," a phrase that has strong echoes of the Christian Church; Zaehner reads the Prophet in the light of seeming, but not always consistent, parallels to postexilic Judaism and to Christianity.

The major difficulties for both Zardushti and foreigner are that the texts are not only incomplete and fragmented but also confusing, poorly transcribed in the past, and difficult to translate. Many foreign scholars have become more immersed in the problems of linguistics than of interpretation and doctrine. Among the Zardushti, differences of opinion result from time to time because the authoritative sources, the Avesta and other scriptures, are open to variant readings. However, in the light of tradition and much exchange of copies of basic texts, the following can be said to be a fair representation of Zoroastrianism as taught by the faithful themselves.

Before the universe was manifest, God existed in a state of dormancy, formless, timeless, and motionless. This state is known as Zravane Akarena (Boundless Time, eternity without beginning and without end). The universe was not yet manifest, there was no time as mankind knows it because the sun, moon, and stars were not yet created. This pre-existence was God's first absolute aspect.

Then the Divine Will moved and spoke, pronouncing the Word that partially manifested God in the universe. Limited Time (or self-created time, which had a measure) came out of the placid ocean of eternity. With His Will at the center, He remained the One, the Omniscient Source of Existence, or, in the common Zardushti term, Ahura Mazdā. The Prophet termed this aspect as "God without a predecessor."

The One became two, spirit and matter, life and form. Zoroastrianism is now to be marked by a duality expressed in various terms; however, rather than duality, "polarity" is more explicit. The universe develops along two lines: Spen (increase) and Angra (decrease). As the real aspects of both are invisible, they are known as mino or mental concepts. Angra-mino was formalized as Satan, and man was asked to discriminate between Good and Evil.

About the question that has always plagued the Zardushti, of how Evil could come from God, the simple explanation is that there is no such thing as absolute evil. Evil is only relative, depending on the viewpoint of the observer. Whatever thwarts the growth of the soul, whatever is against the will of God, is evil.

Ahura Mazdā—God—acts, for administrative purposes, through two great officers, Ahu (ruler) and Ratu (teacher), who govern the temporal and the spiritual spheres, respectively. They are the Will and the Wisdom aspects of God, or Law and Grace.

God Himself shows three aspects: Ahurā (the Creator), Volumana (the Preserver), and Asha Vahista (the Reconstructor). The three hold joint consultations over the appointment of a Savior, and in a Yasht, Ahura Mazdā says, "I am the Creator, the Preserving Nourisher and the Smiter."

Later comes the sevenfold aspect of the Archangels, who dominate seven kingdoms and creatures of Nature: men, animals, fire and the luminaries, the mineral kingdom, the earth, the waters, and the vegetable kingdom. These seven great ministering aspects of Divinity thus supervise and maintain seven creations under evolution; they are "united in thought, word, and deed" and are entities possessing power, intelligence, and love derived from the "One without a Second" and are administrators in the Divine Hierarchy. Ahura Mazdā is One, and Three, and also Seven. Subordinate angels, thirty-three in number, aid the archangels in administration. None is independent of the supreme power—called in Parsee texts the Father—but each carries out His plan as Creator. God is also thirty-three. However, some of these thirty-three angels are also many, for each heavenly body has its own invisible spiritual guardian; the living and the dead, too, have guardian angels.

Ultimately the One becomes innumerable sparks, and they ensoul every atom and every cell, so that in mentioning them, even the Gāthās employ the term Ahura Mazdā in the plural, expressing the Immanent aspect of Divinity. There is no corporeal existence without its indwelling spiritual force.

Despite the multiplicity of divine sparks, from archangels down to the most minute celestial being, the Zoroastrians consider themselves monotheists. The heavenly hierarchy exists to aid in the administration of the universe; the Entities, as they are called, are parts of the One Source.

Later Zoroastrians, apparently under the influence of Christianity, or at least Christian terminology, have translated certain phrases of the Avesta in trinitarian terms. God the Creator is the Father, God the Preserver is the Son, and God the Smiter and Reconstructor is the Holy Spirit. In other passages the Sun is "the most beautiful body of God." Fire is the "Son of God"; the archangel Spenta-Armaiti (Bountiful Wisdom), who rules over the earth, is depicted as the "daughter of God," and in a curious late rubric, Ashishwangh Yasht, Ahurā and Armaiti are considered Father and Mother, who create the abstract progeny religion, blessing, inspiration, truth, and friendship. Such passages are likely to be interpreted as metaphorical.

Sin is a "corrosive or consuming influence." All evil thoughts, words, and deeds are due to lack of intelligence. A sinful man is temporarily insane, and the criminal is a child-soul still without experience and conscience. A Zoroastrian must constantly review his own conduct so as to weigh all causes and effects. The second step is a returning to the right path, renouncing all propensities based on error.

Man is free to sin, but God's will is supreme. Zarathustra, in the Gāthās, said, "The Omniscient Lord is aware of every deed done in the past, or to be done in the future. He is the wise Judge. May that come to pass which He wills." While man is free to oppose the Divine Will, God's plan will ultimately come to pass.

The term asha is a key concept. It means, roughly, "Truth," but it has as well many other meanings, being among them, a comprehensive term that signifies order, symmetry, discipline, and harmony, and includes all acts of piety, truthfulness, and beneficence. Asha is a profound spiritual law in accordance with which the universe has been created and governed. Asha is also a way or path: "Through the most beneficent path of asha, we may see Thee, we may understand Thy various aspects and ultimately may we be united with Thee in true love." (Avesta, Yasna 8). Opposed to asha is druj (the Lie, wickedness, disorder). The sense of druj has shifted: In the Prophet's time, druj as the Lie meant the worship of the daevas (demons). In current usage it implies a lower level of human existence, where man wanders in a state of illusion bound by desire and sin.

Man must transcend such a state, it being his role to overcome false attachments, ignorance, and sensual cravings. Until the soul—the Zoroastrian term is fravashi—discovers the right path of reunion with God, it wanders in deceit and destruction. The only possible choice is to follow the path of asha. The fravashi is preexistent, having descended to the material world of matter to gain experience and peace, wisdom, compassion, and efficiency so that it may be liberated from the bonds of druj.

Reunion with God is described by contemporary Zoroastrians as being identical with that burning desire of the heart of the Ṣūfī, the "meeting of the Beloved," an image found in the Prophet himself, who prayed for "The vision of Thy nature and the heart-to-heart union with Thee." Liberation having been achieved, the soul experiences its resurrection—i.e., its rising from the dead.

MAN. In Zoroastrianism man is composed of matter and spirit. On the one hand is the body, on the other the vital breath, a faculty of discernment, a conscience, a soul created before the body, and also the fravishi, which is a kind of external soul, also preexistent. Only the soul and the fravashi have a life after death. Man is born pure and not defiled by original sin (as most Christians believe). To keep his soul from sin, man is given the power of discernment. Thus he is able to distinguish between good and evil and to choose by free will one or the other. The role of the fravashi is to lead him along the path of righteousness.

The fravashi is one of the important concepts. Not only does man have a fravashi but so does all of creation, animated or not. The duty of the fravashi is to see to the prosperity of the world and its just growth and to accompany man rightly in his terrestrial life.

The Avesta states that there will be life after death, in heaven, hell, and an intermediate domain. The dead will be judged by a triad of brothers, Mithra, Sraosha, and Rashnu (Mehr, Sarish, and Rashn in the popular language today). They chastise the wicked, lead the blessed to heaven, and are invoked by mankind for the forgiveness of sins. Whatever judgments the triad makes is upon the basis of what each individual has done according to his own free will. In the end, resurrection will take place, the body being reunited with the soul. Only the good will survive, for all evil will be destroyed. Thus, because man has to stand before his judges, the Zardushti are enjoined to the three concepts of good thoughts, good words, and good deeds. In the afterworld, each will live in family groups in his original form, exempt from all sin and enjoying eternal bliss.

MYSTICISM. Though a tradition of mystical techniques has existed since the earliest times, esoteric practices are now limited to the priesthood. At the time of the Muslim invasion of Iran, Zoroastrian mysticism was diverted into the Persian form of Ṣūfism (q.v.), and since then, among the Zardushti themselves, mystical, esoteric, and occult practices are confined to the clergy, who base their observances on a form of rhythmical breathing akin to dhikr or prāṇa; even these practices are reported to be rare among the priesthood. In India, Hindu techniques such as yoga (q.v.) are forbidden to the Parsees, though some of the laity nevertheless quietly practice them. Among most Zardushtis the development of yogic powers is regarded with concern, as these forces can be used malevolently.